booksonline

Read this book online today:

With SAP PRESS BooksOnline we offer you online access to knowledge from the leading SAP experts. Whether you use it as a beneficial supplement or as an alternative to the printed book, with SAP PRESS BooksOnline you can:

- Access your book anywhere, at any time. All you need is an Internet connection.
- Perform full text searches on your book and on the entire SAP PRESS library.
- Build your own personalized SAP library.

The SAP PRESS customer advantage:

Register this book today at *www.sap-press.com* and obtain exclusive free trial access to its online version. If you like it (and we think you will), you can choose to purchase permanent, unrestricted access to the online edition at a ve

Here's how to get started:

1. Visit *www.sap-press.com.*
2. Click on the link for SAP PRESS BooksOnline and login (or create é
3. Enter your free trial license key, shown below in the corner of the
4. Try out your online book with full, unrestricted access for a limitec

Discover ABAP™

 PRESS

SAP PRESS is a joint initiative of SAP and Galileo Press. The know-how offered by SAP specialists combined with the expertise of the Galileo Press publishing house offers the reader expert books in the field. SAP PRESS features first-hand information and expert advice, and provides useful skills for professional decision-making.

SAP PRESS offers a variety of books on technical and business related topics for the SAP user. For further information, please visit our website: *www.sap-press.com*.

Horst Keller
The Official ABAP Reference (3rd edition)
2012, 1677 pp., hardcover
978-1-59229-376-6

Tanmaya Gupta
ABAP Data Dictionary
2011, 403 pp., hardcover
978-1-59229-379-7

Horst Keller, Wolf Hagen Thümmel
Official ABAP Programming Guidelines
2010, 398 pp., hardcover
978-1-59229-290-5

Thorsten Franz, Tobias Trapp
ABAP Objects: Application Development from Scratch
2009, 505 pp., hardcover
978-1-59229-211-0

Karl-Heinz Kühnhauser and Thorsten Franz

Discover ABAP™

Bonn • Boston

Galileo Press is named after the Italian physicist, mathematician and philosopher Galileo Galilei (1564–1642). He is known as one of the founders of modern science and an advocate of our contemporary, heliocentric worldview. His words *Eppur si muove* (And yet it moves) have become legendary. The Galileo Press logo depicts Jupiter orbited by the four Galilean moons, which were discovered by Galileo in 1610.

Editor Stefan Proksch
English Edition Editor Kelly Grace Harris
Translation Lemoine International, Inc., Salt Lake City, UT
Copyeditor Emily Nicholls
Cover Design Barbara Thoben, Graham Geary
Photo Credit Gettyimages/Iconica/Geoff Brightling
Layout Design Vera Brauner
Production Graham Geary
Typesetting Publishers' Design and Production Services, Inc.
Printed and bound in the United States of America

ISBN 978-1-59229-402-2

© 2012 by Galileo Press Inc., Boston (MA)

2nd edition 2012

3rd German edition published 2011 by Galileo Press, Bonn, Germany

Library of Congress Cataloging-in-Publication Data
Kühnhauser, Karl-Heinz.
[Discover ABAP]
Discover ABAP / Karl-Heinz Kühnhauser and Thorsten
Franz. — 2nd ed.
p. cm.
Includes bibliographical references and index.
ISBN 978-1-59229-402-2 (alk. paper) — ISBN 1-59229-402-2
(alk. paper)
1. SAP R/3. 2. ABAP/4 (Computer program language)
I. Franz, Thorsten. II. Title.
HF5548.4.R2K84 2011
650.0285'53—dc23
2011041664

SUSTAINABLE FORESTRY INITIATIVE Certified Fiber Sourcing
Label applies to the text stock www.sfiprogram.org

Contents at a Glance

Dear Reader,

The first edition of this book published in 2007, and was an immediate success. There is more to writing a book than providing information and instruction; indeed, the real challenge is to make this information and instruction accessible. The original author of *Discover ABAP*, Karl-Heinz Kühnhauser, answered this challenge with aplomb, and delivered a book that is one of the cornerstones of SAP PRESS' publishing program. However, this did present a problem when it came time to do a new edition; as you can imagine, the question of who could fill Mr. Kühnhauser's shoes was not an easy one to answer.

I wish I could take credit for finding Thorsten Franz. Not only does the man know his ABAP, he *also* knows how to write a book—which is, I assure you, a rarer combination of qualities than one in my profession would like. Alas, the glory goes to editors before me . . . but I'm at least lucky enough to reap the rewards. Reading *Discover ABAP* was truly one of them, which is a sentiment that I trust you, dear reader, will share. Another was simply the opportunity to work with Thorsten, who is possibly the funniest author I've had the pleasure of knowing. (I'll admit that his quality taste in science fiction doesn't hurt either.) I consider myself lucky to call him both a colleague and a friend.

Of course, we at SAP PRESS are always eager to hear your opinion. What do you think about *Discover ABAP*? How could it be improved? As your comments and suggestions are the most useful tools to help us make our books the best they can be, we encourage you to visit our website at *www.sap-press.com* and share your feedback about this work.

Thank you for purchasing a book from SAP PRESS!

Kelly Grace Harris
Editor, SAP PRESS

Galileo Press
Boston, MA

kelly.harris@galileo-press.com
www.sap-press.com

Contents

4 Fields and Calculations 99

5 Modifying Character Strings 121

6 Debugging Programs 141

7 Modifying Transparent Database Tables 173

8 Calculating Dates, Times, Quantities, and Currencies 213

11 Selection Screens 323

Preface to the Second Edition

Like its previous edition, this book is a practical introduction for those of you who are planning to enter the world of ABAP programming. Since presenting you with basic ABAP information is this book's primary goal—and everything else is secondary—*Discover ABAP* intentionally reduces technical and business-related issues to a minimum to simplify the conversation. As it is impossible to cover ABAP to its full extent, this book limits itself to describing a core topic and moving along a common thread throughout the chapters to reach the intended target group: programmers with little or no ABAP knowledge and SAP introduction project developers and team members. In this way, the book is able to impart a feeling of success to ABAP newcomers.

This book should not replace a course in basic SAP principles or advanced literature on specific ABAP-related subjects. It is not exhaustive in any respect. Nor does not aim to be a "dry run," but is instead intended to motivate you to get to know and use the SAP system. All steps that are essential to reaching this goal are comprehensively described through examples, background information, and source code listings.

Who This Book Is For

This book is primarily intended for developers who work in companies that currently implement an SAP system. It addresses consultants and project managers who want to read and understand ABAP source code and implement changes themselves. Last, the book has also been written for students and trainees who are learning ABAP as part of their professional training. You do not need any special knowledge of the topic to understand the material, though some sections are addressed to programmers who have worked with other programming languages.

About This Book

This book will guide you from a simple ABAP report, through important table maintenance tasks in the ABAP Dictionary, to the modularized flow control and complex data transfer structure between different reports. For this purpose, we'll continuously use a business example—a fictitious member management system—throughout this book in order to apply the theoretical aspects to real-life scenarios. So the focus of this book lies on describing and applying ABAP knowledge, not on its business-related context and processes.

Enhancements in the Second Edition

The book has been thoroughly revised for the second edition. The most recent ABAP release at the date of printing (ABAP Release 7.0 EHP2) included many enhancements that are also relevant for ABAP development beginners. In addition, the ABAP programming language has been further developed so that some ABAP language constructs (which previous editions referenced as the usual case) have become obsolete and should no longer be used. Similar to the adage "Orthography and grammar have been carefully adapted to today's common usage," ABAP syntax has been carefully modernized. Nevertheless, do not ignore old or obsolete notations, since it is likely that you'll need to understand, correct, or enhance old programs during your ABAP career. It is critical to recognize and classify both old and new notations, and understand their respective advantages and disadvantages.

Fortunately, the community of ABAP programmers continues to grow, bringing in new experiences in various programming languages. Once upon a time, most newcomers were experienced COBOL programmers and experts without previous programming knowledge; today, Java programmers, developers with experience working with modern script languages, and others contribute to the ABAP community. In light of this, this book includes both links to popular frameworks and tools outside the ABAP world, and sporadic references to object-oriented programming for more experienced readers.

Overall, this second edition entails the most comprehensive revision of *Discover ABAP* since its initial publication. This is an indication of the dynamic nature of the ABAP community, and the broad scope of innovations that extend our knowledge landscape.

Navigational Tools for This Book

Throughout the book, you will find several elements that help you access useful information. We have used the following icons to help you navigate:

> **Tip**: Useful information (as well as special tips and tricks) can make your work easier.

> **Note**: Notes highlight information about advanced topics, other resources to explore, or things you should keep in mind.

> **Warning**: This icon alerts you to common errors and pitfalls.

> **Example**: Here you'll encounter real-life scenarios and exercises.

Additionally, marginal notes provide a useful way to scan the book for topics that interest you. They appear beside a paragraph or section with related information.

This is a marginal note

System Requirements

You'll get the most out of this book if you meet a few requirements. Ideally, you have already familiarized yourself with some SAP basics, such as navigating through the main menu. Experience with general programming logic from other programming languages, macros, or scripts may positively influence your learning efforts. Access to an SAP system (including the relevant authorizations) would be another advantage. The mini-SAP system would be sufficient.

Mini-SAP System

The mini-SAP system, also known as ABAP trial version, is a test version included in various SAP PRESS books (*http://www.sap-press.com*). Alternatively, you can download it free of charge from the SAP website or the SAP Developer Network (SDN) in the DOWNLOADS area. The mini-SAP system provides the ABAP development environment, which is all you need when using this book.

The examples and figures in this book refer to SAP ERP 6.0 EHP5 or ABAP 7.0 EHP2.

What's In This Book?

Chapter 1, ABAP and Getting Started with the SAP System, describes the organizational and technical architecture of SAP systems, as well as the development prerequisites for getting started with ABAP. It shows the division of labor between the runtime environment and application programs, and addresses the structure of ABAP reports.

Chapter 2, ABAP Dictionary, gives you an overview of the purpose of the ABAP Dictionary. Using an example of a transparent table, you'll learn how to create a table, enter and display table entries, and handle data elements, domains, and technical settings.

In **Chapter 3**, Programming in the ABAP Editor, you'll create your first ABAP report, maintain its properties, create the source code, and execute the report. This chapter will teach you about the first ABAP statements and the relevant syntax.

You'll carry out basic arithmetic operations using variables in **Chapter 4**, Fields and Calculations. This chapter will also introduce you to the properties of data objects and differentiate between compatibility and convertibility. In addition, it describes some useful tricks you can use to improve list formats.

In **Chapter 5**, Modifying Character Strings, you'll work with and modify character strings, search for substrings, and carry out different variants of string operations.

Chapter 6, Debugging Programs, focuses on pursuing the program flow and finding program errors. For this purpose, you'll use the ABAP Debugger and its most important modes. In addition, this chapter introduces layer-aware debugging, which is a new function in ABAP 7.0 EHP2.

In **Chapter 7**, Modifying Transparent Database Tables, you'll enhance and modify a transparent table, learn about foreign keys, and implement table content checks. Along the way, you will use fixed values in domains, value tables, and check tables. You'll also learn about the specifics of currency and quantity fields.

In **Chapter 8**, Calculating Dates, Times, Quantities, and Currencies, you will declare and process date and time fields, and examine their specific features. This chapter uses many examples, which are described and traced in the ABAP Debugger.

In **Chapter 9**, Using Data in a Database Table, you'll modify the contents of a database table. It describes how you can insert new rows into the table via ABAP statements and change and delete existing rows. The chapter addresses the risks involved in deleting and manipulating data.

Our sample application gets more complex: In **Chapter 10**, Program Flow Control and Logical Expressions, you'll make some case distinctions, implement control structures and branches, and encounter logical expressions.

Chapter 11, Selection Screens, describes how you can provide a report with input values for the program flow in a selection screen. You will develop simple and complex selections and selection texts, and design the selection screen based on your own requirements. In addition, this chapter describes the meaning of text symbols, messages, and variants as they relate to the selection screen.

Chapter 12, Internal Tables, describes the meaning and types of internal tables. You'll learn what a header line is and how to distinguish between an internal table and a work area. To cement your understanding, this chapter also focuses on tracing the program flow in the

ABAP Debugger and includes important statements about processing the table rows.

In **Chapter 13**, Modularizing Programs, you'll learn about source code modules, internal and external subprograms, and function modules. In this context, the chapter also describes an option for exporting data from the SAP system. The transfer of data and data structures to called modules is also discussed in this chapter.

Chapter 14, Advanced Topics, is completely new in this edition, and gives you an idea of the numerous enhancements in the SAP world. Even though this introductory book won't go into the details of advanced topics (such as Web Dynpro, web services, and business rules), it does provide an overview of them and introduce you to the most important topics of the SAP world.

Code Samples for Download

In order to avoid the time-consuming task of typing source code manually, you can download the source code of all sample listings from the website that accompanies this book at *http://www.sap-press.com/*.

Acknowledgments

I would like to thank my wife and children, who made it possible for me to update this book by managing without me and relieving me of household work.

I also wish to thank Renate Fäcke-Kühnhauser for allowing me to continue the work of her late husband, Karl-Heinz Kühnhauser. He is the original author of this book, and I feel deeply indebted to him. I've tried to revise the book in a way of which he would have approved.

Special thanks are due to Tobias Trapp for mentorship, inspiration, and encouragement.

Last, I hope that you enjoy reading this book, and I wish you much success in learning ABAP.

Thorsten Franz
Software Architect, AOK Systems GmbH, Bonn (Germany)

ABAP and Getting Started with the SAP System

Client-server-based development of business applications—as used in the SAP environment—requires a different way of working and thinking than the development of local executable programs. SAP does not simply process applications; it processes cross-company business applications. Before you begin with ABAP programming, consider the architecture of the SAP system, the ABAP development environment, and the basic structure of ABAP reports as described in this chapter.

 ABAP

> ABAP is the programming language that SAP developed specifically for its dialog-oriented database applications. What began as a general report-formatting processor (abbreviated to "ABAP" in German) now exists as Advanced Business Application Programming and is one of the most important programming languages for business application development worldwide.

Before we examine the ABAP programming language, let's briefly look at the business and technical environment that ABAP programs run in.

Almost every midsize or large enterprise processes and stores millions of data records every day, month, and year. During this process, many users simultaneously work in a common database. The result is special business and technical demands for data security and data protection on the system that processes and stores the data and on the system architecture. The SAP enterprise resource planning system (SAP ERP) offers a business package to companies that use IT to process data on a daily basis. The SAP Business Suite supplements this package with further applications.

30 years is a long period of time in the IT industry, but in some situations, the law requires that business data be traceable for 30 years. That's why SAP consistently relied on independence—from hardware, operating systems, database systems and manufacturers, and programming languages—during the development of ABAP. The very first programs written in ABAP can still be processed by this programming language.

Openness The advantage is that it is an open and unlimited system that can be enhanced with new components in the future and still process data from its earliest days. A computer sold in today's market probably can't process the data on a PC from 1980 (if an operable one still exists). This observation doesn't even consider the problem of being able to trace the history of data changes or read the data from the storage medium.

The price that must be paid for this advantage is called *modularization*. In a technical sense, the work is distributed across several computers, servers, and services. In a business sense, the work is distributed across different software modules and supplemented by solutions for industries or customers. Technically, however, all users work with a common pool of data and in a common database to avoid working with insular solutions and creating redundant data.

Since the introduction of SAP ERP, the ABAP world has become even more open thanks to the SAP NetWeaver Application Server. ABAP can start JavaScript programs and transfer data between ABAP and JavaScript in both directions. Web Dynpro is a tool for creating web-based business applications. The ABAP server also provides powerful tools for generating and processing XML data flows, as well as for providing and calling web services. The resulting up-to-date web applications let users in the Internet or intranet access the functions of the ABAP system via a web browser without any problems. There are specific tools and workbenches for development using web applications and web services, but they are not discussed in this book.

Overview of the Architecture of an SAP System

This section explains the various ways that SAP system landscapes can be characterized and the impact on you as you get started with ABAP. During your career as a developer, you will always encounter terms like *presentation server*.

Technical Architecture

From a technical viewpoint, the SAP system is divided into three layers:

Multilayer landscapes

> Presentation layer
> Application layer
> Database layer

This division creates a *client-server architecture*, which is based on the principle of distribution of labor (see Figure 1.1).

Data input and output and a user's work with dialog screens occur in the intranet on the workplace PC, which is the *client* or *presentation server.* Presentation servers form the presentation layer of SAP. A special program package for the graphical user interface (also known as the SAP GUI; see "Logging On and Off the System") handles communication between the presentation server and the application server. The SAP GUI must be installed locally on the client. Without this program package, it is impossible to directly communicate with the SAP system.

Presentation layer

Data is processed centrally on one or several *application servers*. The application server communicates with the client over a message server and the SAP GUI. Depending on the business requirements, one application

Application layer

server could be sufficient. For larger systems, however, a single application server usually provides some but not all of the necessary services. Here, the message server is responsible for the load distribution and communication between the application servers, as well as for the connection to the presentation layer and users.

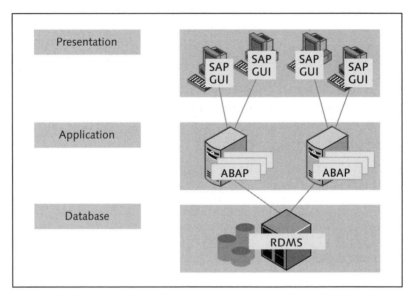

Figure 1.1 Client-Server Architecture

The communication with the database server is implemented via a database management system (Relational Database Management System, or RDBMS). Depending on the physical database, this system operates in the background in different ways. For a developer—that is, for you—the interface for working with different database systems is always the same. Programs, including the first programs you will write as you work through this book, run on application servers that make up the application layer.

 One or Many?

The remaining sections of this book do not distinguish between one application server and several application servers. The distinction is irrelevant when getting started with ABAP.

A common database uses its own server, the *database server*, to store data. Depending on the volume of data, among other factors, one or more computers can house application and database servers. For example, the application server can consist of several physical servers. The remaining sections of this book do not distinguish between common and separate servers for applications and databases.

For web applications, the architecture is quite similar. Instead of the SAP GUI, the web browser plays the role of the client or presentation server. Instead of occurring over the message server, communication with the ABAP system takes place over the *Internet Communication Framework*. Here, as well, the presentation layer is clearly separated from the application layer and data storage.

Database layer

Business Organization Architecture

In addition to a technical view of client-server architecture, the system landscape of SAP is often described in terms of business organization:

> Test and development system

> Consolidation system

> Production system

The principle of division of labor also applies to this multilevel organization. Depending on the quantity of data and the requirements for data security and data protection, two to four system levels appear in the real world. The minimum configuration consists of a test system and a production system. Depending on the operating system and the server's hardware, both systems can run on a single physical computer, but they would be technically separated as individual instances and each would have its own database. In four-system landscapes, two quality assurance systems lie between the development and the production systems.

Basic principle: division of labor

In terms of hardware systems, the sky is the limit, ending in the mainframe area. The decisive factors here include the operating system of the application server and the volume of data. Some operating systems allow the operation of several instances on one physical computer, but others do not. The volume of data (that is, the number of data records to be processed) determines the processing time for the application server and the time spent on read and write access for the database server. The business requirements determine how quickly results must be available. Servers with limited resources quickly reach their limits.

 Sizing

Determination of the optimal hardware architectures, called *sizing*, is its own area of expertise that is not discussed in any more detail here.

Test and development system

The *test and development system*, which stores practice and training data, is used for programming and testing system settings. Customer-specific settings in SAP software, called *customizing*, are first maintained on the test and development system and adjusted to customer-specific needs.

By their very nature, test and development systems are open and un-protected. They are usually accessed by many development users who have extensive authorizations. These users set up and change data and structures that they later stop maintaining and then discard. This system sometimes has a *sandbox area*, or an area in which users can simulate and test business processes. However, it is usually useful to separate "serious" development and configuration tasks in the test and development system from playful, explorative activities in the sand-box, and to provide a specific *sandbox system* for this purpose. The relatively large number of "power" users means that data protection in these systems cannot be guaranteed to the same level required in a production system.

Consolidation system

For the next layer of the system landscape, objects from the test and development system are transferred to the *consolidation* or *quality as-surance system*. As the name indicates, this system ensures the qual-ity of developments. Access, authorizations, data security, and data protection are treated more restrictively than they are on the test and development system.

The consolidation system is almost never used for development itself, but instead for the acceptance of developments after testing. For this purpose, data from the production system is copied to the consolidation system via a transport. Such data might be made anonymous, or data with a similar structure might be set up in the consolidation system. A later, separate transport moves the development to the production system only after the development runs without errors with this real data.

Since the *production system* represents the highest risks for a company, it has the best protection. System parameters cannot be directly changed here. Developments and customizing settings are never performed on the production system. Only objects that have been tested and released are imported into the production system, and only by logged transports.

Production system

This multilevel system distribution produces two results. First, actual data from production can't be lost in a test system. Second, you must be able to determine which developments and settings should be transferred from the test and development system into the production system, and which should not. Moving these objects into a different system running SAP software uses special tools that are combined in the correction and transport system, but we won't delve into the particulars of this specific topic for system administrators here.

Correction and transport system

 Do Not Transport Objects Yourself

As a novice, you need to know that developers themselves are usually not allowed or are unable to transport objects into another SAP system.

The transport system requires a transport number for a transport. A developer can define the request number as early as when the object was initially created and saved. In more restrictive environments, system administrators might prohibit developers from assigning the order number themselves and require that system administrators assign it. In this case, the object (such as a report) can be created only after the transport request number has been assigned. The rest of the path always continues in the same manner. If a request exists, the developer must release it so that it can be picked up. The administrator of the target system now accepts the request and imports it into the target system. The developer never has any direct influence on the process.

Local objects

There are always some objects (such as those you'll create as you work through this book) that are never supposed to be transported at all. These objects are to be saved locally on the test system, which is why they're called *local objects*.

Platform-Independence

Legitimate simplification

Despite the possible technical and content separations of an SAP system landscape, this book treats each SAP system as a technical unit (an instance) and deliberately avoids the distribution of applications and databases on several servers. This is sufficient for our purposes here. (We are also uninterested in the hardware, operating system, and database system on which our SAP system runs. Even the question of setting up several instances on one hardware system has no importance for us here. Advanced ABAP developers might well consider such issues to be of great interest. Think of different levels of performance and stability that arise for large amounts of data and in complex processes.)

As a newcomer to ABAP programming, you might be happy to know that one of SAP's strengths is its ability to run stably regardless of individual system components. You will, of course, encounter certified platforms; that is, combinations of hardware, operating systems, and databases that SAP has checked and accepted. But which of these combinations a beginner works with is unimportant. You'll find all the tools that you need in the SAP interface, which always looks the same, regardless of the actual platform that supports it. The following does not discuss working with database tools made by a database manufacturer or working with tools made by the operating system manufacturer. Instead, it deals exclusively with SAP tools, which guarantees that the statements in our application programs can be cleanly implemented in the corresponding commands.

Application Programs and Runtime Environment

SAP distinguishes between two types of SAP GUI-based application programs: *reports* and *dynpros*.

Reports

> Reports are essentially batch programs that generate lists, supply data interfaces, and so on. Although classic reports can be populated

from a selection screen and starting parameters, they run according to the same program logic. Users cannot intervene during the execution of a program to change its behavior.

> Dynamic programs (that is, dynpros) permit a user to intervene during the execution of a program. Dynpros use a series of dialog screens; the flow of a program depends on which screens users complete or which functions they trigger.

Dynpros

But this distinction has blurred for a long time now. For some recent releases, reports include screen lists with numerous interactive functions. New tools, such as the *SAP List Viewer* (ALV), accelerate this trend.

In this introduction to ABAP, we only have to work with dynpros twice: first, when we create a selection screen for the report, and later when we display the results of a report as a list on a screen (see Chapter 11).

Work Processes

All application programs written in ABAP run in ABAP work processes on the application server, keeping the programs independent of the operating system and the database (see "Technical Architecture"). Work processes are system users of the database system. SAP sets the number of work processes when it starts; this is like setting up a predefined number of connections or channels to the database system, each of which has different properties or is of a different type.

 Dispatcher

The system architecture places no technical limits on the number of users who can log on to the SAP system. In the real world, the number of users is often considerably larger than the number of available work processes, which is why users cannot be assigned fixed work processes while they are logged on. A specific subsystem (*dispatcher*) distributes user requirements to the free work processes.

As much as possible, the dispatcher tries to optimize things so that the same work process receives the sequential dialog steps of an application. If that proves impossible, the individual dialog steps of an application are assigned to different work processes.

Attributes An ABAP work process can execute an application and access the memory areas that contain the objects and data of the application that is running. It also makes three important elements available:

> **Dynpro processor**
  All application programs have flow and processing logic. The dynpro processor is responsible for the flow logic. It reacts to user actions and controls the further flow of the program. In other words, it is responsible for dialogs and dialog control, but cannot perform calculations.

> **ABAP processor**
  The ABAP processor is responsible for the processing logic. It receives screen entries from the dynpro processor and transmits screen outputs. The ABAP processor can perform arithmetical and logical operations, check authorizations, block and release access, and read and write to the database over the database interface.

> **Database interface**
  A database-independent set of SQL-like ABAP statements exists for database access through the database interface, which is collectively called *OpenSQL*. It is used to address the database interface of every database system with a uniform set of SAP commands. This encapsulation means that ABAP programmers don't even need to know which physical database system supports the SAP system.

  You can also address the database directly with your own database-specific SQL statements which will be interpreted directly by the database system without the ABAP system acting as a translator (*native SQL*), but this is generally frowned upon. System administrators usually forbid this practice because it creates higher risks to security and stability. SAP strongly recommends against using native SQL because it introduces platform-dependencies that should be avoided in ABAP programs.

Although it isn't always obvious in everyday programming tasks, the ABAP processor tends to play a subordinate, passive role, and the dynpro processor a more active one. The latter defines the modules (see "Structure of ABAP Programs") and sequence that the ABAP processor uses to execute logic. During these frequently used, standard tasks, dynpros are generated implicitly from the ABAP statements of the processing logic. You must use the appropriate tools and statements for the dynpro processor and the ABAP processor in all other cases.

However, with the recent introduction of more modern programming styles into the ABAP world, developers tend to regard the dynpro processor as an old-fashioned tool and implement as little control logic as possible in it. Instead, they move the control logic into the actual ABAP code whenever possible, in order to benefit from the more powerful ABAP programming language.

 Two Worlds

The ABAP processor and the dynpro processor create two different worlds, each with different tasks, tools, commands, data declarations, and memory areas. For example, the field contents of one world are not automatically known to the other world. Field contents are transferred at defined times and only when fields with the same names exist on the other side. Some statements function only in their own world. Note that the dynpro processor cannot execute any arithmetical operations. Other statements appear in both worlds, although they have different meanings and different supplements in the respective other world.

The combination of the work processes from the ABAP processor and the dynpro processor is called the *ABAP runtime environment*. It controls the screen and processing blocks to the same degree.

Structure of ABAP Programs

Every ABAP program consists of two parts: the declaration part and the processing blocks. The *declaration part* defines types, tables, structures, work areas, fields, and so on. Declarations for global data are available in the overall report with all its subprograms, and are known to all internal processing blocks at all levels. Declarations for local data are just the opposite: They are declared in a procedure and are available only in this procedure. The declaration part also contains the declarations of selection screens.

Declaration part

To summarize, the declaration part contains:

> Declaration statements for global data, tables, and types.

> All definitions and parameters for the selection screen.

> All declarations of classes internal to a program. (If you're working with ABAP Objects, see the following tip on ABAP Objects.)

→ Chapter 12 explains more about ABAP Objects.

 ABAP Objects

ABAP Objects describes the enhancement of ABAP language elements with object-oriented elements. The enhancement enables object-oriented encapsulation, interfaces, inheritance, and so on in ABAP. A grammatical reform that involves a stricter syntax check is linked to the introduction of ABAP Objects.

Processing blocks

The second piece of an ABAP program is its *processing blocks*. In technical terms, these are modular units that the dynpro processor can call according to specific rules. In terms of business, you can think of processing blocks as small, encapsulated subtasks. Processing blocks include:

> **Dialog modules**
Dialog modules and procedures are called by ABAP statements. Examples include the selection screen or list output on the screen.

> **Event blocks**
Event keywords introduce event blocks (events). They implicitly end at the start of the next event or at the end of the program. Starting a new page in a printed list is an event that triggers the printing of the page header. Other events include the selection of a list row by double-clicking on it or pressing a button on a dialog screen.

> **Procedures**
Procedures are methods in ABAP classes, subprograms, or function modules, for example. Function modules are standard subprograms for frequently repeated tasks, such as the uploading or downloading of data. In this context, they are increasingly replaced by ABAP classes (see "ABAP Workbench").

ABAP programs have a modular structure so that individual processing blocks can be assigned to dialog steps that the dialog processor can call. A processing block normally consists of several ABAP statements. If no processing block is explicitly written in the source code after the declaration part, then all the following ABAP statements are, by definition, part of the START-OF-SELECTION event block.

You can learn more about event blocks in Chapter 11.

 Legibility, Transparency, and Maintainability

➜ See Chapter 12 for more about ABAP Objects.

When you first start creating your own programs, you should use modular options in the source code. Legibility, transparency, and maintainability are the criteria for quality in a good program. It's not enough for a program to do what it's supposed to do. That's what everyone expects. To adhere to the principles of programming, a program must be as legible to a third party as a book. That is, the person for whom you are writing the code must understand what's happening in the source code and why. If necessary, the third party must be able to find the location for a required program modification quickly and make the change there. (Of course, this approach assumes that the third party has the required qualifications and authorization.)

Much to your surprise, you will quickly become this third party. Legal and organizational changes make new demands on a program and must be incorporated into it. It's interesting to note that even after six months, you'll have to examine your own programs objectively—that is, as though someone else wrote them.

The dynpro processor calls processing blocks during execution of an ABAP program. The ABAP runtime environment controls the process. A program can be executed only when the runtime environment can call its first processing block, such as LOAD-OF-PROGRAM. A user or the system itself can trigger the execution of a program. In theory, you can assign a transaction code and a menu path to every part of the program, which provides all options for navigation.

A section that requires a change be modularized so that it doesn't have any undesirable side effects. Think of it as a set of building blocks. You can remove one block and replace it with another without destroying the set as a whole. In this way, you exchange one module for another, and the system continues to run with the new module that can do more than the old one.

Building blocks

At all times, we recommend that you remember the basics of ABAP programming: legibility, transparency, and changeability. These will seem like second nature to you once you finish reading this book.

Logging On and Off the System

As is the case with many client-server applications, a program is developed on a local client (presentation server) and then executed on a remote server (application server). (See "Technical Architecture.") Data is processed on a different computer than the one that processes the dialog with the user.

SAP GUI

For communication with the server, development, and the display of results, the client needs a graphical interface. In the SAP environment, the connection to SAP on the application server is set up over the SAP GUI. It is impossible to log on to the SAP system without the SAP GUI. The SAP GUI is available in different versions, depending on the operating system, and can run in a web browser.

Setting up a connection

Installation of the SAP GUI normally puts an icon for *SAP Logon* on your desktop. SAP Logon is the part of the SAP GUI program responsible for connecting to the SAP system. You can start SAP Logon by double-clicking on the icon or (with a Windows client) via the Windows start menu: START • PROGRAMS • SAP FRONT END • SAPLOGON.

SAP Logon

SAP Logon displays a list of all the SAP systems that you can access. Select the test and development system and click LOGON. The SAP GUI sets up the connection to SAP and the system's logon screen is displayed (see Figure 1.2).

Logon

Enter the CLIENT, your SAP user name (USER), your PASSWORD, and the LANGUAGE you want to work in (EN for English) and press [Enter]. The SAP system administrator must enter you as a user, assign the required rights to you, and provide the data you need for these entries. The administrator should also have given you an initial password for logging on. During your first logon, you are asked to enter your password and repeat it for better security (see Figure 1.3).

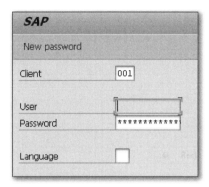

Figure 1.2 Logon Screen

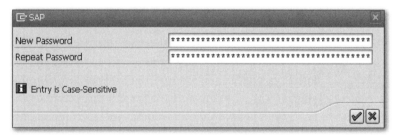

Figure 1.3 Entering Your Password During Your Initial Logon

 Note on Mini-SAP

If you're getting started with ABAP on a mini-SAP system, the logon screen and documentation show two users and passwords.

Confirm the password you have entered twice with Enter . The SAP menu is displayed (see Figure 1.4).

Figure 1.4   SAP Menu

Overview of Business Components

The SAP menu displays entries for Logistics, Accounting, and Human Resources. Depending on the type of the system to which you're logged on, the entries can vary—for example, a *Customer Relationship Management* system (CRM) contains entries for the respective CRM subapplications and any industry solutions or other add-on components that may be installed on your SAP system.

Client and company code

For all the data stored in these applications, the client entered during logon is the top level. In terms of business, the client is comparable to a corporate group. The next level is often the *company code*, or an independent unit with its own balance sheet. Still adhering to our metaphor: If a client is a corporate group, the company code is a subsidiary. Additional levels differ and are specific to customers in individual application areas.

Many objects (like reports) are client-independent: They are available globally in the entire SAP instance. That's why SAP features automatic client-handling and a comprehensive authorization concept that together permit the user to view only data relevant to that user.

Core areas

The traditional SAP ERP system consists of core areas: logistics, accounting, and human resources. Logistics includes areas like materials management, production, and sales and distribution. Accounting contains financials and controlling. Human resources covers business processes for personnel administration and time accounting, for example.

Each of the core areas is extremely comprehensive and requires different kinds of subject matter expertise, but the application data of the core areas is integrated in a common database. You can therefore access material master data from invoicing or production data from human resources. We will not explore the different levels of the core areas any further here.

The OFFICE menu entry includes email and organizer functionalities that you might know from Microsoft Office. Because these functionalities are available only to SAP users, many companies prefer to use other systems for email and task organization. CROSS-APPLICATION COMPONENTS are tasks and functions that apply to several business application areas. In this way, properties such as units of measure are managed uniformly in various areas. The INFORMATION SYSTEMS menu entry includes standard reports for the different business application areas. Standard reports (for example, for statistics) are included in the delivery of the SAP software. We will not discuss these three areas (logisitics, accounting, and human resources) in any more detail.

Additional functionality

 Common Development Environment

What is important here is the common development environment and data pool in the core areas that can be addressed with the ABAP Workbench. There you'll find everything you need to create database tables, write programs, and so on.

ABAP Workbench

You can navigate to the ABAP Workbench via SAP MENU • TOOLS to reach the OVERVIEW, DEVELOPMENT, TEST, and UTILITIES folders (see Figure 1.5).

Figure 1.5 ABAP Workbench

Technical Development Requirements

To work in the ABAP Workbench, you need access to a test and development system and complete installation of the SAP GUI on your client. If you want to create objects, you must be registered as a developer, for which you require an *access key*.

Access key   The system administrator must request the key from SAP for each instance of the SAP system, obtain it, and give it to you. Every system requires entry of this registration number when a new user tries to create objects for the first time (see Figure 1.6).

> **Note on Mini-SAP**
>
> When working with a mini-SAP system (which is the common name of the ABAP trial version), the access key for the standard user is already maintained.

You can only create new objects (reports, database tables, and so on) when the access key is maintained, even if you have other rights in the system. You cannot get started without the access key.

Figure 1.6 Maintaining the Access Key

At first glance, the situation might appear problematic, but it does make sense. This system ensures that changes to objects remain transparent and traceable. Division-of-labor processes in a company absolutely require an ability to trace who created or changed specific objects, and when and in what instance these objects were created or modified. The SAP system offers a number of ways for you to log this work.

Transparent and traceable

Overview of the Most Important Areas
In keeping with the goals of this book, the following section discusses only the areas and tools of the ABAP Workbench that are important for you as an ABAP novice. You can call individual tools from the tree structure of the SAP menu or via a *transaction code* that you can also display in the tree structure (see Figure 1.7). In a certain sense, a transaction code is a brief description of a program.

Transaction code

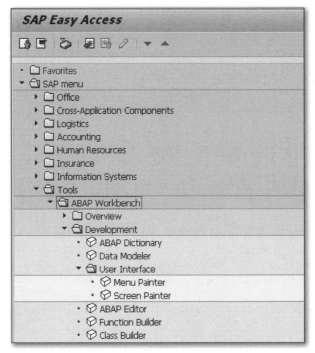

Figure 1.7 Important Components of the ABAP Workbench

➕ Entering Transaction Code

You enter a transaction code in the upper-left section of the screen, in the function code field, to call the initial screen of each tool. You can obtain additional help on the field by placing the cursor on it and pressing [F1].

ABAP Dictionary   As a beginner with the ABAP Workbench, you'll want to read data from tables, write data to tables, create or change tables, check to see if a table exists, and check to see if a table is populated with data. You can use OpenSQL to address only the database tables that are managed with the *ABAP Dictionary*. It is an indispensable information hub for the SAP system that contains a variety of objects and information that are not found on the physical database. For more information, see Chapter 2.

You can navigate to the ABAP Dictionary via SAP MENU • TOOLS • ABAP WORKBENCH • DEVELOPMENT • DICTIONARY or via Transaction SE11.

At first, the *ABAP Editor* will be your most important tool. You'll use it to write and check your first reports. You can start the editor via TOOLS • ABAP WORKBENCH • DEVELOPMENT • ABAP EDITOR or via Transaction SE38.

ABAP Editor

The *Function Builder* tool develops and manages function modules. Think of function modules as standard subprograms for rigidly refined tasks (for example, currency translation). SAP delivers a large number of function modules, but customers can also develop their own. Function modules have defined data interfaces for the input and output of data and should be able to capture errors.

Function Builder

For each function module, the system normally includes documentation that describes the function, input and output, and reaction to errors. You can navigate to the Function Builder via SAP MENU • TOOLS • ABAP WORKBENCH • DEVELOPMENT • FUNCTION BUILDER or via Transaction SE37.

→ See Chapter 13 for more information on working with function modules.

The *Class Builder* is the development tool for global ABAP classes. Global classes are, in many respects, the successors of the function modules: They can also be reused in various programs and are thus ideal for recurring tasks. In comparison to function modules, they offer developers enhanced options for internal modularization due to object-oriented programming.

Class Builder

You can access the Class Builder via SAP MENU • TOOLS • ABAP WORKBENCH • DEVELOPMENT • CLASS BUILDER or with Transaction SE24.

Use the *Menu Painter* tool to design the control portion of the screen (that is, the menu bars, cascades, buttons, and icons). Here you define the function that should be triggered and whether it is triggered by selection of an entry in a menu or by a keystroke.

Menu Painter

We don't necessarily recommend that you navigate directly to the Menu Painter; it is safer and more practical to use forward navigation from the ABAP Editor or from the Object Navigator. That being said, you will come to appreciate both methods while reading this book. If you do want to navigate to the Menu Painter directly, you can do so via SAP MENU • TOOLS • ABAP WORKBENCH • DEVELOPMENT • INTERFACE • MENU PAINTER or via Transaction SE41.

Screen Painter   You use the *Screen Painter* tool to design the input and output parts of the screen. It allows you to declare and position texts, input fields, and output fields, as well as design tabs, tables, and so on.

Our recommendation is the same as for the Menu Painter: use the Object Navigator or forward navigation from the ABAP Editor to navigate to the Screen Painter. Should you wish, you can navigate directly to the Screen Painter via SAP MENU • TOOLS • ABAP WORKBENCH • DEVELOPMENT • INTERFACE • SCREEN PAINTER or via Transaction SE51.

Object Navigator   You will find the *Object Navigator* indispensable when you write your first dialog programs or work on more complex development projects. It creates a common framework for all the related objects of a development. Since we're getting started by writing simple reports, we don't need the Object Navigator. For future work, you can navigate to the Object Navigator via SAP MENU • TOOLS • ABAP WORKBENCH • OVERVIEW • OBJECT NAVIGATOR or via Transaction SE80.

Logging off from the SAP System

To work with the SAP system may be great fun, but the time will come when you want to log off. The following sections introduce various alternatives for logging off the system.

Closing the SAP Window

The easiest and most intuitive method is to close the SAP window. Because it's possible to accidentally click near the top right corner of a window, the system outputs a security request before initiating the logoff process (see Figure 1.8).

Figure 1.8 Security Question for the Logoff Process

The security question does *not* indicate that unsaved data exists that could be lost in the event of a logoff; in fact, the system cannot check for unsaved data during this process. Indeed, the warning is rather general: *If* unsaved data exists, it *will* be lost when you log off. The wording of the warning can easily lead to misunderstandings and is perhaps slightly irritating, but this irritation will probably save you from experiencing severe data loss someday.

Logging off Using the System Menu

You can also use the system menu to log off. For this purpose, select System • Log off (see Figure 1.9). The system then displays the previously mentioned security question.

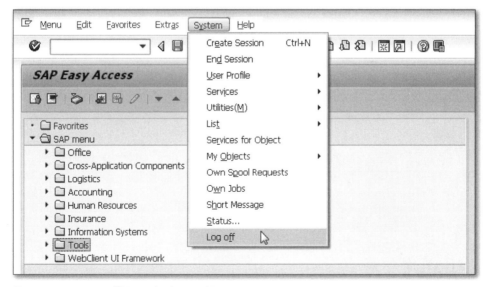

Figure 1.9 Logging off Using the System Menu

Quick Logoff with the/NEX Command

The /NEX command is used for a quick logoff but is not well known. You can enter it in the function code field just like a transaction code (see Figure 1.10). Here, you are logged off immediately without any security question, so be aware that any unsaved data will be lost without warning.

Figure 1.10   Quick Logoff with /NEX

ABAP Dictionary

Even though the standard delivery of the SAP software contains thousands of tables, customers need their own tables to meet their own needs. That's why we'll take a look at the most important work involved, starting with the creation and maintenance of tables.

In this chapter, we will create and populate a table that you'll access again in later chapters. It is the basic table of our example, member management, in which you create, change, and maintain a data record for each member. With each step you'll build on what you learned from previous ones, so you'll be prepared for more difficult steps down the line.

Step by step

 Tables in Real Life

> You won't maintain data in SAP software in a single table, but in many tables that are linked by relationships to a complex data model. To learn the basic principles, however, working with one table will suffice.

Getting Started with the ABAP Dictionary

Transaction SE11   When you navigate to the ABAP Dictionary via SAP Menu • Tools • ABAP Workbench • Development • Dictionary (or using Transaction SE11), the system displays the initial screen of the ABAP Dictionary (see Figure 2.1).

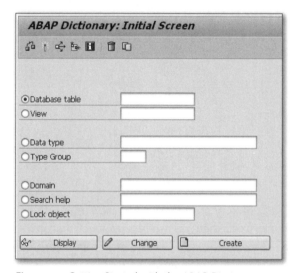

Figure 2.1   Getting Started with the ABAP Dictionary

Database Tables

Dictionary objects   From the initial screen, you can display, change, and create a dictionary object such as a database table, view, data type, type group, domain, search help, or lock object. For now, we're interested only in working with database tables.

There are three types of database tables in SAP software:

> Transparent tables

> Pool tables

> Cluster tables

Pool and cluster tables   With pool and cluster tables, the data is stored in an assigned table pool or cluster in the physical database. Both table types store special data (such as program parameters, dynpro sequences, and documentation), and can store data from several tables in common in a pool or cluster. Pool and cluster tables are not normally used to store business application data; this is generally stored in transparent tables.

 Transparent Tables

As noted, we will work only with SAP tools to create and maintain objects in the physical database. Transparent tables are the only type of tables that create a 1-1 correspondence between the table definition in the ABAP Dictionary and the physical table definition in the physical database.

A table pool consists of a single table in the physical database. All the tables assigned to the pool are called *pool tables*. The pool table stores all the records of the table in the pool, identified by the names of the pool table and the key fields.

A table cluster consists of several *cluster tables*. A cluster table combines data records with the same key in several cluster tables into a physical data record. This lowers the number of data records but lengthens a data record; the result is that you must often create continuation records.

 Only with Open SQL

The 1-1 correspondence found in transparent tables does not apply to pool and cluster tables, so you don't need to maintain any technical settings or indices. The information stored in the ABAP Dictionary is absolutely essential in order to process these types of tables. In an emergency, these types of tables can be processed only with Open SQL, and never with native SQL.

Creating and Maintaining Tables

When you create a new table, you must first think about a name. A table name has a maximum of 16 characters and does not distinguish between uppercase and lowercase. Note that for almost all objects, you must adhere to various *namespaces* for standard SAP objects and customer-specific objects.

According to the naming conventions, the names of customer objects begin with a Z, Y, or a *prefix namespace*. A prefix namespace is a letter sequence enclosed in slashes and uniquely reserved at SAP. It is added as a prefix to the name of the development objects and cannot be used by other SAP customers in their customer-specific objects (for example, /SAPPRESS/). This ensures that object names are unique and that naming conflicts during mergers, for example, do not arise. However, for our training purposes, the well-known customer namespaces Z and Y are sufficient. Enter ZMEMBER01 as the name of your first DATABASE TABLE and click CREATE (see Figure 2.2).

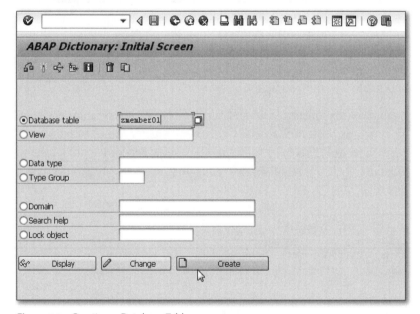

Figure 2.2 Creating a Database Table

The maintenance screen of the ABAP Dictionary contains five tabs: AT-TRIBUTES, DELIVERY AND MAINTENANCE, FIELDS, ENTRY HELP/CHECK, and CURRENCY/QUANTITY FIELDS. In the SHORT DESCRIPTION on the PROP-ERTIES tab, enter an informative, explanatory text, such as "Table of Members." You must complete two fields in the DELIVERY AND MAIN-TENANCE tab:

> **Delivery class**
>
> The delivery class regulates the transport of the table's data records during installations, upgrades, client copies, and transport into another SAP system. SAP and its customers have different write rights, depending on the delivery class.
>
> Enter an "A" in this field for the application table of master and transaction data. Master data (such as material numbers and personnel numbers) changes only rarely. Transaction data, on the other hand, changes often; inventory line items are a good example.
>
> The tables of the various delivery classes are handled differently during client copies, new installations, and upgrades. For example, a client copy generally does not copy master and transaction data.

> **Data Browser/Table View Maintenance**
>
> The settings in the DATA BROWSER/TABLE VIEW MAINTENANCE field regulate the scope that you may use to display and maintain data records with standard SAP maintenance tools. If you limit these rights, you might be unable to create any new data records in the dictionary.
>
> That's why you should select DISPLAY/MAINTENANCE ALLOWED here so that you have all the rights you need to work in the dictionary and can create, change, and delete data records.

But before you begin, save all your work up to this point. Click SAVE or press [Ctrl] + [S] (see Figure 2.3).

Saving a table

In the following dialog, you make an important decision: whether or not your table can be transported into another SAP system. If it can be transported, you must specify a package. A package bundles related objects of the ABAP Workbench and defines the transport layer. The transport layer determines whether objects will be assigned to a transportable change request for a target system, or will instead remain in the local SAP system for the time being.

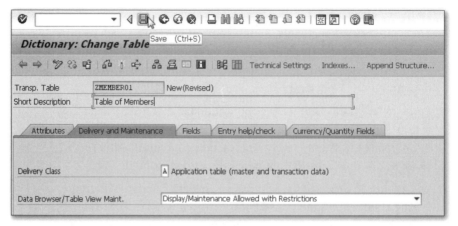

Figure 2.3 Saving the Table

➕ To Transport or Not to Transport?

Carefully consider this. In the real world—that is, in a multilevel system landscape—you would request the name of the package from system administrators and then enter that name because you're creating objects on the test and development system that you'll later use in the production system. For this exercise, that's unnecessary. The table and the initial reports can remain on the local test and development system.

Save the table as a Local Object (see Figure 2.4). It is automatically assigned to package $TMP. Objects of package $TMP are never transported and are not subject to version management.

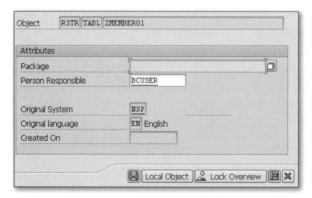

Figure 2.4 Creating an Object Directory Entry

Then enter the table's fields in the FIELDS tab (see Figure 2.5) and determine whether a field is a key field, whether it should have an initial value in the database, and which data element describes the business attributes of the field:

> **Field**
> Though you don't have to take naming conventions into account when selecting a field name, you should make a meaningful selection. Because a table field is always addressed via the table (in the form of `Table_name-Field_name`), the difference between customer fields and SAP fields is not a problem here. The field name has a maximum of 30 characters.

> **Key**
> Here you define whether a field is a key field. Key fields must be located in context at the start of the field and cannot have any gaps. Key fields uniquely identify a row and are used as sort and search criteria. A maximum of 16 key fields are allowed.

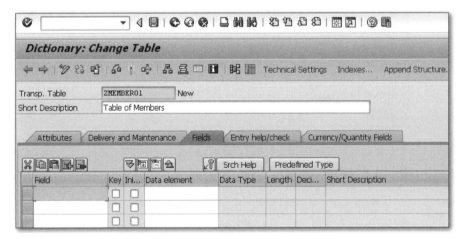

Figure 2.5 Maintaining a Table

> **Initial values**
> This entry is interesting if the field is empty (that is, without a valid value) in a data record. You must make an entry here if you want the field to be populated according to its type and with an initial value (such as zero) in the database. Without an entry here, the field

is actually empty. You can populate the field contents with a value entry at any later time. You should usually always preassign initial values, because otherwise the field in the database may contain null values. In programming, null values can be easily confused with initial values, which can lead to unpleasant errors.

> **Data element**
  Here you either enter the name of the data element or select a default data element. The data element stores some of the attributes of a field, including length, type, and so on.

 Business and Technical Attributes

One characteristic of the ABAP Dictionary is that field attributes are not normally stored directly with the field. Instead, they are stored separately in their own dictionary objects. Notice the distinction between business and technical attributes. The business attributes of a field are found in the related data element, whereas the technical attributes of a field are found in the related domain. Enter the name of the data elements here, and the name of the domains with the data element. We'll deal with this procedure in more detail shortly.

The separation between business and technical attributes provides an advantage: data elements and domains can be reused multiple times. The fields of various tables can point to the same data element, and changes to field attributes can be maintained at a central location. Dependent objects are automatically generated at runtime.

Data Elements and Domains

Using existing elements and domains

In this section, we review the sequence of *field*, *data element*, and *domain*, and the creation of all the objects. Let's begin with a field as an example. The field stores the name of the system client—the client number that you entered on the logon screen. Objects like tables are stored independently of the client and centrally in the database. They can be addressed from multiple clients. Using the correct client is quite helpful when trying to identify the correct data record.

Creating a Data Element

The first field should be called CLIENT and should be a key field. Use the existing element, MANDT, as the data element. Make these entries and click SAVE or press ⌃Ctrl + ⌃S. Then note the gray column of the first row (see Figure 2.6).

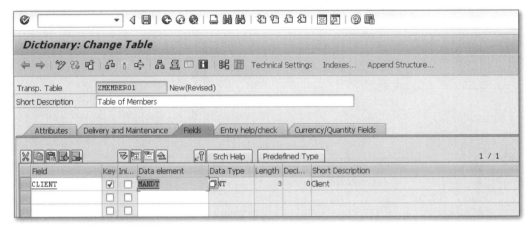

Figure 2.6 Creating a Table Field with an Existing Data Element

Because the MANDT data element already exists and is active, all its attributes and the related domains are accepted automatically. For our exercise, that includes the data type, length, number of decimal places, and a short description. You don't have to do any more work for this table field.

It gets somewhat more complex when you try to create a new data element and a new domain. But remember that you don't have to reinvent the wheel. A sensible alternative is to use existing objects (data elements and domains).

Creating your own elements and domains

The second field of the table should be a unique member number between 1 and 99,999. Enter MNUMBER as the field name. Though you must consider the customer namespace when you work with data elements, you can choose any name you wish—ZMNUMBER, for example—within those limits. Make both entries, and then define the field as a key field and save your work.

Forward navigation   Because the data element does not yet exist, the gray areas behind the data element are not populated at this time. To avoid navigating through the ABAP Workbench when you create a data element, use *forward navigation*. When you double-click on the object that interests you (in this case, the ZMNUMBER data element), the system asks if you want to create a data element (see Figure 2.7). Clicking YES will prompt a dialog for maintaining the data element to be displayed (see Figure 2.8).

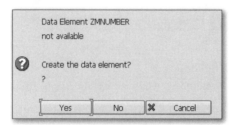

Figure 2.7   Creating the Object

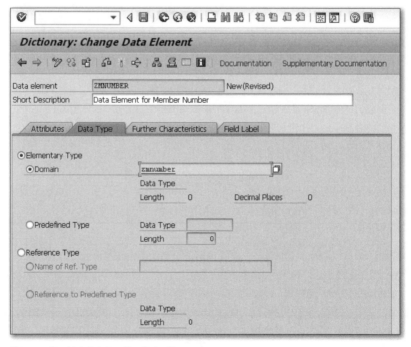

Figure 2.8   Maintaining the Data Element

Data Type

> Enter the name of the linked domain in the DATA TYPE tab. Remember that data elements and domains are different types of objects. You can either select a new name for the new domain or repeat the same name that you used for the data element.
>
> However, you must consider the customer namespace. The DOMAIN object types make it easy for the system to identify the correct object. For the sake of simplicity and uniformity in this example, the domain will also be named ZMNUMBER. Enter the domain in the appropriate field and save the data element.

Enter another SHORT DESCRIPTION of the object. (Use "Data Element for Member Number".) Because the data element is its own object, the system wants to know whether to transport the object. You must enter a package name again, but since you won't transport this initial exercise, save the data element as a LOCAL OBJECT (see Figure 2.9).

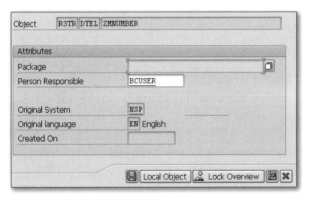

Figure 2.9 Saving the Data Element

In the FIELD LABEL tab, specify the identifier that will later be output in dialog programs and lists. In the screen templates of later dialog programs, you can set up the table field with its short, medium, or long text. The column for the field has a title in lists. Maintain these texts here and populate the related fields of the FIELD LABEL, as shown in Figure 2.10. After you save your entries, the system calculates the

Field label

length of the texts and populates the LENGTH field. You have now done the minimum required to create a data element.

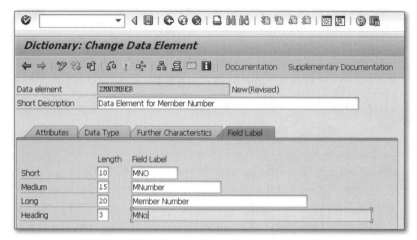

Figure 2.10 Maintaining the Field Label

⊕ Documentation

Developers and users often become frustrated with the poor documentation of programs provided by other developers. We want to create an explanatory text for our data element so that if, later on, someone doesn't know the reason behind the field (even though the name is intuitive), the user can access an explanation and help for the entry or use in custom programs.

All documentation and texts are maintained in the logon language, which is English in this case. When necessary, the texts and documentation are translated into the target language with a separate tool.

Click DOCUMENTATION (see Figure 2.10) to display the screen of another SAP tool, the *SAPscript Editor*. In the world of SAP software, SAPscript is used to design forms; it has its own editor and set of commands. Further detail about the SAPscript Editor is beyond the scope of this book, so just click DEFINITION and enter "Please insert the number of the member (valid from 1 to 99999)" as the help text in the row beneath the entry (see Figure 2.11). Save your entry and press $\boxed{F3}$ to return to maintenance of the data element.

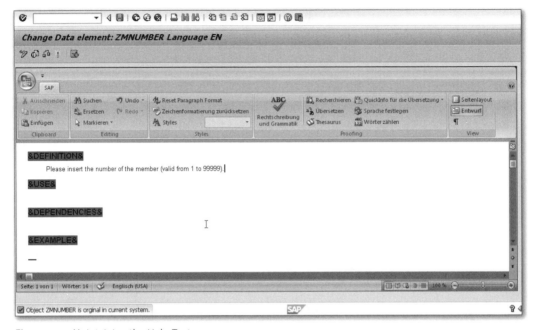

Figure 2.11 Maintaining the Help Text

Creating Domains

You've already maintained the domain name in the DATA TYPE tab of the maintenance screen. So now that we've completed our initial work on the data element, we can focus on creating the domain. We encourage you to work with forward navigation, so just double-click on the domain name, ZMNUMBER.

The system asks if you want to create a domain. If you click YES, the maintenance screen for domains is displayed (see Figure 2.12). But before we look at the tabs of the domain, we must enter a short description: "Domain for Member Number".

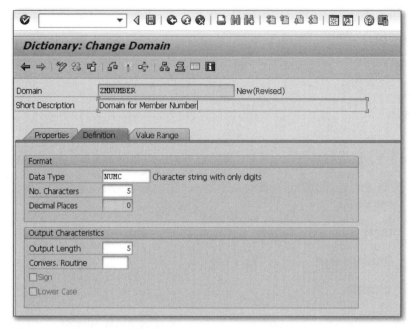

Figure 2.12   Maintaining Domains

Definition   In the DEFINITION tab, you must first specify the data type of the domain. In the real world, decisions about all the attributes of the field were made and documented when the table was designed. But for your information, you can press ⌷F4⌷ to see the data types contained in the dictionary and their attributes. For this exercise, select NUMC as the data type—a numeric character string with an output length of 5. Save the domain object as a LOCAL OBJECT.

Value range   According to the previous declaration of the domain, it might be helpful to limit the range of valid values. The maintenance screen for the domain contains the VALUE RANGE (see Figure 2.13) for this purpose.

In principle, three different types of limitation are supported. If any entries are made here, the system accepts only the value defined here as valid and rejects all other entries. But please note that how the system responds will depend on the data type. Fixed values (single values and intervals) cannot be entered for all data types. Checking entries for dialog screens also depends on the data type:

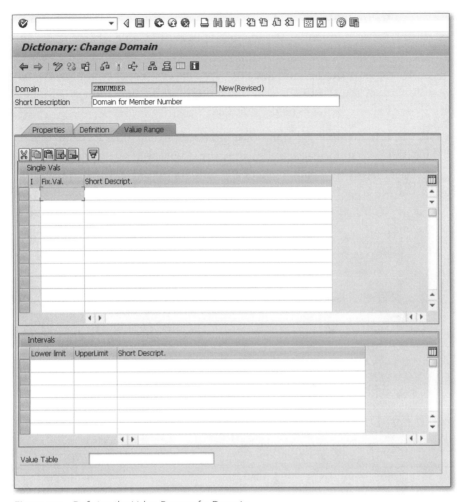

Figure 2.13 Defining the Value Range of a Domain

> **Single values**
> When you maintain single values, you list and describe every valid value. Maintenance of single values in the domain makes sense when the number of permitted entries is relatively small.

> **Intervals**
> If you maintain valid intervals in the domain, the smallest value and the largest value of an interval are specified. All values in between are also valid, including the values at both ends of the interval. Several intervals can be specified for one domain.

→ Chapter 7 deals
with foreign keys
in more detail.

› **Value table**

We recommend that you work with a value table when large quantities of data are involved if you expect input checks for the field to work with a table. Please note that simply populating the value table does not set up a check; this requires implementation of a foreign key on the table field.

Checking the
domain

In this example, we don't cover entering fixed values or value tables, but instead focus on saving domains. To proceed safely and avoid formal errors, you should check the domain in the next step. Follow the menu path DOMAIN • CHECK • CHECK (see Figure 2.14), press Ctrl + F2, or the CHECK button. If you're lucky, the system notifies you that it has not found any inconsistencies. You can then activate the domain.

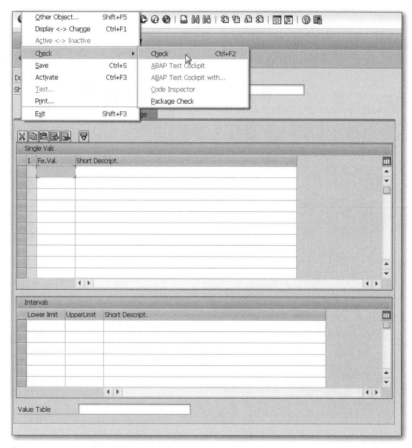

Figure 2.14 Checking the Domain

The domain still has a status of *new* (see Figure 2.15). It must have a status of *active* for you to use it in an active data element; it will become active when you activate it. Navigate via the menu (Domain • Activate), Ctrl + F3, or the Activate button.

Figure 2.15 Activating the Domain

The following dialog window displays an overview of all the currently inactive objects; the domain is already highlighted (see Figure 2.16). If necessary, you can also highlight and activate the other inactive objects. But if the work on these objects has not yet been finalized, you should avoid unnecessary risks and activate only the desired domain.

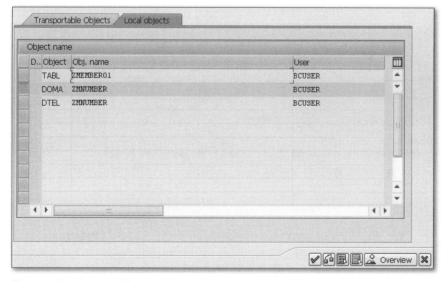

Figure 2.16 Activating Objects

Systemwide use   Confirm your selection with the ENTER button at the lower left or with the appropriate key. The status line notifies you that the object has been activated. To double-check, view the status again and ensure that it is set to active (see Figure 2.17). The domain can now be used globally in the system. Press F3 to leave the maintenance screen and return to the data element.

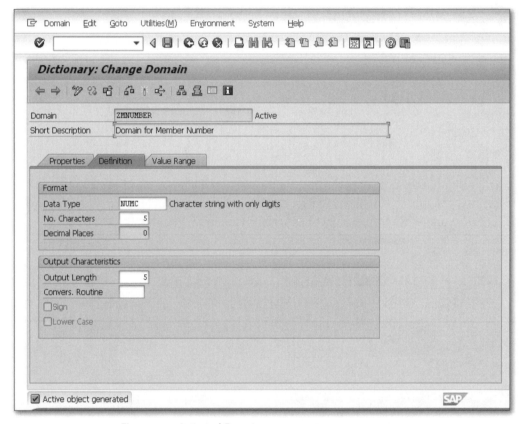

Figure 2.17   Activated Domain

Checking and Activating a Data Element

You should also perform a consistency check before activating a data element. Again, you can navigate via the menu, the key combination, or the CHECK button (see Figure 2.18). Ideally, everything is correct and you can proceed with activating the data element.

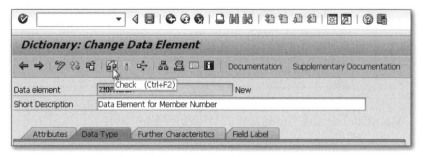

Figure 2.18 Checking the Data Element

The work here corresponds to the work for domains. Activate the data element with the menu or button, confirm your action in the following dialog, and then check the success of the activation by looking for either a status of active for the data element or a notification in the status line. Then use [F3] to return to editing the table fields.

Activating the data element

In order to store data records meaningfully in the table, our exercise requires that you enhance the table with additional fields. You can decide on your own which fields to include in the sample table. You're just practicing here. For our needs, four additional fields are enough to maintain a small data record in the table. The result should look like Figure 2.19.

Completing the table

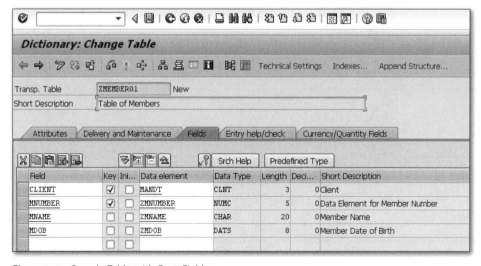

Figure 2.19 Sample Table with Four Fields

> **Checking the Table**
>
> Don't forget to check the table for inconsistencies with the Check button, `Ctrl` + `F2`, or the menu. You should make this important step part of your normal routine and your basic approach.

Maintaining the Technical Settings of the Table

The table is still located only in the dictionary, which is why you have to maintain the technical settings before you activate the table. That's where you define memory parameters, or how (if at all) the data record is stored in a read buffer when the database reads it.

Navigate to the technical settings from the table maintenance screen of the dictionary via Goto • Technical Settings or use the Technical Settings button. The required screen is displayed (see Figure 2.20).

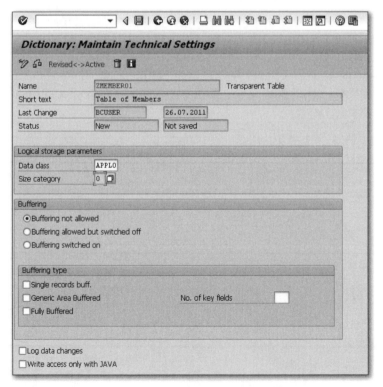

Figure 2.20 Maintaining the Technical Settings of the Table

For the DATA CLASS, use APPL0 (master data in transparent tables). By using this value, you're defining the correct physical area for the table in the database. The physical area, also called the *tablespace*, is an assignment to the directories or disks of the database. Depending on the database system, the data volume, and the number of accesses, the settings made here have an effect on later runtime behavior and should optimize read and write access. Master data or customizing data for the system settings is stored in a separate, dedicated database area.

Data class

Enter "0" as the SIZE CATEGORY because we don't expect a lot of data records for our exercise. The size category sets the size of the initial storage area for the table in the database. If the area you choose is too large, you will reserve unnecessary space. If the area you select is too small, you will have to reorganize more often.

Size category

 Smallest Category

Don't be perplexed by the numbers in the help window. These suggested values depend on the database system used. The smallest of the four size categories is sufficient for our needs.

For buffering, select BUFFERING NOT ALLOWED. In general, buffering means that the table is completely or partially loaded into working memory for reading. In other words, it's read in advance. For good performance, we recommend buffering tables or data records for large tables with many read accesses and relatively few write accesses. Our exercise involves only a very small table.

Buffering

After you make these settings, use F3 to return to table maintenance and activate the table. Success is indicated by a notification in the status line ("Object activated"); the status of the table is now displayed as ACTIVE (see Figure 2.21).

Activating the table

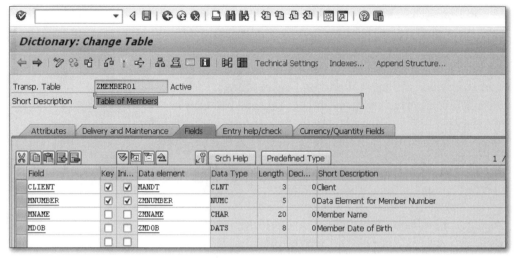

Figure 2.21 Activated Table

Default Values Sufficient

You can classify every table and structure in the ABAP Dictionary using an *enhancement category*, which defines how the table can be enhanced in the future. Don't get frustrated by the warning that is output after the successful activation. It only indicates that the default values from the system have been used for this purpose, which is absolutely sufficient for our case.

Creating Data Records

You can create data records for the table from the maintenance dialog. To write a few data records to the table, navigate via UTILITIES • TABLE CONTENTS • CREATE ENTRIES (see Figure 2.22) to a maintenance dialog in which you can create and save data records (see Figure 2.23).

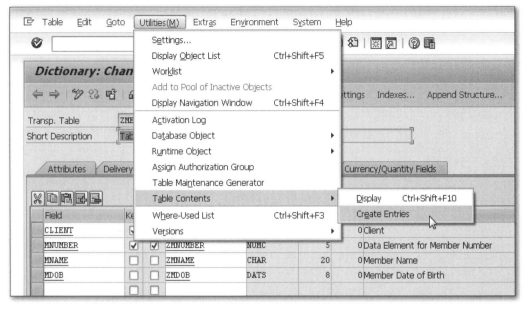

Figure 2.22 Creating Entries in the Table

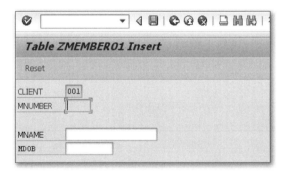

Figure 2.23 Maintenance Dialog for Creating Data Records

Entering Data Records

As a test, enter three data records: a member number (MNUMBER), a name (MNAME), and a birth date (MDOB). The CLIENT field is grayed out and cannot accept entries because automatic client management (which we'll discuss later) has automatically populated this field with the logon client. Key fields (in this example, the member number) appear in yellow. The remaining fields are white.

Gray, yellow, and white

Save each data record individually using the corresponding button. After each save, the status line displays a message: "Database record successfully created."

Monitoring   To check that the documentation is built into the data element, focus on the entry field for the birth date. Click it and press F1. If you have done everything correctly, the business help appears in a new window. If you have anchored fixed values in the domain, you can check them with F4. Then return to the maintenance dialog for the table with BACK or F3.

Displaying the Contents of the Table

From the maintenance dialog, you can view and check the data records of the table. Navigate via UTILITIES • TABLE CONTENTS and select DISPLAY. You can limit selection to specific records, but in this case you want to view all the data records that you have maintained, so click on EXECUTE (see Figure 2.24).

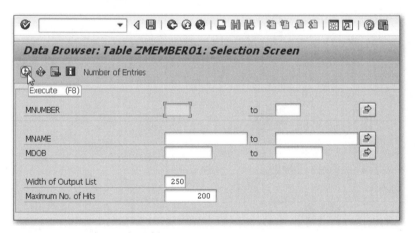

Figure 2.24 Displaying the Table Contents

Initial success   When you see the list shown in Figure 2.25, you'll know that everything has worked properly. Of course, tables in the real world are more comprehensive and involve more effort. We have not explained many options available in the dictionary, but as far as getting starting with

ABAP goes, the worst is already behind you. You have created a table
and populated it with data. Now you can devote all your attention to
ABAP programming.

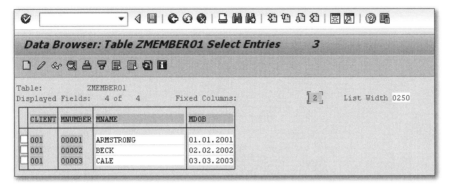

Figure 2.25 Displaying Data Records

Programming in the ABAP Editor

This chapter teaches you how to use the ABAP Editor to create, activate, and execute your first program. It helps you get to know ABAP statements and shows you how to take your first steps in the ABAP Editor.

Everything looks complicated when you first get started, but you'll find that it's usually not half as difficult as you imagined and be proud of your first successful list.

Creating an ABAP Report

You can start the ABAP Editor from the SAP menu (TOOLS • ABAP WORKBENCH • DEVELOPMENT • ABAP EDITOR) or by using Transaction SE38.

Transaction SE38

You must enter a program name in the initial screen that is less than 40 characters long and contains only letters and numbers. Don't use special characters (such as letters with diacritical marks) except for underscores. Remember that you must adhere to the naming convention

One name, one program

for customer objects: The program name must begin with a Z, so name your first report Z_MEMBERLIST01 and click CREATE (see Figure 3.1).

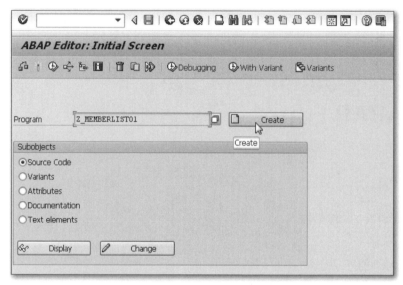

Figure 3.1 Creating an ABAP Report

Maintaining program properties

In the next screen, you define the attributes—the properties of the report (see Figure 3.2)—and give it a descriptive title, such as "First Member List". Specify the original language of the report—in this case, EN for English.

 Original Language

The information on the original language of the report is important, because all texts in SAP, whether in menus or screens, can be maintained in a country-specific manner. SAP provides a proprietary translation tool so you can translate the texts from the original language to the target language without having to change the source code of the program. If developers have done their job correctly, a translator without programming knowledge can translate all the texts.

The status of our program is still *New (Revised)*, which makes sense because we're still creating it. The program will be executable once the status changes to active.

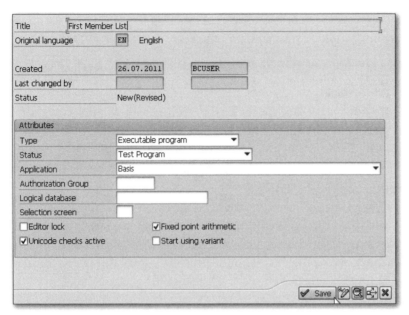

Figure 3.2 Maintaining Program Properties

For the TYPE of program, select EXECUTABLE PROGRAM. An executable program can be started without a transaction code directly, or in the background with a batch job. The invisible runtime environment controls the report. It calls defined processing blocks in a fixed sequence and handles the processes of program execution, such as outputting a list at the end of the report.

Program type

For the STATUS of the program, select TEST PROGRAM from the list and select BASIS for the APPLICATION. Both criteria help program management. They describe the status of program development, for example, if you're dealing with a finished customer program in production or a program in the experimental and testing phase. These criteria also describe the business application area to which the program belongs.

Program status

Leave the next three optional fields blank. You can use the AUTHORIZATION GROUP to assign the program to a program group and then set authorization checks for the group so that only authorized users can start the report. A LOGICAL DATABASE is a higher-level read-program that helps you find and assign data in various tables. It can ensure that data is processed in the right sequence and performs other tasks that are not discussed further here. See Chapter 11 in the section on selection screens for more information on the SELECTION SCREEN VERSION.

Additional attributes

Select the following settings for the four remaining checkboxes:

> **Editor lock**
  Do not set the EDITOR LOCK. You need it only when you want to prevent another user from changing, renaming, or deleting the program. In the real world, this precaution can be helpful because only the author of the last program change can remove the lock.

> **Unicode checks active**
  Check UNICODE CHECKS ACTIVE. As of release 6.10, ABAP supports multibyte coding. Earlier releases used only character sets based on single-byte coding, such as ASCII or EBCDIC codes. In some circumstances, programs without Unicode checks can trigger syntax or runtime errors.

> **Fixed point arithmetic**
  Activate FIXED POINT ARITHMETIC. Otherwise, packed numbers are treated as whole numbers without consideration of decimal places, and intermediate results are rounded in calculations. In other words, if you're interested in exact calculations (as is the case in Chapter 4, Fields and Calculations), you must activate fixed point arithmetic.

> **Start using variant**
  Don't select START USING VARIANT. Variants populate the selection screen with initial values. To ensure that a report is actually populated with the same initial values every time it runs, store the selection screen in a *variant*. If you start the report with the variant, the selection screen is already populated, which significantly reduces the risk of errors.

✚ Beneficial in your Daily Work

The START USING VARIANT option is beneficial in your daily work. In the real world, this kind of selection screen can be quite comprehensive. But right now, starting the report with only a variant will not be helpful. In Chapter 11, we will assign initial values to the report with a selection screen for the first time.

After you save the program, you'll be instructed to create an object catalog entry. Remember to save the object locally, as we noted in Chapter 2, ABAP Dictionary.

Maintaining an object catalog entry

ABAP Editor: Overview

That automatically (and finally) takes you to the ABAP Editor (see Figure 3.3), which has two basic modes: *frontend mode* and *backend mode*.

Frontend and backend mode

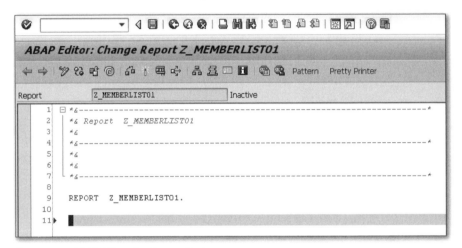

Figure 3.3 ABAP Editors in Change Mode

Modes of the ABAP Editor

The frontend modes load the ABAP source code onto the client, where it is processed locally. In backend mode, the source code is not loaded locally, but instead remains on the server. Saving a change in the source code transmits the change to the server.

Both modes offer the same source code layout and are appropriate for editing ABAP source code. The difference between the two modes lies in their operation and functional scope:

> **Frontend editor (new)**
> The new frontend editor in the source code mode is the most recent editor version. It is available with SAP GUI for Windows 6.40

Operation and functional scope

(Patch Level 10) and requires SAP NetWeaver 7.0 or higher for full support of its functions.

Due to its numerous new functions (such as automatic code completion, source code highlighting, syntax schemas for various programming languages, adaptation of the language syntax using XML configuration files, and other interactive elements), it is a suitable programming tool for all developers.

> **Frontend editor (old)**
> The old frontend editor is similar to a text editor, in that it provides user-friendly context menus and processing functions like cut, copy, paste, and drag-and-drop. However, it lacks the functions of a modern programming environment: source code highlighting and source code completion.

> **Backend mode**
> The traditional backend mode works to accomplish a goal. It processes several rows as a block of rows during cut and paste and requires that you highlight the block with several clicks (we discuss this in more detail in Table 3.2). We recommend using various intermediate buffers so that you can use several clipboards at one time.

➕ Advantages of the New Frontend Mode

Developers from another programming environment (for example, from the Java environment or other modern script languages) who join the ABAP world see the environment as somewhat outdated. The new frontend editor—with its functions for source text completion and visual keyword highlighting, processing blocks, and so on—can make help you get to know the new environment and considerably increase productivity.

That's why we will always use the new frontend mode in the following project, though you can use another mode if it better meets your personal working style.

Switching between change modes

The ABAP Editor always starts in the last mode in which it was operated. If you want to switch from one mode to another, use the UTILITIES • SETTINGS menu to navigate to the dialog for user-specific settings in the ABAP Workbench. Select the new change mode in the ABAP EDITOR tab and confirm your selection with ⌨Enter. The setting remains in effect until you change it again.

Controlling the ABAP Editor

Above the input and output area of the screen used to edit source code, you'll find the control area of the ABAP Editor: two toolbars. The upper toolbar (see Figure 3.4) helps to control the ABAP Editor. Table 3.1 explains the individual icons.

Toolbars as controlling units

Figure 3.4   Toolbar to Control the ABAP Editor

Icon	Function	Description
	Switch between changing and displaying the source code	When you change the source code, the background of the input and output area is white. The background changes to gray once you switch to *Display, but* you cannot change the source code in this mode.
	Switching program status from *active* to *inactive*	Several versions of an object can exist in the real world, but only one of them can be active at any given time. Use this function if you want to deactivate an active version for a time so that you can activate a different version of the object.
	Switching to another object	During a project, developers simultaneously work on several modules that they get to know little by little. Use this function to display a window from which you can quickly control all other objects that belong to your development project. The only type of object you've encountered so far are dictionary objects (such as tables), but advanced developers use this function to navigate to function groups, class libraries, and web objects.
	Enhance	This button can be used to enhance standard programs. Usually, the standard version should not be changed; however, if urgent customer demands require an enhancement of standard programs, you can traditionally modify the source code. The new enhancement concept replaces the traditional enhancement and modification concepts. Because this book is based on custom programs, enhancements and modifications are not necessary.

Table 3.1   Functions of the Toolbar to Control the ABAP Editor

Icon	Function	Description
	Syntax check of the source code	If the system finds a syntax error during a check, it displays a window that indicates the problem areas. It will notify you if no syntax errors were found.
	Activate program	The system creates an active version with this function if the program was once inactive. The correctness of the syntax is checked and an active program version and runtime version are generated. The active object is generated even if the program is already active.
	Execute program in test mode	The program is started in test mode in the Workbench.
	Where-used list of the object	If an object is used in or by other objects, the list shows in which ones the current object is used. You can navigate to the location of the call to check the context in which the object is used there. For example, tables are used in many programs, so it is possible that changes to a table structure have unpleasant side effects. When making changes, we recommend that you gather information about the environment in which an object works.
	Display object list	This function takes you to the view provided by a different tool: the repository browser. You can see all the objects that belong to your development project. You'll work with the repository browser when you require access to several objects for a project.
	Display navigation window	This function is quite practical in complex development projects. An additional window displays the last objects that were edited, so you can quickly navigate among them.
	Full screen on/off	This button lets you activate or deactivate the full screen mode. If you call the program processing using Transaction SE80, the left screen area displays a navigation tree that maps the currently processed program and its elements (such as data declarations, points in time, and subprograms). You can hide or display this navigation tree with the button.
	Help on ...	This function opens a context-dependent window. This window appears in the ABAP Editor when you request help with ABAP terms, like keywords, function modules, and tables.

Table 3.1 Functions of the Toolbar to Control the ABAP Editor (Cont.)

Icon	Function	Description
	Set or delete session breakpoint	It may happen that a program does what it was programmed to do rather than what you want it to do; that is, the end of the program no longer meets expectations and it's time to observe how the program processes in order to make modifications This function sets a stopping point (breakpoint) on a line of source code. The control icon is displayed to the left of the line. When the program runs, it stops at this line and switches to *debugging mode* (see Chapter 6, Debugging Programs). Double-click on the icon at the start of the line to delete the breakpoint.
	Set or delete external breakpoint	When you develop web applications, you need an external breakpoint. You don't use the SAP GUI to log on to web applications but onto a web browser, for example. To have the system switch to debugging mode at the right place in the source code, the breakpoint must be placed before the web logon. This book solely uses session breakpoints.
Pattern	Insert pattern	You must often insert several lines of commands or comment blocks in the source code. This practical function saves you the effort of all that typing. For more information, see Chapter 10, Program Flow Control and Logical Expressions.
Pretty Printer	Pretty printer	Source code can quickly become unmanageable unless visual aids for comments, paragraphs, and insertions are built in. This practical function handles everything for you, freeing you from keeping track of how many spaces you need at the start of a line, for example.

Table 3.1 Functions of the Toolbar to Control the ABAP Editor (Cont.)

The lower toolbar (see Figure 3.5) is used only in backend mode to edit the source code. (The old frontend mode contains a cut-down version of it.) As you can see from the icons, the functions here are similar to those of other interfaces: CUT, COPY, PASTE, and so on. Table 3.2 explains the meaning of the icons.

Figure 3.5 Additional Toolbar to Edit Source Code in the Backend Mode

79

Icon	Function	Description
	Cut line	If you place the cursor on a line in change mode and click this button, you cut the line out of the source code. It disappears from the source code and is stored in the SAP buffer. From there, you can insert the line into another location in the source code. As in word processing, the SAP buffer has only one set of content, which means that new content overwrites old content.
	Copy line	This function copies the line in which the cursor is placed into the SAP buffer. The source code still contains the original line.
	Insert line	In change mode, this function pastes the content of the SAP buffer to the line in which the cursor is placed.
	Selection mode	You use selection mode to edit several lines as a block. To copy a block of lines to another location in the source code, proceed as follows in change mode:
		1. Place the cursor in the first line of the block of lines.
		2. Click on the selection button; the line turns red.
		3. Place the cursor on the last line of the block of lines.
		4. Click on the selection button again. This line and all the lines in between turn red.
		5. Copy the selected block to the X buffer (or to one of the other buffers) via UTILITIES • BLOCK/BUFFER • COPY TO X BUFFER. The status line notifies you that the block was copied to the buffer.
		6. Position the cursor in the target line. Careful programmers often create a blank line for the sake of safety and position the cursor there.
		7. Insert the contents of the X buffer where the cursor has been placed in the source test via UTILITIES • BLOCK/ BUFFER • INSERT X BUFFER.
	Cancel command	This icon lets you cancel the last editor command in change mode.
	Insert new line	In change mode, this icon lets you insert a blank line in front of the line in which the cursor has been placed.

Table 3.2 Functions of the Toolbar for Editing Source Code in the Backend Mode

Icon	Function	Description
	Delete line	Using this icon, you can delete the line in which the cursor has been placed.
	Concatenate lines	In change mode, this function merges the current line with the following line. This option is helpful when editing leaves only one word of a command in the subsequent line.
	Duplicate line/ block	You can use this function to copy lines or blocks in the source code and reinsert them into the original position with a click. Depending on the actual case, it works like a combination of the COPY LINE and INSERT LINE buttons; it highlights a block, copies the block to the buffer, and reinserts the block in front of a line.
	Move line/block	This function moves text. The text in the line is moved five columns to the right. If you don't want to rely on PRETTY PRINTER, you can use this function to ensure better legibility on your own.
	Find	Use this function to search for and replace text in the source code. Whether you're searching for a character string that is a word, for a character string that is part of a larger character string, or for uppercase or lowercase characters, this function will find it if it exists. The cursor in placed on the first line of the hit. You can set the search area at the cursor position or specify a set of lines. You can also search inactive versions of your source code.
	Find next	You usually need this function in combination with the FIND function. If you suspect the presence of additional hits in your source code, you can continue to search with this option.

Table 3.2 Functions of the Toolbar for Editing Source Code in the Backend Mode (Cont.)

In particular, working with buffers differs from working with the clipboards familiar to you from typical desktop applications. In addition to the buffer of the presentation server (client), the SAP system has three additional server-side buffers, which are named the X, Y, and Z buffers.

SAP buffers

Copying within a system and beyond a system

If you're copying in one of these three supplemental buffers, you can also insert the contents into the source code with a different method. Note that in this circumstance, the SAP system must be the same. The buffers are related to the system and are therefore emptied when you quit the editor or log off the system. If you want to copy between systems, you must start from the SAP system and copy to the client's buffer, either via the SAP menu or with [Ctrl] + [C] and [Ctrl] + [V].

The following applies in the line-oriented backend mode: The cursor must be placed on the line that is being edited. A section of a line must be highlighted beforehand. A block that consists of several lines must be highlighted at the beginning and at the end of the block.

Understanding and Editing ABAP Programs

Comments in the source code

Now when you look at the source code (see also Figure 3.3), you might see gray, especially in lines 1-7. The asterisk (*) in the first position makes the entire editing line a comment line. Another way to add comments is to write something after an opening quotation mark ("). Everything after this quotation mark is interpreted as a comment rather than as a command. The section "Notes on the Source Code" provides an example of this feature.

 Multiple Commands in One Line

You can use the period to write two short commands in one line. However, use this option carefully. ABAP will allow you to end each command with a period, but that makes the source code difficult to read and, in addition, runs counter to the convention of placing each new command in a new line.

Make an effort to create good, legible *inline documentation from the beginning*; the business world calls this *adequate documentation*, but this term is not operational. In some situations, it is completely appropriate for comment lines to make up some 30% (or more) of the source code. Bear in mind how quickly your own code can become unfamiliar even to you after a few months, so try to make it as accessible as possible to third parties.

In the ABAP Editor, you'll see black and blue along with gray in line 9. This REPORT statement is the first ABAP statement (also known as a command) that you'll become familiar with. It is always the first statement in an executable program.

REPORT

You'll also see the first operand (or addition) of the command: the program name (Z_MEMBERLIST01).

You can also see a period (.) in the line, because every ABAP statement must end with a period. Even if a statement stretches over several lines or screens, a period must be placed at the end of the statement. However, note that while a period doesn't have a fixed place, such as at the end of a line, it does need to be the last character of the command (that is, it closes the command). Its location in the line is not important. (It also could be placed directly after the last operator.)

One more point

See the following complete statement:

```
REPORT Z_MEMBERLIST01.
```

Tips for Self Help

Even if the REPORT command doesn't offer any explanation, you can easily determine what the statement does and what operands it has. Click on the statement and then press [F1]. A help window opens with *ABAP keyword documentation* that provides you with information on the effects of the command, possible additions, hints, examples, and tips (see Figure 3.6).

Since you want your first ABAP program to materialize quickly, write a short first comment in line 10 (after the REPORT statement):

WRITE

```
WRITE 'This is my first list'.
```

The WRITE statement outputs a list (in this case, a literal 'This is my first list'). A literal is a set character string in the source code that begins with a single quotation mark. Unfortunately, it cannot be maintained as language-dependent. In Chapter 11 we'll start working with text elements that can be translated, but for now just enjoy your immediate success.

Literal

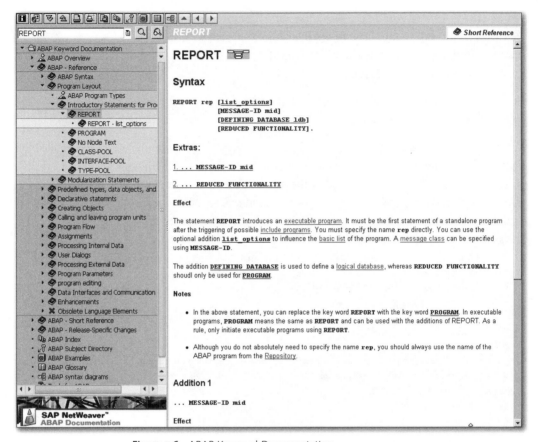

Figure 3.6 ABAP Keyword Documentation

Executing an ABAP Report

Short countdown

Four steps are involved in the execution of your first ABAP program:

> Save

> Check

> Activate

> Execute

Save the program via PROGRAM • SAVE or with the SAVE ([Ctrl] + [S]) button. The status line issues a confirmation. Then check the program via PROGRAM • CHECK • SYNTAX or the CHECK ([Ctrl] + [F2]) button.

If you receive a message in the status line that no syntax errors were found in the program, you can call the program via Program • Activate or with the Activate ([Ctrl] + [F3]) button.

Activation combines several work steps; it checks the correctness of the syntax, generates an active version of the program, generates a runtime environment, and deletes the object from the list of inactive objects. Chapter 2, ABAP Dictionary, already introduced you to the next activation screen. The status line displays the message, "Object was activated." The report is then executable and you can start (execute) it.

There are two ways to perform a required test here. The first way is to navigate via Program • Test • Directly or with the Directly ([F8]) button to start the report from the ABAP Workbench. If the program terminates, you then have to reopen the ABAP Workbench and redisplay the source code on the screen to find and correct errors.

Starting from the ABAP Workbench

The second way is similar to the way that a user would start a report. Usually, users don't have the necessary access rights to work in the ABAP Workbench. User menus can look different based on the rights that a given user has been assigned, but they all have entries for System and Help. That's why a "normal user" can start the report from the SAP menu with System. Let's test this approach.

Starting from ABAP program execution

Open a second session (a second window) via System • Generate Session or with the Generate New Session button. In this session, navigate via System • Services • Reporting to ABAP program execution. In this case, the system has already entered the name of the executable program in the field. You simply have to press the Execute ([F8]) button to start the program.

The advantage of using this approach is that you can see the dump in the second session if the program terminates. If this happens, the system generates a log as a screen list that contains hints about probable causes and an excerpt of the source code that caused the error. If the source code is still in the first session, it's much easier to analyze errors and make corrections.

Did Everything Work?

We're assuming that our first attempt didn't trigger a program termination. If everything worked as expected, you should see the first member
list, as shown in Figure 3.7. You can use the BACK (⌐F3⌐) key to return to
ABAP program execution; then switch back to the session with the ABAP
Editor.

Figure 3.7   First Output of a List

We're not done yet. In the next step, we try to output the data records
of the table that we created and populated in Chapter 2.

Reading and Outputting Database Tables

When you want to work with database tables in a report, you must
declare a work area in the report where you can edit the data from
the table. For our ZMEMBER01 table, you can do this using the following statement:

```
DATA wa_zmember01 TYPE zmember01.
```

TABLES   The DATA statement creates a structure of the same name in the program
with the same data type as the database table: *work area*.

All the fields of the structure have the same names and data types as
the fields in the database table. When reading the data records from
the database table, you can place each of them in the structure and
then work with them.

Obsolete TABLES Statement

Older programs may also contain the obsolete TABLES statement, which defines a table area or table work area. This statement creates a data structure of the same name for the referenced database table in your program. Some commands for database access have a short form that lacks explicit specification of the work area. Instead of using an explicitly named work area, the system implicitly creates a work area that has the same name as the database table in the ABAP Dictionary. To add to the confusion, such implicitly named work areas are frequently misused to type other data objects. This can be confusing because it is not always clear to the reader of a program when the code refers to a work area (a data object in your program's memory), when it refers to a database table, and when it merely refers to the Dictionary structure of said database table for typing purposes. The short form of these ABAP commands establishes no difference among the three. Under certain circumstances, the programming environment outputs an error if you use this kind of obsolete statement. Even though you'll certainly find them in old programs, you shouldn't make a habit of using them.

 The Hyphen

You address the fields of the structure with the names of the work area and their field names; you address the MNAME field of the WA_ZMEMBER01 work area with WA_ZMEMBER01-MNAME. The first part of the name is the structure name; the second part is the field name. Notice the hyphen that separates the parts of the name without any blank spaces. For future work, also note that you should use the hyphen only for this purpose and never with variable names.

Not everyone remembers the type declarations for all the fields of the database tables in use. If you need to refer to them, use forward navigation (double-click on the name of the table) to branch to the dictionary display, where you can see the required information in the FIELDS tab. Then use the BACK button to return to the ABAP Editor.

The following program is the simplest way to output the rows of a database table line-by-line in a list:

SELECT

```
SELECT * FROM zmember01 INTO wa_zmember01.
  WRITE / wa_zmember01.
ENDSELECT.
```

The SELECT statement means that the records from the ZMEMBER01 table are transferred, record for record, into the work area. The asterisk (*) indicates that all the fields of a record are transferred. If you want to transfer only some of the fields, you must specify those fields as a field list instead of using the asterisk.

In this form, the SELECT command corresponds to loop processing. All records of the database table are transferred to the program structure record by record. The loop begins with the SELECT statement and ends with the ENDSELECT statement.

Formatting Lists

The structure contains the statements for processing the records that have been read. In this case, the entire WA_ZMEMBER01 structure will be written to a list for each record. You trigger a new line with a slash (/) in the WRITE command. Please note that you must insert a space before and after the slash.

WRITE /   Since there are three data records in the database table, you have three lines in the list; each line of the list is as long as the structure. The structure is output as a character string in the list. There is no empty column between the fields. The legibility of the list is not optimal; it would be better to see the fields in the desired order (and with some space between them) in the list. You must address the fields of the structure. Consider the following example:

```
WRITE / wa_zmember01-mdob.
```

The slash triggers output of the field on a new line. The following statement, however, places the output of the field at the end of the current line of print; that is, the field is simply added to the line.

```
WRITE wa_zmember01-mname.
```

This approach can produce infinitely long lines. On its own, the system breaks a line on the screen only when the screen settings demand it.

It breaks a line on paper only when the printer output settings or the width of the paper demand it. Accordingly, each developer is responsible for the correct design of a line.

Chain Statement

A WRITE statement is needed for every field of the structure that should be output in the list. Luckily, there is an easy way to avoid writing a statement each time: Simply tell the system that several WRITE statements are to be executed after each other.

Place a colon (:) after the first statement, and separate the statements   WRITE
with a comma instead of a period. Place a period only after the last statement. In our example, the chain statement appears as follows:

```
WRITE: / wa_zmember01-mdob,
         wa_zmember01-mname.
```

Of course, these kinds of chain statements are not limited to WRITE commands.

 Looking Good

> Consider the transparency and readability of the source code. Even when you work with chain statements, you must adhere to the principle of writing each statement to a new line. Avoid writing two or more statements in one line as much as possible.

Lines

For simple list formatting, the ULINE command (without additional   Underline
operands) creates a horizontal line in a new line of the list:

```
ULINE.
```

You can use this command to set off sections of a list and improve its legibility.

Blank Lines

The SKIP statement creates blank lines in a list:

```
SKIP.
```

If you want to create several blank lines, simply specify the number of blank lines. The following statement produces three blank lines:

```
SKIP 3.
```

Writing and Editing Source Code

Type it yourself We recommend that you type your first source code manually (see Listing 3.1) so that you get to know the ABAP Editor. Create empty lines with [Enter]. You can also use the familiar copy and insert functions ([Ctrl] + [C], [Ctrl] + [V], and so on) and practice with the additional ABAP Editor functions for entire lines or blocks of lines, as described in "Controlling the ABAP Editor."

 Download Offer

You can also download the source code in Listing 3.1 from the website for this book at *http://www.sap-press.com/*.

```
1   *&---------------------------------------------*
2   *& Report   Z_MEMBERLIST01                     *
3   *&                                             *
4   *&---------------------------------------------*
5   *&                                             *
6   *&                                             *
7   *&---------------------------------------------*
8
9   REPORT   z_memberlist01                .
10  DATA wa_zmember01
       TYPE zmember01.            " define work area
11  WRITE 'This is my first list'.
12  ULINE.                        " horizontal line
13
14  * loop
15  * each record of the table with all fields
16  * will be printed on a new line of the list
17  SELECT * FROM zmember01 INTO wa_zmember01.
18    WRITE / wa_zmember01.
19  ENDSELECT.
```

```
20   SKIP.                          " one blank line
21
22   * SELECT statement like before
23   * single fields of the record will be printed
24   SELECT * FROM zmember01 INTO wa_zmember01.
25     WRITE / wa_zmember01-mdob.
26     WRITE   wa_zmember01-mname.
27   ENDSELECT.
28   SKIP.                          " one blank line
29
30   * SELECT statement like before
31   *   single fields will be printed like before
32   *   but the WRITE statement is concatenated
         into a chain statement
33   SELECT * FROM zmember01 INTO wa_zmember01.
34     WRITE: / wa_zmember01-mdob,
35              wa_zmember01-mname.
36   ENDSELECT.
```

Listing 3.1   Z_MEMBERLIST01 Report

Notes on the Source Code

Short documentation

Start editing in line 10, right after the automatically inserted REPORT statement. The first 8 lines, which serve as short documentation on the author, creation date, and change history, are automatically generated by the system.

Line 10

```
DATA wa_zmember01 TYPE zmember01. " define work area
```

Accordingly, a data structure (WA_ZMEMBER01) is created that is typed for the ZMEMBER01 database table and thus has the same structure.

The report has a work area (WA_ZMEMBER01) that you can use as the work area for working with data of the ZMEMBER01 table. The statement concludes with a period.

Comment lines

After the blank space, a comment line begins with the quotation mark in the same line: "define work area." The system interprets all characters to the right of the quotation mark as a comment. Even if you write a statement that lasts for several lines, you can still insert comments into individual lines. The comments would appear in the middle of the statement.

Line 11
```
WRITE 'This is my first list'.
```

The text between single quotation marks is output to the current position in the list. Because this is the first WRITE statement, the current position is line 1, column 1.

Line 12
```
ULINE. " horizontal line
```

ULINE produces a horizontal line across the entire width of the list, separating the title from the rest of the list.

Line 13

The blank link should improve the legibility of the list.

Lines 14, 15, and 16
```
* loop
* each record of the table with all fields
* will be printed on a new line of the list
```

These three lines are comment lines that explain the following statements.

Line 17
```
SELECT * FROM zmember01 INTO wa_zmember01.
```

One record after the other

The SELECT statement opens a structure. A loop reads all the data records of the table and transfers them one by one into the work area of the program. The work area contains a complete record of the table. Once the record is processed from the work area, the next record is read. The asterisk means that all the fields of a record are being selected.

Line 18
```
WRITE / wa_zmember01.
```

The slash after the WRITE statement outputs the list to a new line in column 1, rather than to the current print position. Note that you must place a blank space before and after the slash.

Writing the WA_ZMEMBER01 option outputs the table area as a whole; that is, as a character string. The length of the character string is the sum of the lengths of the fields. In the character string, the fields are given according to their type, which means that they are not formatted for printing.

Output as character string

Line 19
ENDSELECT.

The ENDSELECT statement closes the open SELECT structure. Just like other loops have a closing command for every opening command, each SELECT statement (if it's a loop) has an ENDSELECT statement.

 Just Like Math

This process is similar to working with brackets in math. An opening bracket always has a closing bracket; they always appear in pairs. When nesting brackets in mathematic equations, you must make sure that you have assigned them correctly. The same applies to loops in programming. When nesting loop structures, you must also take special care to make sure that the loop is opened in the right position, that the loop processing runs correctly, and that the loop is closed. We have not nested any loops yet, but the principle applies already.

Line 20
SKIP. " one blank line

The SKIP statement creates a blank line in the list. This statement is helpful for improving the legibility of the list.

Improved legibility

Lines 21, 22, and 23
The source text has a blank line and two comment lines here, just as it does in lines 13-16.

3

Line 24

```
SELECT * FROM zmember01 INTO wa_zmember01.
```

All records of the table are reread in a loop, as in line 17. The difference here is in the following record processing.

Line 25

```
WRITE / wa_zmember01-mdob.
```

 Writing Convention

This WRITE statement outputs a field: the MDOB field of the WA_ZMEMBER01 work area. Notice the writing convention (structurename-fieldname). If the field name or the structure name contains a hyphen as part of the name, the system cannot uniquely identify and interpret the statement. That's why you should always work with an underscore (_) when assigning names, as in STRUCTURE_A-FIELD_B.

The slash after the WRITE statement always places the output on a new line in column 1.

Line 26

```
WRITE wa_zmember01-mname.
```

This WRITE statement also outputs a field of the structure: the MNAME field. The output is placed in the current position in the list (in this case, after the MDOB field). The system automatically inserts a line break if fields are written after each other in the same line.

LINE-SIZE   With this kind of output, you must make sure that the line has enough room for the fields that you want in the first line. You could also add LINE-SIZE after the REPORT statement to manipulate the width of the list.

Line 27

```
ENDSELECT.
```

The ENDSELECT statement closes the SELECT loop from line 24—the last one that was opened.

Line 28
```
SKIP. " one blank line
```

As in line 20 of the source code, this insertion of a blank line improves legibility.

Lines 29 to 32
Blank lines and comments are inserted into the source code here.

Line 33
```
SELECT * FROM zmember01 INTO wa_zmember01.
```

The table is read for the third time.

Lines 34 and 35
```
WRITE: / wa_zmember01-mdob,
         wa_zmember01-mname.
```

In the list, the result looks exactly like the second read loop. The difference is in the writing. When several statements that follow each other differ only in the operands, you can use a chain statement. Line 34 has a colon right after the WRITE statement without a space. That tells the system that several WRITE statements now follow each other. The individual statements are not ended with a period, but are separated by a comma. Only the last statement, as usual, is closed with a period.

C as in chain statement; C as in comma

The first statement in our example outputs the MDOB field of the WA_ZMEMBER01 table structure to a new line in column 1. It is closed with a comma. The second statement writes the MNAME field of the same table structure to a list with a blank space after the MDOB field. Because this statement is the last in the chain, it is closed with a period. (Remember that a chain statement can involve several statements right after each other. The principle that a new command belongs in a new line also applies to a chain statement.)

Line 36
```
ENDSELECT.
```

Don't forget to end the loop. This ENDSELECT statement belongs to the SELECT statement from Line 33.

List Screen from Our Sample Source Code

Self-programmed
outputs If you look at the list screen (see Figure 3.8), you can see that the system has generated some outputs on its own (for example, the descriptive text from the program properties). Right now, however, the outputs that we created ourselves are more important:

> The first line is the text, "This is my first list."

> The second line is the horizontal line beneath the text.

> The next three lines present the unformatted output of the table structure. One line in the list corresponds to the complete contents of the structure. Because the table contains three data records, the processing loop is run through three times and three lines are written to the list.

> After the blank line, you can see three lines, each with a birth date and name. Note that the date is output in a different format than it was in the first block. When we declared the field in the table, we defined the DATE field type, which includes a country-specific presentation of the date format. The internal formatting of the field is seen in the output of the table structure: YYYYMMDD. Because only two fields of the table structure should be output, the remaining fields do not appear in the list.

Figure 3.8 List Screen for the z_MEMBERLIST01 Report

> The contents of the third block do not differ from those of the second block. The difference exists only in the source code, where the WRITE command was given as a chain statement.

Did everything work as planned? If so, use the BACK (F3) button to return to the ABAP Editor. In the next step, we'll work with fields and calculations.

4

Fields and Calculations

Be prepared: You never know what you might be forced to include in a calculation. Thankfully, whatever comes up, the SAP system will handle it gracefully and even allow you to operate with date values and character strings. However, in this chapter, you will begin with the simplest task: performing calculations using numbers.

 Preparations

> Before you begin, decide whether you want to create a new report for your first calculations in ABAP or whether you should include them in your old report instead. Although both are possible, we recommend that you use a new report in order to maintain a better overview; you can also copy an existing report and modify it afterwards. This way, you can preserve the old report and save the new one under a separate name.

Preparing the Report

Start the initial screen of the ABAP Editor (SAP MENU • TOOLS • DE-VELOPMENT • ABAP EDITOR). Enter the name of your last report as the program name in the initial screen: Z_MEMBERLIST01. Then start the

Copying and modifying the report

copy process by either selecting PROGRAM • COPY from the menu or clicking the COPY... button ([Ctrl] + [F5]) (see Figure 4.1).

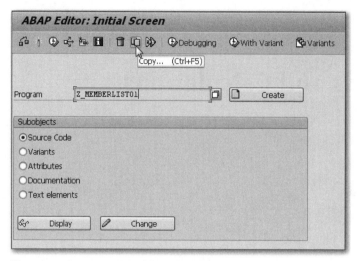

Figure 4.1 Copying an ABAP Program

→ **Chapter 3 provides additional information on naming conventions.**

The system asks you for the name of the target program (see Figure 4.2). The name of the target program must differ from that of the source program, and, of course, meet the requirements of the naming conventions described in Chapter 3.

Figure 4.2 Selecting the Name of a Target Program

Once you have entered the name of the target program, you can continue the copy process by clicking the COPY button or pressing the [Enter] key. Then you can copy other elements from the old program, along with the source code and text elements (see Figure 4.3).

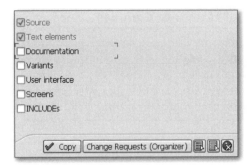

Figure 4.3 Copying Other Elements of an ABAP Report

For now, you can continue this process without checking any of the elements and by clicking the COPY button. Then save your new report as LOCAL OBJECT. After that, the system displays the initial screen of the ABAP Editor again, but with the new program name. The old program was copied, including all selected elements. Take note that the new source code is still inactive.

Ex Copying Elements

For example, if you had stored documentation for the old source code, you could now select and copy this documentation. The elements in this window don't represent separate objects in the database, but are firmly linked with the report. This means that you can't use the documentation for the report multiple times (for instance, for other reports), which would be possible for data elements. Because a data element is a separate object, it can be used multiple times.

Click the CHANGE button to enter the change mode for the source code. What you see now should not be new to you. You already know the old source code. However, you will notice that the REPORT statement is slightly incorrect. Undoubtedly, it was copied correctly, but since the program name in the operand has changed, the first thing you should do with the new source code is to change the program name to the new name: Z_MEMBERLIST02.

Converting Blocks of Lines into Comment Lines

What should you do with program lines that you no longer need? You have two options: You can either delete the lines, or you can convert them into comment lines. Cautious developers will probably opt to convert seemingly superfluous statements into comment lines, which may be needed later to implement a statement. You never know.

You'll do the same here and convert the old statements into comment lines, to be on the safe side. Use the cursor and the cursor keys or the mouse (as you would in any other editor) to select the block of lines that you want to process. The system now displays the selected block in gray (see Figure 4.4).

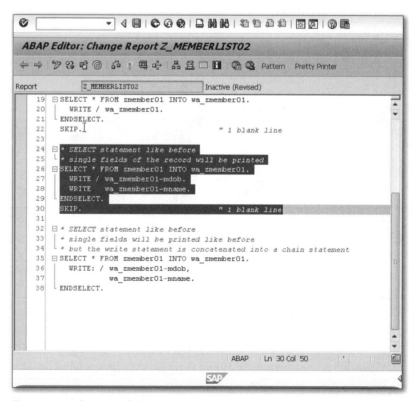

Figure 4.4 Selecting a Block

To convert the entire block into comment lines, select UTILITIES • BLOCK/BUFFER • INSERT COMMENT * (see Figure 4.5). Consequently, all lines of the block contain an asterisk (*) in column 1, which marks them as comment lines. If a line was already a comment line in the previous source code, it now has two asterisks (**).

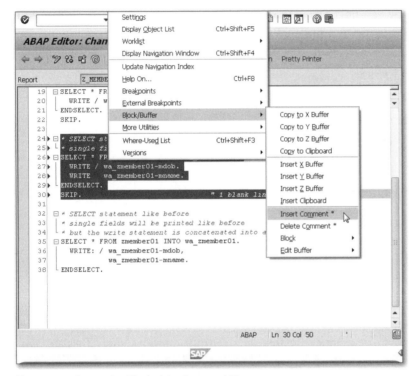

Figure 4.5 Converting Blocks into Comment Lines

Based on Figure 4.5, you can also deduce how to convert a block of comment lines into statement lines if you need to. Highlight both the block and the end of the block and select UTILITIES • BLOCK/BUFFER • DELETE COMMENT *.

Because you won't need the statements beyond line 10, you can delete the block of lines. For this purpose, select the corresponding block again and press the ⌈Delete⌋ key on your keyboard.

Deleting a block of lines

Don't Forget to Save

Remember to save the changes to the source code by clicking the SAVE button every time you have completed an important step and before setting your work aside.

Objective: process numbers and output list

You can now focus on the actual task of this chapter: using ABAP to process two numbers with the four basic arithmetic operations and output the result as a list. To do that, you must carry out the following steps:

> Declare the fields for the numbers

> Calculate the result

> Output the result

Declaring Fields

As it would in real life, our "member management system" requires the processing, enhancement, or analysis of the contents of one or several tables in the report via calculations. For this purpose, we need several fields in the report.

Processing fields

ABAP has rules that dictate how fields are processed. In our example, the system must cache and store the numbers, and then retrieve them for subsequent processing steps. For this purpose, the values are temporarily stored at a specific location or data address in the memory.

In ABAP, these locations are known as *fields* or *data objects*. If the contents of data objects can be changed using ABAP statements, these data objects are called *variables*; if their contents cannot be changed, they are known as *constants*.

Declaring Variables

Assigning names

When assigning names to variables, you should adhere to the following conventions:

> The name should start with a letter or an underscore; that is, it cannot consist only of digits.

> A name can contain a maximum of 30 characters.

> If possible, the name should not contain any special characters except for underscores. The restrictions vary for classic ABAP, Unicode-enabled programs, and ABAP Objects, but avoiding special characters such as the plus sign (+), comma (,), colon (:), and parentheses ((and)) should generally put you on the safe side.

> The names of fields must be different from words that are reserved for ABAP statements or additions, in order to avoid confusion. Again, the strictness of the restrictions imposed by the ABAP language varies depending on the programming context, but using reserved keywords such as DATA or the names of built-in data types such as STRING is at best confusing and at worst grounds for an error message during syntax check.

➕ Mnemonic Variables

In addition, the names of variables should be meaningful (that is, self-explanatory). So if you need to use a variable for a family name, you can call it FAMILYNAME instead of A1, for example. You should also focus on readability and clarity, keeping in mind those third parties who might have to read the source code at some point in the future. After all, you may be in a similar situation someday where you must read source code written by someone else.

Fields should have a symbolic name (such as NUMBER01), a defined length, and a data type. The symbolic names are used to address the memory addresses where the stored contents can be read and processed. Depending on the data type, specific rules apply to the processing itself; however, these rules differ considerably from programming language to programming language.

If you want to be able to change the contents of your nusmber fields, you must first declare your fields using the DATA statement. For your calculations, use two data types for the variables at this point: *integers* and *decimal numbers*.

DATA

For example, if the NUMBER01 field should contain an integer, the statement looks like this:

TYPE i

```
DATA number01 TYPE i.
```

TYPE p Alternatively, if the NUMBER01 field should be a decimal number containing two decimal places, the statement would look like this:

```
DATA number01 TYPE p DECIMALS 2.
```

So it is the intended usage that determines which declaration should be used. Type i fields are typically used for counters or numbers of pieces. Type p fields are often used for arithmetic operations that include decimal places. It is important to know how precise the calculation and calculation display must be, because the level of accuracy determines the number of decimal places required. As an example, just think of currency exchange rates. In such cases, oftentimes up to five decimal places are used, whereas the total number of 14 permissible decimal places is used very infrequently.

Elementary data types Both data types i and p are elementary data types with a fixed length in ABAP. For this reason, you don't need to explicitly specify the field length. These two data types are two out of a total of eight built-in elementary data types with a fixed length in ABAP.

 More Comprehensive Type Concept

You'll encounter an elementary data type with variable lengths later in this book. At this stage, we will restrict ourselves to using the most important data types for a better understanding. Also, we won't describe reference data types and complex data types here. However, you should keep in mind that the type concept used in ABAP for advanced applications is much more comprehensive than what is described here.

If you want to declare two variables in the same way, you must write two statement lines and check that you use the same attributes, as shown in the following simple lines:

```
DATA number01 TYPE p DECIMALS 2.
DATA number02 TYPE p DECIMALS 2.
```

However, the major disadvantage here is that you must always maintain the declaration of NUMBER02 by yourself if the declaration of NUMBER01 changes. This task can become very tedious and laborious if many dependent declarations are used. It is much easier to have the declaration of NUMBER02 reference that of NUMBER01. You can implement that using the LIKE addition:

LIKE

```
DATA number01 TYPE p DECIMALS 2.
DATA number02 LIKE zahl01.
```

This way you can ensure that the declaration of NUMBER02 is always correct because it is linked with the declaration of NUMBER01. If you want to increase the number of decimal places in the future (for example, from two to four), you merely need to change the declaration of NUMBER01, and the declaration of NUMBER02 will be automatically adjusted. Of course, this refers to all variables in a report that reference the declaration of NUMBER01.

This system helps you avoid inconsistencies within a report. However, if identical declarations of variables are required in different reports, the declaration must reference a table field in the ABAP Dictionary, for example. If you want to declare the variable SEQUENTIAL_NUMBER in the same way as the MNUMBER field in the ZMEMBER01 table, you must write the following line of code:

Avoiding inconsistencies caused by automatic adjustments

```
DATA sequential_number TYPE zmember01-mnumber.
```

By using this method, you can avoid having to adjust the variable in different reports. If the length should change in any way, this will only affect the domain of the table field. Then all affected reports will automatically be regenerated during the first startup after the change has been implemented, and not a single line of source code will have to be modified due to that change.

If you wanted to preassign the negative value of -105 to the field, you would include the minus sign (-) in the statement, which would look like this:

```
DATA number01 TYPE i VALUE -105.
```

ZIP Codes

> The relevance of this procedure to real-life scenarios becomes readily apparent if you look at the process of changing from 4-digit to 5-digit ZIP codes in Germany in 1993. Developers sometimes had to search for the ZIP code field in hundreds of programs, and then implement the change and finally recompile the programs. This was a very time-consuming and labor-intensive process, especially since there are many ways to abbreviate the German equivalent of the term "ZIP code" and to declare a variable. The problem would have been solved pretty quickly with our method.
>
> Similar problems arise when companies significantly modify their organizations (for example, due to a merger). Suddenly, the former one-digit region identifier may no longer be sufficient for differentiating between the 500 regions in which the company operates. Or, referring to the ZIP code example, your company is going to operate at an international level and now has to manage not only purely numeric ZIP codes but also ZIP codes that contain both numbers and letters.

This is also relatively easy. If, on the other hand, you want the NUMBER01 variable to represent a decimal number containing two decimal places, the whole matter becomes somewhat more complex. For example, if you want to preassign the value 3.14 to the NUMBER01 variable, you would probably expect to use a statement like this one:

```
DATA number01 TYPE p DECIMALS 2 VALUE 3.14.
```

Unfortunately, this statement doesn't work. You're missing the colon after DATA and you can't use a period as a separator for chain statements or decimal separator.

Basically, this is a good idea because internally, the system does actually use periods as decimal separators, but also uses the period to indicate the end of a statement. So the system would regard the earlier statement as two statements in the same line, and the second statement (14) wouldn't make any sense at all.

Solution: use a literal   For this reason, you should write the preassignment value in a literal in order to obtain a formally correct statement:

```
DATA number01 TYPE p DECIMALS 2 VALUE '3.14'.
```

Correspondingly, if you want to preassign the negative value -4.56 to a variable, the correct syntax would look like this:

```
DATA number01 TYPE p DECIMALS 2 VALUE '-4.56'.
```

Declaring Constants

For the sake of completeness, we should mention at this point that we use a separate statement called CONSTANTS to declare constants (that is, fields whose contents can never be modified), if you need to ensure that the content of a specific field remain unmodified during the runtime of a report. If you encounter such a scenario in your daily work, then the CONSTANTS statement is much more useful than the DATA statement. The system supports this concept, in that it generates syntax or runtime errors once you try to modify the fields in question.

CONSTANTS

However, because the CONSTANTS and DATA statements are essentially identical—with the exception of their intended usage—we won't go into further detail on the CONSTANTS statement at this stage. Thus, regarding simple arithmetic operations, our declarations could look like this for now:

Simple arithmetic operations

```
DATA number01 TYPE p DECIMALS 2 VALUE '-4.56'.
DATA number02 LIKE number01 VALUE '5.67'.
DATA result LIKE number01.
```

The NUMBER01 variable defines data type p as well as the fact that two decimal places will be used. In addition, the variable is assigned the negative initial value of -4.56. With regard to the data type and number of decimal places, the NUMBER02 variable references the NUMBER01 variable and is assigned the initial value of 5.67. The RESULT variable also references NUMBER01, regarding the data type and decimal places.

The advantage of this type of notation is that if you need to change the declaration, you only need to change it for NUMBER01, and the declarations of NUMBER02 and RESULT will be automatically adjusted.

Basic Arithmetic Operations

At this stage, we have already declared all variables needed to carry out addition, subtraction, multiplication, and division operations in ABAP so you can perform arithmetic operations easily by using assignments. For example, if you want to total the contents of the NUMBER01 and NUMBER02 fields, you can use the following statement:

```
result = number01 + number02.
```

Mathematical expression

Concerning the syntax, you should note that the arithmetic operation itself must be written to the right of the equals sign. The result of the operation is inserted into the field to the left of the equals sign, while the NUMBER01 and NUMBER02 fields will continue to contain their initial contents even after the calculation operation. The field to the left of the equals sign, however, will change: After the calculation operation, the RESULT field will have a new content, which replaces the old one.

➕ Blank Characters in Arithmetic Operations

Another important aspect regarding the correct syntax is the use of blank characters. You must put blank characters before and after the equals sign, as well as before and after the arithmetic operator, which was the plus sign (+) in the previous example. If, in the future, you have to use complex expressions and multiple parentheses levels, you must insert blank characters before and after each parenthesis. Note that you must insert at least one blank space, but you can insert multiple blank spaces.

The reason for this convention is that some functions are written directly to the field without any blank characters. Blank characters are essential to helping system distinguish between arithmetic operations and other functions.

Using fixed values

If you want to add a fixed value to the content of the NUMBER02 variable (for example, the value 2), you must structure the corresponding statement like this:

```
number02 = number01 + 2.
```

Again, the old content of the variable to the left of the equals sign is replaced with new content. Of course, you can also add a fixed value to the content of the same variable, for instance by increasing the result by a counter of 1. The corresponding statement would then look like this:

```
number01 = number01 + 1.
```

Once again, the same principle applies: The value of the operation is determined to the right of the equals sign. In the example, we add the number 1 to the content of NUMBER01. The result of the operation is then inserted in the variable to the left of the equals sign. In other words: NUMBER01 has a new content.

Correspondingly, the notation for subtraction, multiplication, and division operations is similar:

```
result = number01 - number02.
result = number01 * number02.
result = number01 / number02.
```

And so you must use the minus sign (-) as the arithmetic operator for subtractions, the asterisk (*) for multiplications, and the forward slash (/) for divisions. Instead of arithmetic operators, we could also use the keywords ADD, SUBTRACT, MULTIPLY, and DIVIDE, but since these keywords are not frequently used in practice, we won't use them in this book.

Statements containing keywords

Now that we've introduced you to the basic prerequisites, we can turn to the details. Here, the old proverb "the devil is in the details" holds true. For example, not all fields have the same attributes or are compatible with each other.

Compatible and Convertible Data Objects

If different fields have the same attributes, they are known as *compatible data objects* because all their technical properties (type, field length, decimal places) are completely identical. If the attributes are compliant, the fields are known as *convertible data objects*. In this case, the data types must be converted in compliance with corresponding conversion rules. The system generates syntax or runtime errors if a conversion isn't possible.

Compatible and convertible data objects

It's comforting to know that many conversion rules are already stored in the SAP system (see "Conversion Rules"). Based on these rules, the

Automatic conversion

system converts one data type into another if you specify the corresponding statements. If these rules generate the results you need, the conversion runs smoothly. Unfortunately, this is not always the case, and the set of available rules doesn't cover all conceivable scenarios.

 Sources of Error

We must grudgingly admit that often the developers themselves are to blame for runtime errors resulting from inconvertible data types; for example, there is no logical reason for trying to save asterisks and special characters in a date field, but it does happen. Even advanced developers are not exempt from generating those errors occasionally, particularly if they have to modify existing applications. The same errors can also occur during data migration from other systems, so there's no need to panic if you encounter one just as you're starting out.

Conversion Rules

What happens if ... The conversion rules define how the content of a source field is entered in a target field. Source fields can have different data types, such as data type p for packed numbers and data type i for integers, which you've already seen. Because there are also other data types available for date and time fields or character strings, the conversion rules specify for each data type the exact way the content of the source field is inserted into the target field. In other words, conversion rules define what happens if you insert a packed number into an integer field, if you add a packed number to the content of a date field, or if you write a packed number into a character field. Let's look at a conversion rule as an example.

Converting a decimal number into an integer If the source type is a data object of type p and the target type is a data object of type i (for example, an integer), the system rounds the decimal places of the source field up or down and inserts the content right-aligned into the target field. If the length of the target is sufficient, the field will be filled with zeros from the left; otherwise, an overflow or runtime error occurs. For example, if you insert the packed number 4.44 into an integer field, the content of the integer field will be 4; if you insert the packed number 5.55 into an integer field, its content will be 6.

If a numerical operation contains several different data types, ABAP converts all data types to the highest data type before executing the operation. Then ABAP carries out the operation using the converted values and inserts the result—if necessary, by using a conversion rule—into the result field.

Converting different data types

 Integers, Packed Numbers, Exponential Numbers

For example, if the operation contains integers, packed numbers, and exponential numbers, the exponential numbers represent the highest data type. In the first step, all integers are converted into packed numbers; then, all numbers are converted into exponential numbers; ultimately, the operation is carried out using exponential numbers. After that, the value of the exponential numbers is inserted into the result field according to the conversion rules. As you can imagine, the accuracy of the calculation depends on the data type of the result field.

To keep things as simple as possible right from the start, you should always make sure to keep your data objects as compatible as possible.

To ensure that we haven't omitted anything germane to conversion, at this point we should mention the COMPUTE keyword, which is the original ABAP command for numerical operations. The syntax for an addition operation using the COMPUTE keyword looks like this:

COMPUTE

```
COMPUTE result = number01 + number02.
```

As you can see, the only difference is that the statement is longer, but its readability doesn't increase. Fortunately, the use of the COMPUTE keyword is optional. In real life, it is hardly ever used outside of research. Most developers use the abbreviated notation, which the system handles in exactly the same way, so we will also opt out of using the COMPUTE keyword in this book and use the abbreviated notation as follows:

```
result = number01 + number02.
```

Good to Know...

There is one case in which it is important to know that the COMPUTE statement exists. If you search the system for the documentation on functions that are rarely used, you'll only find that documentation if you use the COMPUTE statement.

As of SAP NetWeaver 7.0 EHP2 or SAP NetWeaver 7.3, the COMPUTE statement allows for the EXACT addition, which leads to a special behavior in calculations with decimal floating point numbers. This addition is available with the full COMPUTE keyword only.

Special Features of Division Operations

Different cases
With regard to calculations in ABAP, addition, subtraction, and multiplication operations don't pose any problems. However, division operations warrant a closer look. Sometimes you'll want to get a division result that has decimal places, and other times you'll want to divide by integers without a remainder. You might also be interested only in the remainder as a result of a division. ABAP provides different statements for these different variants.

As we already described, the simplest case of a division is represented by a forward slash (/):

```
DATA number01 TYPE p DECIMALS 2 VALUE '4.56'.
DATA number02 LIKE number01 VALUE '5.67'.
DATA result LIKE number01.
result = number02 / number01.
```

Computational accuracy
If you use an electronic calculator to calculate the result, it will output the number 1.243421053. But what will ABAP do? All variables have been declared in the same way. A packed number consists of a maximum of 16 bytes, which is equal to 32 places (including the algebraic sign). The system would provide the exact result—in ABAP, the computational accuracy for packed numbers is represented by a maximum of 14 decimal places—but it will round it in order to reduce the number of decimal places to two in the target variable, which we declared earlier as containing two decimal places. ABAP rounds the value to 1.24.

If you want to get the result of an integral division, you must rewrite the statement and use the `DIV` operator instead of the forward slash: **DIV**

```
result = number02 DIV number01.
```

If all other prerequisites remain unchanged, the integral division outputs the value 1 as a result. Because the target variable has two decimal places, its content will be `1.00` after executing the statement.

In a third scenario, we're interested in the remainder of the integral division. Here, we'll use the `MOD` operand so that the statement is structured like this: **MOD**

```
result = number02 MOD number01.
```

Again, we assume that all other factors remain unchanged so that the result of the integral division is 1, with the remainder 1.11. This remainder, including its two decimal places, is transferred to the target variable, which is assigned the value 1.11 as its content.

 1.5 Hours

→ You can find more examples in Chapters 5 and 8.

You may be wondering whether this kind of calculation is relevant to real life. If you are, consider the fact that in many systems, time is not entered in terms of hours and minutes, but in decimal values (for example, "1.5 hours"). To convert those decimal values into hours and minutes, you must use the different division options described here.

Sample Code for Fields and Calculations

Listing 4.1 introduces some simple arithmetic operations.

```
1  *&---------------------------------------------*
2  *& Report   Z_BASIC_ARITHMETICS              *
3  *&                                            *
4  *&---------------------------------------------*
5  *&                                            *
6  *&                                            *
7  *&---------------------------------------------*
8
9  REPORT   z_basic_arithmetics.
10
11 * Define fields
```

```
12   DATA number01   TYPE p DECIMALS 2 VALUE '4.56'.
13   DATA number02   LIKE number01     VALUE '5.67'.
14   DATA result_addition LIKE number01.
15   DATA result_subtraction LIKE number01.
16   DATA result_multiplication LIKE number01.
17   DATA result_division_exact LIKE number01.
18   DATA result_division_integer LIKE number01.
19   DATA result_division_rest LIKE number01.
20
21   * Processing
22   number01 = number01 + 1.
23   number02 = number01 + 2.
24   result_addition = number01 + number02.
25   result_subtraction = number01 - number02.
26   result_multiplication = number01 * number02.
27   result_division_exact = number02 / number01.
28   result_division_integer = number02 DIV number01.
29   result_division_rest = number02 MOD number01.
30
31   * Output
32   WRITE: / 'number01', number01,
33          / 'number02', number02,
34          / 'result_addition:',
                 result_addition,
35          / 'result_subtraction:',
                 result_subtraction,
36          / 'result_multiplication:',
                 result_multiplication,
37          / 'result_division_exact:',
                 result_division_exact,
38          / 'result_division_integer:',
                 result_division_integer,
39          / 'result_division_rest:',
                 result_division_rest.
```

Listing 4.1 Z_BASIC_ARITHMETICS Report

Notes on the Source Code

Lines 1 to 8

These lines are automatically generated by the system as comment lines.

Line 11

The source code is divided into sections to improve readability. In Listing 4.1, these sections are created using three comment lines: Define fields (lines 11 through 19), Processing (lines 21 through 29), and Output (lines 31 through 39).

Line 12

The NUMBER01 variable is declared as a packed number containing two decimal places. It is assigned the initial value 4.56.

Line 13

The NUMBER02 variable is assigned the initial value 5.67 and the same attributes as NUMBER01.

Lines 14 to 19

The result fields are declared; a separate field is created for each result. Of course, it would also have been possible to create only one RESULT field and then overwrite its value repeatedly, but, depending on the way it is further processed, you may want to reuse the content or a field at a later stage. In addition, you want to output the different calculation results right away.

A matter of further processing

 Be Generous Regarding the Use of Variables

> In any case, the available memory and hardware are no longer a reason for being frugal with variables, since readability and transparency are much more important quality criteria. So if you can improve the quality, you can afford to be generous regarding the use of variables.

Line 21

The processing section begins in this line.

One calculation after the other

Line 22

The value of the NUMBER01 field increases by 1. Before that statement, the content was 4.56; after, it is 5.56.

Line 23

The NUMBER02 field is assigned the content resulting from the addition of NUMBER01 and the number 2. Previously, the content of NUMBER02 was 5.67; now it is 7.56.

Line 24

The RESULT_ADDITION field is assigned the result of the operation NUMBER01 plus NUMBER02 (that is, 5.56 + 7.56, which equals 13.12).

Line 25

The result of the subtraction of NUMBER01 and NUMBER02 is the negative number 2. This number is represented by the value 2.00- in the RESULT_SUBTRACTION result field. (We use the notation in which the number precedes the minus sign because this is the way you will see the system display negative numbers both in the ABAP Debugger and on list screens.)

Line 26

Because the value of NUMBER01 is now 5.56 and the value of NUMBER02 is 7.56, the result of multiplying these two values and rounding them to two decimal places is 42.03.

Line 27

The rounded result of the division of 7.56 by 5.56 is 1.36-. At the same time, this is the new content of RESULT_DIVISION_EXACT.

Line 28

The result of the integral division is 1.00. Due to the formatting, the decimal places that are actually redundant are included here.

Line 29

The remainder of the integral division is 2.00. This value is copied into the RESULT_DIVISION_REST field.

Line 31

The section for preparing the output starts in this line.

Lines 32 to 39

The WRITE statement outputs a literal as text in a new line in column 1, followed by a blank character and the content of the variable. The WRITE statement is written as a chain statement, which actually consists of 16 individual WRITE statements. The WRITE command is followed by a colon; the individual statements are separated by commas. Only the final statement of the chain statement ends with a period.

Once you have edited, saved, checked, and activated the report as described, you can execute it, and the list screen should look like the one shown in Figure 4.6.

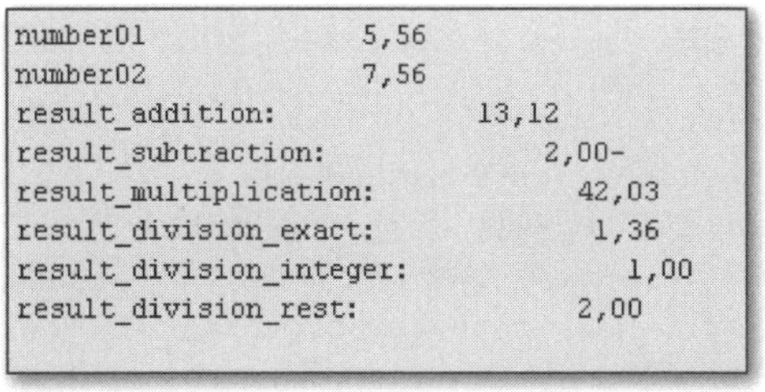

```
number01            5,56
number02            7,56
result_addition:        13,12
result_subtraction:      2,00-
result_multiplication:     42,03
result_division_exact:      1,36
result_division_integer:     1,00
result_division_rest:      2,00
```

Figure 4.6 List Screen for the Example of the Basic Arithmetic Operations

Everything is correct as far as the form and logic go, but it's not very aesthetically pleasing. Because the length of the literals at the beginning of each line is different, the output variables are located in different column positions and hence in different columns. For this reason, we'll take care of changing the column distribution in the final step.

Look and feel needs improving

Improved List Format

You can solve this little problem by telling the WRITE command where (that is, in which position of a line) it is supposed to output the respective variable. If you want to output the variable from column 30 onwards, you must change line 32 of Listing 4.1 in the following way:

Outputting fields of a list in columns

```
WRITE: / 'number01', 30 number01,
```

All you need to do is write the column position of the printed line right in front of the variable in question. Note that there must be at least one blank character between the column position and the variable.

Complex Lists

You can edit the other relevant lines in the same way by inserting the output position in front of each relevant variable. This process is useful if the output lists are short and not very complex. However, if a list is more complex, you could try another method: just think of the reference in data declarations containing LIKE.

UNDER   You can also use a reference to another object with regard to the output position in such a way that you simply reference the position of another variable. If the position of the leading variable changes, then all other referencing variables will change accordingly. You must use the formatting option UNDER with the WRITE command. Edit lines 33 through 39 like this:

```
33          / 'number02', number02 UNDER number01,
34          / 'result_addition:', result_addition UNDER
               number01,
35          / 'result_subtraction:', result_subtraction
               UNDER number01,
36          / 'result_multiplication:',
               result_multiplication UNDER number01,
37          / 'result_division_exact:',
               result_division_exact UNDER number01,
38          / 'result_division_integer:',
               result_division_integer UNDER number01,
39          / 'result_division_rest:',
               result_division_rest UNDER number01.
```

Once you have saved, checked, activated, and executed the report, the list screen should look like the one shown in Figure 4.7.

```
number01                              5,56
number02                              7,56
result_addition:                     13,12
result_subtraction:                   2,00-
result_multiplication:               42,03
result_division_exact:                1,36
result_division_integer:              1,00
result_division_rest:                 2,00
```

Figure 4.7   List Screen with Output in Columns

5

Modifying Character Strings

Words are character strings; however, numbers or dates can also be character strings, depending on the purpose of their display and usage. For this reason, this chapter describes the areas of use, tasks, and operations that relate to character strings.

In previous chapters you learned how to multiply phone or item numbers, but you will probably agree that it doesn't make much sense to apply arithmetic operations to this type of character strings. It would be much more useful to complement a local phone number with a national or international dialing code. To do this, you must be familiar with the basic statements needed to carry out character string operations, so that's what we'll focus on in this chapter. Let's look at the declaration of character strings first.

Basic statements

Declaring Character Strings

From a technical point of view, the different uses of fields are reflected by the different data types. The following elementary data types are provided for character strings in ABAP:

> Data type `c` for character fields of a fixed length

> Data type `n` for numeric character fields of a fixed length

> Data type `string` for character fields of a variable length

TYPE c In most cases, the `string` data type behaves just like data type `c`, but there are other specific aspects that you must consider; these are discussed later in this chapter. Data type `c` is used for alphanumeric characters. Here, the minimum field length is one character, and the maximum field length is 65,535 characters. The initial value is a blank character. Like any other field, character fields must be declared before you can use them. The GENDER field (with a field length of one character) can be declared using the DATA statement, as shown below in full-length notation:

```
DATA gender TYPE c LENGTH 1.
```

The old notation is equivalent, but more difficult to read:

```
DATA gender(1) TYPE c.
```

As you can see, the field length immediately follows the field name without a blank character and in parentheses, and followed by the data type as the operand. Because data type `c` is a generic data type, older ABAP programs also contain the simplified declaration:

```
DATA gender.
```

 Default Settings

In generic data types, missing information is replaced by default settings. If you don't specify a data type, the system automatically uses data type `c`; if you don't explicitly specify the field length for a data type `c`, the system implicitly enters the default length 1. Based on this concept, the mentioned declarations for the GENDER field are identical.

You could also find the following declaration in older ABAP programs. Here, the length of the parentheses notation is specified and the data type is omitted:

```
DATA last_name(20).
```

Caution: Obsolete!

In modern ABAP, it is no longer common to use the default settings as described here because the specification of data type and length is missing. The programmer relied on the system to copy the default settings for the type and length automatically. This means that another developer who has to maintain the program in future has to know the standard behavior of the system by heart in order to understand the behavior of the program correctly. This is dangerous because the system doesn't always do what you expect it to do and sometimes behaves rather bizarrely. So make your declarations as explicit as possible in order to avoid nasty surprises.

Fields of data type n have a special usage. Although these fields are intended for character strings that are treated correspondingly, these character strings can contain only numeric characters. The character strings are written in a right-aligned position to the fields. If the field contains more fields than the character string, the leading places on the left of the field are filled with zeros. Typical examples of these strings include article numbers, item numbers, hierarchy levels, and field or record lengths. Whenever you want to use numbers without carrying out any arithmetic operations, you should use data type n. For this reason, these fields are also known as *numeric text fields*.

TYPE n

Data type n is a generic data type as well. The minimum field length is 1 character, and the maximum field length is 65,535 characters, as is the case for data type c. However, in contrast to the data type c fields, the initial value of the data type n fields is 0.

All other additions of the DATA statement apply to both data types in the same way, particularly the TYPE, LIKE, and VALUE additions. For example, you could declare the LAST_NAME field in the same way as the data element of the MNAME field of the ZMEMBER01 table.

LIKE

```
DATA last_name TYPE zmember01-mname.
```

And so the LAST_NAME field has the same attributes as the MNAME field: data type c and a field length of 20 characters.

The correct statement for assigning the value F to the GENDER field is as follows:

VALUE

```
DATA gender TYPE c LENGTH 1 VALUE 'F'.
```

 Case Sensitivity

The initial value in the previous statement is written as a literal. At this point, it is very important to use uppercase and lowercase letters. This difference is critical, especially with regard to future queries. If you search for an uppercase F in a field that contains a lowercase m, the system won't return any hits.

String Operations

String operations

Frequently occurring *string operations* include, among others, searching for a specific character or group of characters within a string, replacing a character with another one, or shifting the characters of a string to the right or left in order to provide more space or to close gaps. You may even want to complement a character string with characters from a different string, or to cut specific characters out of a string.

 Example: Telephone Numbers

Let's look at a simple example: If you want to declare the TELEPHONE field as a numeric character string containing eight places and assign the initial value 887766 to it, the corresponding statement looks like this:

```
DATA phone TYPE n LENGTH 8 VALUE '887766'.
```

So far, so good. Six places have been assigned, and two more places are being kept in reserve in case you have to process a longer phone number. It appears that you did everything correctly, since phone numbers are normally not used in arithmetic operations. However, in this example, we haven't taken into account that the actual initial value of an eight-digit numeric character string consists of eight zeros. The six-digit initial value of 887766 overwrites six zeros from right to left so that two leading zeros are left on the left-hand side of the field, which means that the field content is actually 00887766.

If you tried to call that number, you probably wouldn't be very successful. Therefore, the two leading zeros must be removed with a string operation.

124

Shifting Character Strings

One possible way to do that is to move the character string to the left until the leading zeros disappear, as in the following statement:

SHIFT phone LEFT DELETING LEADING '0'.   **SHIFT**

The SHIFT statement moves the field content (here, the string 00887766) to the left until all leading zeros have been deleted. After the operation, the field content is 887766☐☐, which means that two blank characters are added to the right of the numbers in the field.

Of course, you can also move a character string in a certain direction and by a specific number of places within a field. For example, if you want to move the phone number two places to the right, you must use the following statement:

SHIFT phone BY 2 PLACES RIGHT.

After that, the field content looks as you initially thought it would (namely, ☐☐887766). You might be wondering why you couldn't have used a type c field right from the start. The reason for this is simple: If you use type c, the system accepts all alphanumeric characters, including letters and special characters. If you use type n, these characters are ignored by the system. If the entire character string consists only of letters and special characters, then the field is set to its initial value. This facilitates the programming of check and error routines that can detect and handle incorrect data entries.

Differences between type c and type n

If you omit the additions of the SHIFT statement that we just described, you get the statement in its shortest form:

SHIFT phone.

 Data Types

> Individual situations will be a major factor when determining which data type is preferable. If an article number consists of alphanumeric characters, type c is the right choice; however, if an article number consists of only numbers—and if you want to avoid using incorrect field contents right from the start—then type n is the better option.

Bookshelf analogy

In that case the system uses default values for the missing operands. The default filling direction is from right to left, and the number of positions is 1. In other words, by default, the field content is shifted by one position to the left, so be careful when shifting field contents. Think of it like a simple bookshelf without side walls: If you shift the books too far to one side, some of them will fall down. The principle of shifting field contents works similarly. If you shift the field content beyond the left or right border, some characters will be irretrievably lost.

Replacing Character Strings

Different task, same procedure

Whether you want to translate a decimal number (including the decimal separator from the German into the American format) or create a new 16-digit material number based on an old eight-digit one, you always have to find and replace specific characters or character groups within a string. You must use the REPLACE statement to do that.

Let's suppose the PHONE_INTERNATIONAL field is a type c field consisting of 25 places and contains the value ☐☐887766. The first two places are blank characters. You now want to replace the leading blank character with the content of the AREA_CODE field.

For this purpose, use this statement:

```
REPLACE ` ` IN phone_international
           WITH area_code.
```

REPLACE

The REPLACE statement finds and replaces the first occurrence of the search term, which is " " (blank character) in this case.

Remembering once again that we are, as is frequently the case in SAP systems, dealing with an international phone number, we observe that the AREA_CODE field is a type n field and consists of five places. It the content 09876, which means that the content of the PHONE_INTERNA-TIONAL field will be 09876☐887766 after the operation. The first blank character was replaced by the area code, but the second blank character was preserved and is now located between the area code and the local phone number.

Single quotation marks and back quotes

You may have noticed something special: Instead of the common single quotation marks, the blank character is enclosed in *back quotes* (`). The reason is that the search term " " (blank character) that is defined in the program text is a character literal. In ABAP, the two types of character literals differ in their data type and how they handle blank characters. Text field literals are of the c data type, and string literals are of the string data type. Both handle closing blank characters differently.

In case of text field literals, closing blank characters are ignored and treated as if they didn't exist. The 'ABC   ' text field literal is treated as 'ABC   ' and a ' ' text field literal as an empty value. The REPLACE statement handles an empty search term by inserting the replacement term before the processed string. The following REPLACE statement with single quotation marks would output the result 09876☐☐887766 with two blank characters, because the replacement term would simply be inserted before the string:

Subtle difference: text field literals and string literals

```
REPLACE ' ' IN phone_international
          WITH area_code.
```

Ex International Area Code

Let's look at another example to better grasp replacing character strings. Let's assume that the content of the PHONE_INTERNATIONAL field is 09876☐887766. While leaving all other conditions unchanged, you want to replace the leading zero with the international dialing code and a zero in parentheses. For Switzerland, the string would be +41-(0), for example. The corresponding statement would then look like this:

```
REPLACE '0' IN phone_international
WITH '+41-(0)'.
```

After the operation, the content of the field would be +41-(0)9876☐887766. If you wanted to replace the remaining blank character between the area code and the local phone number with a minus sign, then you would have to use the following statement:

```
REPLACE ` ` IN phone_international WITH `-`.
```

This statement (as a string literal) searches for a blank character (which it will find in position 12) and replace it with a minus sign. (For minus signs, it doesn't matter whether you use back quotes for a string literal or the usual single quotation marks for a text field literal.) The new field content would then be +41-(0)9876-887766.

In the correct variant with back quotes, closing blank characters are accepted. The `` `ABC ` `` text field literal is actually treated as `` `ABC ` `` and the blank character `` ` ` `` as a blank character, so the REPLACE statement can be executed successfully. The first blank character in PHONE_INTERNATIONAL is identified as identical to the search term and replaced by AREA_CODE. By the way, leading blank characters are accepted by both text field literals and string literals.

Condensing Character Strings

Removing redundant blank characters

Long text fields often contain blank characters that aren't needed. Sometimes these blank characters are created by string operations in long character strings. It is possible to condense the substrings within a field in such a way that all redundant blank characters are removed. Alternatively, you can collect the character strings of multiple fields within one field and condense them there.

Let's look at the first option. Let's assume that the content of the PHONE_INTERNATIONAL field is +41□-(0)9876□□887766. There is one blank character between the international dialing code and the area code and two blank characters between the area code and the local phone number. In total, the string contains three blank characters.

CONDENSE

The CONDENSE statement lets you compact the three parts of the character string in the PHONE_INTERNATIONAL field in such a way that between the international dialing code +41 and the area code, and between the area code -(0)9876 and the local phone number 887766, there is *only one* blank character, regardless of how many blank characters there were previously. Therefore, only the third blank character has been removed; and after the following operation, the field content of PHONE_INTERNATIONAL is +41□-(0)9876□887766.

```
CONDENSE phone_international.
```

 **NO-GAPS**

> If you still think there shouldn't be any blank characters, you can use the
> NO-GAPS addition to remove all blank characters between the character
> strings. In that case, use this statement:
>
> CONDENSE phone_international NO-GAPS.
>
> After that, the corrected field content is +41-(0)9876887766.

Concatenating String Fields

There is, however, an easier way to place string fields into a target field
in any sequence that you choose. Suppose that you want to output
two fields in a list line: NAME and FIRST_NAME. Both fields are c type
fields; the length of each field is 40 characters. Since the two fields
alone would fill 80 columns of the list line, many of which would be
blank characters, it would be more useful to output the contents of
both fields in a separate output field, and to concatenate the character
strings in such a way that only one blank character is left between last
name and first name.

Separate output field

We can also apply this method to our phone number. Suppose that you
want to copy the contents of the INTERNATIONAL_AREA_CODE, AREA_CODE,
and PHONE fields in this very sequence into the PHONE_INTERNATIONAL
field. To do that, you can use the CONCATENATE statement:

CONCATENATE

```
CONCATENATE international_area_code
            area_code
            phone
            INTO
            phone_international.
```

To specify the information on the source fields, the CONCATENATE statement uses position operands in which the sequence of the source fields
determines the sequence of the character strings in the target field.
In other words, if the INTERNATIONAL_AREA_CODE is the first operand,
then the content of the field represents the first part of the character
string in the PHONE_INTERNATIONAL field; correspondingly, the content
of the AREA_CODE field represents the second part of the character string
in the target field, while the content of the PHONE field is the third
part. Leading blank characters are copied; closing blank characters are

ignored by source fields of the c type but accepted by source fields of the string type.

In our example, the content of the source field INTERNATIONAL_AREA _CODE is +41, that of the AREA_CODE field is 09876, and that of the PHONE field is 887766; after the operation, the content of the target field PHONE_INTERNATIONAL will be +4109876887766.

SEPARATED BY Certainly, we know that the readability of this field could be improved by separating the individual components of the phone number by a minus sign. For this end, the CONCATENATE statement provides the SEPARATED BY addition. Here, you must specify a variable or literal, which will be inserted between the individual string components.

 New Notations

SAP NetWeaver 7.0 EHP2 provides new commands and functions for processing character strings. For example, you can concatenate character strings using the & and && operators:

```
phone_international = international_area_code &
                     '-' &
                     area_code &
                     '-' &
                     phone.
```

In addition, it provides numerous new functions for processing character strings. Some of these are similar to existing commands (CONDENSE, CONCAT_LINES_OF, REPLACE, SHIFT_LEFT, SHIFT_RIGHT, SUBSTRING, TO_UPPER, TO_LOWER, and TRANSLATE) but others are completely new functions worth having a look at in the ABAP language documentation, such as the new REPLACE function:

```
phone_international = REPLACE( val  = '09876-887766'
                              sub  = '0'
                              with = '+41-(0)-'
                              occ  = 0 ).
```

This statement replaces all occurrences of the search term 0 with +41-(0) in the character string 09876-887766 and assigns the result to the PHONE_INTERNATIONAL variable. To ensure that only the first zero—instead of all occurrences—is replaced, you can also transfer the value 1 for the occ parameter. Since there aren't any other zeros beyond the first one in this example, the result would be the same: +41-(0)-9876-887766.

In our example, we'll use the literal '-' and write:

```
CONCATENATE international_area_code
            area_code
            phone
            INTO
            phone_international
            SEPARATED BY '-'.
```

For better readability, the statement is distributed across several lines. After the operation, the field content of PHONE_INTERNATIONAL is +41-09876-887766.

Splitting Character Strings

Similarly, a situation that represents the direct counterpart to the CONCATENATE statement might be that we need to split up a large character string into several parts, or that we have to write parts of the character string into a separate field. In the previous example, for instance, the international area code is part of a large character string. However, let's try to split up this string into the international area code, the local area code, and the local phone number.

You can use the SPLIT statement to resolve this issue. This statement distributes a character string into several fields.

SPLIT

```
SPLIT phone_international AT '-'
      INTO
      international_area_code area_code phone.
```

This statement splits the PHONE_INTERNATIONAL field at the separator string. The separator string follows the AT addition and is either given as the content of a variable or as a literal, as in our example. Again, the target fields are written as position operands, so you must explicitly consider the sequence of the target fields. In addition, it is very important that you ensure that the target fields are large enough to accommodate the character strings.

AT

If the content of the PHONE_INTERNATIONAL field prior to executing the statement is +41-09876-887766, then the content of the INTERNATIONAL_AREA_CODE field will be +41, the AREA_CODE field will contain 09876, and the PHONE field will contain 887766 after the operation.

String Operations with Direct Positioning

Another group of tasks requires the use of string operations. Sometimes you may have to add a specific number of characters at a certain position within a string or remove a specific number of characters from a certain position onwards within a string.

Direct positioning

Let's suppose that the PHONE_INTERNATIONAL field contains the string +41-(0)9876-887766; you know that if an international area code is used, the first three characters are the ones that form the international area code. You can access these three characters by direct positioning and specifying the length (in order to place the character string into the target field, INTERNATIONAL_AREA_CODE), using this statement:

```
international_area_code = phone_international+0(3).
```

Put simply, this statement means that the new content of the target field (INTERNATIONAL_AREA_CODE) is the content of the source field (PHONE_INTERNATIONAL), from position 0 onwards and with a length of three characters. The length specification is written without any blank character in between the parentheses directly after the source field.

From the center

Often, the substring in question is located somewhere in the middle of the string, but even if that's the case, this method requires that you know the start position and the length of the relevant part. In our example, you could copy the local area code (which is contained in the international phone number) and place it into a target field. All you need to know is that the local area code always begins after position 4 and that it consists of seven characters. Therefore, you must copy the characters located in positions 5, 6, 7, 8, 9, 10, and 11. To do that, use the following statement:

```
area_code = phone_international+4(7).
```

 Type c Versus Type n

This example demonstrates the difference between the data types. If the type of the target field is c, it will contain (0)9876 after the operation. If, on the other hand, it is a type n field, it will contain the string 09876, because data type n ignores parentheses, which are alphanumeric characters.

This way you can remove characters from a string and manipulate characters within strings. Let's suppose that you want to replace the international area code 41 with 33. If that's the case, then you must write the following statement:

```
phone_international+1(2) = '33'.
```

Because you want to use the plus sign in the new international area code as well, you must replace positions 2 and 3 of the PHONE_INTER-NATIONAL field with the literal '33'.

Sample Code for String Operations

Listing 5.1 shows an example of sample code using string operations.

```
 1   *&---------------------------------------------*
 2   *& Report   Z_MEMBERLIST03                 *
 3   *&                                           *
 4   *&---------------------------------------------*
 5   *&                                           *
 6   *&                                           *
 7   *&                                           *
 8   *&---------------------------------------------*
 9
10   REPORT   z_memberlist03                 .
11
12
13   * Define strings
14   DATA: gender TYPE c length 1 VALUE 'F',
15         last_name TYPE zmember01-mname,
16         phone TYPE n LENGTH 8 VALUE '887766',
17         area_code TYPE n LENGTH 5 VALUE '09876',
18         international_area_ode TYPE c LENGTH 5 VALUE '+41',
19         phone_international TYPE c LENGTH 25.
20
21
22   * Control output original field content
23   WRITE / 'original field content'.
24   WRITE:    30 phone,
25             40 area_code,
26             50 international_area_code,
27             60 phone_international.
```

```
28  ULINE.
29  * SHIFT statement
30  WRITE / 'Shift'.
31  SHIFT phone LEFT DELETING LEADING '0'.
32  WRITE 30 phone.
33  SHIFT phone BY 2 PLACES RIGHT.
34  WRITE /30 phone.
35  ULINE.
36  * REPLACE statement
37  WRITE / 'Replace'.
38  phone_international = '  887766'.
39  REPLACE ` ` IN  phone_international
                WITH area_code.
40  WRITE 60 phone_international.
41  REPLACE '0' IN phone_international
                WITH '+41-(0)'.
42  WRITE /60 phone_international.
43  REPLACE ` ` IN phone_international
                WITH `-`.
44  WRITE /60 phone_international.
45  ULINE.
46  * CONDENSE statement
47  WRITE / 'Condense'.
48  phone_international = '+41 -(0)9876  887766'.
49  CONDENSE phone_international.
50  WRITE 60 phone_international.
51  CONDENSE phone_international NO-GAPS.
52  WRITE /60 phone_international.
53  ULINE.
54  * CONCATENATE statement
55  WRITE / 'Concatenate'.
56  phone = '887766'.
57  SHIFT phone LEFT DELETING LEADING '0'.
58  phone_international = space.
59  CONCATENATE international_vorwahl
                area_code
                phone
60              INTO
61              phone_international
62              SEPARATED BY '-'.
63  WRITE 60 phone_international.
64  ULINE.
65  * SPLIT statement
66  WRITE / 'Split'.
```

```
67   international_area_code = space.
68   area_code = space.
69   phone = space.
70   SPLIT phone_international AT '-'
71          INTO
72            international_area_code
              area_code
              phone.
73   WRITE: 30 phone,
74          40 area_code,
75          50 international_area_code.
76   ULINE.
77   * Direct positioning
78   WRITE / 'Direct positioning'.
79   international_area_code = space.
80   international_area_code =
                     phone_international(3).
81   WRITE 50 international_area_code.
82   telefon_international = '+41-(0)9876-887766'.
83   area_code = space.
84   area_code = phone_international+4(7).
85   WRITE 40 area_code.
86   phone_international+1(2) = '33'.
87   WRITE 60 phone_international.
```

Listing 5.1   Report Z_MEMBERLIST03

Notes on the Source Code

Lines 17 to 20

In real life, when designing the fields and data types, we recommend that you carry out a thorough analysis upfront about which data type best meets your requirements. Errors in the design will be difficult to correct at a later stage. In the example in Listing 5.1, we assumed that the local phone number and the area code consist only of numbers. On the other hand, the international area code contains a plus sign, and the entire international phone number may contain separators such as forward slashes, parentheses, or minus signs in order to improve readability. For this reason, both the international area code and the entire international phone number must be type c.

The design comes first

Lines 23 to 28

These statements are necessary for the list output. For reasons of clarity, we want the content of the PHONE field to start at position 30 of the line, the content of the AREA_CODE field to start at position 40, and the content of the INTERNATIONAL_AREA_CODE and PHONE_INTERNATIONAL fields to start at positions 50 and 60, respectively. Moreover, horizontal lines are used here and later on in order to separate the list into easily readable subject areas.

Line 31

In this line, we shift the string in the numeric field to the left in order to remove the leading zeros. There is another way to solve this task, depending on the requirements, but at this stage we're still in the learning phase.

Line 33

Here, we shift the content of the field by two places to the right.

Line 38

The literal ' 887766' will be the new content of the field. The two leading blank characters on the left are needed for the following example.

Line 39

In this line, we replace the first blank character with the content of the AREA_CODE field. This only works because the search term is of the string type (due to the back quotes), so the contained blank character is considered.

Line 41

In the field, we replace the '0' character at its first occurrence, starting from the left of the field, with the literal '+41-(0)'.

Line 43

In the field, we replace the blank character ` ` with the minus sign `-` at its first occurrence. Here, a string literal is used so that the blank character is not ignored. Otherwise, there would be only one occurrence before the entire string.

Line 48

For this exercise, the PHONE_INTERNATIONAL field is assigned the defined content '+41 -(0)9876 887766'. The field contains a total of three blank characters.

Line 49

The substrings in the field are condensed so that they are separated only by single blank characters.

Line 51

The remaining blank characters in the field are removed as well, and the substrings are condensed without gaps.

Lines 56 and 57

A familiar method is used to set the content of the field to the initial value for the exercise.

Line 58

The PHONE_INTERNATIONAL field is filled with blank characters. For this   SPACE
purpose, the example uses the reserved term SPACE, which is equivalent to text field literal ' ' and thus also to text field literal ''. It has the effect that the PHONE_INTERNATIONAL field has an initial, empty value after the assignment.

Lines 59 to 62

This statement is distributed across four lines. It populates the empty PHONE_INTERNATIONAL field with the contents of the INTERNATIONAL_ AREA_CODE, AREA_CODE, and PHONE fields in the order of their occurrence in the command. For better readability, the substrings are separated by a minus sign in the target field.

Lines 67 to 69

For the exercise, the fields are initialized with the assignment of a blank character.

Lines 70 to 72

The content of the PHONE_INTERNATIONAL field is searched for the '-' separator. Since the field contains this separator in two places, there are three substrings. These substrings are written to the target fields in the order in which the fields are specified as position operands in the statement.

Lines 73 to 75

The fields, which previously contained blank characters, now contain the substrings and are written to the list in correspondence with their position.

Line 80

The INTERNATIONAL_AREA_CODE is filled with the first three characters of the PHONE_INTERNATIONAL field.

Line 84

Seven characters of the PHONE_INTERNATIONAL field, which are located after position 4—namely, those characters in positions 5, 6, 7, 8, 9, 10, and 11—are copied and the system tries to transfer them to the AREA_CODE field. The data type of the source field is c, and it contains parentheses in positions 5 and 7. The data type of the target field is n, which means that it won't accept any numbers and special characters. The automatic type conversion ensures that only numeric characters are transferred to the target field.

Line 86

In the PHONE_INTERNATIONAL field, we overwrite the contents of positions 2 and 3 with the contents of the literal '33'.

Program Output

The list output begins with the original values of the fields from position 30 onwards. This enables you to check the list for correctness. The PHONE field contains two leading zeros, while the PHONE_INTERNATIONAL field doesn't contain any values at all (see Figure 5.1). In the second section, the string was first shifted to the left, and then to the right. The third section presents the results of the operations carried out using the REPLACE statement. First, we replaced the leading zero with the international area code, and then the blank character with a minus sign. In the fourth section, the CONDENSE statement was used to remove the blank characters from the string, and the CONCATENATE command in the fifth section was used to form a string that's separated by minus signs. Then the SPLIT statement was used to split the string across three fields. The final section shows how you can use direct positioning to change the international area code from 41 to 33.

All steps in the screen list

Original field content	00887766	09876	+41	
Shift	887766			
	887766			
Replace				09876 887766
				+49-(0)9876 887766
				+49-(0)9876-887766
Condense				+49 -(0)9876 887766
				+49-(0)9876887766
Concatenate				+41-09876-887766
Split	887766	09876	+41	
Direct positioning		09876	+41	+33-(0)9876-887766

Figure 5.1   List Screen for Z_MEMBERLIST03

6

Debugging Programs

As the number of fields reaches unmanageable levels and the operations become increasingly complex, you can no longer be sure that the fields have the correct content at runtime. Luckily, you don't have to, because there's a tool that handles this task for you: the *ABAP Debugger*. This tool enables you to keep your programs free from errors of various kinds because you can take a look under the hood at full speed and trace the processes in the program in detail.

So far, we've assumed that the fields and their changes are conceptually clear, and that you have checked and compared the results in the on-screen list. But not all field content is output in a list, and you can't possibly trace all input in your head, especially with programs that are constantly increasing in complexity. So the time has come for you to get to know the ABAP Debugger, which allows you to analyze and trace in detail any source code (such as the code used in Chapter 5).

Monitoring and analysis

Overview

The ABAP Debugger allows you to check program logic line by line, execute it one command at a time, and immediately verify the field content and program logic of the result. This step-by-step procedure makes troubleshooting the program much easier.

Breakpoints and watchpoints

You can trace the program right from the start, set *breakpoints* before critical statements, and use *watchpoints* that halt the process when fields are detected that contain predefined content. The ABAP Debugger is capable of much more, but what we have described here will suffice for introductory purposes.

 Classic and New ABAP Debugger

As of release 6.40, you can either work with the classic ABAP Debugger from release 4.7 or use the new ABAP Debugger. The classic Debugger runs in the same windows as the monitored program, which results in some restrictions for advanced developers. The new Debugger runs in a separate session in a separate window. The monitored program is closely linked to this session. The separate session approach for the Debugger provides much more monitoring and analysis options for advanced developers. For example, you can analyze the program status from different perspectives, use multiple tools at the same time, and compare the results.

This chapter describes the new Debugger to the degree that is necessary for getting started with ABAP. As of release 7.0, the new ABAP Debugger is the default debugger. As of release 7.0 EHP2, it contains a number of new features, the most prominent of which (layer-aware debugging) is described in this chapter. Of course, where it makes sense, you can switch between the classic and new debuggers. This can be done in the ABAP Editor via the UTILITIES • SETTINGS menu. You can select the ABAP Debugger on the DEBUGGING tab in the user-specific settings for the ABAP Editor (see Figure 6.1).

Calling the ABAP Debugger

Execute program in debugging mode

You can start the Debugger from within the ABAP Workbench in two ways. If you want to trace the program flow—in our case, Z_MEMBERL-IST01—immediately, start the Debugger from the initial screen of the

ABAP Editor using the DEBUGGING ([Shift] + [F5]) button (see Figure 6.2).

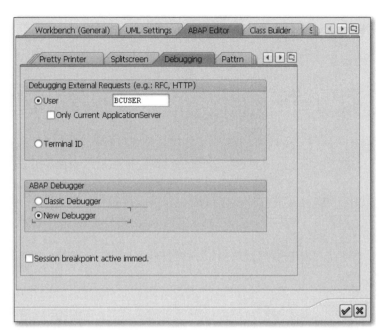

Figure 6.1   Selecting the ABAP Debugger

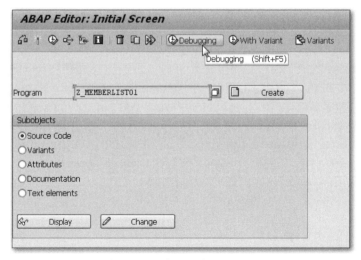

Figure 6.2   Starting the ABAP Debugger from the ABAP Editor Initial Screen

The ABAP Debugger screen is then displayed. The system stops before the first executable statement in the program, which in our case is the REPORT statement, as indicated by the yellow arrow next to the command (see Figure 6.3).

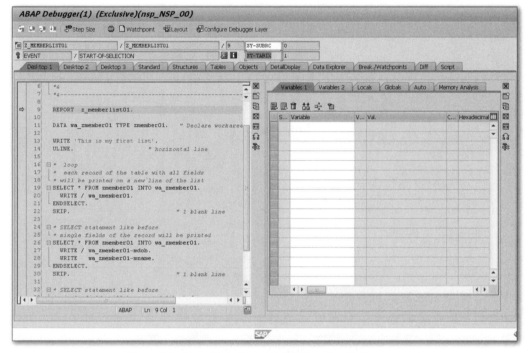

Figure 6.3   Executing a Program in Debugging Mode

Dynamic and static breakpoints

The second method of starting the ABAP Debugger from within the ABAP Workbench is to use breakpoints (which you can set yourself in the source code in the ABAP Editor), either dynamically or statically. For static breakpoints, simply write the BREAK-POINT command into the source code (see "Static Breakpoints"). You can set up and manage dynamic breakpoints without interfering with the source code, which is a significant advantage over static breakpoints.

Session Breakpoints

All dynamic breakpoints are user-specific and are valid only for the current session. In the new ABAP Debugger, these breakpoints are called *session breakpoints*.

They are invisible to other users and cannot be used when the respective user logs on to the SAP system again or after the session has expired.

Let's assume that you want to set a breakpoint before line 31 in the ABAP Editor. To do so, place the cursor in line 19 and click SET/DELETE SESSION BREAKPOINT ($\boxed{\text{Ctrl}}$ + $\boxed{\text{Shift}}$ + $\boxed{\text{F12}}$) (see Figure 6.4).

```
ABAP Editor: Change Report Z_MEMBERLIST01

  ← →   ✏ ✂ 🗋 ©  🔍  ⊟  🖳 ⇩  🔠 🔠 ⬜ ⓘ  🔍🔍 Pattern  Pretty Printer
                                        Set/Delete Session Breakpoint   (Ctrl+Shift+F12)
Report       Z_MEMBERLIST01              Active

   1  ⊟ *&--------------------------------------------------------------*
   2    *& Report  Z_MEMBERLIST01
   3    *&
   4    *&--------------------------------------------------------------*
   5    *&
   6    *&
   7  └ *&--------------------------------------------------------------*
   8
   9    REPORT  z_memberlist01.
  10
  11    DATA wa_zmember01 TYPE zmember01.     " Declare workarea
  12
  13    WRITE 'This is my first list'.
  14    ULINE.                      " horizontal line
  15
  16  ⊟ *  loop
  17    |  *  each record of the table with all fields
  18    └  *  will be printed on a new line of the list
  19  ⊟ SELECT * FROM zmember01 INTO wa_zmember01.
  20      WRITE / wa_zmember01.
  21  └ ENDSELECT.
  22    SKIP.                            " 1 blank line
  23
  24  ⊟ * SELECT statement like before
  25    └ * single fields of the record will be printed
  26  ⊟ SELECT * FROM zmember01 INTO wa_zmember01.
  27      WRITE / wa_zmember01-mdob.
  28      WRITE  wa_zmember01-mname.
  29  └ ENDSELECT.
  30    SKIP.                            " 1 blank line
  31
  32  ⊟ * SELECT statement like before
  33    * single fields will be printed like before
  34    * but the write statement is concatenated into a chain statement
                                                        ABAP   Ln 19 Col  1

  ☑ Breakpoint was deleted                    SAP
```

Figure 6.4   Setting a Session Breakpoint

Stop icon   The system displays a STOP icon beside the relevant line in the ABAP
Editor (see Figure 6.5). Now, if you start the program during the current session in this mode or in any other mode, the system stops before
the command (as indicated by the STOP icon), switches to debugging
mode, and waits for further instructions (see Figure 6.6). You can now
slowly and deliberately check the content of all fields and tablespaces
that are currently known to the system.

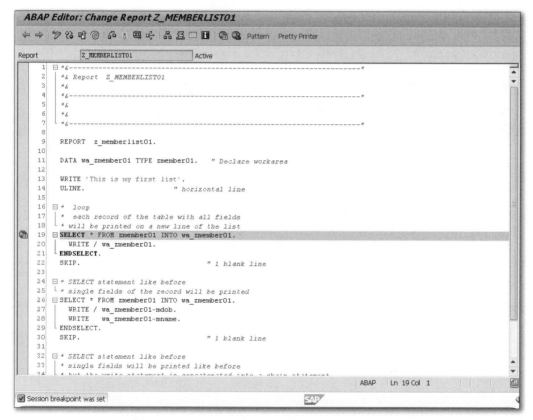

Figure 6.5 Session Breakpoint in the ABAP Editor

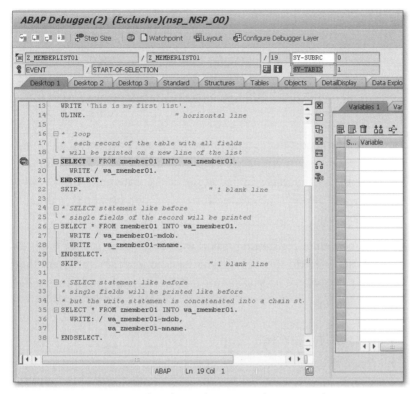

Figure 6.6 System Stops Before the Breakpoint in Debugging Mode

Working with the ABAP Debugger

The ABAP Debugger provides a variety of operating modes and views of the program flow, which you can switch between and combine as your current situation requires. In terms of becoming familiar with ABAP, the most important modes are the tabs of the variables in the DESKTOP 1 tab (in which you trace the program flow and the content of variables) and the STRUCTURES and TABLES tabs (in which you observe the content of work areas and internal tables). In the BREAK-/WATCH-POINTS tab, you can manage and observe breakpoints and watchpoints. These observations and the resulting analyses are indispensable both for troubleshooting and for finding the right points if you have to make changes to source code.

Indispensable for troubleshooting

Desktop 1

Check statements

If you switch from the ABAP Editor to the ABAP Debugger, you are taken by default to the breakpoint location on the DESKTOP 1 tab. If you want to execute each statement one at a time in order to check field content, tablespace content, and so on, click the STEP INTO ([F5]) button.

Step into

The system executes the command beside the yellow arrow only, and then, as previously mentioned, waits for further instructions. In our example, the system has stopped at the WRITE statement. In this way, you can work through the entire source code step by step (see the following text box).

This can be a time-consuming task if the source code is very long, so it makes sense to do this only if you have to analyze a program that you don't know well or you're not initially sure where to insert the breakpoints.

> **Ex** **Look Before You Leap**
>
> The adage "Look before you leap" applies here. If the system is about to call a subroutine, function module, or other object, and then you press [F5], the ABAP Debugger immediately switches to the next-lowest execution level; in other words, it switches to the object in question and proceeds normally. The risk is that the ABAP Debugger may analyze system areas or other modules that you are using as finished components and that you didn't want to debug. Therefore, remember that the [F5] button can take you much deeper into the system than you want to go. *Layer-aware debugging* has offered protection against this since release 7.0 EHP2. This technology is described in more detail at the end of this chapter.

Execute

Based on what you have just read, you can probably already see the difference between [F5] and [F6]. With [F6], if the next executable command is a function module call, a sub-program call, or a call of another object, everything related to this call is executed in the background. The ABAP Debugger remains on the execution level and stops before the next executable statement after the current call is completed.

In our example, the ABAP Debugger has stopped before the SHIFT statement. With this statement, whether you use the F5 or the F6 button is immaterial, since the system stops next at the WRITE statement in both cases.

Consider the F7 button as a lifeline that you can use if you "get lost" with the F5 button. If you have left the program level and aren't sure how deep into the system you've gone, you can use F7 to return to the surface and to your original level. In other words, using the combination of F5 and F7 in this situation has the same effect as using F6 directly.

Step out

The classic ABAP Debugger additionally provides the DISPLAY LIST button (Ctrl + F12), which allows you to trace the development of the list. When the system stops at a breakpoint, click this button to view the current interim status of the list and to check whether everything is as you expected. Then press F3 to return from the list processor to the ABAP Debugger.

Display list

 Run (to Cursor)

As previously mentioned, working through large pieces of source code line by line can quickly become very time-consuming. Therefore, we recommend that you check the system status by setting breakpoints at all the points that you deem critical. There can be any number of statements between these breakpoints. When you press F8, the ABAP Debugger works through all the subsequent statements up to the next breakpoint, where it then stops again. If the program logic doesn't contain any more breakpoints, the program is executed and closed. In our example, the next step is the list output.

The new ABAP Debugger provides two options for viewing the content of fields (such as the current content of the WA_ZMEMBER01-MNAME field). Either double-click the WA_ZMEMBER01-MNAME field in the left part of the screen, or enter the field name in the table in the right part of the screen and press Enter (see Figure 6.7).

Check and modify field content

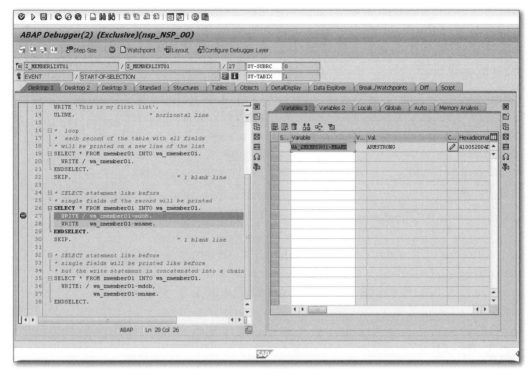

Figure 6.7 Current Field Content in the ABAP Debugger

The field is then transferred to the right part of the screen, with the field name on the left and the current field content on the right. If you now instruct the ABAP Debugger to process the next statement—using the STEP INTO or F5 button—you will see whether the executed statement modified the field content, and if so, how.

In this way, you can trace up to eight fields at once, and view up to four of them simultaneously in the classic ABAP Debugger. You have to scroll to view the remaining fields. The buttons to scroll and the information about which of the eight fields is currently displayed are located in the middle of the screen, over the table. The new ABAP Debugger isn't restricted by these limitations.

Modifying field content
You may want to do more than just view the current field content; you may also want to modify the content of a field so you can test the program logic. For example, in an extreme case caused by the configura-

tion of the test data, dividing by zero may result in the program never producing a list, because the system creates a runtime error before this point. In this case, you could correct the field content so that dividing by zero is avoided and the program creates the required list. Of course, the results in the list are only as good as the test data, but at least you can check whether the list screen is correct and ensure that the non-manipulated fields are producing the required list output.

In the classic ABAP Debugger, proceed as follows: If the field is already contained in the table of eight fields in the lower part of the screen, then the manipulation procedure is very simple. First, click the field content display in the right-hand column. Then overwrite the existing field with the new content and click the CHANGE FIELD CONTENTS button on the extreme right. The new field content has now replaced the old content, and the new content will be used until the program closes. If you restart the ABAP Debugger, you may have to redo the manipulation step.

In the new ABAP Debugger, you double-click on the variable name to change to the DETAIL DISPLAY tab. For this variable, you can use the CHANGE FIELD CONTENT button to change the content of the variable and save it using the ⌷Enter⌷ key (see Figure 6.8).

New ABAP Debugger

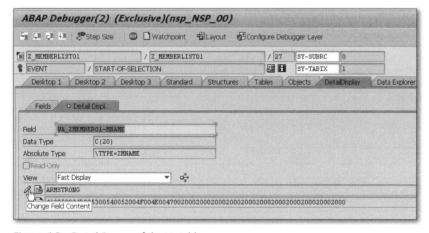

Figure 6.8 Detail Screen of the Variable

➔ See Chapter 10
for more information
on return codes.

In the classic ABAP Debugger below this table, you can see three fields in gray (which indicates that no data can be entered into them) belonging to the table SYST. This is a system table; its fields are named in accordance with the convention SY-[FIELDNAME]. SY-SUBRC, for example, is a field that takes the return value of a statement. When a system statement is executed without any problems, the return value of a command is usually zero. Whether the system returns a return code, what code it returns, and under what error conditions it does so depends on the statement.

Display Options in the Classic Debugger

All display modes in the classic ABAP Debugger have the same basic structure. The upper part of the screen contains the source code, and the lower part contains special information, depending on the mode that has been set. Two modes are of particular significance to us: the DESKTOP 1 tab and the STRUCTURES tab. You're already familiar with the first mode, the DESKTOP 1 tab.

Structures Tab

You use the STRUCTURES tab when you need to make changes to the contents of structured variables, for example. After you've set the breakpoint and the system has stopped program execution, switch to the STRUCTURES tab (see Figure 6.9).

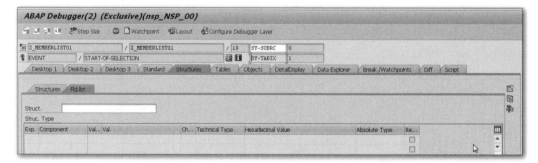

Figure 6.9 Checking the Table Work Area

Monitoring
tablespaces

You can see the input field for the structure name on the FIELD LIST tab. If you want to monitor the WA_ZMEMBER01 work area, for example, enter the structure name into this input field and press ⌈Enter⌋. The second way of displaying the work area is to double-click on the structure name in DESKTOP 1, first in the left part of the screen, then in the right part. This also takes you to the STRUCTURES tab of the ABAP Debugger (see Figure 6.10).

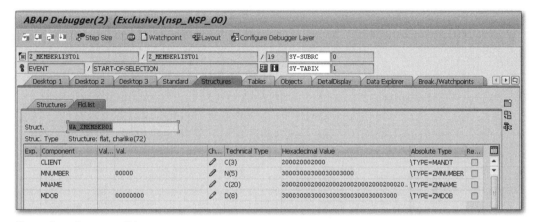

Figure 6.10 Structures Tab

As for variables, you now work through the program using the ⌈F5⌋ key, observing the changes to the table work area as you go (see Figure 6.11). If you want to test the capabilities of the ABAP Debugger right now, you can use the sample report from previous chapters to do so.

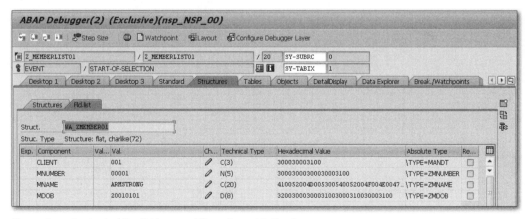

Figure 6.11 Content of the Tablespace After a Record Is Read

Break-/Watchpoints Tab

Another frequently used operating mode of the ABAP Debugger is the *watchpoints mode*. Watchpoints are particularly useful when you're working with large data quantities. While a breakpoint forces the program to stop at a specific point in the source code, a watchpoint monitors the content of a field. With a watchpoint, the system stops program execution as soon as the content of the monitored field matches a value that you predefine.

Create a watchpoint   If you want to use a watchpoint, you first have to create one. For this purpose, use the CREATE WATCHPOINT button on the WATCHPOINTS tab of the BREAK-/WATCHPOINTS tab (see Figure 6.12). The CREATE/CHANGE WATCHPOINT window opens, in which the system proposes the source code as the object to be monitored.

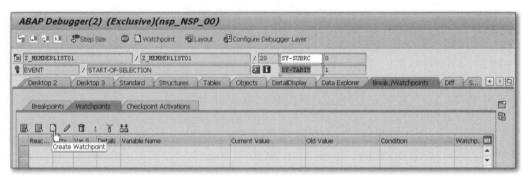

Figure 6.12   Creating a New Watchpoint

 Purpose of Watchpoints

Imagine a file with several thousand data records. In this file, you have set a breakpoint at the point after a record has been read and before it is processed. But how does the breakpoint know whether the record is the one in which the error to be analyzed occurs? The breakpoint always stops at the same point in the source code—that is, before a record is processed. You can see that it would be very time-consuming to manually work through to the error point every time using F5. If, on the other hand, you use a watchpoint, the system always stops where the field content matches the predefined field content, regardless of whether this record is the first or the hundredth in the table.

Enter the name of the field that you want to monitor and the comparison operator as the condition; specify whether the comparison value is contained in a field or whether you will enter it directly (see Figure 6.13).

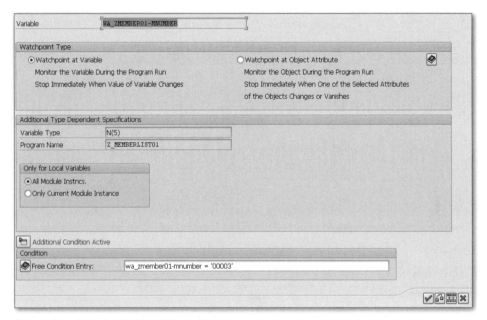

Figure 6.13 Example of a New Watchpoint

Check your entries and confirm them by pressing Enter . The BREAK-/WATCHPOINTS tab displays in the status line that the watchpoint was created successfully (see Figure 6.14).

The lower part of the screen contains an overview of the active watchpoints and their comparison values or comparison fields. The Classic ABAP Debugger used to have the restriction that there could be up to ten watchpoints—linked by a logical AND or OR—in a debugging session. This restriction no longer applies in the new ABAP Debugger. Press F8 to continue program execution. The system stops as soon as it reaches the next breakpoint or watchpoint (see Figure 6.15). The system marks the last reached watchpoint with a yellow arrow. You can now take your time and analyze the system status, field content, table contents, and so on. Of course, as you work, you can switch to any of the other

Detailed analysis

tabs of the ABAP Debugger, depending on which mode is most suitable for each analysis.

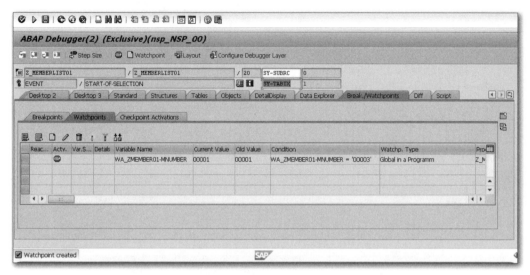

Figure 6.14 Break-/Watchpoints Tab—Watchpoints

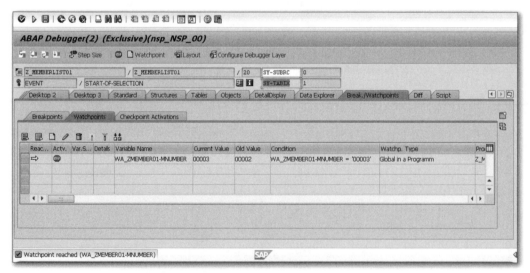

Figure 6.15 System Stop at Watchpoint

Breakpoints Mode

You can also set more breakpoints in the ABAP Debugger by simply double-clicking on a statement line in the DESKTOP 1 tab, for example. The stop icon then appears beside this line. If you double-click on the stop icon, the ABAP Debugger first deactivates the breakpoint; if you double-click on it *again*, the breakpoint will be deleted permanently.

> ### ▶ Manage Dynamic Breakpoints in the Debugger
>
> If you would rather manage the breakpoints in the ABAP Debugger than in the ABAP Editor, use the BREAKPOINTS tab on the BREAK-/WATCHPOINTS tab in the ABAP Debugger to switch to the operating mode for breakpoints (see Figure 6.16). Here, you can carry out all necessary activities for breakpoints (such as creating and deleting them, and so on).
>
> You already know that you only need session breakpoints within the scope of this book. In contrast to the classic ABAP Debugger, the new ABAP Debugger uses not only variables as breakpoints, but also ABAP statements, calls of function modules or subprograms, and much more. Since you don't really need these functions for the scope of this book, we don't discuss them further here.

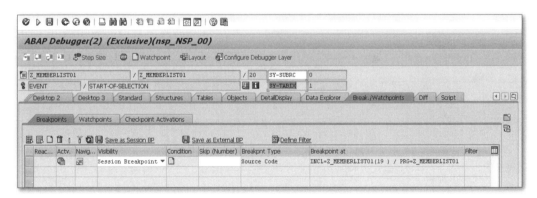

Figure 6.16   Break-/Watchpoints Tab—Breakpoints

The classic ABAP Debugger can manage up to 30 breakpoints, but the new ABAP Debugger doesn't share this limitation. If you no longer require a breakpoint, select the header of the relevant breakpoint on

Deleting a breakpoint

the Break-/Watchpoints tab and delete it with the Delete Breakpoint button.

 Lifetime of Breakpoints and Watchpoints

As we already mentioned, session breakpoints and watchpoints in the ABAP Debugger only "live" as long as the ABAP Debugger session runs, and are deleted when the user closes the ABAP Debugger. If you stay logged on to the system and want to restart the ABAP Debugger, you'll also have to redefine the breakpoints and watchpoints that you set previously. In these situations, you can save your dynamic breakpoints and watchpoints before you close the ABAP Debugger so that they remain available in the same session. To do this, click on the Save as Session BP button. Saved points remain intact until you explicitly delete them or until you log off from the system and thereby end your session.

Close debugging mode

There are two ways to close the ABAP Debugger. The first way is to get the system to process your test program, which you do using the button Run (to cursor) or [F8]. You then automatically return to the level before the ABAP Debugger call, in our case in the calling session, for example, the ABAP Editor. Of course, this assumes that the program has closed properly and that no runtime errors have occurred.

The second way to close the ABAP Debugger is to choose Debugger • Exit Debugger from the menu. This closes the debugging mode immediately and returns you to the mode before the ABAP Debugger call. So if you called the ABAP Debugger from within the ABAP Editor (Transaction SE38), for example, you are returned to that transaction. You then have to restart the ABAP Debugger from there.

Manage dynamic breakpoints in the ABAP Editor

You can also manage dynamic breakpoints in the ABAP Editor. Choose Utilities • Breakpoints • Display to see an overview of all the dynamic breakpoints that are currently available (see Figure 6.17).

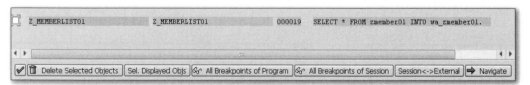

Figure 6.17   Managing Breakpoints in the ABAP Editor

The dialog box then displays the dynamic breakpoints. Click the checkbox to the left of the line to select a breakpoint. You can then use the DELETE SELECTED OBJECTS button to delete the breakpoints you selected. On the other hand, if you double-click on a breakpoint in the list, you are taken to the line of source code that precedes the breakpoint. Click the CONFIRM button or press ⟨Enter⟩ to close the dialog box.

Table 6.1 provides you with a summary of the buttons on the ABAP Debugger screen, along with their descriptions and shortcuts.

Button	Description	Shortcut
	Step into	F5
	Execute	F6
	Step out	F7
	Run (to cursor)	F8
	Display list (only in the classic ABAP Debugger)	Ctrl + F12
Step Size	Step size (change debugging increment)	Ctrl + Shift + F10
STOP	Breakpoint at command, create method	F9
Layout	Save layout	Ctrl + Shift + F3
Configure Debugger Layer	Configure Debugger layer	Ctrl + Shift + F4
Watchpoint	Create watchpoint	Shift + F8
	Delete field name (only in the classic ABAP Debugger)	–
	Change objects	–

Table 6.1 Buttons in the ABAP Debugger

Static Breakpoints

BREAK-POINT This section briefly describes the ABAP statement `BREAK-POINT` for the sake of completeness. During a complex development process, it can be useful to build this statement into the source code for introductory and testing purposes. However, once you have done so, the program execution stops at this point and switches to debugging mode every time, which can become irritating over time.

 Don't Puzzle the End User

As we have mentioned previously, dynamic breakpoints apply only to the respective user and only during the current session. Embedded statements, on the other hand, apply to all users. Therefore, if a user starts this program—for example, a user in a technical department may do so for testing purposes—and the program execution stops at the `BREAK-POINT` command, then the system will switch to debugging mode, as it always does. That user is likely to be very puzzled at this moment. Your job is to spare or at least buffer the user from these potentially confusing moments.

Layer for Layer: Layer-Aware Debugging

Let's suppose that you use the ABAP Debugger to analyze another developer's program. However, the program that you debug not only contains its own program flow logic, but also numerous calls in unknown code located in other programs (for example, in SAP standard libraries for the screen display of tables).

While you try to understand the business logic of your colleague's program in the ABAP Debugger in detail, you may get caught up in the whirlwind of confusing system classes.

Framework debugging It can also be the other way round: Increasingly larger parts of ABAP development are implemented within frameworks, such as Web Dynpro ABAP. Here, the code that contains the actual business application logic is not directly started by the user; thus, the highest level of the call sequence; instead, the framework (for example, the Web Dynpro framework) is called first. It processes a lot of technical framework code until it finally calls the business function that you want to use.

If you manually navigated through the framework code, the debugging session would take too much time; so due to the complexity of the code, it's easily to accidentally skip the essential program part—which is rather small in comparison with the whole program.

The problem is the same in every complex application software: Numerous components, which solve various subtasks like database accesses, calculations, dialog displays, and interfaces, interact with each other and form an overall solution together. During the program flow, which you monitor in the ABAP Debugger step by step, all of these components are processed even though you're probably not interested in all of them. If you have an idea in which area the error hides, you can hide the components that have nothing to do with it or skip their code in the ABAP Debugger.

Hide irrelevant components

Remember that since release 7.0 EHP2, the ABAP Debugger provides layer-aware (targeted) debugging of specific software layers. It lets you simply hide software that you don't want the ABAP Debugger to analyze. The software will still be processed, but in the background; the Debugger does not display any steps in the hidden software layers and only notifies you when it reaches a source code area that you actually want to debug.

New in release 7.0 EHP2

 SAP NetWeaver 7.0 EHP2 Required

Layer-aware debugging is available as of SAP NetWeaver 7.0 EHP2. If it is not available on your SAP system, it's because you're using an older SAP release. In this case, you can ask your administrator whether the system landscape contains a system with a higher release or you can search the SAP Developer Network (*http://sdn.sap.com*) for an up-to-date ABAP trial version for downloading. When this book was printed, SAP NetWeaver 7.02 (SAP NetWeaver 7.0 EHP2) was available for download.

Listing 6.1 shows a slightly modified version of the Z_MEMBERLIST01 program. Although the listing is still several pages away, take a look at the program. Do you already recognize the differences between this version and the previous version? The following sections describe them step by step.

A call of the standard SAP module REUSE_ALV_GRID_DISPLAY, which originally calls a simple list, was added to the program. This module displays an internal table that exists in the main memory of the calling program in a user-friendly way. Also provided are functions for filtering, exporting, changing the layout, and so on. This might be useful if, for example, a helpful colleague added the module but didn't document it sufficiently.

If you execute the Z_MEMBERLIST01_DEBUG program, the table display of the member list (see Figure 6.18) is shown instead of the known list output. This table display is called SAP List Viewer, ALV Grid, or simply ALV. You can find it in numerous SAP dialogs.

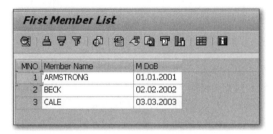

Figure 6.18 Output of the REUSE_ALV_GRID_DISPLAY Module

Table display and additional functions Experiment with the various functions of the list output and try the icons above the table. Here, among other things, you can find functions for sorting, filtering, exporting, and managing layouts. If you double-click on a table row, the system displays a message dialog (see Figure 6.19).

Figure 6.19 Message That Appears When You Double-Click on a Table Row

If you confirm the message by clicking on CONTINUE, you return to the table display. Clicking BACK or pressing ⌹F3⌹ takes you to the known list output of the program, as shown in Figure 6.20. You can then also exit the list output with BACK or ⌹F3⌹.

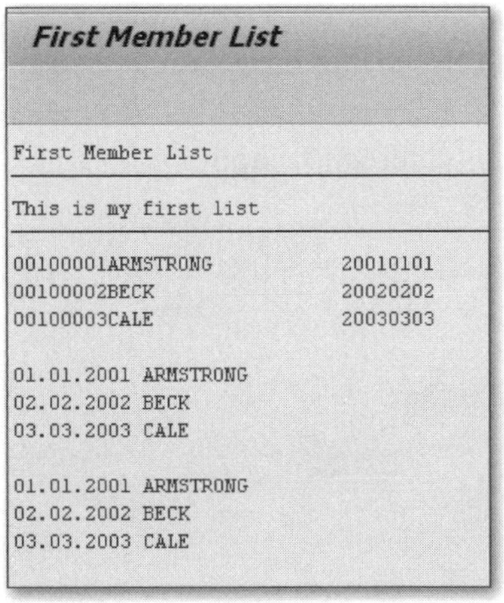

First Member List

```
First Member List

This is my first list

00100001ARMSTRONG        20010101
00100002BECK             20020202
00100003CALE             20030303

01.01.2001 ARMSTRONG
02.02.2002 BECK
03.03.2003 CALE

01.01.2001 ARMSTRONG
02.02.2002 BECK
03.03.2003 CALE
```

Figure 6.20 List Output of the Program

What happened? If you read the program code in Listing 6.1 carefully, you may have noticed that there is a subroutine, CALLBACK_USER _COMMAND, that could be responsible for the output of the message. Even though this subprogram is not called in our program, it nevertheless was processed because the message is displayed when you double-click on a table row on the screen. How is this possible?

The answer is that a callback function is used. In this case, the calling program passes the name of a function (here, the CALLBACK_USER _COMMAND subroutine) to the called program (here, the function module for the table display). This function module then calls the respective program when needed. So the called program calls back and executes a function of its calling program.

Callback

You can often find such constructs in software where frameworks and service modules are created as general solutions for recurring tasks. Even though recurring tasks can be standardized to a large extent, it is sometimes necessary to embed application-specific code in the flow. This is also the case in this example: Our program calls the standard

Callback functions are typical for frameworks

module, and the standard module calls a function of our program at a specific time before the program flow control is returned to the module so that it can continue with its tasks.

Defining object sets   Again, start the program, but this time in the new ABAP Debugger. Click on CONFIGURE DEBUGGER LAYER, as shown in Figure 6.21. Configure the layer-oriented debugging in the dialog box that opens (see Figure 6.22). Here, select the LAYER-AWARE DEBUGGING ACTIVE checkbox. This readies the lower part of the window for input.

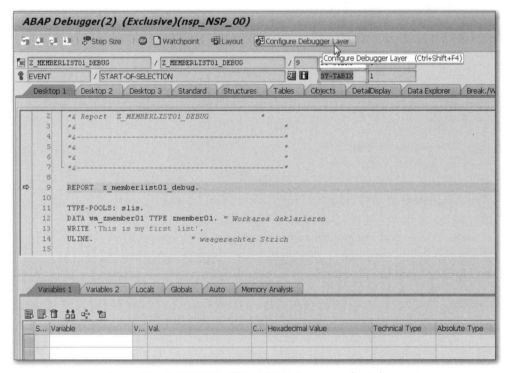

Figure 6.21   Z_MEMBERLIST01_DEBUG Program in the Debugger

The DIRECT DEFINITION OF THE VISIBLE OBJECT SET (LAYER) radio button is selected by default. This is sufficient in our case; if you regularly use the ABAP Debugger in the future, you can store profiles here for periodic access.

Our goal is to debug the program flow, but to have the system display the code in the Z_MEMBERLIST01_DEBUG program itself. The system is supposed to hide the code of the standard SAP module, which is also processed during the program execution.

For this purpose, enter the Z_MEMBERLIST01_DEBUG program name into the PROGRAMS field and select the STOP AT ENTRY checkbox. (Check that the STOP AT EXIT checkbox is not selected.) Then click CONTINUE to confirm the dialog (see Figure 6.22).

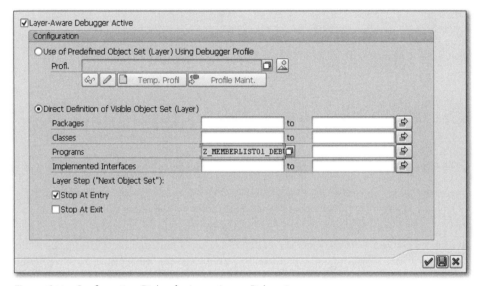

Figure 6.22 Configuration Dialog for Layer-Aware Debugging

Back in the ABAP Debugger, the new button (NEXT OBJECT SET) indicates that layer-aware debugging is enabled (see Figure 6.23).

Next object set

You can now debug some program steps to ensure that the normal debugger functions are still available.

Remember that you specified in the configuration dialog that you want to debug the Z_MEMBERLIST01_DEBUG program when it is accessed. If you click on the new button, NEXT OBJECT SET, then the system will continue executing the program until the next point in the program flow is reached that corresponds to this definition (that is, until the Z_MEMBERLIST01_DEBUG program is accessed again).

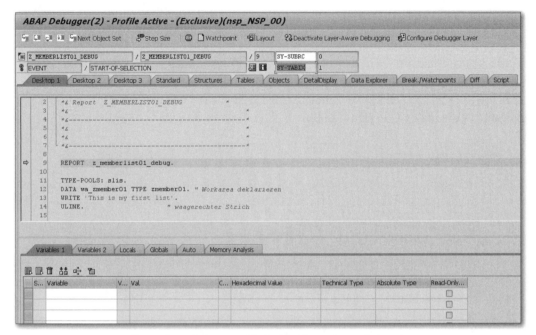

Figure 6.23 Debugger with Enabled Layer-Aware Debugging

Interactive functions   When you click on the NEXT OBJECT SET button, the system exits the ABAP Debugger and shows the table display of the member list. Why does it do this? Because the interactive functions of a program remain intact during the debugging process, and dialog outputs are not suppressed. The processing now continues as usual until the next point in the flow that is supposed to be debugged is reached (that is, when our program is accessed again).

You can also use the sort, filter, and export functions as required without the system displaying the ABAP Debugger, because all of the program code that is processed for these functions is outside the selected object set.

Next object set is reached   Only after you have double-clicked on a table row does the standard SAP module for the table display remember our callback function and navigate to the CALLBACK_USER_COMMAND subroutine of the Z_MEMBERL-IST01_DEBUG program. Based on our definition, our debugging session should also continue, because we are interested in everything that happens in this (and only this) program.

Next Object Set Is Not a Breakpoint

Be wary of comparisons of the NEXT OBJECT SET function (which is reached when an execution point according to the object set defined in the Debugger Settings is entered or exited) to a breakpoint or watchpoint. This analogy is misleading: the ABAP Debugger does not treat the access to and exit from the defined software layers as breakpoints.

So the CONTINUE ($\boxed{F8}$) function does *not* take you to the next object set. For this purpose, you can only use the NEXT OBJECT SET function.

Double-clicking on the table eventually takes you back to the ABAP Debugger. As you can see in Figure 6.24, the system outputs a message that the selected object set was accessed. The system noticed that the execution again reached the Z_MEMBERLIST01_DEBUG program that you want to debug.

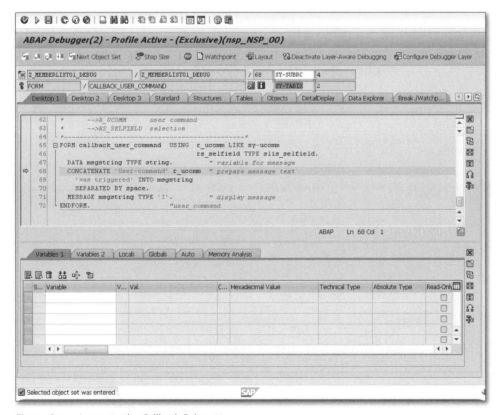

Figure 6.24 Access to the Callback Subroutine

The execution has reached the CALLBACK_USER_COMMAND subroutine, whose name was previously passed to the SAP function module RE-USE_ALV_GRID_DISPLAY as the value for the callback function name parameter.

You can now either trace the program flow in the ABAP Debugger step by step or, by clicking on NEXT OBJECT SET, have the system continue the debugging process, but not until the program is accessed the next time.

 Disabling and Enabling

> You can enable and disable layer-aware debugging at any time in your debugging session. To do so, simply use the ACTIVATE LAYER-AWARE DEBUGGING or DEACTIVATE LAYER-AWARE DEBUGGING button. It is possible that the system disables layer-aware debugging on its own, because when you enable it again, the profile last used is deployed.

Sample Code for Layer-Aware Debugging

```
 1 *&---------------------------------------------*
 2 *& Report   Z_MEMBERLIST01_DEBUG            *
 3 *&                                              *
 4 *&---------------------------------------------*
 5 *&                                              *
 6 *&                                              *
 7 *&---------------------------------------------*
 8
 9 REPORT  z_memberlist01_debug.
10
11 TYPE-POOLS: slis.
12 DATA wa_zmember01 TYPE zmember01.
                         " define work area
13 WRITE 'This is my first list'.
14 ULINE.                  " horizontal line
15
16 * loop
17 * each record of the table with all fields
18 * will be printed on a new line of the list
19 SELECT * FROM zmember01 INTO wa_zmember01.
20   WRITE / wa_zmember01.
```

```
21 ENDSELECT.
22 SKIP.                    " 1 blank line
23
24 * SELECT statement like before
25 * single fields of the record will be printed
26 SELECT * FROM zmember01 INTO wa_zmember01.
27   WRITE / wa_zmember01-mdob.
28   WRITE   wa_zmember01-mname.
29 ENDSELECT.
30 SKIP.                    " 1 blank line
31
32 * SELECT statement like before
33 * single fields will be printed like before
34 *   but the WRITE statement is concatenated
       into a chain statement
35 SELECT * FROM zmember01 INTO wa_zmember01.
36   WRITE: / wa_zmember01-mdob,
37            wa_zmember01-mname.
38 ENDSELECT.
39
40 DATA zmember01_itab TYPE TABLE OF zmember01.
41
42 SELECT * FROM zmember01 INTO TABLE zmember01_itab.
43
44 CALL FUNCTION 'REUSE_ALV_GRID_DISPLAY'
45   EXPORTING
46     i_callback_program   = 'Z_MEMBERLIST01_DEBUG'
47     i_callback_user_command = 'CALLBACK_USER_COMMAND'
48     i_structure_name     = 'ZMEMBER01'
49   TABLES
50     t_outtab             = zmember01_itab.
51
52 *&---------------------------------------------*
53 *&      Form  user_command
54 *&---------------------------------------------*
55 *      -->R_UCOMM     User-Command
56 *      -->RS_SELFIELD  Selection
57 *---------------------------------------------*
58 FORM callback_user_command USING r_ucomm
                              LIKE sy-ucomm
59                                 rs_selfield
                              TYPE slis_selfield.
```

```
60   DATA msgstring TYPE string.   " Variable for
                                        message
61   CONCATENATE 'Usercommand'
       r_ucomm                        " build message
62     'was triggered' INTO msgstring
63     SEPARATED BY space.
64   MESSAGE msgstring TYPE 'I'.   " display message
65 ENDFORM.                        "user_command
```

Listing 6.1   Report Z_MEMBERLIST01_DEBUG

Notes on the Source Code

Line 11

The TYPE-POOLS statement defines the usage of a type group so that the data types defined in the type group can be used in the current program. As of release 7.0 EHP2, this statement is obsolete; it is only used here to make the program executable in earlier releases that can't perform layer-aware debugging.

Lines 40 to 42

An internal table for the display of the member list is defined and populated.

Line 44

Calling the SAP function module REUSE_ALV_GRID_DISPLAY:

> The T_OUTTAB parameter transfers the internal table that is supposed to be displayed.

> The I_STRUCTURE_NAME parameter transfers the name of the ABAP Dictionary table, ZMEMBER01, which the system is supposed to use to display the internal table.

> The I_CALLBACK_USER_COMMAND and I_CALLBACK_PROGRAM parameters are used to transfer the name of the subroutine and the name of the callback program for calling back user-defined functions in the table display.

Line 58

The `CALLBACK_USER_COMMAND` subroutine was specified as a callback function. It must have the interface defined by the `REUSE_ALV_GRID_DISPLAY` module. The `R_UCOMM` parameter is used to transfer the function codes that were triggered by the user. The `RS_SELFIELD` parameter allows you to transfer detailed information on the clicked table row and column.

Line 61

The message that is supposed to be output is created.

Line 64

The message is output.

Modifying Transparent Database Tables

Modifications of database tables fall into several categories. In this chapter you will learn about different options for adding fields to existing tables or making other changes.

Do you remember the transparent database table from Chapter 2, ABAP Dictionary? The table created previously consists of fields for the system client: the name, number, and date of birth of the member. The key fields are CLIENT and MNUMBER (see Figure 7.1).

To prepare for the upcoming steps, you'll modify the table. Even the simplest modification involves the insertion of additional fields. The procedure for non-key fields in customer-specific tables is relatively simple. Inserting items into standard SAP tables is a more involved process because such modifications can be made only with append structures. For customer-specific tables, modifications can be made by manipulating key fields. See "Maintaining Append Structures" for more information.

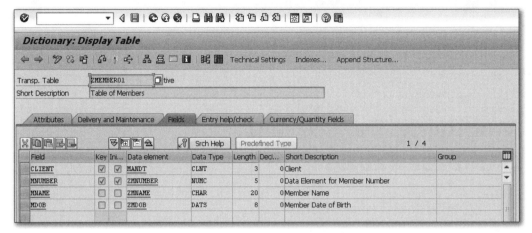

Figure 7.1 Member Table with Four Fields

The risk of lost data When you manipulate key fields, you must also adjust the table in the database. The database system determines whether you can make the adjustment by deleting and creating new items, by changing the database catalog, or via a reimplementation.

➕ Table Conversion

When you change table structures, you usually want to retain the data that is contained in the table. In some cases, the SAP system uses a mechanism called table conversion. Here, the old table (with data) and the new table (without data) temporarily exist in parallel, and the system transfers the data from the old table to the new table using the MOVE-CORRESPONDING ABAP command.

You might have to undertake complex work that involves a lot of reorganization and even the risk of losing data.

Deleting fields from tables is not always easy, especially when these fields already contain data. Of course, you can also copy or delete tables.

Copying a Database Table

Whether you're working with customer-specific tables or standard SAP tables, we recommend that you don't take any risks and therefore begin by copying the table instead of working with the original. Copying a table means that you copy only the table (with its properties and fields). Since only the structure—an empty shell without content—is copied, you can use this copy as a test to see if what you want to happen actually does happen before you make any changes. Even if the copy means a duplicate and redundant storage of data—which you would normally want to avoid—sometimes requirements demand that you copy an entire table structure at least temporarily.

Don't take unnecessary risks

You start the copy process in the initial screen of the ABAP Dictionary with Transaction SE11 or via SAP MENU • TOOLS • ABAP WORKBENCH • DEVELOPMENT • DICTIONARY. Enter the name of the table to be copied, ZMEMBER01 (see Figure 7.2). When you click the COPY ([Ctrl] + [F5]) button to initiate the process, a window is displayed that suggests the source table (see Figure 7.3).

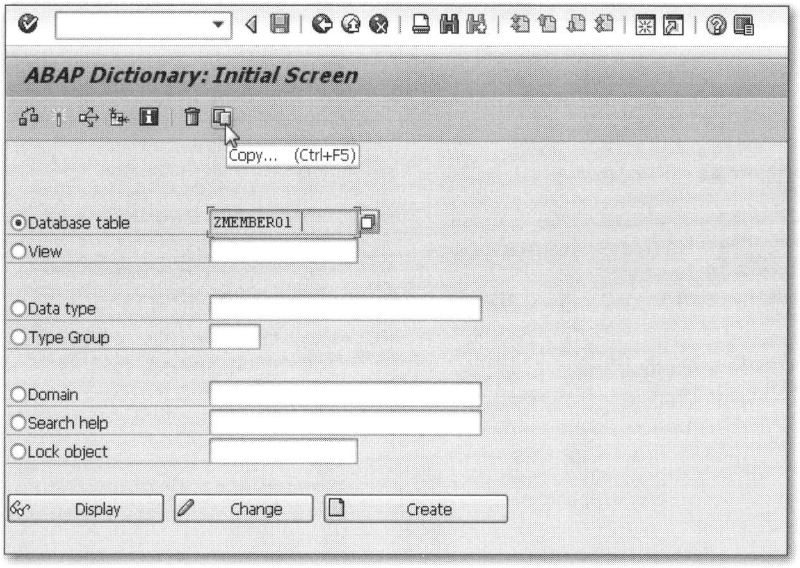

Starting the copying process

Figure 7.2 Copying a Database Table

175

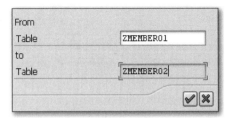

Figure 7.3　Source Table and Target Table During Copying

After you check the source table, enter the name of the target table and press ⌈Enter⌉. In the next screen, the system asks for the name of the package (that is, which group of objects) that your object should belong to (see Figure 7.4).

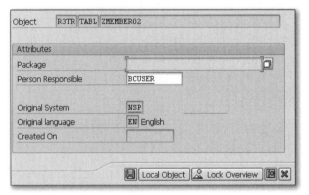

Figure 7.4　Assigning a Target Table to a Package and Saving It

 Package Names

The term "development class" is often used instead of "package." In the real world, of course, you know where you're working. For example, if you're working in financial accounting, you probably know the name of the package for customer-specific applications in financial accounting. If anything is unclear, ask your system administrator about the current naming conventions.

Because all objects are stored as local objects in our exercise, click LO-CAL OBJECT to save the object. The status line displays a notification that the ZMEMBER01 table has been copied to ZMEMBER02. The system automatically entered package $TMP.

After this step, you return to the initial screen of the ABAP Dictionary, which now displays the target (database) table for editing (see Figure 7.5). The copied table has not been activated and therefore cannot be used yet. You must use the CHANGE button to change to the ABAP Dictionary to maintain the table.

Activating the copied table

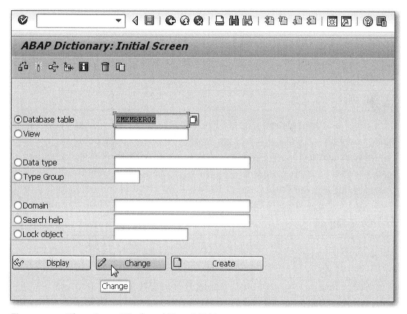

Figure 7.5 Changing a Displayed Target Table

The *new* table status of the target table confirms that the table might not be populated with data yet (see Figure 7.6). If you want the structure and properties of the table to remain unchanged, then click ACTIVATE, and a runtime object is generated for the table.

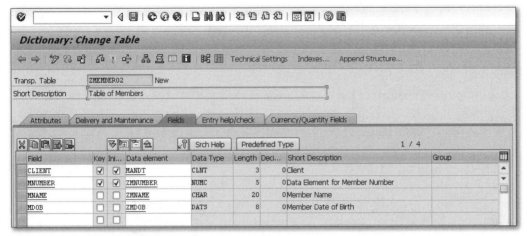

Figure 7.6 Table Status of the Target Table After Copying

 Activation Log

You can have the system display the activation log as necessary. If the system writes activation warnings to the log, you must decide if these warnings have a negative effect on your work with the table. Warnings can also result from formal checks in the system; however, these are irrelevant for the concrete case so they can be ignored. For example, you can ignore the warning that the enhancement category for the table or structure is missing.

Creating a runtime object
The runtime object contains all the information needed for optimum access to ABAP programs and optimized system performance. Only then can you write data records to the table. After successful activation, the status bar displays a message, "object activated."

To double-check that the table does not contain any data records or to quickly find out how many data records a table row contains, we recommend that you display how many rows the table contains. Follow menu path UTILITIES • TABLE CONTENTS • DISPLAY and go to the data browser (see Figure 7.7).

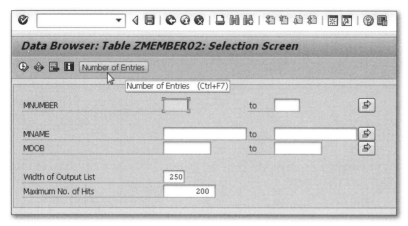

Figure 7.7 Displaying the Table Contents

To check that the data records of the source table weren't copied, use the NUMBER OF ENTRIES button to open a window for the number of table entries to see if the table is empty (see Figure 7.8). Use the CLOSE button to leave the window. From the data browser, use the BACK button to return to the maintenance screen of the table in the ABAP Dictionary.

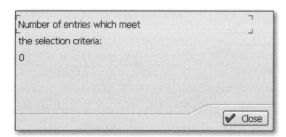

Figure 7.8 Checking the Number of Data Records in a Table

If you start from the DICTIONARY: CHANGE TABLE screen, you can use a simple maintenance dialog to enter data records in the target table (UTILITIES • TABLE CONTENT • CREATE ENTRIES). Branch to the screen to create data records and enter some test data records. We recommend that you enter three to five data records that differ from the content of non-key fields. Because we'll be referring to these data records and the table repeatedly in the following sections, it's important that you can easily identify them manually.

Creating data records with table maintenance

Don't Forget to Save

Save each data record with the Save button. After you enter the last data record, use the Back button to return to the screen for table maintenance.

Enhancing Non-Key Fields

To enhance a customer-specific transparent table with non-key fields, you'll work much like you did when you created fields in a new table, as described in Chapter 2. You assign field names, create new data elements and domains, or reassign existing data elements and domains.

 Consider the Activation Sequence

When you activate the objects, take the activation sequence into account. To activate a table, you must activate all the referenced data elements; to activate a data element, the referenced domains must be activated. That's why you must check all the objects for inconsistencies and only then should you activate the domains, the data element, and then the table. The procedure is the same for each object and must be repeated in each field.

Adding non-key fields

Now try to enhance the table with a few fields. First add a table for the gender of the member. The field should be of the CHAR type (a character string) and have a length of 1. The purpose of the field is to be able to maintain a gender key. Maintaining the field in the table, creating a data element for it, and creating a domain for the data element shouldn't be difficult for you since Chapter 2 already explained the procedure. You can reread the chapter if you have any questions.

Maintaining Fixed Values in Domains

The domains involve a new aspect: only specific values should be permitted for the gender key. Future ABAP programs should offer input help, and the system should reject all other entries so that the gender key field can contain only the values defined for it. One way of meeting this requirement is to store fixed values in the domain. This procedure is quite typical and workable, even for small quantities of values like those of the gender key. Of course, you would work differently with large quantities of values; an alternative approach is presented below.

To store fixed values in the domain, branch to the VALUE RANGE tab in the maintenance screen once you've created the domain and entered the permitted values there (see Figure 7.9).

Maintaining fixed values in the domain

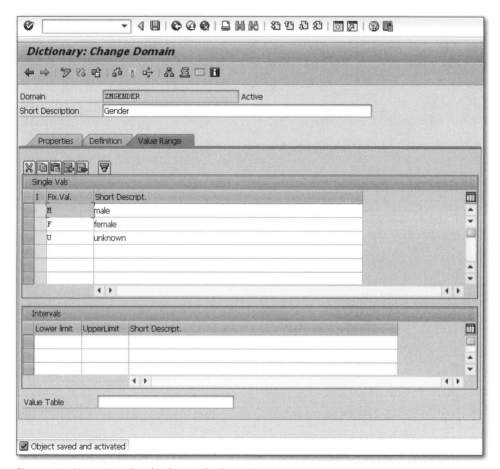

Figure 7.9 Maintaining Fixed Values in the Domain

Maintain three gender keys for male, (M), female (F), and unknown (U) as individual values. Note that you can also maintain fixed values as intervals, but we don't need to address this option for our exercise.

After you maintain the fixed values, everything else should already be familiar to you. You activate the domains, data elements, and table, and then test the effects of the fixed values.

 Input Help Icon in the ABAP Dictionary

When you examine the entry field for the gender even during simple maintenance, you should now see an input help icon next to the field (see Figure 7.10).

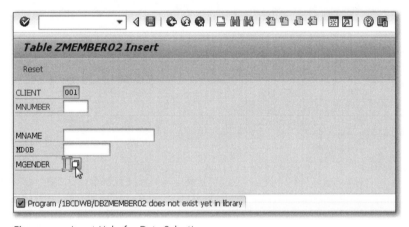

Figure 7.10   Input Help for Data Selection

You can click on the icon or press [F4] to open a window with the list of suggested values (see Figure 7.11).

Input help list   Select the desired value by double-clicking on it or highlighting the row (that is, simply click on the value and then click the COPY button). The value is automatically transferred into the entry field for the gender key.

Figure 7.11 Input Help List

> ## ❶ Entry Check
>
> The simplicity of the options for data entry in the ABAP Dictionary means that no additional validation occurs. That's not a problem, because users don't work in the ABAP Dictionary, but instead in business applications for financials and accounting. You'll notice the full effect of fixed values in the domain when you work with programs and dialogs, which use table fields that refer to the related domains.
>
> An entry check occurs only for data types CHAR and NUMC. With screens, the entry check can ensure that only the entry of fixed values from the input help list is enabled.

→ You can learn more about input checks in Chapter 11.

Important Points for Currency and Quantity Fields

Please note some important points for currency and quantity fields. First, consider the existence of special data types in the ABAP Dictionary, because you enter amounts or quantities in these fields. The data type for currency fields is CURR; the data type for quantity fields is QUAN. Both fields correspond to amount fields of type DEC, with a maximum field length of 31 characters. As you can imagine, information on only the amounts and quantities is not enough.

For currencies, you must know the currency unit that corresponds to the amount. Over 180 hard or soft currencies exist around the world, as do their exchange rates. The currency unit of a specific amount is extremely important to the financial and accounting departments, so

Currency fields

the amount field for currencies with the CURR type must also be linked to a reference field for the currency unit of type CUKY. The field of type CUKY is the reference field for the currency amount; it has a fixed value of five characters.

Quantity fields   A similar situation exists with quantity fields, but the amount field refers to quantity units (like liters or tons) that are entered in fields of type UNIT. The UNIT type fields also have a fixed length of three characters.

As a practical demonstration, enter two additional fields into our table. Use field MFEE for the currency amount and MCURRENCY for the currency unit. Record both fields in the field list and define the corresponding data elements and domains (see Figure 7.12).

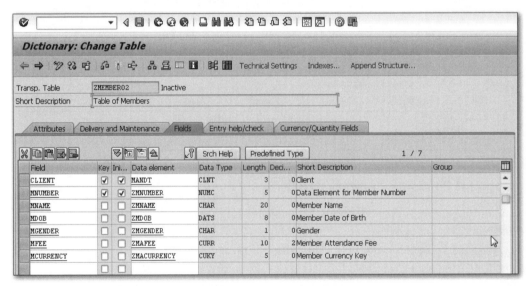

Figure 7.12   Table with Currency Fields

Unlike the example with the fields you have used so far, you cannot simply activate the table with currency and quantity fields. If you try to do so with the ACTIVATE button, you'll get an error message (see Figure 7.13).

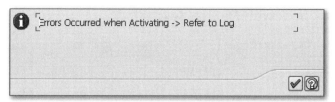

Figure 7.13 Error Message During Activation of a Table

Unfortunately, the entries in the FIELDS tab are not enough. In the maintenance screen, you must also enter a reference field of type CUKY in the table maintenance screen's CURRENCY/QUANTITY FIELDS tab. The dictionary can thus ensure that a currency unit exists for every currency amount and that a quantity unit exists for every quantity amount. The reference table can exist in the same table or in another table. In our simple example, the reference field exists in the table ZMEMBER02 (see Figure 7.14).

Reference fields for amounts with currencies and quantities

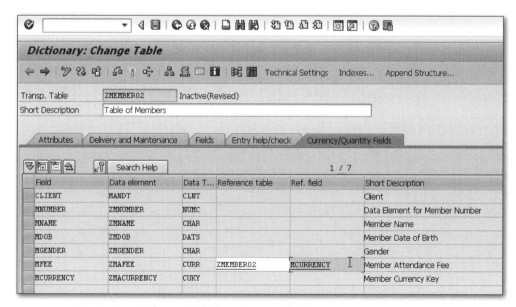

Figure 7.14 Maintaining a Reference Field for a Currency Field

Table activation is no longer a problem after you've maintained the reference field and the reference table. As you have already done several times, test the functionality of the table by entering data records in the maintenance dialog of the ABAP Dictionary.

Entry Check with Foreign Keys

Everything should work just fine now. So far, so good. You can use any abbreviation for any currency that you want, since you haven't built in any entry check yet. But any responsible businessperson would cringe at the thought of this. To ensure that you can maintain only real and valid currency units, you must build in a foreign key.

Maintaining Foreign Keys

The use of a foreign key ensures that you can enter only values from input help. Some preliminary work is required to meet this goal.

For our example, let's begin the preparatory work in data element ZMACURRENCY for table field MCURRENCY. The data element refers to a standard domain for currency units from SAP called WAERS, rather than a domain that you invent yourself (see Figure 7.15).

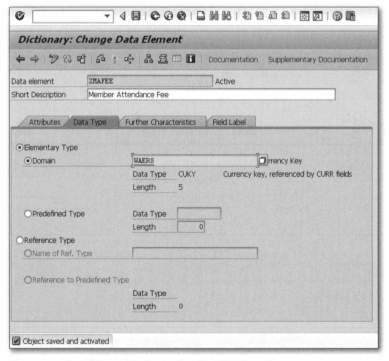

Figure 7.15   Data Element Refers to Standard SAP Domain

If you use forward navigation to branch to the domain and examine it more closely, you can see that the VALUE RANGE tab already contains value table TCURC (see Figure 7.16).

Value table

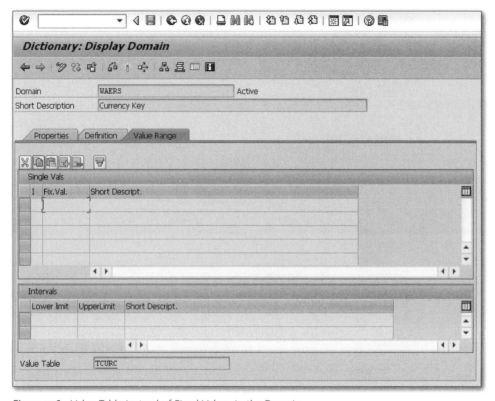

Figure 7.16 Value Table Instead of Fixed Values in the Domain

You have three options to limit valid values with the domain: fixed values, intervals, and the storage of valid values. Whenever there are too many values or it becomes too complicated to store them in the domain, you can maintain the values in a value table (in this case, table TCURC). It contains all the valid currency identifiers in the system, which total to over 200 identifiers (see Figure 7.17).

All valid currency identifiers

If you follow this principle with all the relevant table fields, then the system has only one table that contains the valid currency units.

Central data maintenance with a value table

This means that you have to maintain currency units centrally in one table.

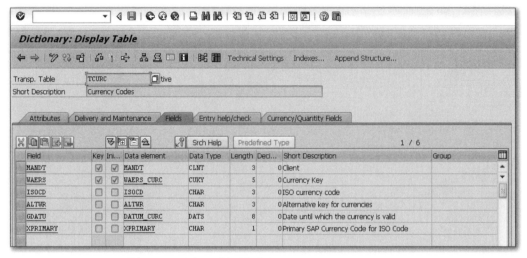

Figure 7.17 Value Table TCURC

To use the value table for entry checks, please note the following regarding the key fields in the value table and the referring domains:

> The field for the currency key must be a key field in the value table. The system looks for a single, unambiguous record with the key fields of the value table.

> In the value table, the data element for the field of the currency key must refer to the WAERS domain. The same domain must serve as the basis for the WAERS field in the TCURC value table and the MCURRENCY field in the ZMEMBER02 foreign key table. The domain is essentially central data that works with the links (see Figure 7.18).

You have now done the preliminary work necessary to maintain a foreign key. So far, we haven't done much for the entry check in table ZMEMBER02 except for specifying a value table instead of fixed values in a domain. But the goal is to activate an entry check that allows only entries that agree with those in the value table.

The contents of table ZMEMBER02 depend on a foreign key and on the contents of another table. The entry check for the MCURRENCY field occurs through comparison with another table (in this case, TCURC). You activate the dependency by maintaining a foreign key in table ZMEMBER02 for field MCURRENCY. In this context, the table in which the foreign key is maintained is called a *foreign key table,* and the table against which the valid entries are checked is called a *check table.*

Foreign key table and check table

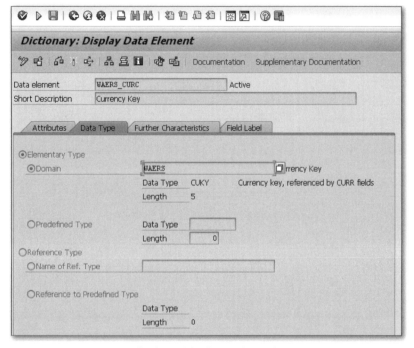

Figure 7.18 Same Domain for the Fields of the Value and Foreign Key Table

You now maintain the foreign key for the MCURRENCY field in table ZMEMBER02 by highlighting the row header and clicking the FOREIGN KEYS button (see Figure 7.19).

Maintaining foreign keys

The system now displays a dialog screen to maintain the foreign key (see Figure 7.20). If you have completed the preparatory work correctly, the system suggests that you accept the value table as the check table.

A value table can also be a check table

189

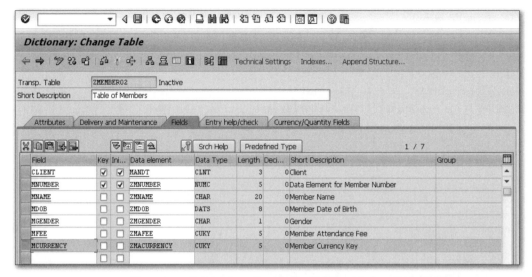

Figure 7.19 Maintaining a Foreign Key Relationship for a Table Field

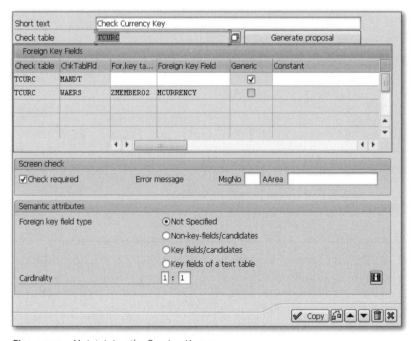

Figure 7.20 Maintaining the Foreign Key

All key fields of the check table are offered for the foreign key. You can select all key fields for the foreign key or just specific key fields. In our simple example, the WAERS field is used as the check table.

Now maintain the short description of the foreign key in the dialog window. In our example, the check table has two key fields. The foreign key fields that should not be checked (in this example, MANDT) are deleted from the list; the related check table field should be marked as a generic key, which produces more hits. In the real world, the risk will depend on the business task. If certain currencies exist only in a certain client, you might have to consider the client as well. If the currency rules are uniform for all clients, you can ignore the client.

 Value Range in the Entry Check

> The entry check should also apply in the relevant dialog screens. Check CHECK REQUIRED in the SCREEN CHECK area.

If you want the system to issue an error message of your choice, you can maintain the message. Chapter 11, Selection Screens, covers messages in more detail. At the moment, you don't have to enter an error message. If you leave the MESSAGE NUMBER and APPLICATION fields empty, the foreign key check automatically generates a generic error message when invalid values are entered.

Defining an error message for incorrect input

In our example, the foreign key field doesn't identify the foreign key table or key field, and it isn't used anywhere else for definitions. As a result, you don't need to maintain any SEMANTIC ATTRIBUTES; the type of the foreign key field is NOT SPECIFIED, the setting suggested by the system.

Attributes of foreign keys

CARDINALITY describes the foreign key relationship in terms of the number of possible hits in the foreign key table and in the check table. A "1" on the left side of cardinality means that there is exactly one record in the check table for every dependent record of the foreign key table. This prevents the existence of records in the foreign key table that don't refer to a record in the check table. A "1" on the right side

Cardinality

of cardinality means that exactly one dependent record exists in the foreign key table for every record in the check table.

These examples should suffice. We won't delve into the special characteristics of generic keys in any more detail. Save the foreign key that you have maintained with the COPY button.

Testing the foreign key

In the ABAP Dictionary, you can now check the table for inconsistencies (just to be safe) and activate it. Then test your settings by maintaining additional entries. You'll notice that the system reacts differently than it did before. If you focus on the MCURRENCY field by clicking on it, a button for input help is displayed (see Figure 7.21).

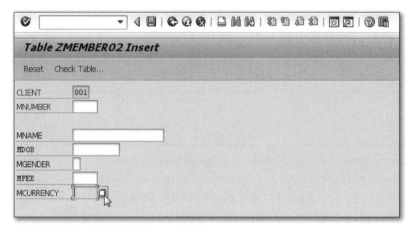

Figure 7.21 Input Help for Currency Unit

Click the button or press [F4] to display a popup window of possible (permitted) entries as an input help list (see Figure 7.22). The procedure to find the correct currency is similar: check it and copy it. As is the case with fixed values, the validation is completely effective only in application dialogs.

Input help and check

At the end of this work, you can once again check in the ABAP Dictionary to see what input help is stored there. Go to the ENTRY HELP/CHECK tab in the table maintenance screen. You can see which input help is activated for a given field in the FOREIGN KEY, CHECK TABLE, ORIGIN OF THE INPUT HELP, and FIXED VALUES columns (see Figure 7.23).

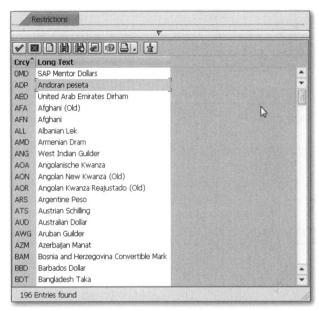

Figure 7.22 Input Help Window for Currency Units

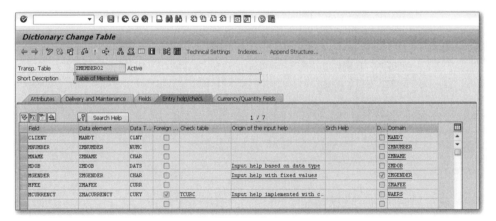

Figure 7.23 Maintained Entry Helps

Maintaining Append Structures

So far, you have maintained additional table fields directly in the field list. For customer-specific tables, you must be authorized to change a table. For standard tables from SAP, you must also have an object key. Even ignoring the amount of work involved, it is extremely risky to set up customer-specific fields in standard tables. A new version of the software might include a field that has the same name as the customer-specific field, and the results cannot be predicted.

 Enhancing Standard Tables

You have other options for avoiding this situation and still being able to enhance tables. You can use *append structures* to enhance both a standard or customer-specific table, which will remain unchanged at the core. The append structure is created especially for any supplemental, customer-specific fields that are needed and thus added (appended) to the table. This technique gives you the ability to enhance every standard table. It also protects customer-specific enhancements from being over-written and destroyed during an SAP software upgrade.

Assigning an append structure

Each append structure is assigned to exactly one table, but each table can have several append structures. The fields created in the append structure are addressed in ABAP programs with `Table_name-Field_name`, just like all other fields. If the fields are linked to dialogs, they are treated just like all other table fields.

Creating an append structure

To explain the principle of the append structure, we'll use a simple example. In the maintenance screen of the ABAP Dictionary, click APPEND STRUCTURE... to create an append structure (see Figure 7.24).

Dictionary: Change Table

← → 🖉 ⅋ ⬚ ⬚ ↑ ⬚ 옳 읇 ⬚ 🈑 🈯 🈯 Technical Settings   Indexes...   [Append Structure...]

Append Structure... (F5)

| Transp. Table | ZMEMBER02 | Active |
| Short Description | Table of Members | |

Attributes │ Delivery and Maintenance │ Fields │ Entry help/check │ Currency/Quantity Fields

✂ ⬚⬚⬚⬚   ⬚⬚⬚⬚   ⬚ Srch Help │ Predefined Type   1 / 14

Field	Key	Ini...	Data element	Data Type	Length	Deci...	Short Description
CLIENT	✓	✓	MANDT	CLNT	3	0	Client
MNUMBER	✓	✓	ZMNUMBER	NUMC	5	0	Data Element for Member Number
MNAME	☐	☐	ZMNAME	CHAR	20	0	Member Name
MDOB	☐	☐	ZMDOB	DATS	8	0	Member Date of Birth
MGENDER	☐	☐	ZMGENDER	CHAR	1	0	Gender
MFEE	☐	☐	ZMAFEE	CURR	10	2	Member Attendance Fee
MCURRENCY	☐	☐	ZMACURRENCY	CUKY	5	0	Member Currency Key
	☐	☐					

Figure 7.24   Creating an Append Structure for a Table

Accept Suggested Names

When you assign a name to the append, remember that the name of the append structure must fit into the customer namespace—that is, it must begin with a `Z` (or with your registered customer namespace, such as `/SAPPRESS/`). When you accept the suggested name with Enter (see Figure 7.25), the system displays the maintenance screen for the append structure. It's similar but not identical to the maintenance screen for the table (see Figure 7.26).

Figure 7.25 Selecting the Name of the Append Structure

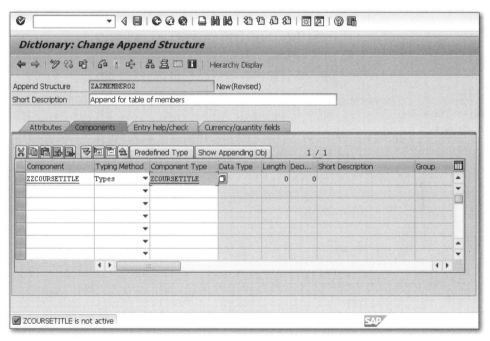

Figure 7.26 Maintaining an Append Structure for a Table

After you enter a short description, you maintain the components of the structure in the COMPONENTS tab (that is, the field named

Naming convention for append components

ZZCOURSETITLE in our example). The ZZ at the beginning of the field name is no accident: The customer namespace for fields in an append structure always begins with ZZ or YY. The reason is actually quite simple. Because some fields in standard tables already begin with Z, and because the fields of an append structure in ABAP and dialog programs are addressed with Table_name-Field_name (that is, fields of standard tables and fields of customer-specific tables are addressed in the same way), conflicts might arise if you can't differentiate between the customer-specific fields of an append structure and the fields of a standard table. The only way to differentiate between the two types of fields is by beginning the names of customer-specific fields with ZZ or YY (or with a registered customer namespace).

Create field ZZCOURSETITLE and data element ZCOURSETITLE. Save the structure and then use forward navigation (double-click on ZCOURSE-TITLE); the system creates the data element. In the next screen, you'll notice a characteristic that differentiates work with structures from work with table fields. In general, structures can contain additional structures or tables (but that doesn't concern us at this time).

Components permitted in an append structure

The components of a structure can also be fields that refer to a data element, as they do in a field. In this special case, the only enhancements allowed in an append structure are those that maintain new fields in the table, define foreign keys, or link search help (see Figure 7.27). Therefore, select DATA ELEMENT as the type, and then save and activate the data element and the domain. Then check and activate the append structure.

Figure 7.27 Creating a Component Type for Components

Activating the append structure

Activation of an append structure also activates the corresponding table; the fields of the append structure are added (appended) to the table in the database. When the table is activated, all the append structures of the table are searched and their fields are appended to the table on the database.

You can check the success of your work in the FIELDS tab in the maintenance screen for tables of the ABAP Dictionary. In the last row, the FIELD column contains .APPEND and the DATA ELEMENT column contains the name of the append, ZAMEMBER02 (see Figure 7.28).

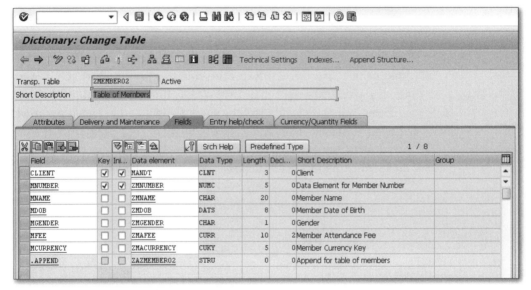

Figure 7.28 Table with Append Structure

Use forward navigation (double-click on ZAMEMBER02) to branch to the structure and view its entries. Use the BACK button to return to the maintenance screen.

Maintaining an Include Structure

An *include structure* offers a second option for enhancing tables. Unlike an append structure, which always belongs to exactly one table, an include structure is a reusable module that can be linked to other tables, structures, ABAP programs, dialogs, and so on as a dictionary object.

Differences and Restrictions

> An include structure must meet certain preconditions in a table so that it can be inserted. A field length can have a length of 16 characters, at most; this is the same length permitted for a field name in a table. The structure must also be flat and cannot contain any substructures.

Preparing an include structure

Insertion of an include structure begins in the maintenance screen of the table in the ABAP Dictionary (see Figure 7.29). If the include structure is to be located at a specific place in the field list, place the cursor *below* the row where you want to insert it. You should note that the include structure is always inserted in the row *above* the cursor. In this case, place the cursor on .APPEND in the FIELD column so that the rows for the include structure will be inserted between the rows for the MCURRENCY field and the .APPEND field. The position of the include structure is important if it contains key fields, because the key fields must be located as a closed unit at the beginning of a table. If the structure doesn't contain any key fields, the position of the include structure depends only on organization and legibility.

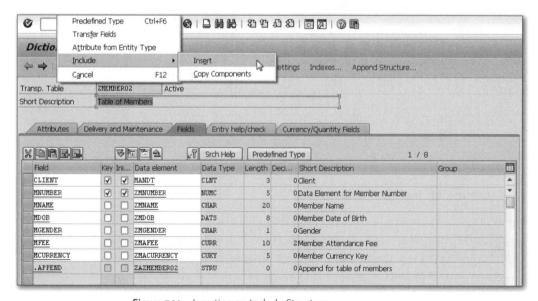

Figure 7.29 Inserting an Include Structure

After you position the cursor, insert the include structure at the desired location with EDIT • INCLUDE • INSERT. In the following screen, the system prompts you for the name of the include structure (see Figure 7.30). If you're working with a customer-specific include structure, make sure that you take the customer namespace into consideration.

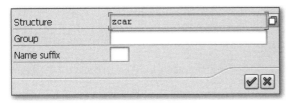

Figure 7.30   Selecting an Include Structure

Let's assume that you want to insert an include structure intended for car data, and you need the data to issue parking permits to the members. Because of reusability, the structure could also be used in other tables for data on employee and customer cars.

Inserting an include structure

Enter ZCAR as the name of the structure. Because the structure doesn't yet exist in the dictionary, the system issues a notification: "ZCAR is not present as active." Once you confirm the notification with ⌷Enter⌷, the system asks if you want to create the structure (see Figure 7.31). Click YES to return to the dictionary maintenance screen of the structure (see Figure 7.32).

Creating an include structure

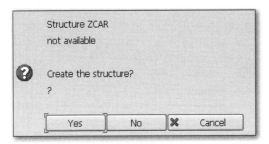

Figure 7.31   Creating a Structure

Create field ZZCARTYPE in the structure maintenance screen, as indicated in Figure 7.32. The field is intended as a key to record the type of car. You can decide whether to add more fields for reusable car

Maintenance screen of the structure

data. If you wish to do so, simply follow the same instructions given for this field.

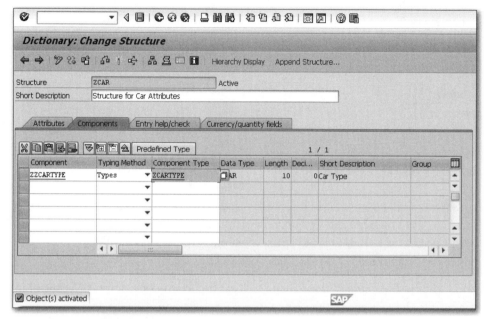

Figure 7.32 Maintaining a Structure

 How Do I Get There?

This is just a reminder. Though we created the new structure with forward navigation, we could have done so from the initial screen of the ABAP Dictionary (see Figure 7.33). From there, you would select DATA TYPE and enter ZCAR as the name of the structure, and, in the next screen, you would indicate that you want to create the structure. Everything else would be the same. Both options are equally valid and lead to the desired result, so you can decide which option is preferable.

Activating the include structure

After you maintain the fields, data elements, and domains, you must activate the domains, data elements, and the include structure. Activation of the structure automatically adjusts all the related tables. Once you have checked and activated the structure, use the BACK button to return to the maintenance screen of the ABAP Dictionary (see Figure 7.34).

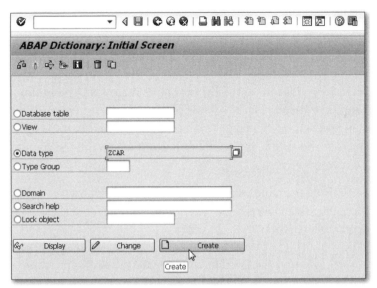

Figure 7.33 Creating a Structure in the Initial Screen of the ABAP Dictionary

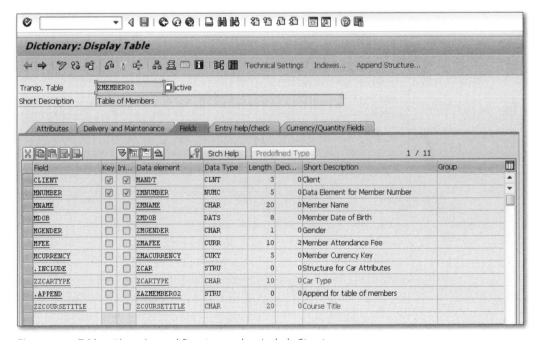

Figure 7.34 Table with an Append Structure and an Include Structure

Using forward
navigation
You then see the activated include structure in the table and can use forward navigation to go to the maintenance screen of the include structure at any time. Alternatively, you could also display the include structures contained in the table by placing the cursor on the row with the include structure and clicking the EXPAND INCLUDE button. The system then displays all the fields of the include structure in the maintenance screen of the table. You can use the COMPRESS INCLUDE button to hide the fields. Both of these buttons are in the FIELDS tab, directly above the first row.

After you activate the table, you can check it in the data browser of the ABAP Dictionary (see Figure 7.35), which you can reach with UTILITIES • TABLE CONTENTS • DISPLAY.

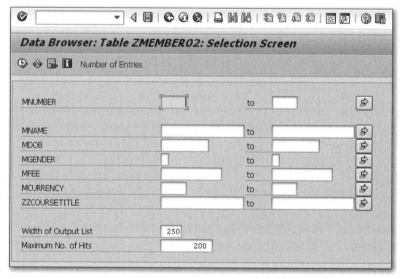

Figure 7.35 ABAP Dictionary Data Browser

Checking a table
with an include
structure
In this interface for testing and development, you see the table fields from the append structure and the fields from the include structure. In the user interface, users cannot tell if the fields come from a standard SAP table or from a customer-specific append without additional insider knowledge.

Manipulating Key Fields of Tables

As long as only non-key fields have been changed in the table and the related structures, you can assume that the changes affect only the ABAP Dictionary and not the physical database.

But every change to key fields affects the physical database and requires an adjustment of the physical table structure. Consider this example: Our first table, ZMEMBER01, had four fields, including two key fields, CLIENT and MNUMBER (see Figure 7.36).

Effects of manipulating key fields

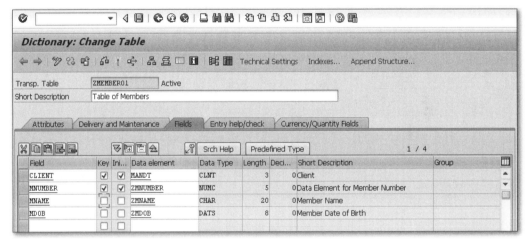

Figure 7.36 Table with Two Key Fields

To be able to define a third key field, first remember that key fields must be located as a block at the beginning of the field list. If the third key field it is something other than the MNAME field, then you must move it into the third row.

Procedure for manipulating key fields

This can be done relatively easily using the CUT, COPY, INSERT, INSERT ROW, and DELETE ROW buttons. These are located in the FIELDS tab, directly above the first row. Place the cursor in the row before the intended place of the insertion and use the INSERT ROW button to create a blank row.

In our example, however, we use the MNAME field as an additional key field. Mark it as a key field and then activate the table (see Figure 7.37).

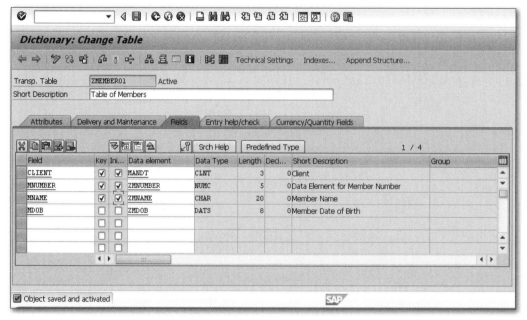

Figure 7.37 Table Enhanced with an Additional Key Field

❗ Risks of Removing Key Fields

After you maintain data records, the table must contain records that clearly differ from each other in terms of key fields, but that otherwise display some partial redundancies (see Figure 7.38). These data constellations can lead to significant problems if you remove or delete key fields. For example, if the MNUMBER field were to become a non-key field, the key for two members whose last name is Ericson might not be unambiguous any longer and their data could be lost.

If you attempt to convert the MNAME field into a non-key field and then try to activate the table, you'll get an error message stating that errors occurred during activation of the table.

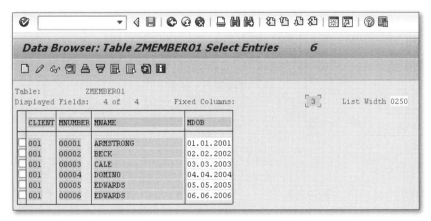

Figure 7.38 Table with Similar Data Records

If you display the error log by clicking YES, you can see that deleting key fields really does require a physical conversion of the table on the database (see Figure 7.39).

Error log

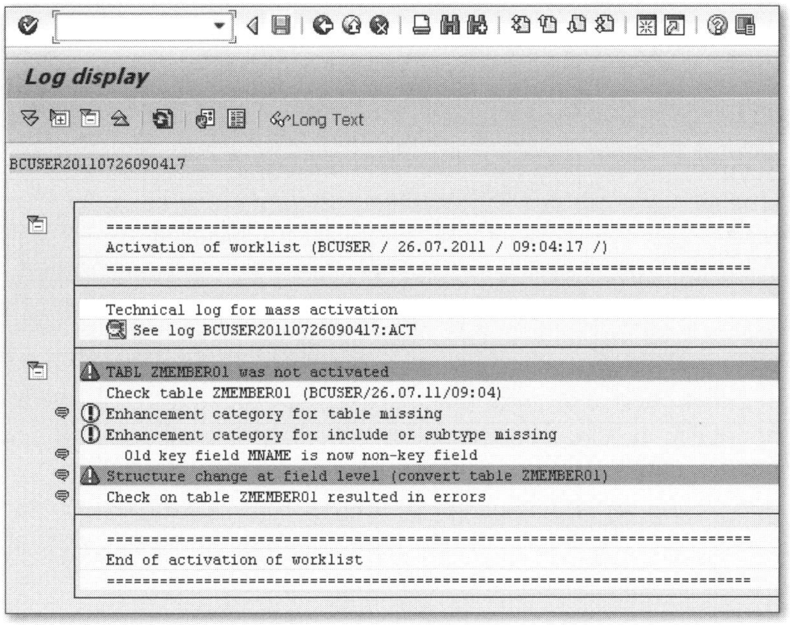

Figure 7.39 Error Log During Activation of the Table

Physical conversion
Perform the physical conversion of the table with the database utility of the ABAP Dictionary, which you can reach with UTILITIES • DATABASE OBJECT • DATABASE UTILITY (see Figure 7.40).

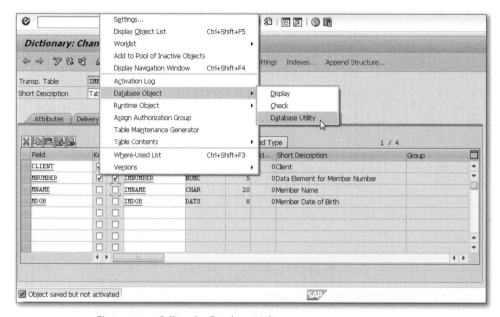

Figure 7.40 Calling the Database Utility

As noted in Chapter 2, ABAP Dictionary, the database utility is the uniform user interface for all certified database systems. You use this tool to adjust the database and activate the table at the same time.

Conversion in dialog
Because we're working with a small table with only a few data records and a small number of dependent objects, the process won't take long; as such, it's best to perform database operations directly. Also, we will try to keep the data (see Figure 7.41). In other instances where you have complex data records, you'll have to reckon with long runtimes, which is why we recommend processing in the background. Here, the DIRECT processing type meets our needs. Start the adjustment and activation with the ACTIVATE AND ADJUST DATABASE button.

Answer the security question (REQUEST: ADJUST) with YES. The status line then displays a message: "Request for ZMEMBER01 executed successfully." If you now go back to the table maintenance screen of the ABAP

Dictionary, you can see that the table has a status of *active* and that all data records of the table are still present.

Figure 7.41 Database Utility

Deleting Table Fields

In rare cases, you might have to delete a field from a table. Please use special care and caution. Problems can occur in the following contexts:

Risks and restrictions

> If key fields are deleted and the table already contains data, then data can be lost.

> If the table is a check table for a foreign key, then none of the table's key fields can be deleted as long as the foreign key relationship exists.

> When the table already contains data, you must convert the table on the physical database after deleting any fields.

> ❯ If the field is used in another table as a reference field, then it cannot be deleted while the link still exists.

> ⓘ **Delete Only When It Is Absolutely Necessary**
>
> For these reasons, you should delete a field from a table only when it is absolutely necessary. We recommend that you carefully plan during the design phase to avoid creating unnecessary fields that may need to be deleted later.

Irretrievable
data loss

You can experiment with our ZMEMBER01 table and delete the MDOB field for practice. In the maintenance screen of the table, highlight the header of the relevant row and remove it with DELETE ROW (see Figure 7.42).

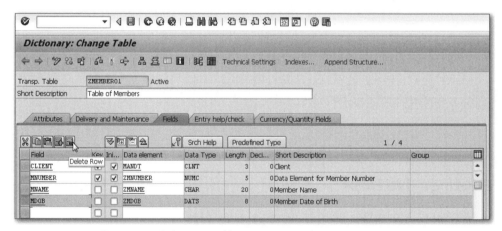

Figure 7.42 Deleting a Field

After the activation of the table, the data that was stored in the deleted field has been lost irretrievably. Notice that the date of birth column has disappeared (see Figure 7.43).

> ⓘ **Different Behavior in Older Releases**
>
> In earlier versions that were released before SAP ERP 6.0, this situation always led to an activation error that required a table adaptation through the database utility.

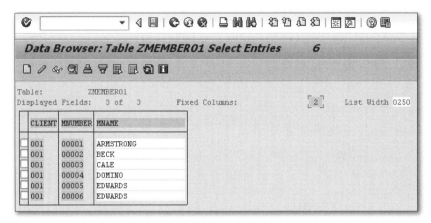

Figure 7.43 Table Content After Deletion of the Date of Birth

Deleting Tables

An equally rare and even riskier case is the deletion of a table from the ABAP Dictionary and the database. Only customer-specific tables and objects can be deleted, and only when they are no longer used in programs or other objects. Before you attempt to delete a table, use the where-used list in the maintenance screen of the ABAP Dictionary (see Figure 7.44) to see if the table may and can be deleted.

A rare and risky case

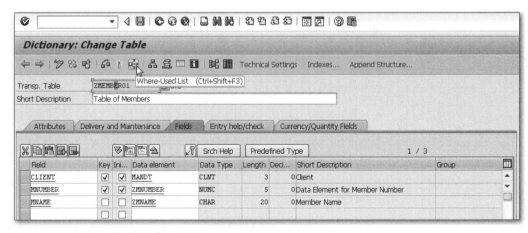

Figure 7.44 Where-Used List for a Table

Checking the
where-used list

Use the WHERE-USED LIST button to reach a dialog window where you can search for the objects that use the table (see Figure 7.45). It's helpful to search in familiar programs. Set the appropriate checks in the dialog window and start the search with Enter. Two hits are displayed here (see Figure 7.46).

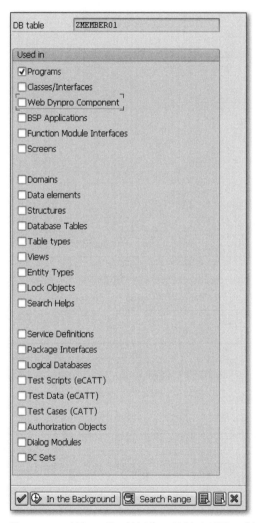

Figure 7.45   Where-Used List for a Table in Other Objects

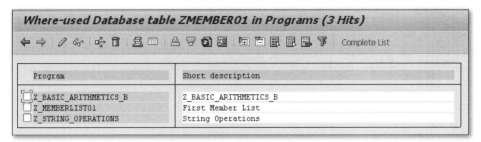

Figure 7.46 Hits for the Where-Used List of a Table

As long as these reports use the table in any form, even if only to define fields, you cannot delete the table. The next step would be to deconstruct all the related objects—an effort that we will not expend here. In an extreme case, reports would be useless and might as well be completely deleted or overwritten. The complexity and risk of this process should already be clear to you.

Restrictions for deleting tables

But to practice deletion of a table, copy the existing table ZMEMBER01 to table ZTABDELETE. See "Copying a Database Table" for instructions. After you see the notification "Table was copied from ZMEMBER01 to ZTABDELETE," activate the table so that the situation is as close to the real world as possible. The fact that the table is empty after it is copied isn't important for our purpose here.

Start the deletion procedure from the initial screen of the ABAP Dictionary with the DELETE button (see Figure 7.47). After you confirm the security question about deleting the table, you receive a notification: "ZTABDELETE was deleted." The table and its potential contents are irretrievably lost.

Sample deletion procedure

 Complex Preliminary Work

The deletion procedure itself is very simple. Most of the work in the real world involves the preliminary work of removing the links to other objects. Before you undertake all this work, be certain that you no longer need the table.

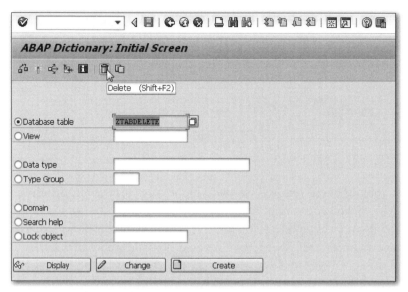

Figure 7.47 Deleting a Table

8

Calculating Dates, Times, Quantities, and Currencies

Although it doesn't make sense to carry out every conceivable computation with dates, times, quantities, and currencies, there are certain calculations that you must perform with these kinds of fields in your daily work. This chapter describes how to do them and what to take into consideration.

As soon as you define date and time fields, you'll notice that these types of data are not numerical, but are character types. So, basically, date and time fields are strings that can be used for arithmetic operations. These mathematical operations are made possible by the automatic type conversion that works in the background.

Field Definitions

In an ABAP report, date fields are defined using the DATA statement and the data type d. A data type d field always contains eight places. The first four places indicate the year, the following two places indicate the

Defining date fields

month, and the last two places indicate the day. The format is presented as YYYYMMDD; the initial value of a date field consists of eight zeros.

> **The Easiest Way To Get Started**
>
> The easiest way to get started with the definition of a date field is to use the TYPE addition to reference the type of the system date of the SAP system (which can be found in the DATE field of the SYST structure). If you use this definition, all attributes of the system field will be automatically applied to your date field, including the output formatting. If you use this reference option, you won't have to be concerned about inserting the period characters between the day, the month, and the year during print formatting, for example, because the output formatting for the SY-DATUM field has already been firmly defined.

For example, if you want to define the INVOICE_DATE field, you can use the following statement:

```
DATA invoice_date TYPE sy-datum.
```

Filling a date field

You can fill the date field using the VALUE addition of the DATA command as a literal; alternatively, you can fill the date field at program runtime by using a separate statement (see the examples below). The statement can be either an arithmetic operation or a string operation.

Defining a time field

Like date fields, time fields are actually character strings. Time fields contain six places; their format is HHMMSS. The first two places indicate the hours, the next two places indicate the minutes, and the last two places indicate the seconds. As is the case with the date field, the initial value of time fields also consists of zeros; the ABAP data type for time fields is t.

You can also find the system time in the SYST structure (namely, in the UZEIT field). Hours, minutes, and seconds are often separated by colons in lists (see the box below). However, if you don't want to deal with output formatting at this stage, we recommend that you reference the SY-UZEIT field when defining a time field. For that reason, the definition of the SESSION_BEGIN field might look like this:

```
DATA session_begin TYPE syst-uzeit.
```

You can fill time fields in the same way as date fields.

 The Customs of The Country

> The display and formatting of date and time fields depends largely on the customs of a country. For this reason, the SYST system structure contains several date and time fields, which format national and international formats in different ways.

In ABAP reports, currency fields are treated like packed numbers, so you must define a currency field like a packed number. Just make sure that you use the correct number of decimal places. The whole matter becomes a little more complex as soon as currency fields from the ABAP Dictionary come into play. To ensure a certain degree of accuracy in the calculation, the number of decimal places should be the same on both sides. But even here you can use a very simple method: referencing the table field definition in your definition on the ABAP side.

For example, if you want to define the TAX_AMOUNT field that calculates the sales tax, you can use the following statement to reference the definition of the relevant amount field in the ABAP Dictionary:

```
DATA tax_amount TYPE zmember02-mfee.
```

The most complex task is the definition of a currency field in the Dictionary. You can, of course, define currency fields in the ABAP Dictionary in a similar way as you would define amount fields, the only difference being that the currency fields have the special data type CURR. However, in this case, you must also define a separate currency key for each currency field. This currency key specifies the currency of the currency amount (currency name), and represents a specific text field of the CUKY type with a field length of 5.

So a currency field in the ABAP Dictionary must reference a CUKY type reference field. In addition, you need both the amount and the currency name (or currency key) for the currency field. After all, you want to know whether an amount is specified in a hard or soft currency and what its purchasing power is. You might also need the exact exchange rate to evaluate and convert the amount into a different currency.

Synchronizing the definitions in ABAP

In the ABAP Dictionary, a CURR type amount field may contain a maximum of 31 decimal places. If you use a CURR type amount field in an ABAP Dictionary table within an ABAP report, the CURR data type of the ABAP Dictionary will be converted into ABAP data type p, taking into consideration the variable field length and the number of decimal places. In ABAP, the CUKY type currency key is converted into a type c with field length of 5.

> **Currency Field**
>
> To create and test the corresponding examples, we added a currency field to Table ZMEMBER02 in Chapter 7.

Using Date Fields in Arithmetic Operations

Key dates and terms

You may be wondering why you should even use date fields in arithmetic operations. But think of determining periods of time, key dates, delivery dates, production cycles, salary agreements between employers and employees, the determination of the exact age of a person, or staff membership in the company on a specific payroll date. All of these cases require using date fields in arithmetic operations.

For this reason, the following sections will guide you step by step through the processing and usage of date fields in arithmetic operations. The following code snippets refer only to this aspect; the sample code listing at the end of this chapter contains the corresponding definitions and DATA statements for the date fields used in the following sections.

Filling a date field

First, you must fill a date value into the INVOICE_DATE field. If you want the INVOICE_DATE field to contain the current value of the system date, use the following statement:

```
invoice_date = sy-datum.
```

If you want the INVOICE_DATE field to contain the date 02/05/2004, the statement must look like this:

```
invoice_date = '20040205'.
```

The easiest way to get started is probably to use short examples so you can get to know the other aspects of this subject. Note that these examples are not the only correct solution; as you know, "many roads lead to Rome" and there are certainly other solutions and examples available. What's most important in the following examples is that you develop a feel for the particular way of thinking that is required when programming in ABAP, or the kinds of problem-solving strategies that work in this environment. Both will come naturally once you become acquainted with the way the SAP system handles the most frequently used variable types.

 Example 1

Invoice date and payment term

> You want to use the current system date as the date of an invoice. The payment term is 30 days. The objective of the program is to determine the payment date.

To solve this task, you must proceed as follows:

> Assign the value of the system date to the INVOICE_DATE date field.

```
invoice_date = sy-datum.
```

> Then assign the value 30 to the integer field, PAYMENT_TERM.

```
payment_term = 30.
```

> After that, add the INVOICE_DATE to the PAYMENT_TERM fields and insert the result into the PAYMENT_DATE field.

```
payment_date = invoice_date + payment_term.
```

 Example 2

First day of the current month

> You want your program to determine the first day of the current month as the key date.

To carry out this task, you must do the following:

> Assign the value of the system date to the MONTH_BEGIN date field.

```
month_begin = sy-datum.
```

> The day is indicated by the last two places in the field. After position 6, you must set positions 7 and 8 to the value 01 and assign them to the MONTH_BEGIN date field.

```
month_begin+6(2) = '01'.
```

First day of the following month

 Example 3

> You want your program to determine the first day of the subsequent month as the key date.

This task is slightly more complex. If each month had the same number of days, it wouldn't even be a problem. Unfortunately, your program must provide correct results at all times, whether in January, February, or in June, and regardless of whether it has to take into account periodic calendar changes such as the end of a month, the turn of the year, or a leap year. Moreover, it is widely expected that the number of source code lines is kept as low as possible (while still maintaining good readability, of course).

Here, we can employ a little trick. You can use the calendar functions of the system and solve the problem in the following way:

> Assign the value of the system date to the MONTH_BEGIN date field.

```
month_begin = sy-datum.
```

> The day is indicated by the last two places in the field. After position 6, you must set positions 7 and 8 to the value 01 and assign them to the MONTH_BEGIN date field.

```
month_begin+6(2) = '01'.
```

"Trick 35"
> Add 35 days to the first day of the current month so that you always end up in the subsequent month. (The use of the number 35 in this "Trick 35" has been chosen arbitrarily. The number must be at least 31 and less than or equal to 58.) The built-in calendar function in the system then automatically provides you with a valid date of the subsequent month, which means that the results are also correct at the end of a month, at the end of a year, and in leap years.

```
month_begin = month_begin + 35.
```

> Again, the day of the subsequent month is indicated by the last two places in the field. Positions 5 and 6 of the field have been assigned the value of the subsequent month. If the change to the subsequent month included a change of years as well, the first four positions indicate the new year. To set the day of the subsequent month to 01, you must set positions 7 and 8 to 01 and assign them.

```
month_begin+6(2) = '01'
```

 Example 4

Ultimo of the previous month

You want your program to determine the last day (ultimo) of the previous month as the key date.

To do that, first determine the first day of the current month, as described in Example 2:

> Assign the value of the system date to the MONTH_BEGIN date field.

```
month_begin = sy-datum.
```

> The day is indicated by the last two places in the field. After position 6, you must set positions 7 and 8 to the value 01 and assign them to the MONTH_BEGIN date field.

```
month_begin+6(2) = '01'.
```

> Once again, you can use the calendar function of the system. By subtracting 1, you move one day backwards from the first day of the current month to the last day of the previous month. This way, leap years and the turn of a year don't pose a problem.

```
month_end = month_begin - 1.
```

 Example 5

Ultimo of the current month

You want your program to determine the last day of the current month as the key date.

Because you don't know in which month your program will be executed, it doesn't make any sense to use the number 31 for the last day. You need a solution that always provides correct results, so you should once again use the calendar function of the system:

> Assign the value of the system date to the MONTH_BEGIN date field.

```
month_begin = sy-datum.
```

> The day is indicated by the last two places in the field. After position 6, you must set positions 7 and 8 to the value 01 and assign them to the MONTH_BEGIN date field.

```
month_begin+6(2) = '01'.
```

> Add 35 days to the first day of the current month so that you end up in the subsequent month. "Trick 35" ensures that you definitely reach into the subsequent month.

```
month_begin = month_begin + 35.
```

> Starting from the first day of the subsequent month, work backwards to the last day of the current month. Again, you delegated problems such as the end of a month or year and leap years to the system calendar.

```
month_begin+6(2) = '01'.
month_end = month_begin - 1.
```

Past days of the current year

 Example 6

> Starting from the current day of the year, you want to know how many days of the current year have already passed and how many days of the year remain.

To answer this question, you must carry out the following steps:

> Assign the value of the system date to the CURRENT_DATE date field.

```
current_date = sy-datum.
```

> Then set both the month and the day to 01 and assign them to the YEAR_BEGIN date field. Set the month and day to 12 and 31, respectively (because December has 31 days), and assign them to the YEAR_END date field.

```
year_begin = sy-datum.
year_end = sy-datum.
```

```
year_begin+4(4) = '0101'.
year_end+4(4) = '1231'.
```

> Subtract `YEAR_BEGIN` from `CURRENT_DATE` and insert the result into
> the `DAYS_PAST` integer field.

```
days_past = current_date - year_begin.
```

> Subtract `CURRENT_DATE` from `YEAR_END` and insert the result into the
> `DAYS_REMAINING` integer field.

Remaining days of
the current year

```
days_remaining = year_end - current_date.
```

Ex Example 7

Determining the
age of a person

> You want to determine the age of a person in relation to the current day.
> How old is the person today if she'd been born on December 23, 1967?
> You want the program to output the age both as a rounded number of
> years and in terms of full years and days.

The first part of solving this task can be carried out in the following
steps:

> Assign the value of the system date to the `CURRENT_DATE` date field.

```
current_date = sy-datum.
```

> Then assign the value 19671223 to the `DAY_OF_BIRTH` date field.

```
day_of_birth = '19671223'.
```

> If you subtract the date of birth from the current date, you will ob-
> tain the difference of the two date values in terms of days. Insert
> this difference into the `AGE_DAYS_I` integer field.

```
age_days_i = current_date - day_of_birth.
```

> To simplify things, we don't consider leap years in this calculation.
> We will go into greater detail on this subject in the Linked Logical
> Expressions section in Chapter 10. So since you base your calcula-
> tion on the assumption that a year has 365 days, you must divide
> the content of `AGE_DAYS_I` by 365. The result must be assigned to the
> `AGE_YEARS_I` field. Because of the type of the field, the integer field
> can only contain integer values; the result is rounded up or down
> to the nearest whole number. At this point, you have solved the

first part of the task: the age of the person is specified as a rounded number of years.

```
age_years_i = age_days_i / 365.
```

In the second part of the exercise, you must pay a little more attention and remember the different division options (see Chapter 4).

Dimension of time periods

By using the forward slash (/), you can obtain the exact result with two decimal places. Depending on the definition of the target field, the result may be processed by an automatic type conversion before it is stored in the target field with the correct type. The division process using the DIV operand results in an integer division with a remainder. The result of the integer division is assigned the correct type and stored in the target field. (In this operation, the remainder is ignored.) The division process using the MOD operand determines the remainder and stores the result with the correct type in the target field as well.

At this point, you have the following options to solve this part of the exercise:

Computational accuracy with date intervals

> If you want to calculate and present the exact age in terms of years and days in the decimal system, you must first calculate the difference between the current date and the date of birth, divide this difference by 365, and save the result in a packed number that contains four decimal places, for example:

```
age_dec4 = ( current_date - day_of_birth )
           / 365.
```

> If the requirement is to specify the age in terms of full years and days, you must determine the number of full years via an integer division using the DIV operand. In that case, it is less important whether the target field is of type i or p since the content consists of integers either way.

```
age_full_years =
     ( current_date - day_of_birth ) DIV 365.
```

> The integer division provided the number of full years, but omitted the remaining days. These can be calculated as the remainder of the integer division by using the MOD operand.

```
age_days_remaining =
( current_date - day_of_birth ) MOD 365.
```

Using Time Fields in Arithmetic Operations

The previous examples using date fields in calculations should have given you a feeling for this odd but useful combination of arithmetic operations and string operations that lets you edit date fields. You can also use these two types of operations to modify time fields. Let's look at some examples again.

 Example 1

Daily working time

The start of work on a specific day is set for 8:15 a.m., and the end for 6 p.m. How much time passes between these two time definitions?

The individual steps towards a solution could look like this:

> The SESSION_BEGIN and SESSION_END fields must be defined using data type t or by referencing SY-UZEIT.

```
DATA session_begin TYPE t.
DATA session_end TYPE sy-uzeit.
```

> In the program flow, you must assign the actual start of work to the SESSION_BEGIN time field, and the end of work to the SESSION_END time field.

```
session_begin = '081500'.
session_end = '180000'.
```

> The time difference between SESSION_END and SESSION_BEGIN is specified in terms of seconds, so the target field could well be an integer field of type i.

Computational accuracy with time intervals

```
time_difference_sec = session_end
                    - session_begin.
```

> If you prefer to have the time difference specified in terms of minutes or hours, a target field of type p with at least two decimal places might be more useful, because the decimal places in such a field allow you to express fractions of hours and minutes as decimal values,

as is commonly done with industry minutes. If you want to specify the time value in terms of minutes, use the following statement:

```
time_difference_min =
  ( session_end - session_begin ) / 60.
```

If you prefer to specify the time difference in terms of hours and minutes, use the following statement:

```
time_difference_hour =
  ( session_end - session_begin ) / 3600.
```

Further processing of time intervals

› Once these processing steps have been completed, the time data is assigned to fields of type i and p. Based on the assumption that the TIME_DIFFERENCE_HOUR field is of type p and contains at least two decimal places, you can easily integrate a lunch break of 45 minutes (that is, 0.75 hours) by assigning the value of 0.75 hours to the BREAK field of type p, which contains two decimal places. Subtract the lunch break time from the time difference to obtain the exact working time.

```
break = '0.75'.
session_time  = time_difference_hour - break.
```

Remaining time

Ex **Example 2**

You want your program to determine how much time remains between the current time and midnight. The remaining time should be calculated in separate fields for hours, minutes, and seconds.

› First you must read the current time from the system time and insert 24 hours (for midnight as end of day) into the MIDNIGHT field:

```
time = sy-uzeit.
midnight = '240000'.
```

› Then calculate the remaining time until midnight in seconds:

```
balance_time = midnight - time.
```

› To specify the number of full hours, you must define the BALANCE_HOURS field using data type i and calculate the value for the hours by using the following statement:

```
balance_hours =
```

```
( midnight - time ) DIV 3600.
```

> To determine the remaining minutes, you must use the remainder of the integer division (specified in seconds) and divide it by 60:

```
balance_minutes =
  ( ( midnight - time )
  MOD 3600 ) DIV 60.
```

> To determine the remaining seconds, you must calculate the remainder for the integer division of the time difference by minutes:

```
balance_seconds =
  ( midnight - time ) MOD 60.
```

> The output of the three fields in a list with explanatory texts might look like this:

```
WRITE: / 'Balance time till midnight:',
  balance_hours, 'hours,', balance_minutes,
  'minutes and', balance_seconds, 'seconds'.
```

Ex **Example 3**

Time period with date change

> A work shift doesn't end until the early morning hours of the following day. How many hours, minutes, and seconds lie between the current time in the afternoon or evening and the end of the work shift? Again, we want to specify the output of hours, minutes, and seconds in separate fields.

> The beginning of this example is as simple as before. You must copy the current time from the system time and define the end of the work shift as 05:20:10 am. Admittedly, this time is not very realistic for the end of a shift, but you don't want to use a straightforward number to specify the seconds at this point. Therefore, all shift workers are asked to be lenient toward you.

```
time = sy-uzeit.
shift_end = '052010'.
```

> Before we proceed with the next step, let's consider some preliminary facts: A day has 86,400 seconds. Although this is a well-known fact, not everybody always has this number always at hand. Moreover, the value for the end of the work shift in this example is

One day = 86,400 seconds

smaller than the current time, which may result in negative times. For example, if you assume that the current time is 21:00 hours (that is, 9 p.m.) and the end of the work shift is at 03:00 hours (that is, 3 a.m.), the resulting time difference would be 6 hours. This is easy for people to understand, but not intuitive for computers.

Time interval in seconds

Therefore, you must separate this process into two steps. First, calculate the difference between the end and the start:

$3 - 21 = -18$

Second, calculate the difference between –18 and 24. This assignment may appear to be trivial; however, this exercise provides you with the correct time difference based on 24 hours and ensures that this time difference is positive.

$| 24 - 18 | = 6$

The corresponding ABAP statement summarizes both steps in one command like this:

```
balance_time =
  ( shift_end - time )
  MOD 86400.
```

Remaining hours

> Based on the remaining time determined in this way, you can calculate the number of full hours:

```
balance_hours = balance_time DIV 3600.
```

Remaining minutes

> Based on the remainder of the integer division, you can calculate the remaining minutes to determine the number of hours:

```
balance_minutes = ( balance_time MOD 3600 ) DIV 60.
```

Remaining seconds

> As in the previous example, you must determine the remaining number of seconds on the basis of the remainder of the integer division to determine the minutes:

```
balance_seconds = balance_time MOD 60.
```

> In the final step, you can output the values in a list:

```
WRITE: / 'Balance time till shift_end:',
  balance_hours, 'hours,', balance_minutes,
  'minutes', balance_seconds, 'seconds'.
```

Real-Life Challenges

In real life, you have to use date and time fields more often than you would expect. This is not limited to a certain field of work. In fact, you will encounter this task in any SAP module and in most different contexts. For this reason, you will certainly benefit from the examples described here in your daily work.

Using Quantity and Currency Fields in Arithmetic Operations

In comparison to using date and time fields in arithmetic operations, the use of quantity and currency fields in calculations is relatively simple, provided you comply with some basic rules. As long as you stay within the boundaries of the ABAP world, you can consider these fields like any other type p field; depending on the specific business requirements, you must use different numbers of decimal places. In real life, the number of decimal places has a great impact on the accuracy of the calculation and can be much higher than the number of decimal places shown in a list. Consider the importance of the accuracy of a calculation with regard to exchange rate conversions between different currencies.

If you link quantity and currency fields from the ABAP Dictionary with calculations on the ABAP side, your freedom is slightly restricted. In those cases, you must harmonize the field definitions in ABAP with the definitions in the ABAP Dictionary in order to avoid a loss of information.

Harmonization of currency fields

This harmonization process includes two particular aspects: the number of decimal places and the associated quantity and currency keys. In the ABAP Dictionary, a currency field corresponds to an amount field of type DEC, but it has its own data type CURR and always references an associated currency key field of type CUKY. Apart from that, currency fields may have a total of 17 places. The currency key fields of type CUKY on the side of the ABAP Dictionary correspond to the string fields of type c in ABAP and have a fixed length of 5 characters. Therefore, we strongly recommend that you don't use any custom definitions when defining the corresponding fields in ABAP. Instead, always reference the definitions in the ABAP Dictionary. Moreover, if a definition changes in the ABAP Dictionary, this won't cause any problem for updating the relevant ABAP reports.

Harmonizing quantity fields

These basic rules apply to both quantity and currency fields; the only difference is that the specific data type for quantity fields in the ABAP Dictionary is QUAN, while the quantity units are mapped in associated fields of type UNIT. In the ABAP Dictionary, the quantity unit fields can contain two or three places and correspond to type c strings of the same length in ABAP. Quantity fields can also contain a total of 17 places in the ABAP Dictionary and must be defined as type p fields in ABAP.

Harmonizing quantity and currency fields

As is the case with currency fields, you shouldn't invent any ABAP definitions for quantity fields; instead, reference existing definitions in the ABAP Dictionary.

Due to the similar structures of quantity and currency fields, we only want to use one example at this stage in order to further demonstrate what has been described so far in this section.

Ex **Calculating the Sales Tax**

You want the program to read the name of the member, the course fee, and the course currency from the members' table. In addition, you want all members to be output in a list; each line of the list should contain the name of the member, the course fee, the tax amount, and the invoice amount.

> In the first step, you must set the percentage of the sales tax and assign it to the TAX_PERCENTAGE field. Since the field must contain the factor for the tax, it is defined with data type p and two decimal places. Of course, in real-life scenarios, such values as the tax percentage are stored in tables and are not hard-coded into the source code, but we'll ignore this bit of reality for this example, and assume a VAT percentage of 19%.

```
tax_percentage = '0.19'.
```

> You must process and output the data from the table record by record. For this reason, you must read the records into a work area one after the other and initiate a loop in order to read all fields of all table records:

```
SELECT * FROM zmember02 INTO wa_zmember02.
```

> If the table contains any data, there is now one data record in the work area. All fields are known and can be addressed. To determine the tax amount, the course fee must be multiplied by the tax factor. The tax amount must then be written to the target field. As already described, the definition of the TAX_AMOUNT field should actually contain a reference to the ABAP Dictionary field, ZMEMBER02-MFEE.

```
tax_amount =
  tax_percentage * wa_zmember02-mfee.
```

> The invoice amount to be paid results from the addition of the tax amount and course fee. Again, the definition of the INVOICE_AMOUNT field should contain a reference to the WA_ZMEMBER02-MFEE field:

Determining an
invoice amount

```
invoice_amount =
  tax_amount + wa_zmember02-mfee.
```

> All required fields have been calculated so that the list line can be output:

```
WRITE: / wa_zmember02-mname,
  wa_zmember02-mfee,
  wa_zmember02-mcurrency,
  tax_amount,
  wa_zmember02-mcurrency,
  invoice_amount,
  wa_zmember02-mcurrency.
```

> Once all table records have been read, processed, and output, the loop can be closed:

```
ENDSELECT.
```

Sample Code for Date, Time, and Currency Fields

Listing 8.1 shows an example of sample code for the date, time, and currency fields.

229

```
1   *&---------------------------------------------*
2   *& Report   DATE_TIME_QUANTITY_CURRENCY                      *
3   *&                                                      *
4   *&---------------------------------------------*
5   *&                                                      *
6   *&                                                      *
7   *&---------------------------------------------*
8
9   REPORT   Z_DATE_TIME_QUANTITY_CURRENCY.
10
11  * Define table work area
12  DATA: wa_zmember02 TYPE zmember02.
13
14  * Define fields
15  DATA: time           TYPE sy-uzeit,
16        age_dec4       TYPE p DECIMALS 4,
17        age_integer    TYPE i,
18        payment_date   TYPE sy-datum,
19        day_of_birth   TYPE sy-datum,
20        year_begin     TYPE sy-datum,
21        year_end       TYPE sy-datum,
22        midnight       TYPE sy-uzeit,
23        tax_amount     TYPE zmember02-mfee,
24        tax_percentage TYPE p DECIMALS 2,
25        month_begin    TYPE sy-datum,
26        month_end      TYPE sy-datum,
27        break          TYPE p DECIMALS 2,
28        invoice_amount TYPE zmember02-mfee,
29        invoice_date   TYPE sy-datum,
30        balance_minutes TYPE i,
31        balance_seconds TYPE i,
32        balance_hours  TYPE i,
33        balance_time   TYPE p DECIMALS 4,
34        shift_end      TYPE sy-uzeit,
35        days_past      TYPE i,
36        days_remaining TYPE i,
37        current_date   TYPE sy-datum,
38        session_begin  TYPE sy-uzeit,
39        session_end    TYPE sy-uzeit,
40        session_time   TYPE p DECIMALS 2,
41        payment_term   TYPE i.
42
43  * Define field values
44  invoice_date = sy-datum.
```

```
45  invoice_date = '20040205'.
46  session_begin = sy-uzeit.
47  session_begin = '081500'.
48  SKIP.
49
50  * Calculate invoice payment date
51  invoice_date = sy-datum.
52  payment_term = 30.
53  payment_date = invoice_date + payment_term.
54  WRITE: / 'invoice_date',          30 invoice_date,
55         / 'payment_term in days', 30 payment_term,
56         / 'Payment date',          30 payment_date.
57  SKIP.
58
59  * Calculate first day of current month
60  month_begin = sy-datum.
61  month_begin+6(2) = '01'.
62  WRITE: / 'first day of current month is',
             month_begin.
63
64  * Calculate first day of following month
65  month_begin = sy-datum.
66  month_begin+6(2) = '01'.
67  month_begin = month_begin + 35.
68  month_begin+6(2) = '01'.
69  WRITE: / 'first day of following month is',
             month_begin.
70
71  * Calculate last day (ultimo) of previous month
72  month_begin = sy-datum.
73  month_begin+6(2) = '01'.
74  month_end = month_begin - 1.
75  WRITE: / 'last day of previour month is',
             month_end.
76
77  * Calculate last day (ultimo) of current month
78  month_begin = sy-datum.
79  month_begin+6(2) = '01'.
80  month_begin = month_begin + 35.
81  month_begin+6(2) = '01'.
82  month_end = month_begin - 1.
83  WRITE: / 'last day of current month is',
             month_end.
84  SKIP.
```

```
 85
 86  * Calculate past days and remaining days of the current
         year
 87  current_date = sy-datum.
 88  year_begin = sy-datum.
 89  year_end = sy-datum.
 90  year_begin+4(4) = '0101'.
 91  year_end+4(4) = '1231'.
 92  days_past = current_date - year_begin.
 93  days_remaining = year_end - current_date.
 94  WRITE: / 'year_begin', year_begin,
 95           'year_end', year_end,
 96           'current date', current_date,
 97         / 'days past', days_past,
 98           'days remaining', days_remaining.
 99  SKIP.
100
101  * Calculate the age of a person
102  current_date = sy-datum.
103  day_of_birth = '19671223'.
104  age_integer = current_date - day_of_birth.
105  WRITE: / 'Age integer in days', 46 age_integer.
106  age_integer = age_integer / 365.
107  WRITE: / 'Age years integer rounded', 46 age_integer.
108  age_dec4 = ( current_date - day_of_birth ) / 365.
109  WRITE: / 'Age years 4 decimal places', 40 age_dec4.
110  age_dec4 = ( current_date - day_of_birth ) DIV 365.
111  WRITE: / 'Age interger division', 40 age_dec4.
112  age_dec4 = ( current_date - day_of_birth ) MOD 365.
113  WRITE: / 'Age integer division rest days ', 40 age_dec4.
114  SKIP.
115
116  * Calculate session time
117  session_begin = '081500'.
118  session_end = '180000'.
119  session_time = session_end - session_begin.
120  WRITE: / 'session_time seconds', 40 session_time.
121  session_time = ( session_end - session_begin ) / 60.
122  WRITE: / 'session_time minutes', 40 session_time.
123  session_time = ( session_end - session_begin ) / 3600.
124  WRITE: / 'session_time hours', 40 session_time.
125
126  * Calculate session time without breaks
127  break = '0.5'.
```

```
128  session_time = ( session_end - session_begin ) / 3600.
129  session_time = session_time - break.
130  WRITE: / 'break hours', 40 break.
131  WRITE: / 'session_time without breaks', 40 session_time.
132  SKIP.
133
134  * Calculate time from now till midnight
135  time = sy-uzeit.
136  WRITE: / 'current time', 40 time.
137  midnight = '240000'.
138  balance_time = midnight - time.
139  WRITE: / 'balance_time till midnight seconds',
                40 balance_time.
140  balance_hours = ( midnight - time ) DIV 3600.
141  WRITE: / 'balance_hours till midnight',
                40 balance_hours.
142  balance_minutes =
        ( ( midnight - time ) MOD 3600 ) DIV 60.
143  balance_seconds = ( midnight - time ) MOD 60.
144  WRITE: / 'balance_time till midnight:',
                balance_hours, 'hours',
145                balance_hours, 'hours',
146                balance_minutes, 'minutes',
147                balance_seconds, 'seconds'.
148  SKIP.
149
150  * Calculate time beyond midnight
151  time = sy-uzeit.
152  shift_end = '052010'.
153  WRITE: / 'current time', 40 time.
154  WRITE: / 'shift_end',      40 shift_end.
155  balance_time =  ( shift_end - time ) MOD 86400.
156  WRITE: / 'balance_time till shift_end seconds',
                40 balance_time.
157  balance_hours = balance_time DIV 3600.
158  WRITE: / 'balance_hours till shift_end',
                40 balance_hours.
159  balance_minutes = ( balance_time MOD 3600 ) DIV 60.
160  balance_seconds = balance_time MOD 60.
161  WRITE: / 'balance_time till shift_end:',
162                balance_hours,   'hours',
163                balance_minutes, 'minutes',
164                balance_seconds, 'seconds'.
165  SKIP.
166
```

```
167   * Calculate with currency fields
168   tax_percentage = '0.19'.
169   SELECT * FROM zmember02 INTO wa_zmember02.
170   WRITE: / wa_zmember02-mname,
                wa_zmember02-mfee,
                wa_zmember02-mcurrency.
171   tax_amount =
          tax_percentage * wa_zmember02-mfee.
172   invoice_amount =
          tax_amount + wa_zmember02-mfee.
173   WRITE : tax_amount, wa_zmember02-mcurrency,
                invoice_amount,
                wa_zmember02-mcurrency.
174   ENDSELECT.
```

Listing 8.1   Report Z_DATE_TIME_QUANTITY_CURRENCY

Notes on the Source Code

Line 9

The name of the ABAP report in Listing 8.1 is Z_DATE_TIME_ QUAN-TITY_CURRENCY. You can generally assign any name you like to your reports, provided you stay within the customer namespace.

Line 12

To use Table ZMEMBER02, a work area is defined.

Lines 15 to 41

All required variables are defined using a chain statement of the DATA statement. The way the variables are defined does not depend on any business-specific requirements; it merely serves the learning objective of this example.

Lines 44 to 47

The variables are assigned values. As an example of a value assignment, the INVOICE_DATE field is first assigned the current system date and then the value 02/05/2004. The SESSION_BEGIN field is treated similarly.

Lines 51 to 56

This is where the process for determining the payment date begins. The INVOICE_DATE field is assigned the current system date, while the PAYMENT_TERM field is assigned the value 30. The payment date is then determined by adding up the payment term and the invoice date. The list output generates the text "Invoice date" in a new line. The IN-VOICE_DATE field is output in the same line from position 30 onward. Payment term and payment date are output in separate lines according to the same pattern (Figure 8.1).

 Everything is Still Hard Coded

> At this point, you should note the following: In compliance with your current level of knowledge, texts are output in lists via "hard-coded" literals that can be maintained independently of a language. Bear in mind that you will actually use text elements in your daily work instead of literals.

→ You can learn more about text elements in Chapter 11.

Lines 60 to 62

To specify the first day of the current month, you insert the system date into the MONTH_BEGIN field. Positions 7 and 8 of a date field always indicate the day. For this reason, you use a string operation after position 6 to insert the string 01 in positions 7 and 8 to indicate the first day of the month. Then, you output the beginning of the current month in the list (Figure 8.2).

Lines 65 to 69

To determine the first day of the subsequent month, the MONTH_BEGIN field is again assigned the value of the system date. Then the field value is set to the first day of the current month. Thirty-five days are added to the date value to determine a day in the subsequent month, while the determination of year and month changes is carried out without any error by the calendar function of the SAP system. In the next step, the day is again set to 01. Because you already carried out the last string operation for the subsequent month, the MONTH_BEGIN field now shows the first day of the next month (Figure 8.2).

Lines 73 and 75

To calculate the last day of the previous month, the date value of the first day of the current month must be determined. Once the MONTH _BEGIN field contains the first day of the current month, subtract one day from this date value. The system automatically determines the previous day, which represents the last day of the previous month (Figure 8.2).

Lines 78 to 83

To calculate the last day of the current month, you must first determine the first day of the subsequent month. By subtracting one day from the first day of the subsequent month, you can determine the previous day, which is actually the last day of the current month (Figure 8.2).

Lines 87 to 94

To determine the days that have already passed in the current year, the YEAR_BEGIN field is first assigned the value of the system date. In a second step, a string operation is used to assign the value 01 to positions 5 and 6 in order to indicate the first month of the year, while positions 7 and 8 are assigned the value 01 to represent the first day of the month. Based on the difference between the current date and the beginning of the year, the number of past days can be determined and inserted in the DAYS_PAST field.

Correspondingly, December 31 of the current year is inserted in the YEAR_END field. Analogous to the procedure for past days, the difference between the end of the year and the current date is used to calculate the number of remaining days in the current year (Figure 8.3).

Line 106

To determine the age of a person in relation to the current day, you need the current date and the date of birth. The difference between these two date values is specified in days. If you divide the number of days by 365, you will obtain the number of years (at least, according to the Gregorian calendar, which is used in the U.S. and Western Europe). Please note that leap years are not taken into account here.

To Keep It Simple: No Leap Years

Here we do not take leap years into account. Although the division by 365 using the forward slash calculates the exact value, the target field will show only the rounded whole number because it is a type i field.

Line 108

If the target field was a type p field containing four decimal places, for example, the division of the difference between the current date and the date of birth would output a decimal number. In this case, the decimal places would represent fractions of years (that is, months and days).

Line 110

In an integer division, the target field always contains a natural number. For this reason, it actually makes sense to use a type i target field. Depending on how the field will be used later, it might also make sense to use a target field of a different type. This decision often depends on the specific business requirements within a company. In this sample code listing, we use a type p field that contains four decimal places because we wanted to demonstrate how this kind of field works.

Line 112

The remainder of the integer division provides the remaining number of years in terms of days. Although the days when we had to be frugal with our resources and therefore had to reuse fields multiple times are gone, we will nevertheless insert the number of remaining days into the same target field in our example in order to simplify things. For those of you who don't want to do, you will have to create a separate variable for the target field (Figure 8.4).

Using fields multiple times

Line 119

In time fields, differences are always indicated in seconds. Sixty seconds constitute one minute; 3,600 seconds make up one hour; and 86,400 seconds equal one day. So after the subtraction, the SESSION_TIME field contains the value of the time difference in seconds.

Line 121

The division by 60 provides the exact value of the time difference in minutes. Depending on the data type of the target field, the result will be inserted into the field with the corresponding accuracy and in the corresponding format.

Line 123

Industry minutes   The division by 3,600 provides the result of the time difference in hours. Depending on the data type of the target field, the result will be inserted into the field with the corresponding accuracy. Decimal places of the target field map the fractions of hours. Depending on the business application you use, these fractions of hours are also known as *industry minutes*.

Line 129

The big advantage of processing hours, minutes, and seconds in the decimal system is that a half hour is not regarded as 30 minutes but as 0.5 hours. This greatly facilitates further processing. In order to determine the pure session time, you simply need to subtract the lunch break from the difference between the end and the beginning of the session (Figure 8.5).

Lines 135 to 139

To calculate the time that is left between now and midnight, the TIME field is assigned the value of the system time. The time field contains six decimal places. Positions 1 and 2 indicate the hours, positions 3 and 4 represent the minutes, and positions 5 and 6 the seconds. And so the literal '240000' in the MIDNIGHT field represents the value of 24:00:00 hours (midnight at the end of the day). The difference between midnight and the current time is measured in seconds and inserted into the BALANCE_TIME field.

Line 140

The integer division of the time difference by 3,600 provides the remaining number of hours until midnight.

Line 142

The remainder of the integer division is measured in seconds as well. The division of this value by 60 provides the number of remaining minutes. The idea behind the procedure applied here is that we want the time to be output in the following format: "There are 3 hours, 4 minutes, and 5 seconds left until midnight."

Line 143

To determine the remaining seconds as well, in addition to the hours and minutes, you merely need to divide the remainder of the integer division by 60, because this remainder is already expressed in seconds. The number of minutes is not relevant at this point. The number of remaining seconds is indicated in the BALANCE_SECONDS field (Figure 8.6).

Line 152

The standard version of SAP ERP contains patterns and templates for work schedules. Nevertheless, oftentimes you must use time intervals that last until after midnight. For this reason, we set the end of the work shift in this exercise to 20 minutes and 10 seconds past 5 am on the subsequent day. This admittedly unrealistic time of a work shift end lets you check whether your program can calculate the remaining time accurately in hours, minutes, and seconds.

Adjusted work schedules

Lines 155 to 160

First we calculate the difference between the end of the shift and the current time. To keep this example simple, we assume that the current time is later than 05:20:10. This means that the time of the shift end is always shorter than the time of the shift start, and the time difference is negative. The remainder of the integer division by 86,400 (that is, the remainder of 24 hours) is written to the BALANCE_TIME field. So the target field contains the real time difference. The remaining calculations are carried out like the ones already described (Figure 8.7).

Line 168

The sales tax used in the example is not specified as a percentage, but as factor '0.19' and is written to the TAX_PERCENTAGE field. Of

Fixed sales tax

course, in real-life scenarios, this value is not hard-coded in the source code, but is read from the corresponding table values where it is also maintained.

Lines 169 to 175

You read and process every single record from the table. The process of reading record after record can be compared to a loop that runs, as long as there is still a record to be read from the table. The loop begins with the SELECT statement and ends with ENDSELECT. Both statements belong together and define the beginning and end of the read structure. In-between these two statements, you can find the statements for processing a record that is read.

In our example we determine the tax amount for each data record by multiplying the course fee by the tax percentage. After that, we add up the tax amount and the course fee in order to obtain the invoice amount. The relevant fields are output as a line in a list; each data record entails a new list line. However, the arithmetic operations used in this example are less important. What is far more interesting here are the data definitions of the fields that are used. Regarding their definition, the TAX_AMOUNT and INVOICE_AMOUNT fields reference table field ZMEMBER02-MFEE in order to avoid conversion errors (Figure 8.8).

Program Output

This section contains the screen outputs that you should get if the program can be executed successfully.

```
invoice_date                30.07.2011
payment_term in days                30
Payment date                29.08.2011
```

Figure 8.1 Payment Date of an Invoice

```
first day of current month is 01.07.2011
first day of following month is 01.08.2011
last day of previour month is 30.06.2011
last day of current month is 31.07.2011
```

Figure 8.2 First and Last Days of a Month

```
year_begin 01.01.2011 year_end 31.12.2011 current date 30.07.2011
days past        210   days remaining        154
```

Figure 8.3 Past and Remaining Days of a Year

```
Age integer in days                 15.925
Age years integer rounded              44
Age years 4 decimal places          43,6301
Age interger division               43,0000
Age integer division rest days     230,0000
```

Figure 8.4 Age of a Person

```
session_time seconds            35.100,00
session_time minutes               585,00
session_time hours                   9,75
break hours                          0,50
session_time without breaks          9,25
```

Figure 8.5 Session Time

```
current time                  12:43:44
balance_time till midnight seconds    40.576,0000
balance_hours till midnight          11
balance_time till midnight:     11  hours      16  minutes      16  seconds
```

Figure 8.6 Remaining Time Until Midnight

```
current time                  12:43:44
shift_end                     05:20:10
balance_time till shift_end seconds    59.786,0000
balance_hours till shift_end         16
balance_time till shift_end:    16  hours      36  minutes      26  seconds
```

Figure 8.7 Remaining Time Until the Next Morning

```
ARMSTRONG          100,00  AUD      16,00  AUD      116,00  AUD
BECK               200,00  CAD      32,00  CAD      232,00  CAD
CALE               300,00  USD      48,00  USD      348,00  USD
```

Figure 8.8 Using Currency Fields in Arithmetic Operations

9

Using Data in a Database Table

As long as you only read data records in tables, you don't need to worry about other system users. But what happens if both you and another user want to modify the same data record at the same time; how are the concurrent access attempts handled? In this chapter, you'll learn about the most important aspects of writing, modifying, and deleting data records.

Concurrent access

Understanding the Principles

> Due to its complexity, the problem of an unknown number of users accessing the same database table is really a topic for advanced users rather than beginners. Nonetheless, you should at least be familiar with the rules and pitfalls of this topic so that you're in a better position to assess the risks. It is also important that you understand the basic principles.

First, remember that you're working in a client-server architecture. This meant that the application and the database are not located on your desktop PC, but on a server (the presentation server). You work from a client. From this client, you start a program on an application server that is located somewhere in the network, which, in turn, accesses a database server that is likewise located somewhere in the network. In other words, many computers are involved in the process, and they all need to be coordinated. As described in Chapter 1, ABAP and Getting Started with the SAP System, the application and the database system communicate via a database interface. (Fortunately, you as the application developer don't need to worry about this technology.)

OpenSQL The programs in the SAP system use OpenSQL to access the database tables independently of the database system. OpenSQL allows you to read and modify data—and also to buffer data on the application server—thus reducing the number of database accesses. The database interface is also responsible for synchronizing the buffer with the database table at predefined intervals. Unfortunately, the buffered data is not always up-to-date, so buffering is most useful for relatively static data, such as Customizing settings and master data.

Division of labor OpenSQL cannot create tables or modify table structures; the ABAP Dictionary handles these tasks. This division of labor is intentional, since normal programs are not supposed to be able to perform the tasks of the ABAP Dictionary. Also, ABAP statements (that is, OpenSQL statements) can be used to access tables that were created and administered in the physical database using the ABAP Dictionary only.

To ensure that the SAP system is genuinely independent of the database system, no database system tools are used to check authorizations and lock concepts in the database. Instead, the system has its own authorization concept and lock concept that are used consistently on the system side for all certified database systems.

Authorization Concept

As a rule, users should be allowed to access only data for which they possess the necessary authorization. The authorization concept is used to define which data (that is, which fields) users can access and how. An activity (for example, display or modify) is specified for every field. This combination of field and activity is stored in an authorization object.

To make the task of managing authorization objects easier, they are grouped into object classes. Object classes are assigned to applications and aggregated to form profiles, which are aggregated to form composite profiles. This process continues until the data views (which are required for the users to be able to complete the tasks assigned to them) are reflected at the work center level, for example.

Authorization object

Fortunately, no one needs to reinvent the wheel here. The standard delivery of the SAP system contains a wealth of profiles and composite profiles that the developer only has to check and, possibly, copy and incorporate minor modifications. For example, a developer may take a profile for an accounting clerk in asset accounting and check in each specific case whether the default profile corresponds to the actual requirements. If not, the developer can copy and modify the profile. The view of the data required for the specific user's work—and the required authorizations—are mapped in what is known as a role.

Authorization profile

For a user to be able to log on to the SAP system, he has to be "created" in the SAP system and have a user master record. Also, one or more roles must be assigned to the user in the user master record. These roles assign the appropriate authorizations to users. They specify what activities a user can execute, and with what data. The job of an application (that is, the executed program) is to check whether or not the user has the required authorizations. The user is granted access to the data in question only if he has the necessary authorizations for it.

User master record

No authorization checks are carried out in the physical database system itself; these checks have to be built into the SAP system in advance. Therefore, for example, an authorization for a transaction can be maintained in the transaction code and checked before the transaction is executed. The transaction then starts only if the corresponding authorizations are entered in the user master record.

No authorization checks

Similar restrictions apply to starting ABAP programs. For example, there is a special authorization object for executing ABAP programs, and this authorization object can be used to assign ABAP programs to groups. Group assignments can then be used to specify that certain users are allowed to execute certain programs and others are not.

Authority-Check

> Self-defined authorization checks can also be built into the ABAP source code using the AUTHORITY-CHECK statement. This statement has to be used if the transaction or the ABAP program itself is not sufficiently protected by authorizations, and to protect the functionality implemented in classes and function modules against unauthorized use.

Lock Concept

When using the lock concept, you have to differentiate between database locks of the physical database and business locks of the SAP system. Database system locks are not sufficient for the requirements of the SAP system. While the database system does set physical locks for data records to which modify statements apply, these locks are valid only for a single SAP system dialog step (that is, a single screen). A transaction consists of a complete business process, and it is therefore clear that the lock concepts of physical database systems are insufficient.

No lock for transactions Imagine that you're creating an order. The full creation process contains several screens. Before you get to the final screen, you notice that some data that you need to complete the order is missing. In such cases, you have to be able to "park" the transaction you have just started without already having posted parts of it to the database: The SAP system lock concept allows data records to be locked across several dialog steps.

Also, a lock cannot apply only to the application server that initiated the lock; it has to apply to *all* application servers in the SAP system. This means that locks have to be recognized by multiple work processes so they can trigger corresponding reactions.

Lock objects For this reason, the SAP system uses its own lock concept that is completely independent of the database system. Lock objects are the basis of this lock concept. Lock objects enable the system to lock data records in multiple database tables for the duration of an entire SAP transaction, provided that they are linked in the ABAP Dictionary via foreign key relationships.

Lock objects have to be created in the ABAP Dictionary, and contain the tables and key fields that are to apply to a shared lock. Two function modules are created automatically: one to lock the lock object, and the other to unlock the lock object. These function modules have to be called at the logically correct point in the ABAP source code. This means that on one hand, you are genuinely independent of any database system lock concepts, but on the other, you are responsible for correctly setting and unlocking locks. Refer to Chapter 13 for general information on how to call function modules.

The function modules for locking and unlocking are executed in a special work process. If an SAP system contains multiple application servers, only one of these servers has this special work process. This application server also manages a central lock table for the entire system. The function modules enter or delete the lock in this lock table (that is, the function modules enter or delete a data record in the lock table). You can use the corresponding function module to delete a lock. You can also do this via a posting or a transaction, but a description of this process exceeds the scope of this book.

The lock is thus *not* placed on the physical data record in the database system; instead, it takes the form of a logical lock in a central lock table. Therefore, all the involved application programs must adhere to the conventions of the SAP lock concept and query the lock table for relevant entries.

Logical lock

There are two types of locks: shared locks and exclusive locks. With a shared lock, other applications may also set a shared lock and gain read access to the data. The only thing that is not permitted with a shared lock is an exclusive lock, which enables the user to modify data records. In addition, exclusive locks prevent all other application programs from reading or writing the locked data for the duration of the lock, or outputting a message to inform other users of this fact.

Shared lock and exclusive lock

Point-in-Time Problem

It is difficult to find the right point in time to set a lock. If you set a lock too soon, you may risk blocking other users unnecessarily. If you set the lock too late, the application may be at a disadvantage and have problems with updating data. Estimating the right point in time to remove a lock is similarly difficult. If you wait too long, other applications will again be blocked unnecessarily.

If you set too many shared locks, it will be very difficult for other applications to gain exclusive access. Similarly, a poorly timed exclusive lock will prevent all other applications from gaining exclusive access. So the right point in time for specific actions depends on the business and technical tasks at hand.

As previously mentioned, locks are removed by the relevant function module. If the call is not explicitly triggered by an error, then locks are automatically removed during the posting process or at the end of the SAP transaction.

 Dialog Programming Is Always An Issue

The information provided here about the problem of the authorization concept and the lock should suffice for an introduction to ABAP, since you usually won't do any dialog programming until later. You will need to take these mechanisms into account and, if necessary, incorporate them when developing ABAP reports later on, as your ABAP skills become more advanced. We will not go into this topic in any more detail at this point; for the rest of this chapter, we will assume that the table belongs to you alone.

We have one request to any advanced ABAP programmers who may be reading these lines: Do not say out loud what you are thinking. Breathe deeply, and remember that each developer will finally understand how inevitable locks actually are when he has to carry out complex troubleshooting because a lock was not been set, if not sooner.

OpenSQL Statements

As previously mentioned, OpenSQL statements are used to modify table content. OpenSQL statements are a special kind of ABAP statement. You are already familiar with one example: the SELECT statement. Via encapsulation, OpenSQL statements use a consistent ABAP syntax for all certified database systems. Programs that contain these statements can run without the need for any adaptation, even if a different system replaces the underlying database system. However, a prerequisite is that all database objects are created and managed using the ABAP Dictionary.

The first key field of a database table for application data is always the client number. (Only system tables are cross-client.) By default, OpenSQL statements have automatic client handling, and thus apply only to the current client. Automatic client handling means that it is not possible to select or modify the data of one client from within another client.

Automatic client handling

In ABAP, the following are the main statements for modifying table content, besides the SELECT statement:

Modifying table content

> To insert new rows (that is, new data records) into a table, use the INSERT command.

> To modify an existing data record, use the UPDATE command.

> Use the MODIFY statement if you don't know whether this record is already contained in the table. If it does already exist, it is modified; in this case, the statement has the same effect as the UPDATE command. If the data record doesn't exist yet, the MODIFY statement has the same effect as an INSERT command.

> To delete the data record from the database table, use the DELETE command. But be careful: the contents of whole tables can be deleted using the DELETE statement and become irretrievably lost.

All the statements listed above return a return code and thus populate the SY-SUBRC system field. The SY-SUBRC field can be checked in the ABAP Debugger or called up in the source code directly after the

Return code

relevant statement. Depending on the content of the table field, the action is evaluated and a decision is made as to how the program will proceed. If the system can formally execute the statement without incurring any problems, the SY-SUBRC field gets the value 0.

By the way, a statement return code with the value 0 is a common value to indicate that everything is OK in other programming languages as well. If the system cannot execute the statement, it usually returns a different return code. In this case, the value of the return code depends on the individual command. You also have to look up which value describes which error in the reference or help text of each command. The further progress of the program is controlled by the program logic, in accordance with the field type. Chapter 10, Program Flow Control and Logical Expressions, provides examples of this. You can find more details in the *The Official ABAP Reference* (SAP PRESS, 3rd edition, 2012).

Creating a New Data Record

INSERT   With the INSERT statement, you can insert one or more new data records into a database table. For the sake of simplicity, we'll restrict ourselves to single data records when discussing this and the other OpenSQL statements.

To use the table content, first define a work area whose structure is identical to that of the table. Then calculate all the field values of the new data record, and enter into the work area the data record that is supposed to be written to the database table as a new row. Next, copy the content of the work area to the database table as a new row.

Ideally, the structure of the work area and the structure of the table area are identical, which you can achieve by referencing the declaration of the table work area in the declaration of the work area. Work areas are defined using the DATA statement.

Defining a work area   When assigning names to work areas, you are restricted only by the general naming conventions, as before. However, for the sake of readability in the source code, we recommend that you start all names with the prefix WA_. If you want to create the work area WA_ZMEMBER02 with the same structure as table ZMEMBER02, the DATA statement looks like this:

```
DATA wa_zmember02 TYPE zmember02.
```

There is a subtle difference between the definition with TYPE and with LIKE: If you use LIKE, the definition refers to a concrete data object that exists in your program; if you use TYPE, the definition refers to a data type that can be defined either in your program or in the ABAP Dictionary.

ZMEMBER02 has two roles here. As a database table in the ABAP Dictionary, it is a global data type and should be referenced with TYPE; due to the definition as a table work area with the obsolete TABLES statement, there is a data object with the same name in the program, which you could reference with LIKE. For reasons of clarity, however, you should not use such implicit double roles.

After declaring the work area, you determine the values for the fields of the new record and store the results in the work area. Once the new record has been fully created in the work area, it is transferred from there to the database table; in our example, the work area WA_ZMEMBER02 is filled. The new data record in the database table ZMEMBER02 is inserted using the following code:

```
INSERT zmember02 FROM wa_zmember02.
```

The name of the database table could also be specified dynamically using this syntax. In this case, the statement contains a field name instead of the table name and the content of the field is the name of the database table. If we assume that the field ZTARGETTABLE is of type c and has ZMEMBER02 as content, the statement could be as follows:

```
INSERT (target_table) FROM wa_zmember02.
```

The variable in which the table to be filled is located—in our example, variable TARGET_TABLE—has to be placed in brackets without any space characters.

If the transfer is successful, the work area is initialized using the CLEAR statement, if necessary, and recreated for the next data record. So you keep the work area for the last-read table record and the work area for the new table record completely separate.

 Greater Flexibility

> Using work areas offers other benefits, as well. For example, work areas allow for a much greater degree of flexibility, as you will see in Chapter 12. As a result, as your level of knowledge increases—especially in the course of this book—you'll use work areas more and more.

If you want to write a new row to table ZMEMBER02 using the traditional method (without work area), as you can still find it in older programs, first use the TABLES statement to define a table work area:

```
TABLES zmember02.
```

This not only declares the use of table ZMEMBER02 in your program, but it also creates a data object that has the characteristics of a global variable and the same structure as the database table—as if you'd defined the following:

```
DATA zmember02 TYPE zmember02.
```

 TABLES Statement

> The TABLES statement is regarded as obsolete and is only supported outside of ABAP classes and for downward compatibility reasons. In the context of ABAP Objects—that is, in ABAP classes—the TABLES statement is no longer allowed and, therefore, neither are table work areas. These table work areas have been replaced by specially defined work areas. However, the traditional syntax still exists in practice in customer-specific programs and in some standard reports. We have mentioned it here for this reason, and also because it aids in the understanding at the introductory stage.

If a table work area is declared, it thus implicitly acts as the work area for the respective table. This means that you don't have to specify the work area when you use the INSERT statement; the system always uses the implicitly declared work area that has the same name as the database table:

```
INSERT zmember02.
```

In the modern notation, this would have the same meaning as the following statement:

```
INSERT zmember02 FROM zmember02.
```

Only the name of the database table has to be specified directly in this abbreviated form (without specification of the work area). As described, directly after the command, you can query the return code that was entered in the SY-SUBRC system field. If it is 0, then the system executed the statement formally, without any problems. If the system cannot add a new row to the database table because it already contains a data record with the same primary key, then SY-SUBRC is set to 4.

Unfortunately, using the table work area as a buffer for a new data record involves some risks. For example, if fewer fields are filled in the new data record than in the old data record, you must ask yourself how you can ensure that all fields in the record structure get the correct new content and that no undesirable hybrid forms are created. Another example is if, in order to calculate results or interim results, you need values from both the old and the new record; how do you ensure that you will be able to access the old record structure as long as you need to and create the new structure at the same time?

Risks

The solution to the problem in the first example is relatively straightforward: Before you start filling the new record structure, delete the content of the table work area using the CLEAR statement. If you want to delete the table work area for the ZMEMBER02 table, the statement is this:

CLEAR

```
CLEAR zmember02.
```

The CLEAR statement resets all fields of the table area to its type-specific initial values. For example, fields with the data type c (character fields) get a space character (' ') as their initial value, and fields with the data type d (data fields) get the initial value '00000000'.

See Listing 9.1 (later in this chapter) for a sample listing of inserting records.

Modifying an Existing Data Record

UPDATE Another way of modifying multiple data records simultaneously is by using an UPDATE command; however, we'll restrict ourselves to modifying a single record here. If you use a work area, modify the work area and update the corresponding row of the database using the following code:

```
UPDATE zmember02 FROM wa_zmember02.
```

 Specifying The Name of The Database Dynamically

> The name of the database table could also be specified dynamically. The same principles apply to automatic client handling and the CLEAR command.

In the traditional notation, you create the table work area accordingly and modify each row in the database table. In our example, you modify the table work area for ZMEMBER02 and update the corresponding row in the database table:

```
UPDATE zmember02.
```

If there is a data record in the database table with the same primary key, this record is updated and the return code has the value 0. If the system doesn't find a record with this primary key in the database table, then the table remains unmodified and the return code has the value 4.

See Listing 9.2 (later in this chapter) for a sample report demonstrating how to update existing records.

Modifying a Data Record

MODIFY Since the MODIFY command is used both to create a new record and to modify an existing one, it has two modes of operation, but in terms of performance, it is not as good as the specialist commands INSERT and UPDATE. For this reason, you should use it only if the program logic requires that you make both modes available; in general, INSERT and UPDATE are preferable to MODIFY.

For the `MODIFY` statement, you usually use a work area to make your code compatible with ABAP Objects and enable it to run in the context of ABAP classes like in the following:

```
MODIFY zmember02 FROM wa_zmember02.
```

With this syntax, all other rules and comments apply similarly to the comments on `INSERT` and `UPDATE`.

Of course, you can also use the `MODIFY` statement in the traditional syntax (that is, in combination with a table work area that is declared via the `TABLES` statement. In this case, you have to specify the table statically). In our example, the statement is as follows:

```
MODIFY zmember02.
```

The primary key of the data record is derived from the field contents of the table work area. If none of the data records in the database table has this primary key, a new row is created. If there is a data record with this primary key, the content of the table work area is added to the corresponding row. In both cases, the value of the return code is 0. The return code is 4 only if the row cannot be processed at all.

See Listing 9.3 (later in this chapter) for a demonstration of how to modify records.

Deleting a Data Record

As we mentioned in this chapter's introduction, you can do a lot of damage by using the `DELETE` command. However, this possibility should not deter you from using the delete function. Instead, you simply need to plan, develop, and test everything in a particularly risk-aware fashion when deleting one or more data records—even retroactive program modifications.

DELETE

Let's start with the normal case: deleting a data record from the database table with reference to the work area. Not all fields in the work area must have the right content; specifying the relevant primary key will suffice. In our example with the table ZMEMBER02, the primary key consists of the client and the member number. Thanks to automatic client handling, you don't need to worry about the correct client. All you have to do is specify the member number to identify the primary key. In the work area, enter the member number to be deleted into the member number field, and then delete the corresponding row in the database table:

```
DELETE zmember02 FROM wa_zmember02.
```

With this syntax, you can again specify the database table name dynamically; all other rules and comments apply similarly to the comments on INSERT, UPDATE, and MODIFY.

In our example (shown in Listing 9.4, later in this chapter), a data record is deleted with reference to a table work area in a similar way. Fill the MNUMBER field in the table work area and delete the row in the database table like this:

```
DELETE zmember02.
```

With this syntax, you again have to specify the table name statically. The primary key of the data record to be deleted is derived from the field contents of the table work area. If the system finds a row in the database table with this primary key, it is deleted and the return code is set to 0. If the system doesn't find a row like this, the return code is set to 4.

❗ Extreme Care Needed

As we mentioned earlier, the DELETE statement should be handled with extreme care. With the previous method, you always addressed the data records in the table ZMEMBER02 via the primary key. With this statement, you should practice addressing the "correct" rows using a condition rather than the primary key.

Also keep in mind that the numerous variants of the INSERT, MODIFY, and DELETE commands are dangerous sources of error. Slightly varying syntax variants enable you to manipulate internal tables with or without header line and database tables with table work area or work area. After the FROM addition, you can find the name of the database table, of a work area, or even of an internal table.

So before deleting a database table by accident, even though you just wanted to process an internal table, first take a look at the documentation and handle DELETE with extreme care.

If you extended your table as suggested in "Maintaining Append Structures" in Chapter 7, course descriptions and titles have been saved. If a
course is canceled—the "Network Technology" course, for example—
and you consequently have to delete all the members of this course
from the table, you can achieve your goal faster by using a condition.
However, you have to program this condition very carefully so that
you don't accidentally delete the wrong data records.

Capitalization, for example, can be a small but nasty stumbling block at
this point, because the condition is specified as a literal, and in literals
lowercase letters and uppercase letters are handled as different characters. So you have to be very familiar with the detailed field content
of the database table; otherwise, the system won't be able to find the
rows that you want or may delete the wrong rows, and both cases are
equally annoying.

In our example, therefore, the syntax of "SAP01" is central to the success of the code. You should think carefully about how you want the
literal to look. Should it be called 'sap01' or 'SAP01'? In the case of
the latter, your statement would look like this:

```
DELETE FROM zmember02
  WHERE zzcoursetitle = 'SAP01'.
```

 Get Rid of It All!

> In our example, if you decide to forget the WHERE condition and instead
> write only the following line of code, you can delete all the rows of our
> example table with one "nice little command":
>
> DELETE FROM zmember02.

Comfortable Alternative: Object Services

If you have already gained experience with the development of business applications in other object-oriented programming languages, you
may have come across an object-relational persistency service. Popular
examples are the persistency frameworks Hibernate and JPA in the
Java world. These services are supposed to facilitate the developer's

programming work regarding persistency aspects by taking over complicated and recurring programming tasks. Some examples are database accesses for load and save processes, the management of pending and already executed database accesses, the management of a cache in the main memory, and the mapping between database tables, on the one hand, and object instances in object-oriented programming, on the other.

If you know this kind of services from other environments, you'll probably glad to hear that there is an equivalent in the ABAP environment: Object Services. Discussing them in detail would go far beyond the scope of this introduction book, so only the most important features are described here. If you want to know more, refer to the book *Object Services in ABAP* (SAP PRESS, 2010).

It doesn't make sense to use Object Services for simple database accesses. But if you want to develop database accesses in very demanding scenarios with enormous data volumes, you have to use every trick of the trade, and manual programming becomes rather complicated. This is where Object Services provide support by taking over complex technical cross-functional tasks, such as caching, bundling of database updates, usage of update tasks, and so on. This enables you to focus on the business functionality.

Object Services include a *persistency service* for the management of objects that are stored in the database, a *transaction service* that provides enhanced options for the control of transactions (nested and linked transactions), and a *query service* for searching for and loading persistent objects.

Sample Code for INSERT

```
1   *&---------------------------------------------*
2   *& Report   Z_MEMBERLIST09_INSERT             *
3   *&                                             *
4   *&---------------------------------------------*
5   *&                                             *
6   *&                                             *
7   *&---------------------------------------------*
```

```
 8
 9  REPORT   z_memberlist09_insert.
10
11  * Define work areas
12  DATA: wa_zmember02 TYPE zmember02.
13
14  * Define tables
15  TABLES zmember02.
16
17  * Define fields
18  DATA: mnumber TYPE zmember02-mnumber.
19
20  * Content of table before insert
21  SELECT * FROM zmember02 INTO wa_zmember02.
22    WRITE: / wa_zmember02-mnumber,
23             wa_zmember02-mname,
24             wa_zmember02-mdob,
25             wa_zmember02-mgender,
26             wa_zmember02-mfee,
27             wa_zmember02-mcurrency,
28             wa_zmember02-zzcartype,
29             wa_zmember02-zzcoursetitle.
30  ENDSELECT.
31  mnumber = wa_zmember02-mnumber.
32  SKIP.
33
34  * Create new record from table work area
35  mnumber = mnumber + 1.
36  CLEAR wa_zmember02.
37  wa_zmember02-mnumber = mnumber.
38  wa_zmember02-mname = 'Davis'.
39  wa_zmember02-mdob = '19840404'.
40  wa_zmember02-mgender = 'F'.
41  wa_zmember02-mfee = '400'.
42  wa_zmember02-mcurrency = 'EUR'.
43  wa_zmember02-zzcartype = 'SUV'.
44  wa_zmember02-zzcoursetitle = 'SAP04'.
45  INSERT zmember02 FROM wa_zmember02.
46  WRITE: / 'Sy-subrc of Insert is', sy-subrc.
47
48  * Create new record from table work area
49  mnumber = mnumber + 1.
50  zmember02-mnumber = mnumber.
51  zmember02-name = 'Emerson'.
```

```
52   zmember02-mdob = '19850505'.
53   zmember02-mgender = 'M'.
54   zmember02-mfee = '500'.
55   zmember02-mcurrency = 'JPY'.
56   zmember02-zzcartype = 'Pick Up'.
57   zmember02-zzcoursetitle = 'SAP05'.
58   INSERT zmember02.
59   WRITE: / ' 'Sy-subrc of Insert is', sy-subrc.
60   SKIP.
61
62   * Content of table after insert
63   SELECT * FROM zmember02 INTO wa_zmember02.
64     WRITE: / wa_zmember02-mnumber,
65              wa_zmember02-mname,
66              wa_zmember02-mdob,
67              wa_zmember02-mgender,
68              wa_zmember02-mfee,
69              wa_zmember02-mcurrency,
70              wa_zmember02-zzcartype,
71              wa_zmember02-zzcoursetitle.
72   ENDSELECT.
```

Listing 9.1   Report Z_MEMBERLIST09_INSERT

Notes on the Source Code

Line 12
For the sake of logical separation between table and work area, this row defines a work area that has the same structure as the table in the ABAP Dictionary and makes reference to this table type.

Line 18
In the traditional syntax, the TABLES statement is used to create a table work area—a data object in the program that has the same name and structure as the database table and is implicitly used as the work area for this database table. Using the table name multiple times can be confusing, so in new programs you should use explicitly defined work areas with specific names instead of the TABLES statement. This way it is always clear when the work area and when the table is processed.

Lines 22 to 29

These lines output the old table content so that the table content can be compared before and after.

Line 31

This line enters the last-read member number (that is, the highest one) into the field MNUMBER. This information is important because the member number is a key field.

Line 35

This line increases the member number by 1. The new record is then inserted with the next-highest member number, without any gaps.

Line 36

The last-read record in the table is still in the work area. This row initializes the work area before it is refilled, so that the new record will contain only the correct data and no old content will be transferred to it.

Lines 37 to 44

These lines fill the work area with the new record content.

Lines 45 and 46

The new record is written to the database table, and as a precaution, the return code of the command is output with a comment. Of course, in practice, the return code is queried in a program rather than output in a list. In the case of a positive result, processing is continued or the error-handling process is triggered, depending on the content. You will learn how this works in Chapter 10; for now, the stopgap solution will suffice.

Stopgap solution

Line 49

This line writes another new record to the database. The member number is incremented accordingly.

Lines 50 to 57

This time, these lines create the field content for the new record in the table work area, rather than in the work area. If it is to be used multiple times, this table work area must also be initialized before new content is written to it. In our example, the work area is used only once, so we don't need the CLEAR statement here.

Lines 58 and 59

The database table gets a new record from within the work area. As a safety measure, the return code of the command is also output in the list.

Lines 62 to 72

For checking purposes, all records of the database table are reread after the database is modified and written to the list. This time you also use the work area instead of the table work area in the SELECT statement.

Program Output

The activities carried out so far caused three data records to be added to the database table. Records 4 and 5 were then added after the two INSERT statements (see Figure 9.1).

```
00001 ARMSTRONG          01.01.2001 M      100,00  AUD   SUV          SAP01
00002 BECK               02.02.2002 F      200,00  CAD   SEDAN        SAP02
00003 CALE               03.03.2003 M      300,00  USD   STATION W.   SAP03

Sy-subrc of Insert is    0
Sy-subrc of Insert is    0

00001 ARMSTRONG          01.01.2001 M      100,00  AUD   SUV          SAP01
00002 BECK               02.02.2002 F      200,00  CAD   SEDAN        SAP02
00003 CALE               03.03.2003 M      300,00  USD   STATION W.   SAP03
00004 Davis              04.04.1984 F      400,00  EUR   SUV          SAP04
00005 Emerson            05.05.1985 M      500,00  JPY   Pick Up      SAP05
```

Figure 9.1 List Screen for INSERT Example

Sample Code for UPDATE

```
 1  *&---------------------------------------------*
 2  *& Report   Z_MEMBERLIST09_UPDATE              *
 3  *&                                             *
 4  *&---------------------------------------------*
 5  *&                                             *
 6  *&                                             *
 7  *&---------------------------------------------*
 8
 9  REPORT  z_memberlist09_update.
10
11  * Define work areas
12  DATA: wa_zmember02 TYPE zmember02.
13
14  * Define tables
15  TABLES zmember02.
16
17  * Define fields
18  DATA: mnumber TYPE zmember02-mnumber.
19
20  * Content of table before update
21  SELECT * FROM zmember02 INTO wa_zmember02.
22    WRITE: / wa_zmember02-mnumber,
23             wa_zmember02-mname,
24             wa_zmember02-mdob,
25             wa_zmember02-mgender,
26             wa_zmember02-mfee,
27             wa_zmember02-mcurrency,
28             wa_zmember02-zzcartype,
29             wa_zmember02-zzcoursetitle.
30  ENDSELECT.
31  mnumber = wa_zmember02-mnumber.
32  SKIP.
33
34  * Change record from work area
35  mnumber = mnumber - 2.
36  CLEAR wa_zmember02.
37  wa_zmember02-mnumber = mnumber.
38  wa_zmember02-mname = 'Cash'.
39  wa_zmember02-mdob = '19830303'.
40  wa_zmember02-mgender = 'M'.
41  wa_zmember02-mfee = '301'.
42  wa_zmember02-mcurrency = 'EUR'.
```

```
43   wa_zmember02-zzcartype = 'SUV'.
44   wa_zmember02-zzcoursetitle = 'SAP03'.
45   UPDATE zmember02 FROM wa_zmember02.
46   WRITE: / 'Sy-subrc of Update is', sy-subrc.
47
48   * Create new record from table work area
49   mnumber = mnumber - 1.
50   zmember02-mnumber = mnumber.
51   zmember02-mname = 'Davis'.
52   zmember02-mdob = '19840404'.
53   zmember02-mender = 'F'.
54   zmember02-mfee = '401'.
55   zmember02-mcurrency = 'JPY'.
56   zmember02-zzcartype = 'Pick Up'.
57   zmember02-zzcoursetitle = 'SAP04'.
58   UPDATE zmember02.
59   WRITE: / 'Sy-subrc of update is', sy-subrc.
60   SKIP.
61
62   * Content of table after Update
63   SELECT * FROM zmember02 INTO wa_zmember02.
64     WRITE: / wa_zmember02-mnumber,
65              wa_zmember02-mname,
66              wa_zmember02-mdob,
67              wa_zmember02-mgender,
68              wa_zmember02-mfee,
69              wa_zmember02-mcurrency,
70              wa_zmember02-zzcartype,
71              wa_zmember02-zzcoursetitle.
72   ENDSELECT.
```

Listing 9.2   Report Z_MEMBERLIST09_UPDATE

Notes on the Source Code

Lines 21 to 30
For comparison reasons, all table records are output in the list before any modifications are made.

Line 31
The highest last-read member number is transferred to the MNUMBER field; in our example, it is the value 8.

Line 35

The value of the member number is reduced by 2 (that is, from 8 to 6).

Line 36

This line initializes the table work area. This has to be done because in the example, the sixth record in the table is modified via the work area.

Lines 37 to 44

These lines modify the record fields as follows: the member is changed, and the name, date of birth, gender, and course price are reset.

Lines 45 and 46

The UPDATE of the record with the corresponding key in the database table is done using the values of the work area. Here, too, the value of the return code is output in the list as a precaution.

Line 49

This line respecifies the member number for the key field value.

Lines 50 to 57

These lines create the record in the table work area, and modify the date of birth.

Lines 58 and 59

These lines update the record using the values of the table work area. The return code that specifies whether the modification was successful is also output in the list for checking purposes.

Lines 62 to 72

All table records are again written to the list for comparison purposes. This time you also use the work area instead of the table work area in the SELECT statement.

Program Output

The number of records in the table has remained the same, but one record has been modified: In the third record, the old content has been replaced by Mr. Cash and other data, and in the second record the birthday has changed, for example (see Figure 9.2).

```
00001 ARMSTRONG          01.01.2001 M      100,00  AUD  SUV          SAP01
00002 BECK               02.02.2002 F      200,00  CAD  SEDAN        SAP02
00003 CALE               03.03.2003 M      300,00  USD  STATION W.   SAP03
00004 Davis              04.04.1984 F      400,00  EUR  SUV          SAP04
00005 Emerson            05.05.1985 M      500,00  JPY  Pick Up      SAP05

Sy-subrc of Update is    0
Sy-subrc of update is    0

00001 ARMSTRONG          01.01.2001 M      100,00  AUD  SUV          SAP01
00002 BECK               02.02.2002 F      200,00  CAD  SEDAN        SAP02
00003 Cash               03.03.1983 M      301,00  EUR  SUV          SAP03
00004 Davis              04.04.1984 F      401,00  JPY  Pick Up      SAP04
00005 Emerson            05.05.1985 M      500,00  JPY  Pick Up      SAP05
```

Figure 9.2 List Screen for UPDATE Example

Sample Code for MODIFY

```
1   *&---------------------------------------------*
2   *& Report   Z_MEMBERLIST09_MODIFY              *
3   *&                                             *
4   *&---------------------------------------------*
5   *&                                             *
6   *&                                             *
7   *&---------------------------------------------*
8
9   REPORT  z_memberlist09_modify.
10
11  * Define work areas
12  DATA: wa_zmember02 TYPE zmember02.
13
14  * Define tables
15  TABLES zmember02.
16
17  * Define fields
```

```
18   DATA: mnumber TYPE zmember02-mnumber.
19
20   * Content of table before modify
21   SELECT * FROM zmember02 INTO wa_zmember02.
22     WRITE: / wa_zmember02-mnumber,
23               wa_zmember02-mname,
24               wa_zmember02-mdob,
25               wa_zmember02-mgender,
26               wa_zmember02-mfee,
27               wa_zmember02-mcurrency,
28               wa_zmember02-zzcartype,
29               wa_zmember02-zzcoursetitle.
30   ENDSELECT.
31   mnumber = wa_zmember02-mnumber.
32   SKIP.
33
34   * Create new record from work area with Modify
35   mnumber = mnumber + 1.
36   CLEAR wa_zmember02.
37   wa_zmember02-mnumber = mnumber.
38   wa_zmember02-mname = 'Feliciano'.
39   wa_zmember02-mdob = '19860606'.
40   wa_zmember02-mgender = 'F'.
41   wa_zmember02-mfee = '600'.
42   wa_zmember02-mcurrency = 'RUR'.
43   wa_zmember02-zzcartype = 'Compact Car'.
44   wa_zmember02-zzcoursetitle = 'SAP06'.
45   MODIFY zmember02 FROM wa_zmember02.
46   WRITE: / 'Sy-subrc of Modify is', sy-subrc.
47
48   * Change record from table work area with Modify
49   mnumber = mnumber - 1.
50   zmember02-mnumber = mnumber.
51   zmember02-mname = 'Ellington'.
52   zmember02-mdob = '19850505'.
53   zmember02-mgender = 'M'.
54   zmember02-mfee = '501'.
55   zmember02-mcurrency = 'USD'.
56   zmember02-zzcartype = 'Station W.'.
57   zmember02-zzcoursetitle = 'SAP05'.
58   MODIFY zmember02.
59   WRITE: / 'Sy-subrc of Modify is', sy-subrc.
60   SKIP.
61
```

```
62   * Content of table after Modify
63   SELECT * FROM zmember02 INTO wa_zmember02.
64     WRITE: / wa_zmember02-mnumber,
65                wa_zmember02-mname,
66                wa_zmember02-mdob,
67                wa_zmember02-mgender,
68                wa_zmember02-mfee,
69                wa_zmember02-mcurrency,
70                wa_zmember02-zzcartype,
71                wa_zmember02-zzcoursetitle.
72   ENDSELECT.
```

Listing 9.3   Report Z_MEMBERLIST09_MODIFY

Notes on the Source Code

Up to Line 33

The report is created in the same way as the INSERT and the UPDATE example.

Line 35

First, the MODIFY command is used to create a new data record, and so the MNUMBER key field is incremented by 1.

Lines 36 to 44

These lines initialize the work area and fill the record fields.

Lines 45 and 46

The MODIFY statement is used to find the database table record with the corresponding key fields and to fill the record from within the work area. Because the MNUMBER key field was also incremented, there cannot be any record with this key in the database. Therefore, a new record is created. The return code of the command is output in the list for checking purposes.

Line 49

We now want to use the reverse effect of the MODIFY statement. This way, the member number is modified to the key of an existing record.

Lines 50 to 57

The record to be modified is created in the table work area, and the field content for the currency is modified.

Lines 58 and 59

This time, the MODIFY statement finds an existing record in the database. The record is updated and the return code is written to the list. The system successfully executes both MODIFY statements, and the value of SY-SUBRC is 0 in both cases.

Lines 62 to 72

These lines output the modified table rows in order to represent the content of the table before and after the MODIFY statements.

Program Output

Record 6 was created from scratch by the MODIFY command because a record with the corresponding key didn't exist. Record 5, on the other hand, *was* modified: the unit of currency was changed from the Euro (EUR) to the US dollar (USD; see Figure 9.3).

```
00001 ARMSTRONG          01.01.2001 M     100,00  AUD   SUV         SAP01
00002 BECK               02.02.2002 F     200,00  CAD   SEDAN       SAP02
00003 Cash               03.03.1983 M     301,00  EUR   SUV         SAP03
00004 Davis              04.04.1984 F     401,00  JPY   Pick Up     SAP04
00005 Emerson            05.05.1985 M     500,00  JPY   Pick Up     SAP05

Sy-subrc of Modify is    0
Sy-subrc of Modify is    0

00001 ARMSTRONG          01.01.2001 M     100,00  AUD   SUV         SAP01
00002 BECK               02.02.2002 F     200,00  CAD   SEDAN       SAP02
00003 Cash               03.03.1983 M     301,00  EUR   SUV         SAP03
00004 Davis              04.04.1984 F     401,00  JPY   Pick Up     SAP04
00005 Ellington          05.05.1985 M     501,00  USD   Station W.  SAP05
00006 Feliciano          06.06.1986 F     600,00  RUR   Compact Ca  SAP06
```

Figure 9.3 List Screen for MODIFY Example

Sample Code for DELETE

```
1   *&---------------------------------------------*
2   *& Report   Z_MEMBERLIST09_DELETE              *
3   *&                                             *
4   *&---------------------------------------------*
5   *&                                             *
6   *&                                             *
7   *&---------------------------------------------*
8
9   REPORT  z_memberlist09_delete.
10
11  * Define work areas
12  DATA: wa_zmember02 TYPE zmember02.
13
14  * Define tables
15  TABLES zmember02.
16
17  * Define fields
18  DATA: mnumber TYPE zmember02-mnumber.
19
20  * Content of table before delete
21  SELECT * FROM zmember02 INTO wa_zmember02.
22    WRITE: / wa_zmember02-mnumber,
23             wa_zmember02-mname,
24             wa_zmember02-mdob,
25             wa_zmember02-mgender,
26             wa_zmember02-mfee,
27             wa_zmember02-mcurrency,
28             wa_zmember02-zzcartype,
29             wa_zmember02-zzcoursetitle.
30  ENDSELECT.
31  mnumber = wa_zmember02-mnumber.
32  SKIP.
33
34  * Delete record from work area
35  CLEAR: wa_zmember02, zmember02.
36  wa_zmember02-mnumber = mnumber.
37  DELETE zmember02 FROM wa_zmember02.
38  WRITE: / 'Sy-subrc of Delete is', sy-subrc.
39
40  * Delete record from table work area
41  mnumber = mnumber - 1.
42  zmember02-mnumber = mnumber.
```

```
43  DELETE zmember02.
44  WRITE: / 'Sy-subrc of Delete is', sy-subrc.
45
46  * Delete record under condition
47  DELETE FROM zmember02 WHERE zzcoursetitle = 'SAP01'.
48  WRITE: / 'Sy-subrc of Delete under condition
        is', sy-subrc.
49
50  * Content of table after Delete
51  SELECT * FROM zmember02 INTO wa_zmember02.
52    WRITE: / wa_zmember02-mnumber,
53             wa_zmember02-mname,
54             wa_zmember02-mdob,
55             wa_zmember02-mgender,
56             wa_zmember02-mfee,
57             wa_zmember02-mcurrency,
58             wa_zmember02-zzcartype,
59             wa_zmember02-zzcoursetitle.
60  ENDSELECT.
61
62  * Delete all records of the table
63  DELETE FROM zmember02.
64  WRITE: / 'Sy-subrc of Delete all records is',
        sy-subrc.
65  SELECT * FROM zmember02 INTO wa_zmember02.
66    WRITE: / wa_zmember02-mnumber,
67             wa_zmember02-mname,
68             wa_zmember02-mdob,
69             wa_zmember02-mgender,
70             wa_zmember02-mfee,
71             wa_zmember02-mcurrency,
72             wa_zmember02-zzcartype,
73             wa_zmember02-zzcoursetitle.
74  ENDSELECT.
```

Listing 9.4 Report Z_MEMBERLIST09_DELETE

Notes on the Source Code

Lines 35 and 36

The key field for the record to be deleted is entered in the work area, and so this area is initialized. Next, the member number of the last-read record is entered as a key field in the work area.

Lines 37 and 38

These lines find the corresponding record with this key in the database table and delete it. The return code is output in the list for checking purposes.

Lines 41 and 42

These lines identify the key for the next record to be deleted and place it in the table work area.

Lines 43 and 44

These lines delete the corresponding record in the database table. As before, SY-SUBRC is output in the list for checking purposes.

Line 47

Watch out for typing errors

We don't want to delete just one record from the database table; we want to delete all records that fulfill the condition that the field ZZCOURSETITLE contain the content "SAP01". If a typing error is made and the literal 'SAP01' contains both lowercase and uppercase letters, or the corresponding record field in the database contains upper-case letters only, the command will not find any matches. In other words, the condition is not fulfilled and no records are deleted.

Line 63

Be warned that this statement deletes all records in the database table. Compare rows 47 and 63: the only difference between them is the condition. If you omit the condition, the DELETE command will do its worst. You can see, therefore, how a fleeting mistake can have serious consequences in practice.

Lines 65 to 74

The remaining records in the database table are written to the list as a test (although, in our example, these are only empty records).

Program Output

Originally, there were six records in the database table. The first DELETE statement deleted the last record, and the second DELETE statement deleted the penultimate record (of the original six). The DELETE statement with the condition deleted all the remaining records apart from two, and these two were then deleted when all records were removed. In the end, the database table is empty (see also Figure 9.4).

```
00001 ARMSTRONG              01.01.2001 M         100,00  AUD   SUV            SAP01
00002 BECK                   02.02.2002 F         200,00  CAD   SEDAN          SAP02
00003 Cash                   03.03.1983 M         301,00  EUR   SUV            SAP03
00004 Davis                  04.04.1984 F         401,00  JPY   Pick Up        SAP04
00005 Ellington              05.05.1985 M         501,00  USD   Station W.     SAP05
00006 Feliciano              06.06.1986 F         600,00  RUR   Compact Ca     SAP06

Sy-subrc of Delete is       0
Sy-subrc of Delete is       0
Sy-subrc of Delete under condition is         0
00002 BECK                   02.02.2002 F         200,00  CAD   SEDAN          SAP02
00003 Cash                   03.03.1983 M         301,00  EUR   SUV            SAP03
00004 Davis                  04.04.1984 F         401,00  JPY   Pick Up        SAP04
Sy-subrc of Delete all records is       0
```

Figure 9.4 List Screen for DELETE Example

Program Flow Control and Logical Expressions

Making decisions in programming isn't easy. Sometimes common sense and logical expressions seem to contradict each other. Why doesn't your machine ever do what you want it to? This chapter describes the rules that you must adhere to with regard to the program flow.

In Chapter 9, Using Data in a Database Table, you had to write the return code of the DELETE statement into the list. There was no other alternative. This wouldn't have changed the program flow if an error had occurred and the return code had returned a value other than zero. Instead, the program would have generated the same list, but with rather useless results.

When it comes to practical usage, it makes far more sense to make a case distinction in order to identify errors, for example, and to handle them separately. In certain cases, it may be preferable not to generate a list and to terminate the program with a message instead. This chapter provides you with the tools you need to address those specific cases: the *program flow control* and *logical expressions*.

Case distinctions

Control Structures

A program is designed to solve a task which, in turn, consists of sub-tasks. Some of the subtasks must always be performed, others need to be performed only under certain conditions, and some subtasks are optional. Each contains statements, which are summarized into statement blocks. A statement block may consist of a single command, such as a WRITE statement, or several complex processes.

Condition and action

A statement block is run through general conditions that are regulated by program flow control statements, which are known as *control structures*. The control structures contain the condition and the action associated to it. The program flow control is responsible for linking subtasks with each other by using control structures in a useful way. You can use control structures for case distinctions and repetitions.

> **Ex** **Control Structures in Real Life**
>
> This may sound rather abstract to you, but it isn't—these kinds of control structures exist in real life as well. For example, we go to the movies if we have the time, if someone joins us, and if we like the movie; otherwise, we stay home and read a book. The only difference is that in real life, few people express this decision-making process like this:
>
> ```
> IF time and company and interest,
>   THEN movie_theater,
>   ELSE stay at home reading,
> ENDIF.
> ```

Structure start and end

A control structure has a structure start and a structure end. In the previous example, the structure start is represented by the IF statement, while the ENDIF statement represents the structure end. Both control statements belong together, like parentheses in math. The statement blocks for the subtasks are located between the two statements. Control structures either branch to the relevant statement blocks or repeat certain statements within a loop.

Using Patterns

Like all other ABAP statements, you must also include the statements for the control structures in the source code. Under certain circumstances, it may make sense to use patterns for that because *patterns* insert predefined structures into the source code from the cursor position onwards.

To insert a pattern, you must position the cursor in the line from which you want to insert the pattern going forward, and click the PATTERN button, as shown in Figure 10.1.

Inserting patterns

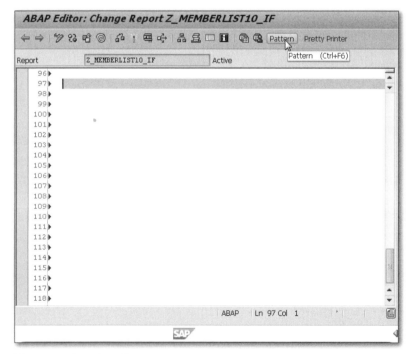

Figure 10.1 Inserting a Pattern

The system then opens a window from which you select a pattern from a range of frequently used patterns, such as the SELECT statement. Other patterns such as the IF structure can be obtained via the OTHER PATTERN field. Because you want to insert an IF structure, you must enter IF in that field (see Figure 10.2) and click the CONTINUE button (the green arrow icon). The system then inserts the complete IF structure description into the source code (see Figure 10.3).

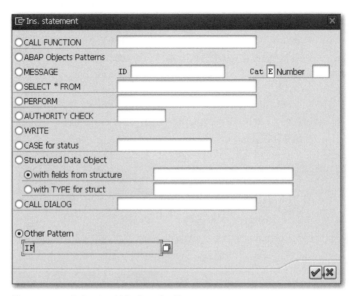

Figure 10.2 Selection Window for Patterns

Figure 10.3 IF Structure Inserted into the Source Code Using a Pattern

Initial adjustments

Lines that aren't needed should be deleted or converted into comment lines, and missing parts (such as conditions and statement blocks) should be added. If you aren't certain of the exact name of the pattern, you can click on the HELP button after placing the cursor in the OTHER

PATTERN field (see Figure 10.4). The system then displays another window containing a list of possible patterns. The list begins with different patterns for comment lines; it contains the statements for the control structures described in this chapter, as well as additional patterns (see Figure 10.5).

⊡ Ins. statement	✕
○ CALL FUNCTION	
○ ABAP Objects Patterns	
○ MESSAGE	ID	Cat E Number
○ SELECT * FROM	
○ PERFORM	
○ AUTHORITY CHECK	
○ WRITE	
○ CASE for status	
○ Structured Data Object	
⊙ with fields from structure	
○ with TYPE for struct	
○ CALL DIALOG	
⊙ Other Pattern	
	✔ ✕

Figure 10.4 Selecting Other Patterns

Select the relevant pattern from the list—either by double-clicking on it or by highlighting it and clicking the SELECT button—so that the pattern is copied into the selection window. All other steps are the same as described above.

 Complete Insertion of a Structure

→ Chapter 13 provides additional information on function modules.

> Inserting patterns always involves a complete insertion of the entire structure. If, in individual cases, it is easier and faster to write the structure statements manually into the source code, then you're welcome to do so. On the other hand, using patterns for inserting structures ensures a straightforward nesting of the structure across all levels. Later on, when using function modules, you will certainly come to appreciate the use of patterns, because using the insert pattern function to generate the skeleton code for function module calls will save you a lot of work.

```
List of ABAP/4 statement structures

 *
 **
 **1
 **2
 **3
 **4
 **5
 *-*
 *-*1
 *.*
 *F
 *M
 CASE
 DO
 FORM
 FUNCTION
 IF
 LOOP
 MESSAGE
 MODULE
 REPORT
 SELECT
 SELECT-OPTIONS
 SHIFT
 SORT
 SUBMIT
 TRANSFER
 WHILE
 WINDOW
```

Figure 10.5   List Window for Patterns

Branches

A branch corresponds to the "either-or" statement in normal language. The critical factor for your decision is a condition. This condition could simply be a state (for example, "it's raining") or a complex condition that consists of numerous nested conditions (such as "Quality class 1 is regarded as achieved, if quality criteria 1 through n are met. Quality criterion 1 is met if quality attributes 1 through n are met. Quality attribute 1 is met if ...").

Formulating operational conditions

However, what all these cases have in common is that certain actions—statement blocks in the source code—can be processed only if the con-

280

dition is met. Whereas our normal language leaves us some room for interpretation with regard to what a condition looks like and when it is addressed, in ABAP source code, you can only use and check operational (measurable) conditions and states. For this purpose, fields and field contents must either be compared with each other or linked by logical expressions.

When you query field content, you have to ensure that the exact content is used. For the computer, upper-case letters, lower-case letters, the number of blank characters, or the spelling of abbreviations lead to completely different field content. For example, if you search for the field content "sap01" but the actual field content is "SAP01", the required condition is not met.

Taking into account the writing conventions of field content

 Unattractive Notation

As you can imagine, there are numerous options for filling field content in such a way that a human still knows what is meant but, for formal reasons, the computer thinks that the condition is not met. You now might better understand why the unattractive notation with only upper-case letters persists: In a data field that only allows upper-case letters, it's harder to generate double entries or mixed upper- and lower-case entries that cannot be assigned correctly. Consider this when having a look at the screens in this chapter.

IF Structure

In ABAP, the simplest control structure for a branch begins with the IF statement and a condition, and ends with the ENDIF statement. These two statements include the commands that will be executed if the condition is fulfilled. At this point, you merely check a field content, but during the course of this chapter, you'll learn that you can use complex logical expressions for the conditions of the IF structure.

Let's suppose that you want to count only the members of the "SAP01" course. You could do that in the following way: First process all records of the table in the usual way. But whenever a record meets this specific condition, increase the number of members by 1.

IF... ENDIF

```
IF wa_zmember02-zzcoursetitle = 'SAP01'.
```

```
  counter_sap01 = counter_sap01 + 1.
ENDIF.
```

If the content of the field for the course title is "SAP01", the condition is fulfilled and the statement block (in this case, only one line) will be executed. In this way, the program counts how many people will attend the "SAP01" course.

ELSE A branch that follows the principle "either A or B" contains the additional structure statement ELSE, which represents the "or" in the "either-or" case. If the condition of the IF statement is fulfilled, the first statement block is executed; otherwise, it is the second statement block after the ELSE statement that is executed.

In the first statement block of our example, we count the members of the "SAP05" course. In the second statement block, we create a counter for all other members. This means that a count is made in any case. Which counter will be increased simply depends on the condition.

```
IF wa_zmember02-zzcoursetitle = 'SAP05'.
  counter_sap03 = counter_sap03 + 1.
ELSE.
  counter_otherwise = counter_otherwise + 1.
ENDIF.
```

ELSEIF The third method of using an IF statement once again checks a condition. If that condition is not met, a second condition is checked using the ELSEIF statement. If that second condition is not fulfilled, a third condition is checked using the ELSEIF statement, and so on. This process can continue endlessly until you use an ELSE statement to stop it.

Let's look at the following example:

```
IF wa_zmember02-zzcoursetitle = 'SAP01'.
  counter_sap01 = counter_sap01 + 1.
ELSEIF wa_zmember02-zzcoursetitle = 'SAP02'.
  counter_sap02 = counter_sap02 + 1.
ELSEIF wa_zmember02-zzcoursetitle = 'SAP03'.
  counter_sap03 = counter_sap03 + 1.
ELSE.
  counter_otherwise = counter_otherwise + 1.
ENDIF.
```

The first condition is fulfilled if the field for the course title contains the value "SAP01". This means that the members of the "SAP01" course are counted in the first processing block. After that, the system doesn't check any other conditions; instead, it goes directly to ENDIF and continues the program flow with the first statement after the IF structure.

If the first condition is not fulfilled, the program checks whether the second condition is fulfilled (that is, whether the course title is "SAP02"). If the second condition is fulfilled, the second statement block is executed so that the counter for the members of the SAP02 course increases. If the second condition is also not fulfilled, the program checks the third condition ("SAP03"). If this condition is met, the counter for the members of this course increases.

One, two, or three

And if the third condition is also not fulfilled, then the "otherwise" case applies, which means that the counter for those courses and course members increases who haven't been recorded so far. After that, the system goes to the ENDIF statement and then to the next command that follows the IF structure.

 Collective Pit

Simply put, the ELSE statement ensures that at least one condition is always fulfilled: Either the data runs through the processing steps and statement blocks of the IF and ELSEIF structures, or it runs through the statement block for the conditions that haven't been fulfilled up until that point. So the ELSE statement can be regarded as the "collective pit" for all those cases that didn't meet any condition within the structure.

Of course, IF structures can also be nested, but if you do this, you must ensure that the start and end of a structure match each other. Similar to the different parentheses levels in math, you must clearly separate the different nesting levels. The extent to which you want to replace nested IF structures by linking multiple logical expressions depends on your personal way of working, the relevant programming conventions, and the required level of transparency. Let's look at two examples:

Nesting IF structures

Ex   **Example 1: Nested IF Structures**

```
IF condition_1.
  IF condition_2.
*   statement_block_1
  ENDIF.
ENDIF.
```

Ex   **Example 2: Linked Logical Expressions**

```
IF condition_1 AND condition_2.
*  Statement block_1
ENDIF.
```

Logical expressions

Regarding the contents, both examples are identical: `Statement_block_1` is executed only if both conditions are fulfilled.

As a rule, however, transparency comes before genius (that is, it's better to write a simple but readable program than an incredible program that nobody can read). If the linking of logical expressions produces structures that fill several pages on your screen, then remind yourself that third parties will have to understand and modify these structures. In those cases, you should check whether nesting the statements may produce better readability, transparency, and changeability. If so, choose nesting over the linking of logical expressions.

CASE Structure

CASE ... ENDCASE

To describe the `CASE` structure, we should take another look at a real-life situation. Pedestrian traffic lights can show either red or green light. If the light is red, we stop; if the light is green, we walk. Note that we only consider the traffic light; right now, no other condition is relevant to us. (Although the consequences of such tunnel vision can prove fatal in real life, for the purpose of this example, we won't take that into account.)

Like the single-minded pedestrian, the `CASE` structure only "looks at" an object. For the pedestrian, the object is the pedestrian light; for the

CASE structure, the object is a field—a data object. In this context, a case distinction is made and the content of the field is queried. If the condition corresponds to the field content, then—and only then—the associated statement block is executed. A CASE structure only ever processes one statement block. Once the statement block has been processed, the system branches to ENDCASE without checking any other field contents. After that, it proceeds to the first command after the CASE structure, where it continues the program flow.

So while the IF structure can check complex logical conditions, the CASE structure makes case distinctions based on the contents of a single field. In other words, if you use an IF structure, it's possible that it be rainy and sunny at the same time. The CASE structure doesn't allow for this situation; either it rains or the sun is shining.

Differences between IF and CASE structures

As is often the case, it all depends on what you want to do. The CASE structure is always very useful if you can match a condition unambiguously with field content.

Unambiguous correspondence

In the example in which we want to count the members of a course, you could easily use a CASE structure. You want to check the content of table field ZMEMBER02-ZZCOURSETITLE (using the WA_ZMEMBER02 work area; depending on the field content, the program branches to the corresponding statement block.

After that, the system proceeds to the ENDCASE statement and continues the program flow with the first command after the CASE structure. In this context, the structure statement WHEN OTHERS has the same function as the ELSE statement in an IF structure. Just compare the following sample code:

```
CASE wa_zmember02-zzcoursetitle.
  WHEN 'SAP01'.
    counter_sap01 = counter_sap01 + 1.
  WHEN 'SAP05'.
    counter_sap05 = counter_sap05 + 1.
  WHEN OTHERS.
    counter_otherwise =  counter_otherwise + 1.
ENDCASE.
```

Application case:
return code

A typical application case for the CASE structure is the analysis of the return code. It is clear which statement returns a return code, which values can be contained in the return code, and which errors the return code refers to. Depending on the success or failure of a statement, the content of SY-SUBRC is unique; this content is queried using the CASE structure.

Differentiating
error cases

So you can write separate statement blocks for the success case and for all documented error cases. For each ABAP statement, it is defined whether a return code is generated, which return code can be returned, and which error cases it defines. Correspondingly, you can structure the statement blocks. The goal of these efforts is to ensure that the program comes to a "proper" end even if an error occurs, or that it at least initiates alternative processes that make sense.

For example, if you use the SELECT command to search data in a table, the command will return the return code 0 if it was able to read at least one record in the table. If it couldn't read a single record, the statement returns the return code 4. This means that return code 0 is followed by the statement block for the OK case. If the return code is 4, then the error-handling routine is started. Take a look at the following snippet of code:

```
CASE sy-subrc.
  WHEN 0.
*   Okay case
    WRITE: / counter_sap01,
             'booked session SAP01'.
  WHEN 4.
*   Error case
    WRITE: / 'Nobody booked session SAP01'.
WHEN OTHERS.
*   not possible, no other sy-subrc provided by statement.
ENDCASE.
```

Like IF structures, CASE structures can also be nested. Make sure to clearly separate the different levels. You can also combine IF and CASE structures with each other.

Differentiating Various Fields

> Some statements can return a number of different error codes, thus distinguishing between multiple errors that could occur during their execution. Function modules often return distinct error messages as well. CASE structures containing six or eight different error-handling blocks are frequently used in practice.

Loops

Loops, also known as repetitions, are used to execute statement blocks multiple times. In this context, a distinction is made between loops without conditions and those with conditions.

SELECT Loop

You already know the SELECT statement, which is a loop that lets you link a condition to the statement. When reading individual records within a table, you can use a selection condition as a filter and read only the records that fulfill this condition.

SELECT ... ENDSELECT

If you want to read only the records in the member table that are assigned the course title "SAP01", you must write the following lines:

```
SELECT * FROM zmember02
        INTO wa_zmember02
        WHERE zzcoursetitle = 'SAP01'.
  counter_SAP01 = counter_SAP01 + 1.
ENDSELECT.
```

Here, the statement block, which consists of only one line—following the condition that increases the number of members—is executed only for the matching records.

DO Loop

The structure of the DO loop begins with a DO statement and ends with ENDDO. In-between these two statements there is the statement block to be repeated.

DO ... ENDDO

```
DO.
* statement_block
ENDDO.
```

 Beware of Endless Loops!

At this stage, you should be alarmed—the above statement doesn't give any indication as to how the statement block is supposed to be executed, whether it should be repeated endlessly, or when the processing should terminate. But don't worry. In the following sections, we'll describe several options that let you limit the number of loop runs and cancel entire loops.

Condition within the DO loop

The most important aspect about the DO loop is that when it executes the statement block in the structure for the first time, the system doesn't carry out any prior check of a condition. Even if you include a condition for terminating the loop, the commands that are located before the termination condition will be executed at least once. For this reason, the location of the termination condition within the statement block is essential for the program logic.

TIMES

In order to limit the number of loop runs, you can define an upper limit of runs. For example, if you want a loop to be run 12 times, you must use the following statement:

```
DO 12 TIMES.
```

Instead of defining a fixed number of runs, you can also store this value as a variable. For instance, if you assign the MONTHS value of type i the value 6, you can use the following statement:

```
DO months TIMES.
```

The loop will be run six times before the program continues with the first statement after ENDDO.

SY-INDEX

While the statement block is being repeated within the loop, the system automatically executes a loop counter. The SY-INDEX field shows the current value for each loop run (that is, the first run is indicated by the number 1, the second one by number 2, and so on). This loop counter can be very useful for troubleshooting in debugging mode and as a termination condition.

DO loops can be nested, and if they are, the system maintains a separate SY-INDEX field for each level. But here, as well, you should act with care. The nesting of loops can quickly cause a considerable workload on the system, as the following example shows:

```
DO 50 TIMES.
*  statement_block_1
   DO 100 TIMES.
*    statement_block_2
     ENDDO.
ENDDO.
```

The above example contains an inner and an outer loop. The outer loop is executed 50 times. For each run of statement block 1, the inner loop is executed 100 times, which means that statement_block_2 is executed 100 by 50 times (that is, 5,000 times).

Nested DO loops

To better understand how quickly the number of loop runs can sprawl, you can look at a clock (that is, at its flow logic). A day has 24 hours, an hour has 60 minutes, and a minute has 60 seconds. If we map this "program logic" in ABAP, we obtain three nested loops. The center is represented by a statement block, which transmits the calculated time to the display. In this example, the statement block consists of only one line—the WRITE statement as a representation of the display formatting:

Flow logic of the clock

```
DO 24 TIMES.
  minute = 0.
  DO 60 TIMES.
    second = 0.
    DO 60 TIMES.
      WRITE: / hour, minute, second.
             second = second + 1.
    ENDDO.
    minute = minute + 1.
  ENDDO.
  hour = hour + 1.
ENDDO.
```

The core-processing block, which is used to display the time, is executed 60 by 24 times a day (that is, 86,400 times). This would result in a list output containing 86,400 lines. Based on the estimation that one

1,440 pages

page contains 60 lines, the entire list would consist of a total of 1,440 pages! To avoid the possibility of producing a list with so many pages right from the start, you should proceed with utmost care: Thoroughly plan the use of loops, trace the loops using the ABAP Debugger, and include termination conditions.

WHILE Loop

WHILE ...
ENDWHILE

In contrast to the DO loop, the WHILE loop checks a condition before it executes the statement block for the first time. If the condition is met, the statement block will be executed. Then the system checks again whether the condition is still met. If so, the statement block is executed once again, and so on. This process continues endlessly unless the condition is no longer met, for instance, because it was modified within the statement block or a termination condition has been reached.

Condition before
the WHILE loop

The syntax of the WHILE loop is relatively simple. The structure begins with a WHILE statement and a condition, followed by the statement block, which will be executed if the condition is fulfilled. The end of the structure is indicated by an ENDWHILE statement.

```
WHILE condition.
* statement_block
ENDWHILE.
```

Stopwatch

In the following example, a stopwatch runs backwards and starts with a preliminary period in seconds. Once the value for the seconds has counted down to 0, the execution is supposed to begin. If we disregard the issue of how to count the number of quartz vibrations so that a second maps the right time unit in the program, and focus only on the programming logic, the following applies: As long as the number of seconds is greater than 0, one more second should be deducted. So these are the statements for the loop:

```
WHILE second > 0.
  WRITE: / second.
  second = second - 1.
ENDWHILE.
```

Of course, you must set the value for seconds, and the system checks whether the field content is greater than 0 before the loop starts. If so, it outputs the value and deducts it by 1. After that, another check is carried out to determine whether the value is greater than 0, and so on. Once the SECOND field reaches the value 0, the statement will no longer be executed and the program branches to ENDWHILE. Then the system continues to execute the program by processing the first statement after ENDWHILE.

As is the case with the DO loop, the number of loop runs is logged in the SY-INDEX field. SY-INDEX can be read in the statement block and evaluated for the program control.

SY-INDEX

Of course, you can also nest WHILE loops, just as you can nest DO loops. In this context, the descriptions previously provided for the DO loops apply in the same way to the WHILE loops.

 Loop Construction

To determine which loop structure is the most appropriate, you need to decide what you want to do. When constructing loops, you should focus primarily on the basic difference between the two types of loops. If you use a WHILE loop, the system first checks a condition. Only if this condition is met will the system execute the first statement in the loop. If you use a DO loop, the system executes the first statement of the loop without a prior condition check.

Termination Statements for Loops

To terminate loops, you can use various termination statements in ABAP.

The first termination statement, CONTINUE, can only terminate a statement block within a loop. If the CONTINUE statement is located in the middle of a statement block, the remaining statements of this block won't be executed and a new loop run will start, provided the conditions for a new run are still fulfilled. Because the command doesn't check any condition by itself, it is often included in a branch based on whose condition the program flow is controlled. If the condition is fulfilled, the CONTINUE command is executed, the statement block is terminated, and a new run is checked and possibly started. The structure of the CONTINUE statement is relatively simple:

CONTINUE

```
IF condition_1.
  CONTINUE.
ENDIF.
```

For example, in order to process the data records of the course members who were born after January 1, 1985 in the member table, you can write the following lines:

```
SELECT * FROM zmember02 INTO wa_zmember02.
  IF wa_zmember02-mdob LT '19850101'.
    CONTINUE.
  ENDIF.
* statement_block_1
ENDSELECT.
```

LT   The condition that follows the IF statement is a logical expression. LT is the operand for "less than," which is used for comparing the two values with each other. If the system reads a record that contains a date of birth before January 1, 1985, then statement_block_1, which won't be further described here, won't be executed and the next record is read instead. Only the data records containing a date of birth on or after January 1, 1985 will be included in the processing of the statement block.

CHECK   The second termination statement, CHECK, is more powerful. If the statement is executed within a loop, the processing of the statement block terminates and the next loop run starts, provided the relevant conditions are still fulfilled. So we can regard the CHECK statement as a combination of the IF and CONTINUE statements. You can simply write the following:

```
CHECK condition.
```

If the condition is fulfilled, then all statements of the statement block that follow the CHECK command will be executed. However, if the condition is not fulfilled, then all subsequent commands of the statement block will be skipped and a new loop run starts after the conditions have been checked.

Selection by the gender key   If you're interested in the number of male and female course members, for example, you could select the data records in accordance with the gender key:

```
SELECT * FROM zmember02 INTO wa_zmember02.
  CHECK wa_zmember02-mgender = 'F'.
* statement_block
ENDSELECT.
```

A check is then carried out within the loop in order to determine whether the condition is fulfilled. If it is, the statement block will be executed; if not, the next record will be read and checked.

 CHECK Outside of a Loop

Don't be surprised if you find the CHECK statement outside of a loop within the source code. Not only can CHECK terminate loop runs, but you can also use it to check other processing blocks such as methods, subroutines, or events. The CHECK statement has various effects, depending on when and where it is executed: In a loop, it can terminate the current loop run; if it is outside of a loop, the current processing block may be exited. The confusion this may cause is the reason why the use of CHECK outside of loops is regarded as obsolete and should no longer be used in new programs.

The third statement, EXIT, is also rather efficient. Not only does it terminate the statement block, but it terminates the loop processing in its entirety. The system branches to the end of the structure and continues the program execution with the first statement to follow the end of the structure. The command always refers to the level at which it is executed. It terminates the processing at this level and initiates the continuation of the program at the next higher, outer level.

EXIT

For example, if the EXIT statement to be executed is located in the inner loop of two nested loops, the inner loop terminates and the program continues by executing the statement that comes first after the end of the inner loop's structure. In other words, the program continues one level higher (that is, in the outer loop). However, if the EXIT statement is located and executed in the outer loop, then the outer loop terminates and the program continues by executing the first statement to follow the end of the outer loop's structure.

To illustrate the above, let's take another look at the time measurement example. This time, however, we won't execute the time

Deliberate timeout

measurement completely, but will terminate the loops using the EXIT statement in order to see what happens. The innermost of the three loops contains a statement block. If the value of SY-INDEX for the innermost loop is 3, then that loop terminates and the system branches to the second loop. However, the statement block was executed prior to that. If the value of SY-INDEX for the middle loop is 3, then the subsequent statements of the middle loop won't be executed, which means that the third loop and its statement block will be skipped. The system goes to the outer loop and starts the next loop run at that level. If the value of SY-INDEX for the outer loop is also 3, then this loop will terminate as well.

```
DO 24 TIMES.
  IF sy-index = 3.
      EXIT.
  ENDIF.
  minute = 0.
  DO 60 TIMES.
    IF sy-index = 3.
      EXIT.
    ENDIF.
    second = 0.
    DO 60 TIMES.
*       statement_block
      second = second + 1.
      IF sy-index = 3.
        EXIT.
      ENDIF.
    ENDDO.
    minute = minute + 1.
  ENDDO.
  hour = hour + 1.
ENDDO.
```

Termination conditions are context-sensitive

As is the case with the CHECK statement, the effect of the EXIT statement depends on the structure (that is, on the level at which it is executed). If the statement is run within a loop, then the loop will terminate. If the statement is executed in a method or subroutine, then the processing block terminates and the program continues to run in the parent structure of that block. The same holds true for events. If you execute an EXIT command in an event, then the event terminates and the system continues by processing the next event. This double function of the EXIT command can easily lead to errors if an EXIT statement that previously was in a loop is now—after a program modification—outside of a loop so that the subroutine or method is exited. To clarify the developer's intention, you should use the RETURN statement to exit a subroutine or method.

If no other events have been defined or statements provided, then the program will terminate. There are more options available with regard to terminating events, but we won't elaborate on them here.

 For All Loop Types

> The termination conditions described here work in the same way with all loop types. For this reason, we provided only one example for each termination condition.

Logical Expressions

In reality, we must always make decisions. However, human decisions are not always logical. But until computers intuitively understand what we want, we have to formulate clear, measurable, and reproducible conditions for a program flow.

This ... or that?

 The Difficulty of Mapping Complexities

> Admittedly, it is difficult to map the complex processes of everyday life or business life on a logical program-based level. When doing so, you must ensure that different contents are mapped and that different data types and field contents can be compared with each other. You also have to anticipate system reactions.

Simple Logical Expressions

Let us first take a look at the *logical operators* in Table 10.1. These logical operators allow you to formulate conditions in order to compare two fields. Example:

Logical operators

```
IF NUMBER01 > NUMBER02.
* statement_block
ENDIF.
```

Provided that the attributes of the two fields are compatible or convertible, the condition is met if the content of NUMBER01 is greater than the content of the NUMBER02 field and the statement block will be executed. In the source code, you can either use logical operators or the corresponding symbols for the logical expressions.

Logical Operator	Symbol	Description
EQ	=	equal to
NE	<>	not equal to
LT	<	less than
LE	<=	less than or equal to
GT	>	greater than
GE	>=	greater than or equal to

Table 10.1 Logical Operators for Data Objects

Automatic type conversion

However, the greater the difference between the fields to be compared, the more important it is to know the system-internal conversion rules. Type c strings of different lengths, for example, are compared from left to right, according to the relevant code table. This sounds rather simple, but do you always know the exact position of a blank or special character in the code table in relation to the lowercase letters, and do you know whether the lexical sort order is identical to the code table? Dealing with these details can be quite confusing and annoying.

If the data types are different, the system carries out an automatic type conversion prior to the comparison. For example, if you want to compare a type c field with a type n field, both fields are converted into type p prior to the comparison. But even here, the system may surprise you. Theoretically, it works without a problem, but if you don't know or adhere to the rules, things won't go so smoothly. So try to harmonize the attributes of the fields that you want to compare.

Special Logical Operators

> Special logical operators are available for character strings. You can use
> them to formulate conditions in order to find out whether a string con-
> tains certain characters and so on. Other operators are available for other
> specific tasks. In this context, however, only the check for an initial value
> of a field and the check for an interval are worth mentioning.

The condition that a subtask should only be executed if the field value **IS INITIAL**
is initial is used relatively often. In this context, the specific task that
you want to perform determines whether the initial value remains unchanged from the start, or whether it is set using a statement during
the program execution, as was the case in our previous examples.

In both cases, the statement block should be executed under this
condition:

```
IF number01 IS INITIAL.
* statement_block
ENDIF.
```

The statement block is only processed if the field content of NUMBER01
is the initial value. If the field already has content, then the condition
is not fulfilled and the statement block will not be executed.

During a check for an interval, the field content is checked for a lower **BETWEEN**
and an upper limit. If the field content lies between or on one of the
two limits, the condition is met and the statement block will be executed. The upper and lower limits of the interval can be specified
either as literals or as variables; if the limits are specified as variables,
the limit values—that is, the field contents—that you define must make
sense (for example, the value of an upper limit must be higher than
the value of a lower limit).

If, in our example, we want to start a specific processing run for the
members who were born in 1984, then we must check whether the date
of birth lies within the period between 01/01/1984 and 12/31/1984. If
this condition is fulfilled, the statement block should be executed.

```
IF wa_zmember02-mdob
    BETWEEN '19840101' AND '19841231'.
*    statement_block
ENDIF.
```

If a person's birthday is exactly on January 1, 1984 or on December 31, 1984, the condition is also fulfilled for that person, and the corresponding data record will be processed in the statement block.

Linked Logical Expressions

Your work can get really exciting if you want to or have to map complex conditions by linking multiple logical expressions. This is somewhat like walking a tightrope; on one hand, you have to map the complexity, and on the other, you need to maintain the transparency, readability, and changeability of the source code. For this purpose, you should primarily obey the rules for linking logical expressions.

 OR in Real Life

If you use two conditions and the logical OR as the linking operator, one or both of the two conditions must be fulfilled in order for the statement block to be processed. Let's suppose that you want to borrow and read a book. You know two people and ask both of them if you can borrow it. You can borrow the book and read it if only one person lends it to you, or if both of them do.

In ABAP, the logical OR is mapped by the OR operand. The basic structure is the same as with the simple IF: There is the branch structure, IF...ENDIF, and the condition c1.

```
IF c1.
* statement_block
ENDIF.
```

The only difference is that c1 is made up of other conditions (such as c2, c3, and so on), which are linked with each other using a logical operand, as in this example:

```
c1 = c2 OR c3
```

Parenthesized levels This way of resolving conditions can continue in any way. It can be combined with other logical operands and can contain multiple parenthetical levels. As a result, you can map very complex conditions; however, few people can continue can this kind of activity as long as a machine can. If these conditions fill multiple screen pages, you can quickly lose sight of the big picture. Since small changes to logical expressions can have a huge impact on the program flow, you should always consider the principles of readability, transparency, and changeability of the source code.

If you want to process the data records of all members of the courses "SAP03" and "SAP04" in a separate statement block, you should formulate the logical OR condition like this:

```
IF wa_zmember02-zzcoursetitle = 'SAP03' OR
   wa_zmember02-zzcoursetitle = 'SAP04'.
*    statement_block
ENDIF.
```

The field that is assigned the course title must either contain "SAP03" or "SAP04" so that the condition is fulfilled. The way in which the condition is structured ensures that the field cannot meet both conditions at the same time. This would require two different fields.

The link established by the logical AND is more rigid than that of the logical OR. If you use two conditions, this means that both conditions must be met at the same time in order for the statement block to process. If you want to go on a vacation, you need both time and money. If either time or money is missing, you can't go.

AND

In ABAP, the logical AND is represented by the AND operand. Let's look at another simple example. Suppose that you want to process the data records of all male members in course SAP03 in a separate statement block. The corresponding ABAP source code would look like this:

```
IF wa_zmember02-mgender = 'M' AND
   wa_zmember02-zzcoursetitle = 'SAP03'.
*    statement_block
ENDIF.
```

There are two fields—one for the gender and one for the course title—and both of them must have a specific content to meet the condition so that the data records are processed by the statement block.

An even more rigid link is established by the NOT operator, which represents a negation. If you've ever received queries such as "Don't you want

NOT

to save this change?", then you know what the problem of a negation is. Many people find it difficult to answer negated queries and conditions, particularly in complex situations and when they are under pressure. For this reason, avoid using negations as much as possible in your daily work. Instead, use positive formulations wherever possible.

 Negations Are Not Always Avoidable

> How many negations do you find in the header of this box? Seriously, sometimes you cannot avoid using negations (for example, in the context of queries on initial field values). As you have seen, it's not hard to query whether or not a field has an initial value. But it's almost impossible to check all field contents that may exist. Sometimes it's enough to know that a field contains a value that differs from the initial value—in other words, that it does not contain the initial value—in order to execute a statement block.

With regard to the structure of the formulation, you should note that the negation NOT must always be placed before the condition. If a statement block is supposed to be executed only if the condition c1 is *not* fulfilled, the corresponding line would look like this:

```
IF NOT c1.
```

In the following example, we want to process the data records of all members that do not attend any SAP courses in a separate block. Consequently, you must write the following ABAP lines:

```
IF NOT wa_zmember02-zzcoursetitle(3) = 'SAP'.
*    statement_block
ENDIF.
```

The condition is that the first three characters of the course title *not* be "SAP" for the data records to be processed by the statement block. ·

To conclude this section, combine your new knowledge about linking logical expressions in a small example.

 Leap Years

> Determine whether a year is a leap year.

In our calendar, a year is considered a leap year if the number of days it contains can be divided by 4 in an integer division without a remainder. Whenever it can be divided by 100 without a remainder, it is not a leap year. However, it *is* a leap year if it can be divided by 400 without a remainder.

366 days—but when?

To implement this in ABAP, we must first create three conditions:

> `c1`: The year can be divided by 400 without remainder.
> `c2`: The year can be divided by 100 without remainder.
> `c3`: The year can be divided by 4 without remainder.

A year is a leap year if `c1` or `c3` is fulfilled, but in that case, `c2` must not be fulfilled. Using a shorter and clearer notation, the condition can be formulated as follows:

```
c1 OR c3 AND NOT c2
```

We don't need to include any parentheses here because in the hierarchical order of the operands, the negation establishes the strongest link; the logical AND is the second strongest operator, and the logical OR is the weakest one. But if you want to improve the overall readability, you may, of course, use parentheses. In that case, the condition would read as follows:

```
c1 OR (c3 AND NOT c2)
```

You should note that by placing the parentheses in different positions, you can change the entire logic of the condition.

For the final implementation in ABAP, you could use separate fields to store the results of the checks as to whether or not a year can be divided in an integer division without a remainder. The condition could then read like this:

```
IF year400 = 0 OR ( year004 = 0 AND NOT year100 = 0 ).
*   statement_block
ENDIF.
```

The sample code for `WHILE` and logical expressions in this chapter has further explanations on this topic.

Sample Code for IF

Listing 10.1 demonstrates the use of the IF statement for control flow.

```
1   *&---------------------------------------------------------*
2   *& Report   Z_MEMBERLIST10_IF                              *
3   *&                                                          *
4   *&---------------------------------------------------------*
5   *&                                                          *
6   *&                                                          *
7   *&---------------------------------------------------------*
8
9   REPORT   z_memberlist10_if.
10
11  * Define work area
12  DATA wa_zmember02 TYPE zmember02.
13
14  * Define fields
15  DATA: counter_sap01      TYPE i,
16        counter_sap02      TYPE i,
17        counter_sap03      TYPE i,
18        counter_sap05      TYPE i,
19        counter_otherwise TYPE i,
20        counter_all        TYPE i.
21
22  * Display content of table
23  SELECT * FROM zmember02 INTO wa_zmember02.
24    WRITE: / wa_zmember02-mnumber,
25             wa_zmember02-mname,
26             wa_zmember02-mdob,
27             wa_zmember02-mgender,
28             wa_zmember02-mfee,
29             wa_zmember02-mcurrency,
30             wa_zmember02-zzcartype,
31             wa_zmember02-zzcoursetitle.
32  ENDSELECT.
33  SKIP.
34
35  * Select table content under condition
36  SELECT * FROM zmember02 INTO wa_zmember02
37             WHERE zzcoursetitle = 'SAP04'.
38    WRITE: / wa_zmember02-mnumber,
39             wa_zmember02-mname,
```

```
40              wa_zmember02-mdob,
41              wa_zmember02-mgender,
42              wa_zmember02-zzcoursetitle.
43   ENDSELECT.
44
45   * Select all records but process records under condition
46   SELECT * FROM zmember02 INTO wa_zmember02.
47     IF wa_zmember02-zzcoursetitle = 'SAP01'.
48       counter_sap01 = counter_sap01 + 1.
49     ENDIF.
50   ENDSELECT.
51   SKIP.
52   WRITE: / counter_sap01, 'booked session SAP01'.
53
54   * Select all records, calculating a subtotal and total
55   SELECT * FROM zmember02 INTO wa_zmember02.
56     IF wa_zmember02-zzcoursetitle = 'SAP05'.
57       counter_sap03 = counter_sap03 + 1.
58     ELSE.
59       counter_otherwise = counter_otherwise + 1.
60     ENDIF.
61   ENDSELECT.
62   counter_all = counter_sap05 + counter_otherwise.
63   SKIP.
64   WRITE: / counter_all, 'Members total.',
65          / counter_sap05, 'booked session SAP05.',
66          / counter_otherwise, 'booked other sessions'.
67
68   * Initialize reused counters
69   CLEAR: counter_sap02,
70          counter_sap01,
71          counter_sap03,
72          counter_otherwise.
73
74   * Select all records, calculating subtotals and total
75   SELECT * FROM zmember02 INTO wa_zmember02.
76     IF wa_zmember02-zzcoursetitle = 'SAP01'.
77       counter_sap01 = counter_sap01 + 1.
78     ELSEIF wa_zmember02-zzcoursetitle = 'SAP02'.
79       counter_sap02 = counter_sap02 + 1.
80     ELSEIF wa_zmember02-zzcoursetitle = 'SAP03'.
81       counter_sap03 = counter_sap03 + 1.
82     ELSE.
83       counter_otherwise = counter_otherwise + 1.
```

```
84    ENDIF.
85  ENDSELECT.
86
87  SKIP.
88  WRITE: / 'Distribution of persons to the sessions:',
89         / counter_sap01, 'SAP01',
90         / counter_sap02, 'SAP02',
91         / counter_sap03, 'SAP03',
92         / counter_otherwise, 'other sessions'.
```

Listing 10.1 Report Z_MEMBERLIST10_if

Notes on the Source Code

Lines 35 to 42

Only the data records that fulfill the condition that the course title field contain the value "SAP01" will be processed. This processing is simulated by a list output.

 Advantage: Preselection

> This preselection is a significant advantage because it is very efficient in specific situations. As you can imagine, the larger the table, the more useful it is to be able to select only the "right" data records from the table. The drawback of this type of selection with a condition could be that the other data records, which might also have to be processed, aren't read and consequently are unavailable for processing. It all depends on what you want to do.

Lines 45 to 49

All records of the table are read. You could use a statement block between lines 45 and 46, which apply to all data records. In addition, the records that meet the condition "SAP01" are processed by a separate statement block and are counted.

Line 52

Key principle

Here you can see an important principle, though perhaps only at second glance. A loop runs in lines 45 to 49. The number of members of the "SAP01" course is calculated in lines 47 to 49 in this loop. The output of the result—that is, the total number of course members—occur after the loop because if the result was output within the loop, it would represent only a preliminary result. This may be useful in other situations, but not here. Remember the following:

> *Calculating* totals: always *within* the loop

> *Outputting* totals: always *after* the loop

Lines 55 to 61
Again, all data records of the tab are read, and two totals are calculated. If the field `WA_ZMEMBER02-ZZCOURSETITLE` contains the value "SAP05", the total number of members of this course increases. Otherwise, the total number of members of other courses will increase.

Lines 62 to 66
The overall total is created from both group totals. The list contains the total number of course members, the number of members in course "SAP05", and the number of members in other courses.

Lines 69 to 72
The totals fields are needed for future examples, which is why they are initialized here.

Lines 76 to 85
All data records of the database table are selected. For each record, the conditions are checked one after the other. If a record fulfills the first condition, then the first statement block is executed and the system branches to ENDIF. If the record does not fulfill the first condition, the system checks whether it fulfills the second condition and so on. A distinction is made between several cases, and group totals are built for the courses "SAP01", "SAP02", and "SAP03". The remaining course members are included in the total for other courses.

Lines 88 to 92
The group totals and corresponding texts are written into the list after the SELECT loop.

Program Output

Enhancing
readability
using SKIP

For control purposes, all records of the table are read first. Our example contains 8 records (see Figure 10.6). After that, the hits are output via the SELECT statement and associated condition, followed by the output of group totals for the individual examples. To improve readability, the SKIP command was used to insert blank lines, while other optical formatting methods were deliberately not used.

```
00001 ARMSTRONG           01.01.2001 M      100,00 AUD  SUV         SAP01
00002 BECK                02.02.2002 F      200,00 CAD  SEDAN       SAP01
00003 Cash                03.03.1983 M      301,00 EUR  SUV         SAP03
00004 Davis               04.04.1984 F      401,00 JPY  Pick Up     SAP04
00005 Ellington           05.05.1985 M      501,00 USD  Station W.  SAP05
00006 Ellington           05.05.1985 M      501,00 USD  Station W.  SAP05
00007 Ellington           05.05.1985 M      501,00 USD  Station W.  SAP05
00008 Feliciano           06.06.1986 F      600,00 RUB  Compact Ca  SAP06

00004 Davis               04.04.1984 F SAP04

        2  booked session SAP01

        8  Members total.
        3  booked session SAP05.
        5  booked other sessions

Distribution of persons to the sessions:
        2  SAP01
        0  SAP02
        1  SAP03
        5  other sessions
```

Figure 10.6 List Screen for IF Example

Sample Code for CASE

Listing 10.2 demonstrates the use of the CASE statement to differentiate between multiple branches.

```
1   *&--------------------------------------------------------*
2   *& Report   Z_MEMBERLIST10_CASE                           *
3   *&                                                        *
4   *&--------------------------------------------------------*
5   *&                                                        *
```

```
6    *&                                                        *
7    *&------------------------------------------------------*
8
9    REPORT   z_memberlist10_case.
10
11   * Define work area
12   DATA wa_zmember02 TYPE zmember02.
13
14   * Define fields
15   DATA: counter_sap01     TYPE i,
16         counter_sap03     TYPE i,
17         counter_sap05     TYPE i,
18         counter_otherwise TYPE i.
19
20   * Display content of table
21   SELECT * FROM zmember02 INTO wa_zmember02.
22     WRITE: / wa_zmember02-mnumber,
23              wa_zmember02-mname,
24              wa_zmember02-mdob,
25              wa_zmember02-mgender,
26              wa_zmember02-mfee,
27              wa_zmember02-mcurrency,
28              wa_zmember02-zzcartype,
29              wa_zmember02-zzcoursetitle.
30   ENDSELECT.
31
32   * Select all records, calculating subtotals
33   SELECT * FROM zmember02 INTO wa_zmember02.
34     CASE wa_zmember02-zzcoursetitle.
35       WHEN 'SAP01'.
36         counter_sap01 = counter_sap01 + 1.
37       WHEN 'SAP05'.
38         counter_sap05 = counter_sap05 + 1.
39       WHEN OTHERS.
40         counter_otherwise = counter_otherwise + 1.
41     ENDCASE.
42   ENDSELECT.
43   SKIP.
44   WRITE: / 'Distribution of persons to the sessions:',
45          / counter_sap01, 'SAP01',
46          / counter_sap05, 'SAP05',
47          / counter_otherwise, 'other sessions'.
48   SKIP.
49
```

```
50  * Initialize reused counters
51  CLEAR: counter_sap01.
52
53  * Control return code of SELECT statement with CASE
54  SELECT * FROM zmember02 INTO wa_zmember02.
55         WHERE zzcoursetitle = 'SAP01'.
56    counter_sap01 = counter_sap01 + 1.
57  ENDSELECT.
58  CASE sy-subrc.
59    WHEN 0. "record(s) found
60      WRITE: / counter_sap01, 'booked session SAP01'.
61    WHEN 4. "no record found
62      WRITE: / 'nobody booked session SAP01'.
63    WHEN OTHERS.
64  * not possible, no other sy-subrc provided by statement
65  ENDCASE.
```

Listing 10.2   Report Z_MEMBERLIST10_CASE

Notes on the Source Code

Lines 32 to 41
All records of the member table are read. Depending on the content of the course title field, the counters for the different courses (that is, "SAP01", "SAP05", and other courses) are increased.

Lines 43 to 46
The group totals are output after the SELECT loop. Again, we apply the principle that we increase the totals *within* the loop, whereas we output the totals *after* the loop.

Line 49
The group totals field for members of the "SAP01" course will be filled once again in the following section, and therefore must be initialized at this point.

Lines 52 to 55
All table records that meet the condition that the course title field contain the value "SAP01" are read. The content of the table is manipulated

in such a way that one program run contains hits, whereas no hits can occur in a second program run.

Lines 57 to 66

Immediately after the SELECT statement has finished, its return code is evaluated using the CASE structure. The return code must always be evaluated immediately after the command, whose return code is supposed to be evaluated. If a different command, which also provides a return code, were placed between the CASE structure that begins in line 58 and the ENDSELECT command in line 57, for which the return code is supposed to be evaluated, we would have a problem. We would query the "wrong" return code with the CASE structure. So to be on the safe side, don't place any other statements between the two, or use a statement that doesn't meet SY-SUBRC. Fortunately, the SKIP command is one such command.

The CASE structure in this example distinguishes between an OK case and an error case. If the value of SY-SUBRC is 0, the table readout contains hits. In this case, statements are processed for these hits in the first statement block. In the example, the statement block contains only one statement, but it could also contain the call of a subroutine (or something similar) and map the "normal" processing.

OK case and error case

The CASE structure considers it an error case if the value of SY-SUBRC is 4. The SELECT statement returns the return code if no hit was found during the readout of the table records. Our example does not have any record whose course title field contains the value "SAP01" because those table entries were deleted prior to the program start.

Consequently, the statement block for the SY-SUBRC with content 4 is executed. In this example, the error-handling process merely consists of a different list output, but in real life, error handling can be as complex as the "normal" processing run.

Program Output

The upper section of the two list screens displays the complete table content. Figure 10.7 shows two members for the "SAP01" course, which is why the third SELECT statement ends with return code 0 and

the "normal" processing run is executed. This creates the last line of
the list.

```
00001 ARMSTRONG            01.01.2001 M    100,00  AUD   SUV          SAP01
00002 BECK                 02.02.2002 F    200,00  CAD   SEDAN        SAP01
00003 Cash                 03.03.1983 M    301,00  EUR   SUV          SAP03
00004 Davis                04.04.1984 F    401,00  JPY   Pick Up      SAP04
00005 Ellington            05.05.1985 M    501,00  USD   Station W.   SAP05
00006 Ellington            05.05.1985 M    501,00  USD   Station W.   SAP05
00007 Ellington            05.05.1985 M    501,00  USD   Station W.   SAP05
00008 Feliciano            06.06.1986 F    600,00  RUB   Compact Ca   SAP06

Distribution of persons to the sessions:
      2   SAP01
      3   SAP05
      3   other sessions

      2   booked session SAP01
```

Figure 10.7 List Screen for CASE Example with Return Code 0 for the Third SELECT
Statement

No members found   In the second list screen in Figure 10.8, you can see that the table contains no members for course "SAP01". For this reason, the third SELECT
statement returns return code 4 so that the statement block for this
error case is executed. Consequently, the last line of the output reads
that nobody booked this course.

```
00003 Cash                 03.03.1983 M    301,00  EUR   SUV          SAP03
00004 Davis                04.04.1984 F    401,00  JPY   Pick Up      SAP04
00005 Ellington            05.05.1985 M    501,00  USD   Station W.   SAP05
00006 Ellington            05.05.1985 M    501,00  USD   Station W.   SAP05
00007 Ellington            05.05.1985 M    501,00  USD   Station W.   SAP05
00008 Feliciano            06.06.1986 F    600,00  RUB   Compact Ca   SAP06

Distribution of persons to the sessions:
      0   SAP01
      3   SAP05
      3   other sessions

nobody booked session SAP01
```

Figure 10.8 List Screen for CASE Example with Return Code 4 for the Third SELECT
Statement

Sample Code for DO and Termination Conditions

Listing 10.3 demonstrates how to use loops to control the flow of the program.

```
 1   *&---------------------------------------------------*
 2   *& Report   Z_MEMBERLIST10_DO                        *
 3   *&                                                   *
 4   *&---------------------------------------------------*
 5   *&                                                   *
 6   *&                                                   *
 7   *&---------------------------------------------------*
 8
 9   REPORT   z_memberlist10_do.
10
11   * Define work area
12   DATA: wa_zmember02 TYPE zmember02.
13
14   * Define fields
15   DATA: second TYPE i,
16         minute TYPE i,
17         hour   TYPE i.
18
19   * Display content of table
20   SELECT * FROM zmember02 INTO wa_zmember02.
21     WRITE: / wa_zmember02-mnumber,
22              wa_zmember02-mname,
23              wa_zmember02-mdob,
24              wa_zmember02-mgender,
25              wa_zmember02-mfee,
26              wa_zmember02-mcurrency,
27              wa_zmember02-zzcartype,
28              wa_zmember02-zzcoursetitle.
29   ENDSELECT.
30   SKIP.
31
32   * Select all records but process records under condition
33   SELECT * FROM zmember02 INTO wa_zmember02.
34     IF wa_zmember02-mdob LT '19850101'.
35       CONTINUE.
36     ENDIF.
37     WRITE: / wa_zmember02-mnumber,
38              wa_zmember02-mname,
39              wa_zmember02-mdob,
```

```
40              wa_zmember02-mgender,
41              wa_zmember02-mfee,
42              wa_zmember02-mcurrency,
43              wa_zmember02-zzcartype,
44              wa_zmember02-zzcoursetitle.
45   ENDSELECT.
46   SKIP.
47
48   SELECT * FROM zmember02 INTO wa_zmember02.
49     CHECK wa_zmember02-mgender = 'F'.
50     WRITE: / wa_zmember02-mnumber,
51              wa_zmember02-mname,
52              wa_zmember02-mdob,
53              wa_zmember02-mgender,
54              wa_zmember02-mfee,
55              wa_zmember02-mcurrency,
56              wa_zmember02-zzcartype,
57              wa_zmember02-zzcoursetitle.
58   ENDSELECT.
59
60   * Example for logical watch with exit statement
61   WRITE: / hour, minute, second. "sy-index.
62   SKIP.
63   DO 24 TIMES.
64     IF sy-index = 3.
65       EXIT.
66     ENDIF.
67     minute = 0.
68     DO 60 TIMES.
69       IF sy-index = 3.
70         EXIT.
71       ENDIF.
72       second = 0.
73       DO 60 TIMES.              "seconds
74         WRITE: / hour, minute, second.
75         second = second + 1.
76         IF sy-index = 3.
77           EXIT.
78         ENDIF.
79       ENDDO.                    "seconds
80       minute = minute + 1.
81     ENDDO.                      "minutes
```

```
 82    hour = hour + 1.
 83   ENDDO.                          "hours
 84   SKIP.
 85   WRITE: / hour, minute, second.
 86
 87   * Program abort, otherwise a list with 86400 lines
 88   EXIT.
 89
 90   * Initialize reused fields
 91   CLEAR: second,
 92          minute,
 93          hour.
 94   * Example for logical watch for one day
 95   WRITE: / hour, minute, second.
 96   SKIP.
 97   DO 24 TIMES.
 98     minute = 0.
 99     DO 60 TIMES.
100       second = 0.
101       DO 60 TIMES.
102         WRITE: / hour, minute, second.
103         second = second + 1.
104       ENDDO.
105       minute = minute + 1.
106     ENDDO.
107     hour = hour + 1.
108   ENDDO.
109   SKIP.
110   WRITE: / hour, minute, second.
```

Listing 10.3   Report Z_MEMBERLIST10_DO

Notes on the Source Code

We cannot repeat it often enough: When using literals, you should note that case sensitivity and the adherence to form is critical. For example, if you want to check whether the gender key is male, the correct way to do that is to use a capital M. If the field happens to contain a lowercase m, the record will be treated differently in the condition. So be as discerning as possible when dealing with literals that are checked against date fields, as well as with all character strings.

Case sensitivity

For All Loops

Basically, the termination conditions we have described can be executed in all ABAP loops. If the effects of a termination condition are described based on a specific loop, this applies to all other ABAP loops as well.

Lines 33 to 45

All records of the table are read. It is conceivable that each record between lines 33 and 34 was processed by a general statement block. After that, the condition as to whether the date of birth is less (that is, earlier than 01/01/1985) is checked in line 34. If the condition is met, the system terminates processing the respective data record and starts reading the subsequent one. Only if the date of birth is greater (that is, later than 01/01/1985) will a record be passed on to the processing block between lines 37 and 44. If the date of birth falls on 01/01/1985, the data record will also be passed on.

Lines 48 to 58

Again, all records of the table are read in a loop. In line 49, the current data record is checked to see whether the GENDER field contains the gender key F. If it does, all subsequent statements in lines 50 to 57 will be executed; otherwise, the system terminates processing the record and begins reading the subsequent one. In other words, the statements in lines 50 to 57 are executed only for the records of female course members, and data records of male members will not be processed.

Lines 65 to 86

From inside to outside

The termination control via SY-INDEX ensures that the loops for hours, minutes, and seconds aren't really processed 24 or 60 times, respectively. To demonstrate this, the processing run is terminated and exited in each loop once the value of SY-INDEX is 3. This control function works "from the inside, out," so to speak. As soon as SY-INDEX for the seconds loop has the value 3, the seconds loop terminates and the system continues by executing the minutes loop. Once the value of SY-INDEX for the minutes loop is 3, the system terminates the minutes loop and executes the hours loop. When SY-INDEX for the hours loop has reached the value 3, the system terminates this loop as well and continues executing the program from line 87 onwards.

Line 88
The EXIT command is located outside of a loop. The program terminates immediately and the system processes the list output. If you want the subsequent program lines to be executed, you must invalidate line 88 (for example, by turning it into a comment line).

Lines 97 to 108
A simple flow logic for nesting hours, minutes, and seconds could be structured as shown here. When executing this part of the program, don't be surprised by the long runtime. As you know, it may take awhile to process the 86,400 seconds in each day.

Program Output

For better reproducibility, the system first lists all table records (see Figure 10.9). The second block of the list contains the data records of course members who were born on or after January 1, 1985. The third section of the list contains the data records of female course members.

The figure columns in the last section of the list represent the list output for hours, minutes, and seconds. Because of the limitation of SY-INDEX and the loop termination, there are two hours in a day, two minutes in an hour, and three seconds in a minute.

The position of the termination condition within the loop determines whether or not (and to what extent) the processing of data records takes place within the loop; the position of the WRITE command in the loop defines whether the values that are calculated last will be included in the list. For example, try to place the list output and termination conditions in different positions and see what happens. You can play around with that a little, but just make sure that you don't accidentally produce an endless loop.

```
00003 Cash               03.03.1983 M    301,00  EUR   SUV          SAP03
00004 Davis              04.04.1984 F    401,00  JPY   Pick Up      SAP04
00005 Ellington         05.05.1985 M    501,00  USD   Station W.   SAP05
00006 Ellington         05.05.1985 M    501,00  USD   Station W.   SAP05
00007 Ellington         05.05.1985 M    501,00  USD   Station W.   SAP05
00008 Feliciano         06.06.1986 F    600,00  RUB   Compact Ca   SAP06

00005 Ellington         05.05.1985 M    501,00  USD   Station W.   SAP05
00006 Ellington         05.05.1985 M    501,00  USD   Station W.   SAP05
00007 Ellington         05.05.1985 M    501,00  USD   Station W.   SAP05
00008 Feliciano         06.06.1986 F    600,00  RUB   Compact Ca   SAP06

00004 Davis              04.04.1984 F    401,00  JPY   Pick Up      SAP04
00008 Feliciano         06.06.1986 F    600,00  RUB   Compact Ca   SAP06
        0          0          0

        0          0          0
        0          0          1
        0          0          2
        0          1          0
        0          1          1
        0          1          2
        1          0          0
        1          0          1
        1          0          2
        1          1          0
        1          1          1
        1          1          2

        2          2          3
```

Figure 10.9 List Screen for DO Example and Termination Conditions

Due to the EXIT command in line 88, there is no list output for the nested loops for hours, minutes, and seconds. Otherwise, the list would be slightly longer.

Sample Code for WHILE and Logical Expressions

Listing 10.4 demonstrates how to use the WHILE command for conditional loops.

```
1  *&---------------------------------------------------*
2  *& Report   Z_MEMBERLIST10_WHILE
3  *&                                                    *
```

```
 4  *&---------------------------------------------------*
 5  *&                                                   *
 6  *&                                                   *
 7  *&---------------------------------------------------*
 8
 9  REPORT  z_memberlist10_while.
10
11  * Define work area
12  DATA wa_zmember02 TYPE zmember02.
13
14  * Define fields
15  DATA: year004 TYPE i,
16        year100 TYPE i,
17        year400 TYPE i,
18        second  TYPE i.
19
20  * Define field value
21  second = 10.
22
23  * Decremental stopwatch
24  WHILE second > 0.
25    WRITE: second.
26    second = second - 1.
27  ENDWHILE.
28  WRITE: / second.
29  SKIP.
30
31  * Display content of table
32  SELECT * FROM zmember02 INTO wa_zmember02.
33    WRITE: / wa_zmember02-mnumber,
34             wa_zmember02-mname,
35             wa_zmember02-mdob,
36             wa_zmember02-mgender,
37             wa_zmember02-mfee,
38             wa_zmember02-mcurrency,
39             wa_zmember02-zzcartype,
40             wa_zmember02-zzcoursetitle.
41  ENDSELECT.
42  SKIP.
43
44  * Select all records and check field value for initial
45  SELECT * FROM zmember02 INTO wa_zmember02.
46    IF wa_zmember02-mdob IS INITIAL.
47      WRITE: / wa_zmember02-mnumber, wa_zmember02-mname,
```

```
48                   'Day of birth is missing, please maintain'.
49     ENDIF.
50  ENDSELECT.
51  SKIP.
52
53  * Select all records and check field value for interval
54  SELECT * FROM zmember02 INTO wa_zmember02.
55    IF wa_zmember02-dob BETWEEN '19840101' AND '19841231'.
56      WRITE: / wa_zmember02-mnumber, wa_zmember02-mname,
57                 wa_zmember02-mdob.
58    ENDIF.
59  ENDSELECT.
60  SKIP.
61
62  * Select all records and check logical OR
63  SELECT * FROM zmember02 INTO wa_zmember02.
64    IF wa_zmember02-zzcoursetitle = 'SAP03' OR
65       wa_zmember02-zzcoursetitle = 'SAP04'.
66      WRITE: / wa_zmember02-mnumber, wa_zmember02-mname,
67                 wa_zmember02-zzcoursetitle.
68    ENDIF.
69  ENDSELECT.
70  SKIP.
71
72  * Select all records and check logical AND
73  SELECT * FROM zmember02 INTO wa_zmember02.
74    IF wa_zmember02-mgender       = 'M' AND
75       wa_zmember02-zzcoursetitle = 'SAP03'.
76      WRITE: / wa_zmember02-mnumber, wa_zmember02-mname,
77                 wa_zmember02-mgender, wa_zmember02-zzcoursetitle.
78    ENDIF.
79  ENDSELECT.
80  SKIP.
81
82  * Select all records and check logical NOT
83  SELECT * FROM zmember02 INTO wa_zmember02.
84    IF NOT wa_zmember02-zzcoursetitle(3) = 'SAP'.
85      WRITE: / wa_zmember02-mnumber, wa_zmember02-zzcoursetitle.
86    ENDIF.
87  ENDSELECT.
88  SKIP.
89
90  * Select all records and check leap year
```

```
91  SELECT * FROM zmember02 INTO wa_zmember02.
92    year004 = wa_zmember02-mdob(4) MOD 4.
93    year100 = wa_zmember02-mdob(4) MOD 100.
94    year400 = wa_zmember02-mdob(4) MOD 400.
95    IF NOT wa_zmember02-mdob IS INITIAL.
96      IF year400 = 0 OR year004 = 0 AND NOT year100 = 0.
97        WRITE: / wa_zmember02-mnumber,
                    wa_zmember02-zzcoursetitle,
98                  wa_zmember02-mname, wa_zmember02-mdob(4).
99      ENDIF.
100   ENDIF.
101 ENDSELECT.
```

Listing 10.4 Report Z_MEMBERLIST10_WHILE

Notes on the Source Code

Lines 21 to 27
In the flow logic for the seconds counter that runs backwards, the initial value is set to 10 seconds. As long as the number of seconds is greater than 0, the system outputs the field value for seconds and reduces the number of seconds by 1. Because the WRITE statement in the loop doesn't contain a forward slash to indicate the start of a new line, the backward-counting seconds are output in a print line until the system inserts a line break by itself.

Lines 45 to 50
All records of the table are read. For each record, the system checks whether the date of birth is initial; that is, if the record of the course member doesn't contain a date of birth. If that's the case, the corresponding record will be included in the list so that the list contains the data records of all course members for whom the date of birth needs to be added. You can therefore use this method to find fields that haven't been maintained within data records and output these fields in a list.

Finding non-maintained fields in data records

Lines 54 to 59
Again, all data records of the table are read. The first record is checked to determine that the date of birth is between 01/01/1984 and 12/31/1984

(limit values included). If the condition is met, the data record is processed by an additional statement block, and all course members who were born in 1984 are included in the list.

Lines 64 to 68

The system checks whether the course title field of a data record contains the value "SAP03" or "SAP04". If this condition is met, a separate statement block processes the data record. The field may contain only one value; two of the possible values are permitted and fulfill the condition.

 Case Sensitivity

Please note that case sensitivity is important here: Records that meet the condition will be included in the list. If the notation doesn't exactly match that of the field content, the record doesn't fulfill the condition and will *not* be included in the list.

Lines 74 to 78

Two fields are checked for this condition. The condition is met if the gender field contains the gender key M and the course title field contains the value "SAP03". Therefore, the statement block will process the data record if it belongs to a male member of the "SAP03" course. The list output will contain only those records that correspond to this condition.

Lines 84 to 86

The condition is that the first three characters of the course title must *not* read "SAP". If this condition is met, the data record will be included in the list. Thus, the list will contain all members of non-SAP courses (that is, people who don't attend SAP courses).

Lines 92 to 94

The YEAR004 field is used to store the remainder of the integer division of the year of birth by 4; the year of birth is indicated by the first four characters of the date of birth in the format YYYYMMDD. If the year of birth can be divided by 4 in an integer division, then the remainder is zero (and so the field content of YEAR004 is 0).

The same happens with the YEAR100 and YEAR400 fields. These three lines correspond to the formulation of the three individual conditions.

Line 95

This condition checks whether the date of birth has been maintained. If it has been maintained, the year of birth has something other than the initial value. If the date of birth has been maintained, the system continues by processing the data record in the next statement block and by checking the next condition.

Line 96

This condition checks whether the remainders of the integer divisions equal 0. The condition itself represents the linked logical expression of the three individual conditions. If the condition is met, the year of birth is a leap year and the data record is passed on to the statement block. To keep a better overview, we used a simple WRITE statement in our example. Therefore, the list will contain the data records of all course members who were born in a leap year.

Remainders equal 0?

Program Output

First the backward-counting seconds are continually output in a print line, followed by a list of the table records (see Figure 10.10).

The last data record is incomplete because the date of birth hasn't been maintained. The second block of the list contains the data records in which the date of birth hasn't been maintained. That's only one record in our example. The third block contains the course members who were born in 1984. Again, there's only one hit.

The fourth block contains the records of the members that attend the courses "SAP03" or "SAP04". Please note that the exact spelling of the course names is important.

10	9	8	7	6	5	4	3	2	1
0									
00003 CASH		03.03.1972 M	301,00	EUR	SUV	SAP03			
00004 Davis		04.04.1984 F	401,00	JPY	Pick Up	SAP04			
00005 ELLINGTON		05.05.1980 M	501,00	USD	Station W.	SAP05			
00006 Ellington		05.05.1985 M	501,00	USD	Station W.	SAP05			
00007 Ellington		05.05.1985 M	501,00	USD	Station W.	SAP05			
00008 Feliciano		06.06.1986 F	600,00	RUB	Compact Ca	SAP06			
00009 IRVING		00.00.0000	0,00			BASIC			
00009 IRVING		Day of birth is missing, please maintain							
00004 Davis		04.04.1984							
00003 CASH		SAP03							
00004 Davis		SAP04							
00003 CASH		M SAP03							
00009 BASIC									
00003 SAP03		CASH	1972						
00004 SAP04		Davis	1984						
00005 SAP05		ELLINGTON	1980						

Figure 10.10 List Screen for WHILE Example and Logical Expressions

The fifth section of the list contains the male members that attend the "SAP03" course. The sixth section looks similar to the fifth one, but it has a completely different content. It contains only the data records of members who don't attend an SAP course.

The seventh and last block contains the data records of members that were born in a leap year.

11

Selection Screens

Until now, we've *hard coded* the starting values for fields. In this chapter, you'll learn how to use a few instructions at the start of the program to inform the ABAP report of values it should work with. These include, for example, whether or not a list should be generated, how often loops will be executed, and what data should be selected from the database.

In ABAP, there are three specific dialog screens: classic dynpros (which you should know from typical application transactions), selection screens (which are usually displayed before the execution of a report for parameters input), and list outputs (which are usually output at the end of the processing of a report).

Two dialog screens

The creation of *classic dynpros* is an art in itself, and requires you to be familiar with a specific graphical editor, the *Graphical Screen Painter* (also known as the Dynpro Painter) and with a special variant of the ABAP language that has been developed specifically for the programming of *screen flow logic*. However, this variant is not discussed in detail here. The creation of *list outputs*, in contrast, is rather simple, and you'll learn a lot about it in this chapter.

The main focus of this chapter is the *selection screen*. It is used to supply a report with starting values using a user dialog before the program is actually executed. So far, you've had to assign the variables values in the source code, but in the selection screen, you can enter these values using a dialog.

List Output on the Screen

However, once you have populated and submitted the selection screen, the report runs just as it did before, and finally produces a result (for example, a list output). In other words, while the report is running, you cannot continue to control it. By default, the list output is no longer on paper, as it used to be, but in a screen list. This output produces its own dialog program: the *list processor*.

If you want to print the screen list to paper, you have to request the output from the screen list using SYSTEM • LIST • PRINT; another option is to direct the output immediately to the printer in the ABAP source code with special instructions, such as `NEW-PAGE PRINT ON`. We won't delve into the particulars of paper production here, however.

Implicit generation

The feature specific to list outputs and selection screens is that they are not designed and written by developers as classic dynpros (dynamic programs) with the Graphical Screen Painter, but are implicitly generated using ABAP instructions (for example, the list screen with the `WRITE` instruction). So their generation is particularly easy and programmer-friendly. For newcomers to ABAP, this has the advantage that the screen flow logic, which has to be programmed manually for classic dynpros, is generated and processed by the system in the background.

Special dynpros

All screens—selection screens and classic dynpros—are components of programs. There are various program types; program types that can contain screens are *executable programs*, *function groups*, and *module pools*. Module pools are rather obsolete and can only be found in older applications. Selection screens are usually included in executable programs (also called reports) and classic dynpros in function groups (for better modularization). However, details about these advanced technologies exceed the scope of this book. In this chapter, we'll look at the selection screen, which appears before an ABAP report starts.

For reports, the standard selection screen dynpro is automatically called and controlled by the runtime environment during program execution, always as dynpro number 1000. For the user, however, the dynpro is only visible when input parameters are provided in the report using ABAP statements. Only these ABAP statements can cause the dynpro to be generated for the selection screen in the background and to be made visible with the input parameters.

For this reason, we won't go into a tremendous amount of detail about the world of dialog programming, but you should still learn about a few basic relationships. You will need this knowledge to understand both selection screen processing and the events related to the selection screen.

Events

Events are processing blocks. The structure of an event starts with the event keyword, but the end of the structure is merely implicit. An event ends, for instance, when a new event starts, a subprogram starts, or the report ends. Therefore, once you have started controlling a report program using events in the source code, you have to keep the style; otherwise, all the ABAP statements would count as part of the last event to fire, and would be executed there.

 Event Keywords

> The structure of the event includes the ABAP statements it contains. Events are looked for in the source code of the report and executed by the runtime environment in a predetermined order. So from a technical standpoint, it doesn't matter in which order the events appear in the report; however, from a practical point of view, reports are much more readable when the events are arranged in a logical sequence.

Order of Events

The flow for program start and program execution is fixed by the run-time environment. If you start a report, this is a simplified form of the control flow after the program is loaded:

> `LOAD-OF-PROGRAM`
Immediately after the program loads, the `LOAD-OF-PROGRAM` processing block is executed, if it is defined in the report.

> `INITIALIZATION`
Then the `INITIALIZATION` event is looked for in the report and executed. For instance, statements that determine values for the selection screen, or modify these values, are placed in this event. However, the event is run only once—the first time the program starts.

Next, the runtime environment checks whether a selection screen is defined in the report. This is the case when you define at least one input field using ABAP statements. Then control passes to the selection screen processor, which is a special dynpro processor. Before the selection screen processor sends the screen to the users, it takes the field values determined in the `INITIALIZATION` event and places them into the input fields. Other events can also trigger the selection screen processor before the user sees the selection screen.

> `AT SELECTION-SCREEN`
After the user sees the screen, fills it out, and submits it, the selection screen processor triggers the `AT SELECTION-SCREEN` event.

This event has a basic form and several variants, and this is a good place to perform more involved input checks. If you discover an error during this check, you can prevent the report from starting to work with the "wrong" data. Instead, you can have the selection screen displayed again, but with an appropriate error message, forcing a "correct" input.

> `START-OF-SELECTION`
Then, control passes back to the ABAP processor, and the `START-OF-SELECTION` event is looked for in the report and processed.

If there are no more events built into the source code, control passes to the list processor for list output at the end of the report. The list processor can then look for and execute certain events in the source code.

Examples of Events

Let's return to a practical application. If you want to enter a new member in our member table, for example, it would be useful if you didn't always need to manually check for the next free member number.

Suggesting the next free number is precisely the kind of task the INITIALIZATION event can handle for us; it is processed before the selection screen is displayed. Look at the following sample code:

Next free number

```
INITIALIZATION.
  SELECT * FROM zmember02 INTO wa_zmember02.
    mnumber = wa_zmember02-mnumber.
  ENDSELECT.
  mnumber = mnumber + 1.
  new_memb = mnumber.
```

First, we simply read the member table and count the numbers in the field MNUMBER. The last line contains the highest number, so the next highest number is free for a new member. This number will appear as a suggestion in the input field on the selection screen, and is therefore written into the NEW_MEMB parameter.

Suggested value in an input field

The runtime environment processes this event before the selection screen is displayed. As described, it starts at the INITIALIZATION event keyword, and ends implicitly. If the report should execute statements after the selection screen, then the following line must contain a different event keyword.

For example, the AT SELECTION-SCREEN event could check the inputs made on the selection screen. The input verification could involve all the fields on the selection screen, or simply individual fields.

If you want to ensure that the new member number used is larger or equal to the new member number suggested, then prevent the input of a "wrong" member number. To do this, write a special input verification for the field NEW_MEMB, which is provided for the new member number:

Checking screen input

```
AT SELECTION-SCREEN ON new_memb.
* Check new member number
  IF new_memb < mnumber.
*    Statement block for error handling
  ENDIF.
```

If a user tries to enter an existing member number for a new member, the selection screen will continue to be displayed with a message in the status bar until a valid member number is finally entered. The exact details of how this error handling works will be explained in "Completing Text Objects." This example and another one for the downwards-counting second timer can also be found in the source code Z_MEMBERLIST11_B (see "Sample Code for Selection Screen (Extended Form)").

Message in the status bar In our example, the AT SELECTION-SCREEN event involves only the NEW_MEMB input field. After the user clicks the EXECUTE button in the selection screen, it is called by the selection screen processor. If the input value is less than the suggested member number, the statement block for error handling is executed. This statement block often consists of a message in the status bar and instructions for reentry. How you manage and send these messages is also described in "Sample Code for Selection Screen (Extended Form)."

 Don't Forget the Implicit End of an Event

If the condition is not satisfied, execution resumes after the ENDIF statement. Don't forget the implicit end of an event. If the report processes the data entered, the following line must contain the event keyword START-OF-SELECTION or a corresponding event keyword.

Simple Selections

The decision to work with or without a selection screen is made in the definition part of the report. Instead of defining fields with the DATA instruction, we use the PARAMETERS or SELECT-OPTIONS statements.

PARAMETERS Statement

To assign a field a value through the selection screen, all you need is the PARAMETERS statement. As far as the definition of the field name, data type, and field length are concerned, the definition in the PARAMETERS statement is the same as that in the DATA statement, except that the length of the variable name is limited to eight characters. Except for data type f—that is, a *floating-point number* (float) or exponential number—all elementary data types can be defined with the PARAMETERS statement. References to field definitions of a table in the dictionary are also possible. Any variable defined with PARAMETERS is shown on the selection screen, along with its name or a selection text and an input field; the fields appear in the order in which they are defined. One possible stumbling block, as usual, is uppercase versus lowercase. Without a special addition, all input is converted to uppercase.

PARAMETERS

Let's take the example from Chapter 10: the countdown second timer. The set value was hard-coded, and the start value in the source code was set to 10. To get an input field on the selection screen instead, define a parameter. The data type will remain as i. The statement in the definition part of the report will be:

Second timer with input field

```
PARAMETERS second TYPE i.
```

The field displayed is still empty; there is no suggested value and no required field (see Figure 11.1). You are responsible for filling in the selection screen (for example, you could enter "10" again).

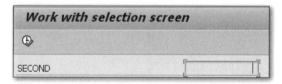

Work with selection screen

SECOND

Figure 11.1 Selection Screen with Parameters and Empty Input Field

If you would like to allow only a certain range for the value given for the second counter, you can also do this using a custom input test. If the value entered is outside that range, we want a message to appear

Range for the suggested value

in the status bar. The selection screen will be displayed again and again until a "correct" entry is given.

```
AT SELECTION-SCREEN ON second. * Check field value of second
  IF second < 5 OR second > 20.
*   Statement block for error handling
  ENDIF.
```

In this example, the AT SELECTION-SCREEN event only involves the SEC-OND input field. If the input value is less than 5 or greater than 20, the statement block for error handling is executed. Error handling should force a "correct" entry, and display the selection screen until the input is accepted.

Additions to the PARAMETERS Statement

DEFAULT   If you want to provide the user with a suggestion value in the field, use the addition DEFAULT, so that the statement looks like this:

```
PARAMETERS second TYPE i DEFAULT 10.
```

 PARAMETERS and DATA

> Note that there is a difference between the PARAMETERS and the DATA statement. If you want to supply an initial value in a DATA statement, the addition you should use is VALUE, but the equivalent addition for the PARAMETERS statement is DEFAULT. The initial value is only a suggested value, which the user can overwrite or delete (see Figure 11.2).

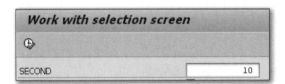

Figure 11.2 Selection Parameter with Suggested Value

OBLIGATORY   You can force input in a field by making it a required field using the OBLIGATORY addition:

```
PARAMETERS second TYPE i DEFAULT 10 OBLIGATORY.
```

A required field like this is marked with an icon in the selection screen (see Figure 11.3). Don't be fooled by the symbol. It disappears as soon as you enter a value into the field.

Figure 11.3 Required Field with Indicator Symbol

 Making Entries in All Required Fields

If an attempt is made to start the report with a required field left empty, the system generates the message "Make an entry in all required fields" in the status bar. The runtime environment will not run the report without input, and the selection screen appears again.

The link to the ABAP Dictionary works smoothly. If a PARAMETERS definition with the TYPE addition refers to a Dictionary field, then all the help texts, value help, foreign key relationships, and verification tables also apply for that field. The Dictionary field can be a field of a transparent table, a field of a structure, or a data element. This help continues to be available via the F1 key or the F4 key. In the following example, you define the field GENDER and refer to the definition in the ABAP Dictionary using the TYPE addition.

TYPE

```
PARAMETERS gender TYPE zmember02-mgender.
```

 TYPE and LIKE

In older programs, you'll often find the LIKE addition instead of TYPE. The difference between these two typing methods is that TYPE refers to a data type and LIKE to a data object. These aspects were often blurred in classic ABAP but should be carefully separated in modern ABAP. So you should only use the LIKE addition for typing if you actually want to refer to a specific data object and not to a data type.

Because table ZMEMBER02 and its columns are regarded as data types here, TYPE is used correctly, though the code would also work with LIKE.

In the member table, fixed values are stored in the domain for the genders. If you focus on that field in the selection screen, the help button appears on the right edge. You can click this or call up help using the [F4] key (see Figure 11.4). In the help window, the fixed values configured are offered for selection, but the system will accept any input—that is, it won't check whether you stay with the selection list or enter a completely new value.

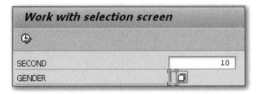

Figure 11.4 Selection Parameter with Value Help Key

VALUE CHECK   If you want to force only the values stored—only the valid values—to be accepted, you need the VALUE CHECK addition:

```
PARAMETERS gender TYPE zmember02-mgender
           OBLIGATORY VALUE CHECK.
```

With this definition, if there is an attempt on the selection screen to enter something that doesn't match the valid value, the system shows ENTER A VALID VALUE on the status bar and redisplays the selection screen.

 VALUE CHECK and OBLIGATORY

> The two additions, VALUE CHECK and OBLIGATORY, are generally used together. If it's important that only valid entries are given, you must ensure that there is something to enter.

LOWER CASE   Differentiating uppercase from lowercase can be problematic, depending on the suitability of the data. All input on the selection screen is converted to uppercase by default. That means that *only* the records that contain *only* uppercase letters in the corresponding fields will be selected. If you define an input field COURSE for a course name and provide the initial value "SAP01", then all lowercase letters will still be converted to uppercase and selected in the table.

```
PARAMETERS course TYPE zmember02-zzcoursetitle
                 DEFAULT 'SAP01'.
```

If an input field differentiates between uppercase and lowercase, you need the LOWER CASE addition.

```
PARAMETERS course TYPE zmember02-zzcoursetitle
                 DEFAULT 'SAP01' LOWER CASE.
```

Here, the system will differentiate between uppercase and lowercase. Though it won't convert the entries into uppercase letters, it will select exactly what is entered on the selection screen.

 Back-and-Forth Effect

Depending on your data configuration, however, the whole thing can have a back-and-forth effect. On one hand, you search and find only selected records with fields in uppercase; on the other, you select only those records. It's important to think about uniform rules for capitalization when creating your data inventory. In fact, it's not unusual to find a rule that all fields used for selection be entered exclusively in uppercase. You can already specify this when defining the data element on which the table column is based. Otherwise, you can run into problems. It's possible to use string operations or the TRANSLATE statement to help, but we won't go into that level of detail here.

It is very convenient for the user when the selection screen is provided with checkboxes, which can be used for control program execution or data selection. From a technical standpoint, these fields are type c with length 1. Their content is either an "X" or a blank (" "). On the selection screen, you can click on these fields and set a checkmark.

AS CHECKBOX

In the following example, the field ALLREC is defined using the AS CHECKBOX addition in order to control whether the complete list output of the table should be displayed (see Figure 11.5):

```
PARAMETERS allrec AS CHECKBOX.
```

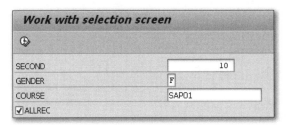

Figure 11.5 Selection Parameter as Checkbox

If the field is selected, you see the list on the screen; if the field is not selected, this output block is omitted. In the source code, wrap the corresponding section in an IF structure, with a condition to test whether the field is initial. If it is initial, nothing happens; if it is filled in, it will be output.

```
IF NOT allrec IS INITIAL.
*   Statement block for list output
ENDIF.
```

Radio button Another option for program control is the radio button, also known as the selection button (see Figure 11.6). Where checkboxes allow users to make multiple selections, radio buttons limit their options.

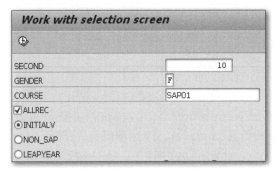

Figure 11.6 Selection Parameter with Radio Buttons

 Radio Buttons

The name "radio button" refers to the mechanical tuning buttons on older car radios. When you pushed one button, the other popped out. You could select any of your preset stations, but only one at a time!

From a technical standpoint, radio buttons are associated with a group in which only one button is selected and the others aren't. Behind every button in the group, there is another field of type c with length 1, which again can receive the contents "X" or " ". For a group of three radio buttons, therefore, you have three fields which you can use for program control flow: the first, the second, or the third field. In the following code example, the buttons are called INITIALV, NON_SAP, and LEAPYEAR, and are assigned to the group RAD1 using the RADIOBUTTON GROUP addition. Don't be irritated by the (still) cryptic parameter IDs; long descriptions of the function of these radio buttons will be provided later in this chapter.

"X" or " "

```
PARAMETERS: initialv  RADIOBUTTON GROUP rad1,
            non_sap   RADIOBUTTON GROUP rad1,
            leapyear  RADIOBUTTON GROUP rad1.
```

By default, the first button in the group is always selected. If you select another button in the group, the previously selected button is deselected.

In the source code, radio buttons are checked for initial values using an IF structure. Only one button in the group can have anything other than the initial value; only the corresponding statement block will be executed. In a simplified form, this structure can look like this:

Querying radio buttons

```
IF NOT initialv IS INITIAL.
*   Statement block_1
ENDIF.
IF NOT non_sap IS INITIAL.
*   Statement block_2
ENDIF.
IF NOT leapyear IS INITIAL.
*   Statement block_3
ENDIF.
```

 Not Ready for Prime Time

Don't be confused by the appearance of the selection screen. The names of the fields and their arrangement are not ready for prime time and still need to be tweaked. We'll be looking at graphical presentation in later sections of this chapter.

Complex Selections

Until now, you've only supplied individual fields on the selection screen with initial values. Now we'll look at what you have to do when you want to permit valid ranges or several possible single values for input.

Internal tables in working memory Assignment of field contents to individual variables won't get you any further at this point. Instead, you'll need to work with a table in which you can enter valid single values or ranges. So for the first time, you won't be working with a database table, but with an internal table in working memory. A significant difference between the two is that the data in an internal table is volatile (it "lives" only as long as the report does) and is therefore called *temporary data*.

SELECT-OPTIONS Statement

Selection table For the selection screen, you can use the SELECT-OPTIONS statement to use the special form of internal table provided by the system. The name of this internal table, also called a *selection table*, can have eight characters at most. The four fields in the selection table are predefined by the system: SIGN, OPTION, LOW, and HIGH (see Table 11.1). Every selection (each range or single value) entered in the table generates one row in the internal table. The internal table can have any number of rows.

Field	Description
SIGN	The SIGN field contains the logical operand. For a single value, this can be an equals sign (=), a greater-than sign (>), or a less-than sign (<), and so on, depending on what you're defining as a valid entry in the selection screen. For a range, this would be the following combination: <>.
OPTION	The OPTION field specifies how the boundary values are to be handled; for example, for ranges, this field specifies whether the range limits are included or excluded.
LOW	The LOW field is the lower limit for a range; for a single value, it is simply the value.
HIGH	The HIGH field is the upper limit for a range; for a single value, it is left empty.

Table 11.1 Fields in the Selection Table

Each new SELECT-OPTIONS statement defines a new internal table. In this definition, the system also needs to know which field is assigned to the internal table. If the LOW and HIGH values, for instance, refer to a field in a database table, then the field attributes of that field automatically apply to the input fields on the selection screen.

Of course, in our example, you can also create a variable for the date of birth using the PARAMETERS statement, but then you could only enter a single birth date in the selection screen to be used for selection. With the SELECT-OPTIONS statement, on the other hand, you can enter as many individual birth date values and ranges as you want, select a corresponding number of records, and process them—or simply generate an appropriate list. So for the internal table for the values of birth dates, it makes sense to define date of birth (DOB) and refer to the work area for the table field ZMEMBER02-MDOB.

Because you want to avoid the obsolete TABLES statement, you should define an explicit work area. You can use the SELECT-OPTIONS statement to refer to it without problems, like this:

```
DATA: wa_zmember02 TYPE zmember02.
SELECT-OPTIONS dob FOR wa_zmember02-mdob.
```

Using the two entry fields in the selection screen, the selection table is supplied with single values or upper and lower limits for ranges (see Figure 11.7).

Single values or ranges

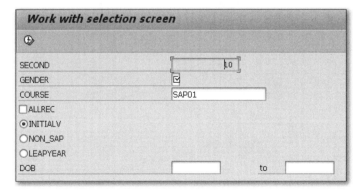

Figure 11.7   SELECT-OPTIONS with Internal Table DOB

In the selection screen, you can enter a single value into the LOW field to the left to be written to the internal table behind SELECT-OPTIONS. If you want to enter a range, enter the HIGH value on the right. Make sure that the HIGH value of the range is larger than the LOW value.

If you leave both fields blank, there will be no limitation of selections, and all values will be considered valid values.

Multiple Selections

Formulated positively or negatively

The system always allows *multiple selection* (that is, several single values and several ranges can be selected). It is possible to formulate the selection either positively or negatively. Positive formulation means, for instance, with a range, that the valid values within the range lie within the boundaries; negative formulation means that all values are valid except those within the range, and that the boundaries values would also be invalid.

If you want to work with multiple selection, click the MULTIPLE SELECTION button in the selection screen (see Figure 11.8). The system displays an additional window with four tabs. Depending on the task required, you would select these tabs, one after the other, to specify the selection criteria.

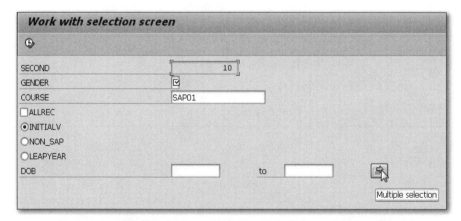

Figure 11.8 Multiple Selection in SELECT-OPTIONS

For example, if you enter two values on the SELECT SINGE VALUES tab and accept them with the corresponding record, then you can use these values comfortably for further processing. One possible use would be in a logical condition of an IF structure. In either case, the data to be tested against the condition would fulfill it if they match any of the single values that were previously entered as single values. This statement block contains one of those entries from the date of birth selection table in the appropriate table field (see Figure 11.9). An IF structure is that case might look like this:

Selecting multiple single values

```
IF wa_zmember02-mdob IN dob.
*   statement_block
ENDIF.
```

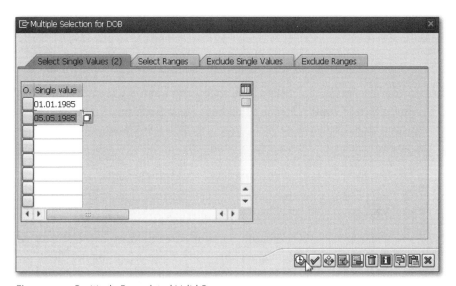

Figure 11.9 Positively Formulated Valid Ranges

You work analogously when you want to select multiple ranges. For positive formulation, select the SELECT RANGES tab with the green traffic light in the window for the multiple selection and enter one or more ranges there. Then accept the selected entries again with the COPY button (see Figure 11.10). Below the tabs, you see buttons with familiar functions such as INSERT LINE to manage the entries.

Selecting multiple ranges

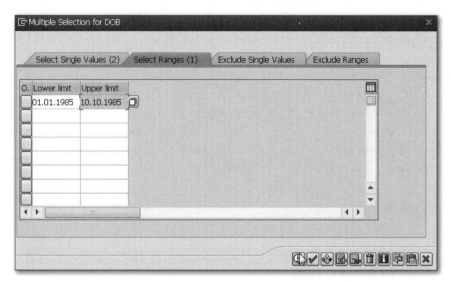

Figure 11.10 Positively Formulated Valid Single Values

Accepting multiple selections

After accepting the entries, you're returned to the selection screen. To denote that multiple selections have now been made, the MULTIPLE SELECTION button now has a green tinge. Here's a summary of what we've learned:

> The internal table DOB contains all valid single values and ranges.

> The internal table behind the SELECT-OPTIONS statement has as many rows as you enter on the different tabs.

> The internal table refers to the work area field WA_ZMEMBER02-MDOB and thus defines the values that will be permitted for this field.

> The WA_ZMEMBER02 work area is typed for the ABAP Dictionary table, ZMEMBER02, and thus inherits all characteristics of this table, such as search help attachments. Accordingly, these are also available to the work area.

> During processing, each record is checked for whether the field contents of WA_ZMEMBER02-MDOB are valid according to the contents of DOB.

> If the field content of WA_ZMEMBER02-MDOB is valid, then the condition is met and the record is passed on to an appropriate statement block.

➕ Combination of Multiple Entries

You can combine multiple entries in several tabs, but note that this should be undertaken with great care. If you overdo it, the resulting program flow and processing can be quite confusing until you recall the logical combinations you specified on the tab entries. Once the tab entries can be reproduced, you can resolve any confusion that arises from combining multiple entries.

Additions to the SELECT-OPTIONS Statement

The additions DEFAULT, OBLIGATORY, and LOWER CASE, which were already introduced for the PARAMETERS statement, are also valid for the SELECT-OPTIONS statement, and so will not be repeated here. Their properties and effects are comparable for the two statements. The SELECT-OPTIONS statement's NO-EXTENSION addition, however, deserves a more detailed examination.

NO-EXTENSION

If you want to prevent multiple selection based on the task requirements, you can qualify the SELECT-OPTIONS statement with the NO-EXTENSION addition:

```
SELECT-OPTIONS dob FOR wa_zmember02-mdob
               NO-EXTENSION.
```

Now, the system will only permit the entry of one row (one single value or one range) on the selection screen. As you can see in Figure 11.11, the MULTIPLE SELECTION button is now missing. Thus multiple selection is automatically prevented, and the internal selection table has only one row.

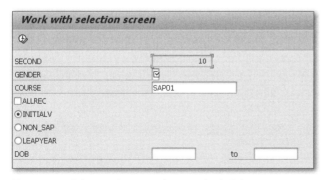

Figure 11.11 Selection Screen without Multiple Selection

Using Selection Texts

Up to now, the selection screen has shown the technical field names of the parameters and the names of the internal SELECT-OPTIONS tables. In the source code, you will continue to work with these technical names, but for the user, you should display better, more descriptive texts. To do this, use special text elements called *selection texts*.

Overview of Text Elements

Text pool

Every ABAP program has its own subobjects, like text elements. The *text pool* contains all the text elements of the program. The original language is the login language in which the program was written, from which the text elements can be translated into other languages without changing the source code. Programs are thus language-independent and the translation itself requires no programming expertise. This local language management capability applies to selection texts as well.

Types of text elements

There are three kinds of text elements:

> **Text symbols**
  You can use these elements in source code in place of hard-coded literals.

> **Selection texts**
  You can display these elements on the selection screen in place of the technical names of parameters and selection tables.

> **List headings**
  You can use these elements to build list headers.

Creating Selection Texts

There are different ways to get to text elements in order to edit them. From the starting screen of the ABAP Editor, you can reach text elements by entering the report, selecting its subobject TEXT ELEMENTS, and clicking the CHANGE button (see Figure 11.12).

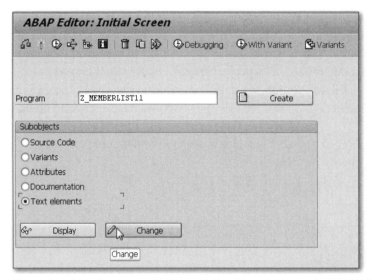

Figure 11.12 Introductions to Working with Text Elements Using the ABAP Editor

➕ Jumping to Text Elements

If you're already working in the source code editor and want to jump to the text elements, use the menu GOTO • TEXT ELEMENTS • SELECTION TEXTS (see Figure 11.13).

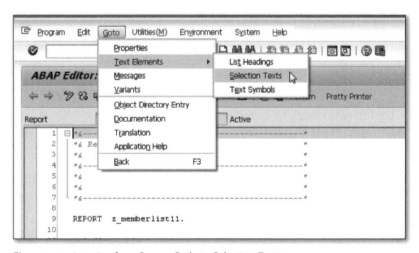

Figure 11.13 Jumping from Source Code to Selection Texts

Editing selection
texts
In the editing screen for text elements, you see three tabs: TEXT SYM-BOLS, SELECTION TEXT, and LIST HEADINGS. In the SELECTION TEXTS tab, in the example, the system has already entered all the technical names of the parameters and selection tables used in the selection screen (see Figure 11.14); in addition, we have jumped from the ABAP Editor from the source code ZMEMBERLIST11 into SELECTION TEXTS using the menu.

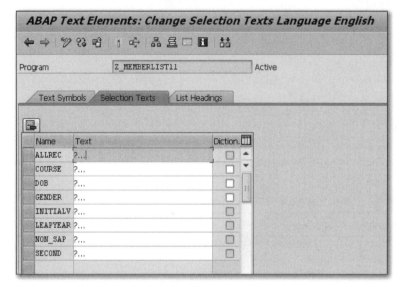

Figure 11.14 Edit Screen for Selection Texts

Some of the parameters used and the selection table are defined by reference to ABAP Dictionary elements. For this reason, the system allows you to take their texts from the dictionary and binds them to the selection screen (see Figure 11.15). These texts have already been edited in the data element in the FIELD LABELS tab as long texts. If you want to accept the texts from the dictionary, set the checkmark in the DICTIONARY column. The texts will be accepted and shown with a gray background in display mode.

Activating
selection texts
The remaining selection texts are edited individually in the fields provided, and can be a maximum of 30 characters in length. The text elements are then in the program's text pool. Since this subobject, too, can only use current contents in active form, after editing the selection texts you can't simply jump back to the source code, but must first activate

the text elements (see Figure 11.16). Only then will the text pool of the ABAP report be activated and available in its current form for the selection screen, as shown in Figure 11.17. As you can see, the screen is much more readable and understandable for users.

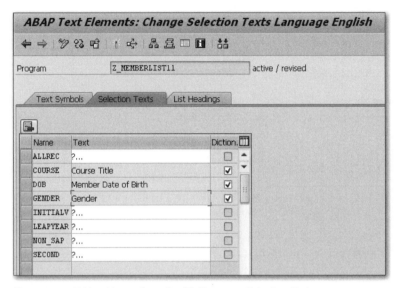

Figure 11.15 Taking Names from the Dictionary as Selection Text

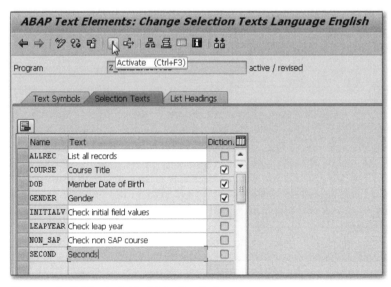

Figure 11.16 Editing Individual Selection Texts

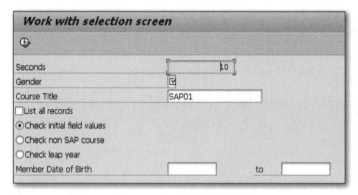

Figure 11.17 Selection Screen with Selection Texts

Saving the Selection Screen

In reality, we repeatedly work with the same reports, at greater or smaller intervals of time. Some of these reports are started daily, and others are done only once a year. The selection screen must be filled in as different technical requirements demand.

Difficult and unreliable
It would be extremely difficult and unreliable if you had to rethink the entries for every selection each time. Furthermore, some selection screens are more than a single screen page long. So you shouldn't have to be the one to determine how the selection screen is filled in for a given technical requirement.

 Payroll

Imagine a payroll accounting run. In many companies, payroll runs happen at different times for individual personnel groups and plants. (Some personnel groups such as shop floor workers may have their payroll run in the middle of the month, while others may have their payroll run at the beginning or end of the month, and yet another group may even have weekly payroll runs.) The individual accounting runs require different forms and so on. Despite this, there are relatively few programs that handle all the mechanical work. With selection screens, you can collect the parameters required to determine which forms must be used for which personnel groups.

Creating Selection Variants

So that you don't have to start from scratch and repeat the necessary entries every time you start the program, you can mark the selection screen as a template after it is filled in and save it as a variant. For each selection screen, you can save any number of different variants. Like text elements, variants are also assigned to the program as a subobject.

Templates

Variants are very useful for even relatively simple selection screens, or for documentation of test data and test runs during program development. In fact, many companies require the consistent use of variants in certain cases.

To create a variant, there are two basic methods. The first is through the ABAP Workbench and the starting screen of the ABAP Editor. After entering the program name, you can also edit the VARIANTS of the selection screen (see Figure 11.18).

Editing variants using the ABAP Workbench

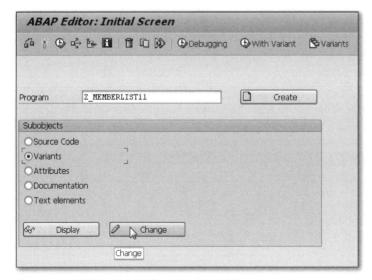

Figure 11.18 Editing Variants from the ABAP Editor

347

You then reach the starting screen of variant editing, where you can either enter the name of an existing variant or use the CREATE button to create a new variant. An existing variant can also be found using the value help button ([F4]) on the variant name. For this variant, for instance, you can have the values displayed by selecting the VALUES subobject and clicking DISPLAY (see Figure 11.19).

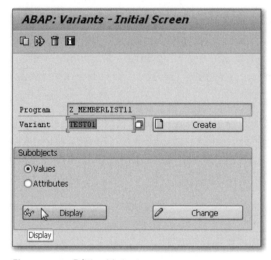

Figure 11.19 Editing Variants

Editing the values of a variant You now see the screen that shows which values this variant enters in the selection screen (see Figure 11.20).

ABAP: Selections of Variant TEST01

Catalog ✎ Values ⚒ Attributes

Objects for selection screen

Selection Scrns	Field name	Type	I/E	Option	frm	to
1000	Seconds	P			5	
1000	Gender	P			F	
1000	Course Title	P			SAP01	
1000	List all records	P				
1000	Check initial field values	P				
1000	Check non SAP course	P				
1000	Check leap year	P			X	
1000	Member Date of Birth	S	I	BT	01.01.1984	10.10.1985

Figure 11.20 Displaying the Values of a Variant

From here, use the DISPLAY ATTRIBUTES button to jump directly to the display of the variant attributes (see Figure 11.21). Now you can see, for example, which fields of this variant are protected, which fields are hidden, and so on. The BACK key (F3) takes you to the edit screen for the values of the variant.

Editing the attributes of a variant

Variant Attributes

| Variant Name | TEST01 |
| Description | Variant for test |

Scrn Assignm.

	Created	Selection Scrns
☐ Only for Background Processing	☑	1000
☐ Protect Variant		
☐ Only Display in Catalog		
☐ System Variant (Automatic Transport)		

Objects for selection screen

Selection Scrns	Field name	Type	Protect field	Hide field	Hide field 'BIS'	Save field without values	Switch GPA off	Required field	Sele
1.000	Seconds	P	☐	☐	☐	☐	☐	☑	
1.000	Gender	P	☐	☐	☐	☐	☐	☑	
1.000	Course Title	P	☐	☐	☐	☐	☐	☐	
1.000	List all records	P	☐	☐	☐	☐	☐	☐	
1.000	Check initial field values	P	☐	☐	☐	☐	☐	☐	
1.000	Check non SAP course	P	☐	☐	☐	☐	☐	☐	
1.000	Check leap year	P	☐	☐	☐	☐	☐	☐	
1.000	Member Date of Birth	S	☐	☐	☐	☐	☐	☐	

Figure 11.21 Displaying Variant Attributes

➕ Editing Variants through the Selection Screen

We always recommend the method using the ABAP Workbench for editing variants independently of program execution. The second method for creating a variant comes directly from the selection screen of the report. Once you have carefully filled it in, check the entries again and use GOTO • VARIANT • SAVE AS VARIANT (or the SAVE AS VARIANT... icon) to jump to variant editing (see Figure 11.22).

349

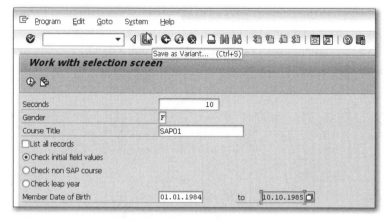

Figure 11.22   Saving Selection Screen as a Variant

In the SAVE AS VARIANT screen (see Figure 11.23), you first give the variant a name (VARIANT NAME) and a DESCRIPTION. Then you can edit the properties of the variant in the upper part of the screen.

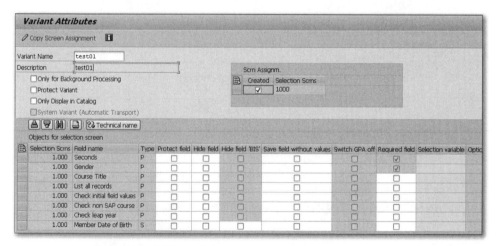

Figure 11.23   Editing a Variant

> **Only for background processing**
> Here, you can specify that the variant only be used for background processing and not be available to the user in dialog operation. Many reports are automatically started at night or at certain times of the day. Starting with a variant is the only option for supplying

the selection screen of such a report with sensible field contents for program execution.

> **Protect variant**
> If another user should not be allowed to make changes to the variant, it makes sense to protect it. On the other hand, if the variant is only used as a template to be completed, you don't need to protect the variant as a whole.

> **Only display in catalog**
> If this attribute is active, the variant is kept as a subobject, but it is not shown in the value help list (F4). In a sense, it is inactive.

➕ **Reduced Risk of Error**

In the lower part of the screen, you can check exactly which properties you also need to give the variant: whether a field in this variant should be hidden, protected from overwriting, or not filled on the selection screen. These settings influence the appearance of the selection screen—possibly drastically—and reduce the input options of the user, and thus the risk of error.

Just for practice, protect the field SECONDS in the variant (see Figure 11.24) so that it is displayed on the selection screen with a gray background and cannot be overwritten.

Protecting variants in part or in whole

Variant Attributes

🖉 Copy Screen Assignment ℹ️

| Variant Name | TEST01 |
| Description | test01 |

☐ Only for Background Processing
☐ Protect Variant
☐ Only Display in Catalog
☐ System Variant (Automatic Transport)

Scrn Assignm.
| | Created | Selection Scrns |
| 🗎 | ☑ | 1000 |

Objects for selection screen

Selection Scrns	Field name	Type	Protect field	Hide field	Hide field 'BIS'	Save field without values	Switch GPA off	Required field	Selectio
1.000	Seconds	P	☑	☐	☐	☐	☐	☑	
1.000	Gender	P	☐	☐	☐	☐	☐	☑	
1.000	Course Title	P	☐	☐	☐	☐	☐	☐	
1.000	List all records	P	☐	☐	☐	☐	☐	☐	
1.000	Check initial field values	P	☐	☐	☐	☐	☐	☐	
1.000	Check non SAP course	P	☐	☐	☐	☐	☐	☐	
1.000	Check leap year	P	☐	☐	☐	☐	☐	☐	
1.000	Member Date of Birth	S	☐	☐	☐	☐	☐	☐	

Figure 11.24 Saving an Edited Variant

After the variant is saved with the SAVE button, you can see the selection screen in its modified form (see Figure 11.25). You can test your settings immediately by starting the report as normal with the EXECUTE button.

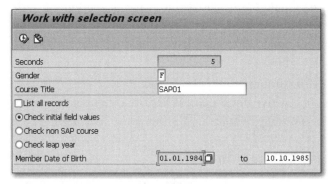

Figure 11.25 Selection Screen with Protected Field

Starting a Report with a Variant

Starting a report with a variant from the ABAP Workbench

To start a report with a variant, there are at least three methods.

For tests and development, you can start reports directly from the ABAP Workbench with a variant. The EXECUTE WITH VARIANT (⎡Shift⎦ + ⎡F6⎦) button shows you a window where you can select the variants (see Figure 11.26). Then the report starts with the corresponding selection screen.

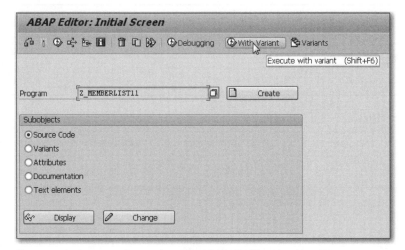

Figure 11.26 Starting a Report from the ABAP Workbench with a Variant

But a user really can't start the report from the ABAP Workbench because he won't have the necessary privileges in the production system. So the usual method is to proceed through program execution, the SAP menu, or a specific transaction code if one has been assigned to the report. If the report is entered in the SAP structure, the user can start the report like any other report through the SAP menu, or via SYSTEM • SERVICES • REPORTING. In the ABAP program execution screen, the user can enter the program name and click the WITH VARIANT button to select a variant with which the selection screen can be filled in (see Figure 11.27).

Starting a report with a variant from ABAP program execution

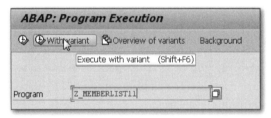

Figure 11.27 Program Executions with Variant

Many users first call up the selection screen and then retrieve the appropriate variant from there (see Figure 11.28). The GET VARIANT (⎡Shift⎤ + ⎡F5⎤) button or GOTO • VARIANTS • GET menu also shows you the variant selector.

Starting a report with a variant from the selection screen

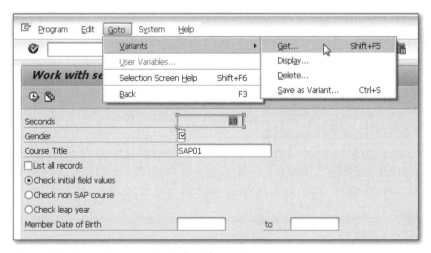

Figure 11.28 Retrieving Variants via the Selection Screen

After variant selection and acceptance, the system displays the corresponding selection screen again. You start the report with the EXECUTE button, as usual.

Completing Text Objects

Before you can set up the selection screen completely on your own, you need a few more tools: text symbols and messages.

Creating Text Symbols

You're already familiar with text objects from "Using Selection Texts," which also described how to reach the text element editing dialog.

Editing text symbols   In this context, there is a third type of text element: the *text symbol*. Text symbols can replace literals (for example, in the WRITE statement, enabling reuse and translation of variable texts). The hard-coding of literals in the source code is therefore superfluous and should be avoided.

Test symbols are essentially placeholders for text. In the ABAP source code, for example, you would no longer write this:

```
WRITE: / 'Member'.
```

Instead, you can simply write this:

```
WRITE: / text-001.
```

The name of a text symbol consists of TEXT- and a three-digit number. For a report, you can use up to 1,000 text symbols in one language, and each text symbol can have as many as 132 characters. When editing text symbols, you either go through the ABAP Workbench to the text elements—as described for selection texts—or from the ABAP Editor through forward navigation. By double-clicking a text symbol, you can reach the edit screen for the text symbols; in Figure 11.29, the list is already active and the text symbols have already been created.

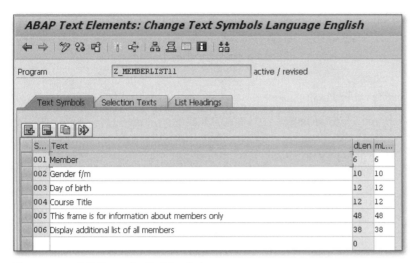

Figure 11.29 Edit Screen for Text Symbols

 Activating Text Symbols

Since it's not hard to create text symbols, as it is analogous to creating selection texts, we won't explain it again here. Just don't forget to enable the text symbols using the Activate button after editing.

The system has already created rows for all text symbols used; the row number corresponds to the number of the text symbol. You only need to enter the text into the corresponding row that you want to see in the selection screen later.

To see the entries in the modified text pool in the selection screen later, you first have to activate the text pool (Ctrl + F3). Only then will the F3 key take you back to the ABAP Editor.

Creating Messages

Messages are primarily used to provide feedback on program control to the user (for example, when noting incorrect entries in the selection screen). In order to send messages to the user, messages must be stored in a message class in system table T100. The message class groups messages according to task area and technical viewpoints; for customers,

T100

the customer namespace should be noted. Customer-specific message classes start with Z or a registered namespace prefix. The language key can also be used to maintain country-specific messages.

 Message Class

> In contrast to text elements, messages are not subobjects of a report, but are stored by group in a central system table. All programs can work with this shared message pool. There are two options: Either the report must be bound to the corresponding message class using the MESSAGE-ID addition on the REPORT statement, or the message class must be added to the command as an operand when sending the message. The ABAP statement MESSAGE is used to send a message.

Editing messages   The start screen for message editing is reached from the ABAP Editor via the GOTO • MESSAGES menu or Transaction SE91. Forward navigation from the source code (double-clicking on the message) is also possible. If the message class does not yet exist, enter the name and create it using the corresponding button. The name of the message class can have up to 20 characters and must start with Z for the reasons mentioned; for now, call your message class ZABAP (see Figure 11.30).

Figure 11.30 Starting Up the Message Editor

For a new message class, you must first edit the properties (see Figure 11.31) and then the messages in the appropriate tab.

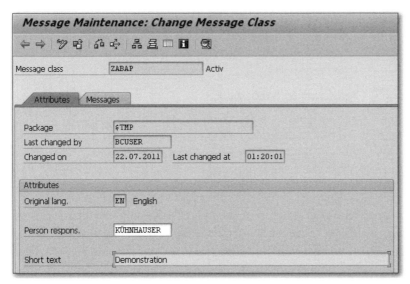

Figure 11.31 Editing Attributes of the Message Class

Every message class has rows 000 through 999. Select the appropriate row and enter your message there. Its text can have a maximum of 72 characters (see Figure 11.32). Don't forget to save your message and the message class after editing so that the new entries will also be stored in table T100.

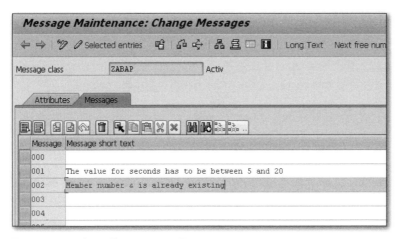

Figure 11.32 Editing Short Message Text

MESSAGE   Now we will finally go into the details of error handling during input verification in the AT SELECTION-SCREEN event, and will examine the appearance of the statement block for error handling.

> **Addition to MESSAGE**
>
> As mentioned earlier, in the event of an error, a message is sent to the user with a hint about the "right" entry or about the error itself. To send messages, use the ABAP MESSAGE statement. As additions, they each need the message type, the message number, and the message class.

Message type   The message type comes with its own risk. It is context-sensitive, so it works differently depending on the location of the MESSAGE statement. For example, in selection screens, message type E (as in error) causes an interrupt in selection screen processing. The selection screen is sent again, and the message appears in the status bar with a red background. The input fields addressed with the AT SELECTION-SCREEN event are ready for input again and must be filled in. This process is repeated until the entries pass the tests; only then does the report continue to execute.

Forcing usable input   To force "correct" entries in the field for the new member number, write the following in the statement block for error handling for member numbers:

```
MESSAGE e002(zabap).
```

To force "correct" entries in the field for seconds, write the following in the statement block for the error handling of the seconds:

```
MESSAGE e001(zabap).
```

The MESSAGE command in this case has the following additions:

> e
>
>   The message type E on the selection screen interrupts the selection screen processing and resends the selection screen with the message in the status bar with a red background.

> 001
>
>   The message number has the content "Seconds must be between 5 and 20" from the message class specified.

> (zabap)

This customer-specific message class ZABAP must be written in parentheses.

The addition WITH of the MESSAGE statement can be used to send up to four operands as position operands in a field list for the message. The content of the first field in the field list is used instead of the first placeholder in the message text; the content of the second field is used in place of the second placeholder, and so on. But this only works if placeholders actually exist for these operands in the message. The ampersand symbol (&) is used for placeholders in the message text. If, for instance, the message text is "Member number & already exists," the MESSAGE statement might look like this:

WITH

```
MESSAGE e002(zabap) with wrong_memb.
```

The content of the field WRONG_MEMB is provided for the variable message text.

➕ Unpleasant Side Effects of MESSAGE

Even seasoned SAP experts don't always know which effect a specific message type has on the program flow in a certain context.

It is possible that a function that has been developed only for use in dialogs is called in a background processing program. In this case, messages that are directly output can lead to a deviating system behavior.

If you add the INTO addition to your MESSAGE statement, the entire message is passed as a string to a variable so that the program flow is not affected. This is useful for generating log outputs; it is also advantageous because you can control the program flow with the appropriate commands.

Consequently, always check your programming to see if the direct output of messages with MESSAGE is actually useful or if you should instead opt to use a logger service—such as the application log (BAL)—to output success and error messages and program the program flow control explicitly. As a rule of thumb, reports can contain MESSAGE but function modules and classes should only contain MESSAGE ... INTO.

Call Transaction SBAL_DOCUMENTATION to get more information on the application log.

Free Layout of the Selection Screen

Blocks are used for clarity

In a preliminary remark about the free layout of the selection screen, we would like to start by pointing out the possibilities and limitations. You can position input fields, print free text in the selection screen, and define input blocks. These are logical groups of information that the user sees as belonging together. You can draw frames around these blocks and label them.

Behind the input fields, however, there are still PARAMETERS or SELECT-OPTIONS statements. The additions for and effects of these statements are unchanged; the same goes for working with variants.

 Limited Freedom

Because of the client-server architecture and distributed applications, you should stick with a grid of rows and columns when working with free positioning. Furthermore, multilined texts, superscripts, and subscripts in texts cannot be used. You also have very little freedom to choose fonts or font sizes.

Formatting Single Lines

SELECTION-SCREEN

To format a line, you need a structure that has a defined start and a defined end. In between are the statements that determine how the line is to be formatted. For each new line, a new structure is needed.

BEGIN OF LINE

The structure starts with SELECTION-SCREEN BEGIN OF LINE and ends with SELECTION-SCREEN END OF LINE, as you can see in this sample code:

```
SELECTION-SCREEN BEGIN OF LINE.
* Statement block for line design
SELECTION-SCREEN END OF LINE.
```

END OF LINE

In the statement block, there are special statements for comments on the screen, position and length specifications, and also the familiar PARAMETERS and SELECT-OPTIONS statements. You can't work with literals for free texts; only text elements (or, more accurately, text symbols) are permitted. *Text symbols* are comparable to variables or fields, except that the content is stored outside the actual source code in a separate text pool. Recall that the name of a text symbol consists of the string TEXT- and a number between 000 and 999, for instance, TEXT-123. Consequently, every ABAP report can manage up to 1,000 text symbols in a language.

For example, if a free text should appear in one line as a comment, the statement SELECTION-SCREEN COMMENT is required. For a comment starting in position 24 in the line with a length of 60 characters, and the name of the text symbol containing the text is TEXT-005, you would write this in ABAP:

COMMENT

```
SELECTION-SCREEN COMMENT 24(60) text-005.
```

If the comment should be left-justified in the line and written with length 16, the statement would be:

```
SELECTION-SCREEN COMMENT (16) text-005.
```

 You Can't Make It Any More Succinct

Unfortunately, formatting single lines cannot be any more succinct; the output length is the very least you have to specify.

Until now, the texts on the selection screen have had no relationship to parameters or selection tables; for instance, the [F1] key has no help to pull up for them. If you associate the text with the parameter or selection table, you receive the help for the text that you'd receive if you focus on the input field and press the [F1] key. The text is associated using the FOR FIELD addition.

FOR FIELD

For instance, if you want to bind text symbol 002 to the parameter GENDER, write:

```
SELECTION-SCREEN COMMENT (20) text-002
  FOR FIELD gender.
```

The text is displayed as left justified and has a length of 20. The functionality of this statement (here, the documentation regarding the gender key) can only be seen when you focus on the text in the selection screen and, for instance, press the [F1] key.

POSITION When displaying text, the statement contains specifications regarding the position and length relative to the current line. However, you can also use the POSITION addition to determine the position for the next output freely. For instance, if the next output, whether text or parameter, is to appear in the line starting in position 24, then in the statement block you write:

```
SELECTION-SCREEN POSITION 24.
```

 Too Time-Consuming

This method allows you to generate any number of outputs in one line, but it is rather time-consuming. You also have to pay close attention to the position specifications. Backwards positioning is possible, and the system will overwrite old position specifications without blinking an eye. If you overdo it, the result might end up being something that you weren't expecting.

A statement block for line layout could look like this:

```
SELECTION-SCREEN COMMENT (20) text-002
   FOR FIELD gender.
   SELECTION-SCREEN POSITION 24.
   PARAMETERS gender TYPE zmember02-mgender
             OBLIGATORY VALUE CHECK.
```

In the line, TEXT-002 is written at the left margin with a length of 20; the next output will be positioned in column 24 in the same line, and from that position on, the parameter GENDER will be displayed. Each line on the selection screen can be formatted in this way, which, as we mentioned earlier, can be necessary but time-consuming.

Formatting a Line Block

One or more lines that belong together can also be defined as a block. A block is set off in the selection screen by a different color, and can have a frame and a frame label.

Again, you need a structure for this that defines a block start and block end; in other words, the SELECTION-SCREEN BEGIN OF BLOCK and SELEC-TION-SCREEN END OF BLOCK statements exist for this reason.

BEGIN OF BLOCK

So the structure, which is defined using the BLOCK addition, represents the outer frame. The BLOCK structure, in turn, consists of several lines, which are defined using the LINE addition. A line can contain individual elements, such as parameters and comments.

For example, if you want to group two lines together as block B1, you would build the structure like this:

```
SELECTION-SCREEN BEGIN OF BLOCK B1.
   SELECTION-SCREEN BEGIN OF LINE. "Line 1
*    Statement block for line design line 1
   SELECTION-SCREEN END OF LINE. "Line 1
   SELECTION-SCREEN BEGIN OF LINE. "Line 2
*    Statement block for line design line 2
   SELECTION-SCREEN END OF LINE.
SELECTION-SCREEN END OF BLOCK B1.
```

The block name (B1) must appear in the statements at both the start and the end of the block structure. Otherwise, the statement for the block is syntactically incomplete.

END OF BLOCK

In addition, a block can have a frame and a frame label in the upper left corner of the block. If you want such a frame, add the addition WITH FRAME. If you also want a frame label, store the text in a text symbol and use the addition FRAME TITLE. If the frame text were stored in text symbol 001, then this statement would be:

WITH FRAME, TITLE

```
SELECTION-SCREEN BEGIN OF BLOCK member
                WITH FRAME TITLE text-001.
```

 Context-Sensitive

> SELECTION-SCREEN statements are also context-sensitive. Some statements only make sense within a line, and others only within a block. Of course, blank lines and lines for the selection screen are also possible, but we won't cover these options here.

Sample Code for Selection Screen (Simple Form)

Listing 11.1 demonstrates the definition of a selection screen.

```
 1  *&---------------------------------------------*
 2  *& Report   Z_MEMBERLIST11                      *
 3  *&                                              *
 4  *&---------------------------------------------*
 5  *&                                              *
 6  *&                                              *
 7  *&---------------------------------------------*
 8
 9  REPORT   z_memberlist11.
10
11  * Define table work area
12  DATA wa_zmember02 TYPE zmember02.
13
14  * Define fields
15  DATA: year004 TYPE i,
16        year100 TYPE i,
17        year400 TYPE i.
18
19  * Define selection screen
20  PARAMETERS: second TYPE i DEFAULT 10 OBLIGATORY,
21              gender TYPE zmember02-mgender
                        OBLIGATORY VALUE CHECK,
22              course TYPE zmember02-zzcoursetitle
                        DEFAULT 'SAP01' LOWER CASE,
23              allrec AS CHECKBOX,
24
25              initialv RADIOBUTTON GROUP rad1,
26              non_sap  RADIOBUTTON GROUP rad1,
27              leapyear RADIOBUTTON GROUP rad1.
28
29  SELECT-OPTIONS dob FOR wa_zmember02-mdob NO-EXTENSION.
30
31  * Decremental stopwatch
32  WHILE second > 0.
33    WRITE: second.
34    second = second - 1.
35  ENDWHILE.
36  WRITE: / second.
37  SKIP.
38
39  * Check checkbox
```

```
40   if not allrec is initial.
41   * Display content of table
42     SELECT * FROM zmember02 INTO wa_zmember02.
43     WRITE: / wa_zmember02-mnumber,
44             wa_zmember02-mname,
45             wa_zmember02-mdob,
46             wa_zmember02-mgender,
47             wa_zmember02-mfee,
48             wa_zmember02-mcurrency,
49             wa_zmember02-zzcartype,
50             wa_zmember02-zzcoursetitle.
51     ENDSELECT.
52     SKIP.
53   endif.  "not allrec is initial
54
55   * Check Radiobutton
56   IF NOT initialv IS INITIAL.
57     SELECT * FROM zmember02 INTO wa_zmember02.
58     IF zmember02-mdob IS INITIAL.
59       WRITE: / zmember02-mnumber, zmember02-mname,
60               'Day of birth is missing.',
61               'please maintain'.
62       ENDIF.
63     ENDSELECT.
64     SKIP.
65   ENDIF.
66
67   * Check Select Options
68   SELECT * FROM zmember02 INTO wa_zmember02.
69     IF wa_zmember02-mdob IN dob.
70       WRITE: / wa_zmember02-mnumber, wa_zmember02-mname,
71               wa_zmember02-mdob.
72     ENDIF.
73   ENDSELECT.
74   SKIP.
75
76   * Check Parameters with logical AND
77    SELECT * FROM zmember02 INTO wa_zmember02.
78     IF wa_zmember02-mgender = gender AND
79        wa_zmember02-zzcoursetitle = course.
80       WRITE: / wa_zmember02-mnumber,
                  wa_zmember02-mname,
81               wa_zmember02-mgender,
                  wa_zmember02-zzcoursetitle.
82     ENDIF.
```

```
83   ENDSELECT.
84   SKIP.
85
86   * Check Radiobutton
87   IF NOT non_sap IS INITIAL.
88     SELECT * FROM zmember02 INTO wa_zmember02.
89       IF NOT wa_zmember02-zzcoursetitle(3) = 'SAP'.
90         WRITE: / wa_zmember02-mnumber,
                       wa_zmember02-zzcoursetitle.
91       ENDIF.
92     ENDSELECT.
93     SKIP.
94   ENDIF.
95
96   * Check Radiobutton
97   IF NOT leapyear IS INITIAL.
98     SELECT * FROM zmember02 INTO wa_zmember02.
99       year004 = wa_zmember02-mdob(4) MOD 4.
100      year100 = wa_zmember02-mdob(4) MOD 100.
101      year400 = wa_zmember02-mdob(4) MOD 400.
102      IF NOT wa_zmember02-mdob IS INITIAL.
103        IF year400 = 0 OR year400 = 0 AND NOT year100 = 0.
104          WRITE: / wa_zmember02-mnumber,
                         wa_zmember02-zzcoursetitle,
105                      wa_zmember02-mdob(4).
106        ENDIF.
107      ENDIF.
108    ENDSELECT.
109    SKIP.
110  ENDIF.
```

Listing 11.1 Z_MEMBERLIST11 Report

Notes on the Source Code

Line 21

The OBLIGATORY and VALUE CHECK additions make the input field a required field, and the system checks the entries according to the ABAP Dictionary. If fixed values are stored in the domain, as in the example, only these stored values will be accepted by the system as valid inputs. The user can only leave the selection screen after entering a valid value, unless the transaction is completely canceled. This ensures that only valid entries for this field will be processed.

Lines 25 to 27

The fields are defined as radio buttons and grouped as RAD1. The group name is arbitrary.

Line 29

The SELECT-OPTIONS statement for the selection table DOB uses the NO-EXTENSION addition to prevent multiple selections. If the addition is omitted, selection of multiple values is automatically activated.

Line 32

The parameter SECOND receives an initial value in the selection screen. If the entry is greater than 0, the program reacts as we would expect.

Line 40

The parameter field ALLREC was defined as a checkbox in the selection screen. If it is visually marked with a checkmark, the field contents are no longer initial. The following statement block will be executed.

Line 56

The radio button INITIALV is checked for an entry. If it was selected in the selection screen, the system executes the corresponding statement block.

Line 69

Basically, this line means that the condition is satisfied when the date of birth read from the current record appears in the DOB selection table. For instance, the condition is satisfied when the date of birth appears as a single value in the selection table, exactly as read from the record, or if there is a range given in the selection table that contains the date of birth read.

Lines 78 and 79

The two parameter fields, GENDER and COURSE, are used in a logical AND combination. The condition is satisfied when both the field for the gender in the record read is identical with the content of the GENDER parameter, and the field for the course title is identical with the contents of COURSE.

Lines 86 and 96

The second and third radio buttons are checked. As far as content is concerned, the procedure is analogous to Line 56; for demonstration purposes, the checking of radio buttons is distributed in the source code. There is no technical reason to check the group of radio buttons in a single structure. In practice, it is better for the readability, transparency, and changeability of the source code if you don't spread this check over multiple locations your code, as we did here. Instead, as far as possible, we recommend that you check a group of radio buttons as a coherent statement block in one single location. Other people forced to deal with your source code will thank you for it.

Program Output

In Figure 11.33, there are still no selection texts entered. However, the NO-EXTENSION addition prevents multiple selection. In addition, the entry field for the gender already has some input. In Figure 11.34, you see the selection screen, which is analogous to Figure 11.33, except for the selection texts entered.

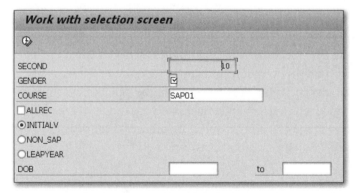

Figure 11.33 Selection Screen with Technical Names (without Multiple Selection)

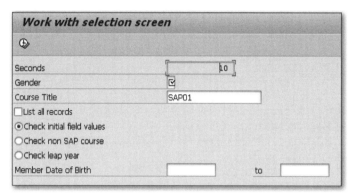

Figure 11.34 Selection Screen with Selection Texts

Sample Code for Selection Screen (Extended Form)

Listing 11.2 illustrates how to take more control over the design of the selection screen and how to use events to control the flow of program execution.

```
 1   *&----------------------------------------------------*
 2   *& Report   Z_MEMBERLIST11_B                          *
 3   *&                                                    *
 4   *&----------------------------------------------------*
 5   *&                                                    *
 6   *&                                                    *
 7   *&----------------------------------------------------*
 8
 9   REPORT   z_memberlist11_b.
10
11   * Define table work area
12   DATA: wa_zmember02 TYPE zmember02.
13
14   * Define fields
15   DATA: mnumber     TYPE zmember02-mnumber,
16         wrong_memb TYPE zmember02-mnumber,
17         year004 TYPE i,
18         year100 TYPE i,
19         year400 TYPE i.
20
21   * Define selection screen
```

```
22  PARAMETERS: second TYPE i DEFAULT 10 OBLIGATORY,
23              case,
24              initialv RADIOBUTTON GROUP rad1,
25              non_sap  RADIOBUTTON GROUP rad1,
26              leapyear RADIOBUTTON GROUP rad1.
27
28  * Block on selection screen with frame and frame text
29  SELECTION-SCREEN BEGIN OF BLOCK member
30                   WITH FRAME TITLE text-001. "Member
31  * Comment line in frame
32  SELECTION-SCREEN BEGIN OF LINE.
33  SELECTION-SCREEN COMMENT 24(60) text-005.
34  *                 'This frame is for information about
                      members only'
35  SELECTION-SCREEN END OF LINE.
36  SELECTION-SCREEN SKIP.
37  * Line with comment and two parameters
38  SELECTION-SCREEN BEGIN OF LINE.
39  SELECTION-SCREEN COMMENT (20) text-002 FOR FIELD gender.
40  *                 'Gender f / m'
41  SELECTION-SCREEN POSITION 24.
42  PARAMETERS gender TYPE zmember02-mgender
                         OBLIGATORY VALUE CHECK.
43  SELECTION-SCREEN COMMENT 32(16) text-004. "Coursetitle
44  PARAMETERS course TYPE zmember02-zzcoursetitle
45          DEFAULT 'SAP01'
46          LOWER CASE.
47  SELECTION-SCREEN END OF LINE.
48  * Line with comment and selection table
49  SELECTION-SCREEN BEGIN OF LINE.
50  SELECTION-SCREEN COMMENT (16) text-003. "Day of birth
51  SELECTION-SCREEN POSITION 21.
52  SELECT-OPTIONS dob FOR wa_zmember02-mdob NO-EXTENSION.
53  SELECTION-SCREEN END OF LINE.
54  * Line with comment and parameter
55  SELECTION-SCREEN BEGIN OF LINE.
56  SELECTION-SCREEN COMMENT (47) text-006.
57  *                 'Display additional list of all members'
58  PARAMETERS allrec AS CHECKBOX.
59  SELECTION-SCREEN END OF LINE.
60  SELECTION-SCREEN END OF BLOCK member.
61
62  * Parameter beyond the frame
```

```
63   PARAMETERS new_memb TYPE zmember02-mnumber.
64
65   INITIALIZATION.
66 * Calculate field value for suggestion new member number
67     SELECT * FROM zmember02 INTO wa_zmember02.
68       mnumber = wa_zmember02-mnumber.
69     ENDSELECT.
70     mnumber = mnumber + 1.
71     new_memb = mnumber.
72 * Check field value of second
73   AT SELECTION-SCREEN ON second.
74     IF second < 5 OR second > 20.
75       MESSAGE e001(zabap).
76     ENDIF.
77 * Check new member number
78   AT SELECTION-SCREEN ON new_memb.
79     IF new_memb < mnumber.
80       wrong_memb = new_memb.
81       new_memb = mnumber.
82       MESSAGE e002(zabap) WITH wrong_memb.
83     ENDIF.
84     .
85
86   START-OF-SELECTION.
87 * Decremental stopwatch
88     WHILE second > 0.
89       WRITE: second.
90       second = second - 1.
91     ENDWHILE.
92     WRITE: / second.
93     SKIP.
94 * Check checkbox allrec
95     IF NOT allrec IS INITIAL.
96 * Display content of table
97       SELECT * FROM zmember02 INTO wa_zmember02.
98         WRITE: / wa_zmember02-mnumber,
99                  wa_zmember02-mname,
100                 wa_zmember02-mdob,
101                 wa_zmember02-mgender,
102                 wa_zmember02-mfee,
103                 wa_zmember02-mcurrency,
104                 wa_zmember02-zzcartype,
105                 wa_zmember02-zzcoursetitle.
```

```
106      ENDSELECT.
107      SKIP.
108    ENDIF. "not allrec is initial
109  * Check radiobutton initialv
110    IF NOT initialv IS INITIAL.
111      SELECT * FROM zmember02 INTO wa_zmember02.
112        IF wa_zmember02-mdob IS INITIAL.
113          WRITE: / wa_zmember02-mnumber, wa_zmember02-mname,
114                    'Day of birth is missing,
                        please maintain'.
115        ENDIF.
116      ENDSELECT.
117      SKIP.
118    ENDIF.
119  * Check select options dob
120    SELECT * FROM zmember02 INTO wa_zmember02.
121      IF wa_zmember02-mdob IN dob.
122        WRITE: / wa_zmember02-mnumber, wa_zmember02-mname,
123                  wa_zmember02-mdob.
124      ENDIF.
125    ENDSELECT.
126    SKIP.
127  * Check parameters gender and course with logical AND
128    SELECT * FROM zmember02 INTO wa_zmember02.
129      IF wa_zmember02-mgender = gender AND
130         wa_zmember02-zzcoursetitle = course.
131        WRITE: / wa_zmember02-mnumber,
                    wa_zmember02-mname,
132                  wa_zmember02-mgender,
                    wa_zmember02-zzcoursetitle.
133      ENDIF.
134    ENDSELECT.
135    SKIP.
136  * Check radiobutton non_sap with logical NOT
137    IF NOT non_sap IS INITIAL. "Easy version:
                                    If non_sap is 'X'.
138      SELECT * FROM zmember02 INTO wa_zmember02.
139        IF NOT wa_zmember02-zzcoursetitle(3) = 'SAP'.
140          WRITE: / wa_zmember02-mnumber,
                      wa_zmember02-zzcoursetitle.
141        ENDIF.
142      ENDSELECT.
143      SKIP.
```

```
144     ENDIF.
145   * Check radiobutton leap year
146     IF NOT leapyear IS INITIAL.
147       SELECT * FROM zmember02 INTO wa_zmember02.
148         year004 = wa_zmember02-mdob(4) MOD 4.
149         year100 = wa_zmember02-mdob(4) MOD 100.
150         year400 = wa_zmember02-mdob(4) MOD 400.
151         IF NOT wa_zmember02-mdob IS INITIAL.
152           IF year400 = 0 OR year004 = 0 AND NOT
                  year100 = 0.
153             WRITE: / wa_zmember02-mnumber,
                         wa_zmember02-zzcoursetitle,
154                      wa_zmember02-mdob(4).
155           ENDIF.
156         ENDIF.
157       ENDSELECT.
158       SKIP.
159     ENDIF.
```

Listing 11.2 Z_MEMBERLIST11_B Report

Notes on the Source Code

The source code in the extended form differs from the source code in the simple form in two significant ways: The selection screen has been formatted freely, and events are used for control. The definition part of the report contains not only the PARAMETERS and SELECT-OPTIONS statements, but also statements for block and line layout.

Lines 29 and 60

The block beginning is defined; the name of the block is required for the definition. However, you only need it to open the block named and to close it again. In addition to the block name, it is determined that the block should have a frame and a title. The title text is stored in the text symbol TEXT-001.

Comments on the command

Line 32

The first line is defined.

Line 33

In the first line starting in position 24, with a length of 60 characters, we print a text. The text itself is stored in the text symbol TEXT-005.

Line 35

The definition of the line is ended.

Line 36

Now we generate a blank line. This statement demonstrates that there are SELECTION-SCREEN statements, which don't make sense within a line. This is because you can't generate a blank line in a line; you can only generate a blank line between two lines in a block.

Line 38

Here we define the third line.

Line 39

A text is printed with left justification (that is, starting in column 0, with a length of 20 characters) and associated with the input field GENDER. This allows the help functions of the F1 and F4 to apply not only to the input field, but also to the associated text.

Test the functionality in the selection screen. Place the focus on the text (by clicking on it) and call up the help function. The same help will appear as for the input field.

Line 41

In the same line, the positioning for the next field is defined as column 24. Here, the next output occurs in the selection screen. But be careful with positioning. "Clever" positioning can result in previous texts or fields on the line being overwritten, truncated, or covered up entirely.

Line 42

Also in line 3, the parameter field GENDER is displayed at the current position in the selection screen for input.

Line 43

Starting in position 32, with a length of 16, the text that is printed is stored in text symbol `TEXT-004`.

Line 44

Still in line 3, the input field `COURSE` is written to the selection screen.

Line 47

The structure for line 3 is finally closed.

Lines 49 to 53

The structure and content of line 4 is defined.

Lines 55 to 59

The structure and content of line 5 is defined.

 Unwritten Rules

> Many developers write the text stored as a comment on the command to improve the readability of the source code. Consider this an unwritten rule that you should follow. The definition of the block end can be found in line 60. In between are the structures for the line layout of the lines in the block.

Line 65

We live in the age of event orientation. The event keyword `INITIAL-IZATION` causes the runtime environment to execute the first processing commands of the report even before the selection screen appears. All statements behind the event keyword belong to the event and are executed. The event is a structure, but it has no explicit statement for the end of the structure—that is, no statement comparable to `ENDIF`, `ENDCASE`, `ENDDO`, `SELECTION-SCREEN END OF LINE`, and so on. In other words, if the next event keyword in line 71 were missing, these statements would also belong to the `INITIALIZATION` event.

Age of event orientation

An event ends when an event keyword defines a new event, a subprogram starts, or the report ends, for example. So after the first event keyword appears in the source code, you are forced to continue working with event keywords. From now on, you will also be working with events and will get to know a few more. They simplify work; in fact, some advanced solutions are just impossible without them.

Lines 67 to 71

This statement block is executed on the INITIALIZATION event. As an example of processing, the member table is read, and the last (that is, the highest) member number is determined. Then the member numbers are incremented until a suggestion value is yielded for the number of the next member. This suggested value can be automatically used when entering a new member record.

Line 73

The new event AT SELECTION-SCREEN provides a boundary for the coding of the previous event, INITIALIZATION. The AT SELECTION-SCREEN event block is still processed in the selection screen in order to check the user's input before diving deep into program execution. As long as the checks performed during this event output any error messages, the selection screen will remain ready for the user's input. In this example, the field SECOND is checked to ensure that the entry made is accepted as valid input.

If the checks do not output any error messages, program execution continues according to the user's choice. For example, if the user has triggered the AT SELECTION-SCREEN event by pressing the F8 key in order to start the program, execution continues with the START-OF-SELECTION event.

Lines 74 to 76

The input test itself is processed. If the value entered is less than 5 or more than 20 seconds, then the following processing block—the error-handling block—is executed.

In this example, this statement block is nothing more than line 75, where the MESSAGE statement sends a message to the user. The message has number 001 from message class ZABAP. The message text is stored in table T100 in the corresponding message class. The message type (in our case, E for error) controls the effect of the message. Remember that the message type is context-sensitive. We already described how this message type works in combination with a selection screen, so we won't list all the options of all message types and their effects here. You can find more details in *The Official ABAP Reference* (SAP PRESS, 3rd edition, 2012).

Message type is context-sensitive

Lines 77 to 83

There is an input check for the new member number. If there is an attempt to give a new member a preexisting member number, then error handling is triggered. Further processing is cancelled and the selection screen is sent again. As part of the incorrect entry hint, the message includes the invalid member number. This invalid number is inserted in the MESSAGE statement in line 82, with the addition WITH and the field WRONG_MEMB. The message 002 has an ampersand (&) at the appropriate point in the text.

Line 86

The new event keyword START-OF-SELECTION again places a boundary on the previous event. Under this event appear statements you already know from previous examples.

 Event Orientation

Without event orientation, you wouldn't be able to execute your own processing blocks before the appearance of the selection screen, or to define your own input verifications.

Program Output

In Figure 11.35, you see that the block in the selection screen has a gray background, a frame, and a frame text on the left. The first line in the block consists of a free text without reference to an input field. The second line is blank.

In the third line, there are two input fields: GENDER F/M and COURSE TITLE. The text in front of the GENDER input field is associated with the input field, so that the association registers when you focus on the text and press the help keys F1 or F4. Then the help for the input field also appears for the text, exactly as stored in the ABAP Dictionary. In the second input field, COURSE TITLE, the text is not associated. The help keys F1 and F4 function only when the focus is on the input fields, and not on the text. Compare this with the relevant points in the source code, lines 39 and 43.

The fourth line contains the selection table without multiple selection, but the fifth line is a little more interesting. Usually, checkboxes are left justified, and their selection texts follow immediately. Free layout allows you to reverse this order and position the text and the checkbox wherever you want on the line.

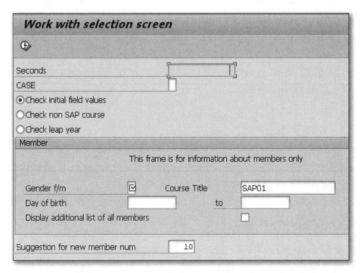

Figure 11.35 Selection Screen with Free Text Layout and Free Parameter Positioning

 Multiple Blocks in One Selection Screen

After the end of the block, more input fields or blocks can be defined in the input screen, as seen in this example. Depending on the requirements, it can certainly make sense for you to define multiple blocks in one selection screen.

In Figure 11.36, you see an attempt to execute the report without filling in the required field for the gender. The system has interrupted processing and displayed the selection screen again with the message "Fill in all required entry fields."

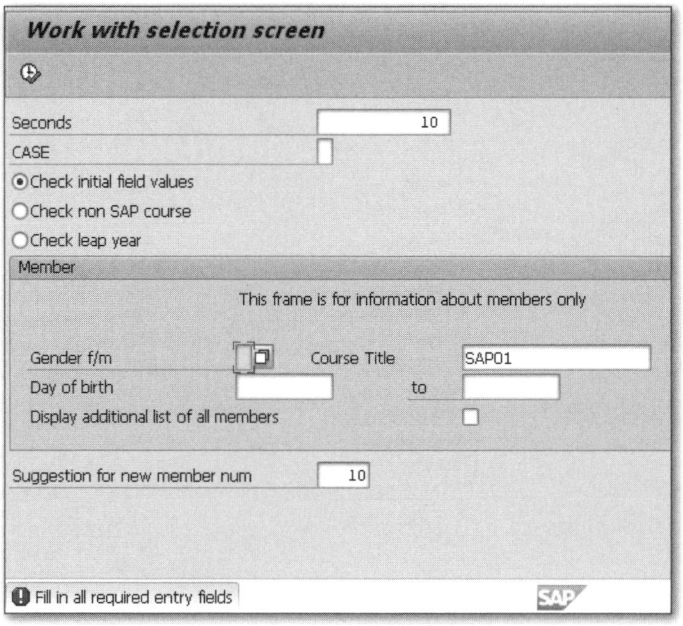

Figure 11.36 Selection Screen with Error Message (1)

Figure 11.37 shows an attempt to execute the report with an invalid input for the seconds. In the AT SELECTION-SCREEN event, there is a specially coded input verification for the field SECOND, which requires that a valid value for the seconds lie between 5 and 20. Because that does not apply here, a message appears on the status bar. This message should be formulated in such a way that it helps the user make valid entries. Based on the formulation of the event, not only is the SECOND field ready for input again, but all of the other fields are only visible in display mode.

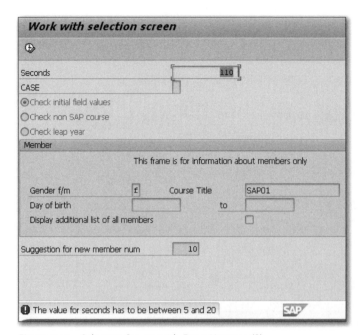

Figure 11.37 Selection Screen with Error Message (2)

12

Internal Tables

You're probably familiar with using tables in the database, but perhaps not with using tables in the memory. You have both of these options in the SAP system. In this chapter, you will come to know and appreciate the tables in the memory.

So far in this book, you have learned about database tables and work areas. You have defined the structure of a database table or field list using the structure of the database table in the ABAP Dictionary and simply referring to it for work areas. Consequently, the structures of work areas and database tables in the previous examples were identical. However, the ABAP Dictionary is only one of two options that you can use to define structures.

The other option is found in the ABAP programs directly: While the structure in the ABAP Dictionary is saved permanently, the structure in the ABAP source code is saved only temporarily. It is defined only when you call the program. The required memory areas are then reserved and the structure is available in the memory only during the runtime of the ABAP program. You can fill and change work areas while executing the program. If the program ends, all reserved memory areas are released again and may be deleted or overwritten.

Only when the program is called

The internal tables behave in almost exactly the same way as the structures defined in ABAP. The only difference is that a temporary structure (a work area) has only one line, while an internal table can have any number of lines. Like a database table, all lines of the internal table have the same line structure.

Purpose of Internal Tables

Temporary tables Internal tables are defined in the ABAP source code, so they only exist temporarily in the memory. Internal tables are defined when you start the program and modified while you are processing the program; when you end the program, the contents and structure cease to exist. Interim results or calculations for list outputs (and so on) are not saved. However, they don't need to be, since the end results were preferably stored in another medium, such as an output list, document, file, data medium, or database table. In addition, the data required for the calculation is still on the database, which means that you can reproduce the end results at any time.

 Processing Speed

When it comes to processing speed, internal tables are beneficial if you want to process complex data structures or large volumes of data in the form of structured data records. Because internal tables are located in the memory, a table entry or a table field of an internal table is accessed considerably faster than it would be on a database table.

Flexibility Internal tables can contain any number of defined structures, so you can group the structures of several database tables into the structure of an internal table, for example. However, you would only be able to compile the structure of the internal table from fields that are defined in the ABAP program. Combinations are also possible, for which program-specific fields are added to the ABAP Dictionary structures.

This approach enables you to set up a data record in such a way that all relevant data for this record is located in a single internal table entry. It is immaterial in this case, from how many database tables and additional calculations the fields of the internal table entries were originally filled. You can easily process and print the complete record from here. You can also sort the entire internal table according to specific criteria (for example, for various forms or lists) without any problems.

You can also refer to the content of an internal table as the table body. In the past, internal tables also contained a header line in addition to their table body; without specific declaration of an additional data object, the header line fulfilled the function of a work area. These days, this construct is obsolete, and is only supported for compatibility reasons. Today, we use explicitly declared work areas instead. The table body contains the table entries, where a table entry corresponds to a data record. Like a database table, all lines have the same setup and structure. To process where data records are read, each data record from the table body must be placed in the header line or work area. Further processing is then performed from there. To process where data records are written, you first set up a line in the header line or work area and then transfer it to the table body by adding or inserting it.

Table body and work area separated

These types of processing frequently occur in a loop for all lines. Individual records can also be processed, of course.

The now obsolete method with header lines was similar to the use of TABLES statements, which is also prohibited in modern ABAP. In both cases, you implicitly define a work area that has the same name as the internal or transparent table and allows access to this table using short forms of the corresponding ABAP statements. On one hand, it saves developers the effort of all that typing; on the other, code in which aspects such as work area and table objects are as mixed up as in these constructs is regarded as less transparent and hard to maintain.

n-dimensional tables are possible

Furthermore, the topic of separating the table body and work area opens up new possibilities: For example, you can create internal tables whose line type is an internal table. From a technical perspective, multi-dimensional table processing is no longer a problem with several work areas. A single, flat structure for use as a header line would mean that the world of internal tables, in this respect, would have remained flat (two-dimensional) as well; however, n-dimensional table processing is a separate topic and will not be discussed here any further.

Simple Use with Fields

You use the fields of internal tables in the same way as fields of database tables. The fields of an internal table are also accessed using `Tablename-Fieldname`. But don't forget that, like with a database table, you only use it to access the contents of the field currently in the work area or header line. The work area must already be filled accordingly before the contents are accessed.

Any number of lines   An internal table can have any number of lines. The limits are set by the SAP architecture at approximately 2 gigabytes and by the system installation and its constraints related to hardware, operating systems, and so on.

 Processing Speed

Of course, the processing speed tends to decrease when the number of lines and table sizes increase and when the system is searching for individual records, for example. Depending on business requirements and the expected table size, you should pay attention to the type when you create the internal table. The individual table types are described in the following section.

Structure and Types of Internal Tables

In internal tables, the data is stored in the *table body*. If the tables include header lines, they additionally have a *header*. Otherwise, you have to define a work area and then transfer a data record from the table to the work area to be able to process it. The table body consists of any number of identically structured lines.

Line type   The line type is an ABAP data type, a structure, or an internal table. If you have a simple case—for example, where a line consists of a flat structure of fields—the fields correspond to the columns of the internal table. However, an internal table can also have a deep structure as the line type. In deep structures, the components (the "fields") have their own structure and can contain multiple fields or even internal tables themselves.

Working with keys is another important difference that arises with internal tables. Although, like a database table, the key is used to identify a line, internal tables may have unique or non-unique keys. We also differentiate between standard keys and user-defined keys.

Access key

A *unique key* means that a line can only appear once, not multiple times. This is similar to a database table. A *non-unique key* means that a line can also appear multiple times in an internal table. The *standard key* depends on the line type of the table. If we continue with the simple assumption that the line consists of a structure with fields, the standard key is composed of all fields of the structure. In this case, a *user-defined key* is compiled from any freely definable subset of fields of the structure.

Depending on the access type, internal tables can be assigned to different table types:

Access types

> **Standard tables**

Standard tables can be accessed using the key or an index. When you access a table using a key, the access time and number of lines are correlated linearly (that is, the greater the number of lines, the longer it takes to get a response). Therefore, access to large internal tables is provided using an index that is maintained internally. The access time in this case only increases logarithmically, not linearly.

A unique key cannot be defined for a standard table, so it's possible to have identical lines that appear multiple times. Standard tables can be filled very quickly in this case, because a duplication of existing keys is not checked. For example, the table could be filled first and then sorted in line with the intended purpose. Depending on the form of access, the search effort would then also only increase logarithmically.

Due to easy handling, the standard tables are still the most frequently recurring table type in practice. You will work with standard tables and key access in the following examples in this chapter.

> **Sorted tables**
>
> Sorted tables are always stored in sorted format according to a key. Unlike for the standard tables, the key can be unique for sorted tables. Tables are accessed using either the key or an index. When you access a table using a key, the access time increases—although only logarithmically—with the number of lines.
>
> We recommend that you use sorted tables rather than standard tables if you want the lines to be sorted when the internal table is being filled. Duplications of lines are already common at this stage. Depending on the contents of the return code of the ABAP statement and the composition of the error handling in the source code, a runtime error is triggered or the system branches into an error-handling routine.

Index tables | Because sorted tables and standard tables both have an internal index, they are also referred to as *index tables*.

> **Hashed tables**
>
> Hashed tables are not accessed using an index (by specifying a line number); neither does the system internally use a linear index to locate records. They are only accessed using a unique key. We recommend using this table type for large tables. Because the system uses a special type of algorithm known as a *hash algorithm*, the response time is constant, regardless of how many lines are contained in the table. The hashed table is the fastest of the three internal table types for large tables. For very small tables, even shorter access times are possible with a different table type in some circumstances.
>
> Simply put, a hash algorithm is ultimately a function for a checksum process that identifies—as uniquely as possible—and briefly describes a data record. There are several hash algorithms, but we won't discuss these further here. Hash algorithms are also used for digital signatures and in cryptology.

Traditional and modern syntax | Sorted tables, hashed tables, and keys for internal tables have existed for well over a decade, since SAP R/3 4.0. These table types and the type concept created new possibilitie s for defining tables and processing tables. This is why, in practice, you will also find various syntax forms for similar tasks and functions. The same also applies for standard tables; there are both traditional and modern syntaxes for statements that have the same meaning.

 Use the Modern Syntax

Although this chapter introduces both the modern variant and the traditional (obsolete) variant, you should always opt to use the more modern syntax. The obsolete variants cannot process all table types and can lead to syntax errors in the context of ABAP Objects. The ABAP environment will continue to support obsolete language constructs for many years due to compatibility reasons. But ABAP Objects is increasingly used in all applications of the SAP system; the places where it makes sense to use non-object-oriented ABAP are quickly decreasing in terms of number and extent.

ABAP Objects is also used for current and future SAP developments. For this reason, we recommend that you get started directly with the modern syntax and only become acquainted with the obsolete variants because you'll still find them in old code. So the following examples first use the modern syntax to complete the task and then illustrate the traditional syntax.

Creating an Internal Standard Table

Let's first look at the common creation of a standard table.

Object-Oriented Syntax with Work Area

The modern syntax clearly distinguishes between *data object*—to which concrete values are assigned—and *data type*. A data type is a structure description that serves as a pattern for the declaration of data objects and can be reused in various data objects. Data types can be elementary (a single field) or complex (consisting of other data types). If a data type is complex, that is, consists of other data types, then those data types can also be elementary or complex. This composition upholds the "modular design principle" that lets you create complex data types that consist of other data types. This is the only way, for example, to create an internal table that contains an internal table, and so on.

Modular design principle

To define an internal table, you need four levels for the object-oriented approach and syntax:

› Defining a line type
› Defining a table type
› Defining the table
› Defining the work area

At first, this may seem like a great deal of effort, but looks can be deceiving: In large and complex programs, the advantage of reusing the type definitions of tables and table lines prevails. They can be used for other tables or for interfaces; you can nest them as required and integrate them into new types.

Defining a line type

Based on our first example, you would first define the line type `LINE01_TYPE` with the `TYPES` statement to define the internal table `ITAB01`:

TYPES

```
TYPES: BEGIN OF line01_type,
         zzcoursetitle TYPE zmember02-zzcoursetitle,
         mfee TYPE zmember02-mfee,
       END OF line01_type.
```

The line type consists of two fields, `ZZCOURSETITLE` and `MFEE`. Reference is made to the ABP Dictionary for their definition. The fields (strictly speaking, the field types) are also defined here using the `TYPES` statement, not the `DATA` statement. The `TYPES` statement is structured as a chain statement in the example.

Defining a table type

You also define the table type with the `TYPES` statement. The `ITAB01_TYPE` table type should always be a standard table type with the `LINE01_TYPE` line type. A standard table always has one non-unique key, so the addition for the key can be omitted. In most cases, the addition for the initial memory space of the internal table can also be omitted. This makes sense only if you could already accurately estimate the expected number of lines for this table type at this stage (and if the estimate would be indicative of a good performance of your program in any way). However, this is only the case for very large tables or tables that are generated multiple times. The addition to use for this purpose is INITIAL SIZE n. You can omit it if you use the value 0 for n, and you want the system to determine how to manage the memory space. You need the STANDARD TABLE OF addition to define the table type. If you want to create the ITAB01_TYPE type for a standard table with the line structure of type LINE01_TYPE, you write:

```
TYPES itab01_type TYPE STANDARD TABLE OF line01_type.
```

Simply for comparison purposes and for a better understanding of the subject, the following is a brief note about defining an internal, sorted table with a unique key: If we assume that the internal table is supposed to be a sorted table with a unique key, you have to define the table type differently. The table type would then be SORTED TABLE. You then define the unique key (in the example, the ZZCOURSETITLE field) using the WITH UNIQUE KEY addition:

```
TYPES itab01_type TYPE SORTED TABLE OF line01_type
  WITH UNIQUE KEY zzcoursetitle.
```

 Key Must Be Unique

Note that the key in this example must really be unique. You cannot have two lines with the same key (that is, with the same field contents of the key fields). The key itself can consist of several components, which are written as a field list and separated by a space.

This completes the required type definitions. As mentioned, you can reuse these type definitions for other internal tables and type definitions. Unfortunately, you'll only first see the benefits of these type definitions when you use them in practice, rather than in small sample programs like the ones here.

Still missing are the definitions of the internal table and those of the assigned work area.

Defining the internal table

You define the `ITAB01` table without a header line with the statement:

```
DATA itab01 TYPE itab01_type.
```

Defining the work area You define the work area for the `ITAB01` table using the `LINE01_TYPE` line type:

```
DATA wa_itab01 TYPE line01_type.
```

Technically speaking, the work area is not linked to the internal table, so you can use it as you wish. But you must use the appropriate statements to ensure that the work area has the right contents at the right time. Whether you subsequently use these contents for processing internal tables or for other purposes is up to you.

Obsolete Syntax with Header Line

The obsolete syntax used to define an internal table uses only the `DATA` statement. It doesn't use the `TYPES` statement because it doesn't distinguish between data type and data object; furthermore, there is no work area independent of the internal table but instead a *header line* that is linked with the table and fulfills this function. You use additions of the `DATA` statement to create a structure that indicates the beginning and end of the internal table. In between are the fields that describe a line. The structure and fields are defined as a chain statement with the `DATA` statement.

DATA If you want to create an internal table called `ITAB01`, which must have fields for the course title and course price, you define this table like this:

```
DATA: BEGIN OF itab01 OCCURS 0,
      zzcoursetitle LIKE zmember02-zzcoursetitle,
      mfee LIKE zmember02-mfee,
      END OF itab01.
```

BEGIN OF ... END OF You use the `DATA: BEGIN OF itab01` statement to define the beginning of the structure (in other words, the beginning of the internal table). You use the colon (:) after the `DATA` statement to introduce the chain statement. The `BEGIN OF` addition identifies the beginning of the `ITAB01` internal table. The definition of the ITAB01 internal table ends with the DATA statement and the END OF addition.

After the name of the internal table, you use the OCCURS addition to give an estimate of how many lines the table is expected to have. The system then reserves a corresponding memory area. If the reserved memory area is too big, you waste resources; if the reserved memory area is too small, the system automatically extends the memory. The first extension is created with the duplicated size of the reserved memory, up to a maximum of 8 kilobytes; each subsequent extension is created with 12 kilobytes. The system uses the OCCURS 0 addition to decide how big it will create the first, initial memory area. You can use this option frequently.

The OCCURS addition is also very important for another reason. It differentiates an internal table from a flat structure or work area when you define a table. If the addition is missing, the definition applies to a work area; however, if the addition is available, the system creates an internal standard table with a header line.

The DATA statement as a chain statement starts with the colon and ends with a comma. Only the last statement of the chain ends with a period. In the sample code, the END OF itab01. statement after the field definitions ends the structure.

The structure contains the statements for defining the table fields of the internal table. They describe a line. The line type could be described by a structure or a combination of structures. The general rules of the DATA statement apply for defining individual fields.

➕ Fields with Identical Names

> To help you work with internal tables, you might find it useful if fields with identical significance have names that are identical to the corresponding fields of the database tables. For technical reasons, however, this isn't necessary. The same also applies for the attributes of fields with an identical name. The next section provides relevant examples.

Filling an Internal Standard Table

This section describes the methods for filling an internal table. There are different methods for the various types of tables; these are explained in greater detail in the next sections.

Filling an Internal Table with a Work Area

First, we fill an internal table without a header line that has been generated with modern ABAP. For this purpose, we use a work area. Other methods allow you to directly access data records within an internal table, but you usually don't need to access the lines of an internal table directly. It is much more comfortable and secure to use a work area that has been generated for this purpose only. In the work area, you can then take your time to prepare the data record that you want to add to the internal table or change and transfer it to the table in another step. Since the work area is technically separated from the internal table, the work area and internal table are only linked explicitly in the program's statements that you created yourself, and not implicitly (as is the case with tables with header lines).

 Example 1

> You want to transfer the content of the ZMEMBER02 database table line by line into the fields with the identical names in the WA_ITAB03 work area. The work area can only accept the content of a line. The ITAB03 internal table should be filled from there.

Defining a line type
For a better understanding, we will again first describe the ITAB03 internal table, the assigned types, and their work areas. The line type of the internal table is described by the following three fields: COURSE_TITLE, FEE, and MAX_PERSONS.

```
TYPES: BEGIN OF line03_type,
  course_title TYPE zmember02-zzcoursetitle,
  fee TYPE zmember02-mfee,
  max_persons TYPE i,
END OF line03_type.
```

The table type of the internal table is a standard table with a non-unique key:

```
TYPES itab03_type TYPE STANDARD TABLE OF line03_type.
```

The "internal table" data object is defined using:

```
DATA itab03 TYPE itab03_type.
```

The "work area" data object is defined with:

```
DATA wa_itab03 TYPE line03_type.
```

These are the prerequisites under which you transfer (using a SELECT loop) each line of the database table into the work area WA_ZMEMBER02 explicitly created for this purpose. You then assign the field contents. For example, the WA_ITAB03-COURSE_TITLE field of the work area for the internal table receives the content of the WA_ZMEMBER02-ZZCOURSETITLE field from the work area of the database table.

After the work area of the internal table is completely filled, the APPEND statement appends the field contents of the work area to the ITAB03 internal table:

```
SELECT * FROM zmember02 INTO wa_zmember02.
  wa_itab03-course_title = wa_zmember02-zzcoursetitle.
  wa_itab03-fee = wa_zmember02-mfee.
  APPEND wa_itab03 TO itab03.
ENDSELECT.
```

Ex Example 2

You again want to transfer the content of the database table line by line and the contents of the fields with the identical names into the internal table.

Again, you do this using the work area of the database table and the work area of the internal table. The line type for the ITAB01 internal table consists of the two fields ZZCOURSETITLE and MFEE, both of which refer to the corresponding fields of the database table in their definition. The field properties in both tables are therefore also the same.

```
TYPES: BEGIN OF line01_type,
         zzcoursetitle TYPE zmember02-zzcoursetitle,
         mfee TYPE zmember02-mfee,
       END OF line01_type.
```

The table type provided for the internal table must be a standard table again with the LINE01_TYPE line type:

```
TYPES itab01_type TYPE STANDARD TABLE OF line01_type.
```

The ITAB01 internal table is defined without a header line:

```
DATA itab01 TYPE itab01_type.
```

You define the required work area using:

```
DATA wa_itab01 TYPE line01_type.
```

In the processing section, you first fill the work area of the WA_ZMEMBER02 database table in a SELECT loop. All field contents of a database line are still contained there. You then transfer the fields with the identical names from the work area of the database table into the fields of the internal table.

 Checking for Identical Names Only

Note at this point that the system only checks for fields with identical names, not for fields with identical properties. In most cases, we advise that you link the field properties through the ABAP Dictionary. This is the only way you can also guarantee that the field properties of the internal table and its work area will correspond to the field properties of the database table in future.

Transferring a work area

The updated contents of all fields with identical names are subsequently contained in the WA_ITAB01 work area. From there, they are appended to the body of the internal table using the APPEND statement:

```
SELECT * FROM zmember02 INTO wa_zmember02.
  MOVE-CORRESPONDING wa_zmember02 TO wa_itab01.
  APPEND wa_itab01 TO itab01.
ENDSELECT.
```

Example 3

> Unlike the two previous examples, you want the lines of the database table to be transferred into the internal table block by block, not line by line.
>
> As mentioned, the block-by-block transfer is the fastest way of filling the internal table.

Although the work areas of the database table and internal table are not accessed for a block-by-block transfer, we will describe their definitions here to help you better understand the following examples.

The line type is defined using:

```
TYPES BEGIN OF line02_type.
    INCLUDE TYPE line01_type.
    TYPES min_persons TYPE i.
TYPES END OF line02_type.
```

This type definition is not presented as a chain statement. The INCLUDE statement is a standalone ABAP statement and not an addition for the TYPES statement. The LINE01_TYPE data type corresponds to the type from Example 2. The type still also contains the MIN_PERSONS field for the minimum number of course members.

Chain statement

The data type for the table is a standard table with the LINE02_TYPE line type:

```
TYPES itab02_type TYPE STANDARD TABLE OF line02_type.
```

The internal table is defined without a header line using:

```
DATA itab02 TYPE itab02_type.
```

The work area for the internal table also corresponds to the LINE02_TYPE line type:

```
DATA wa_itab02 TYPE line02_type.
```

In the processing section of the report, you fill the internal table using a single command. All contents of fields with identical names are transferred in blocks (that is, one after the other and all at once) from the database table into the internal table:

Array fetch

```
SELECT * FROM zmember02
  INTO CORRESPONDING FIELDS OF TABLE itab02.
```

The system only checks for fields with identical names. Remember that this is not a structure syntax, such as a loop, for example. There is therefore no ENDSELECT statement in this case.

Filling an Internal Table with a Header Line

As already mentioned, this method is obsolete in modern ABAP and leads to syntax errors in the context of ABAP Objects. Nevertheless, we introduce it here because in your daily work with the SAP system, you will often be confronted with old program systems that still use this method. You should be able to understand these programs, correct them if errors occur, and maybe someday modernize them and implement ABAP Objects.

In these internal tables, the header line is always used both for writing and reading data. When the internal table is being filled, a line is created completely in the header line and then appended to the table body. When the data records are being read from the table body, the situation is reversed: The data record to be processed is transferred completely into the header line, where all manipulations and accesses will occur.

There are several options for filling the internal table. The following section describes some examples that frequently occur.

Filling an internal table record-by-record

 Example 1

You want to transfer and append the contents of the ZMEMBER02 database table in a loop, one record at a time, to the lines of the body of the ITAB03 internal table. You achieve this by accessing the contents of the database table record by record, using the work area of the database table and then copying each record to the header line of the internal table. Each time a record has been copied to the internal table's header line, you append it to the internal table's body.

You should define the internal table as follows:

```
DATA: BEGIN OF itab03 OCCURS 0,
        course_title TYPE zmember02-zzcoursetitle,
        fee TYPE zmember02-mfee,
        max_persons TYPE i VALUE 10,
      END OF itab03.
```

You use two fields of the internal table to refer to the field attributes of a database table. The field names COURSE_TITLE and FEE in the internal table should initially differ from the field names of the database table. In reality, there may indeed be reasons to name field names in internal tables differently, but we're mainly doing it here for comprehension and demonstration purposes. You define the third field MAX_PERSONS for the maximum number of members as the integer and assign it the initial value 10.

The internal table is filled in a SELECT loop. Each record is placed in the work area of the ZMEMBER02 database table.

```
SELECT * FROM zmember02 INTO wa_zmember02.
* Fill internal table
ENDSELECT.
```

The fields are then supplied with values in the header line of the internal table. This is done by assigning field values from the work area of the database table. For a different task, you would have to use other processing steps here.

Taking tasks into account

```
* Fill internal table
itab03-course_title = wa_zmember02-zzcoursetitle.
  itab03-fee = wa_zmember02-mfee.
```

The ITAB03-COURSE_TITLE field obtains the content of the WA_ZMEMBER02-ZZCOURSETITLE field and the ITAB03-FEE field obtains the content of the WA_ZMEMBER02-MFEE field. The third field of the internal table is already predefined with its initial value and should be copied as is for the sake of simplicity. At the end of this process, the header line of the internal table is filled entirely. The new data record is complete.

Now we are only missing a smaller but more important step: You must transfer the content of the header line to the table body. The new data record is appended to the table body as a new line for a standard table with a standard key.

APPEND

This also occurs in the SELECT loop in the statement block for filling the internal table using the following statement:

```
APPEND itab03.
```

Note that, unlike in the first example, the work area from which the data record is appended to the internal table is not specified here. If you work with this APPEND statement for internal tables with header lines, the header line of the same name (which is linked to the table) is implicitly used.

This step is easily overlooked amid the stress of work. Then we wonder why the internal table consists of only a single line. On closer reflection, even that is incorrect because the internal table doesn't have a line at all; only the header line contains the content of the last processing step and acts like a work area. This confusing property of tables with header lines is one of the reasons why the construct is considered obsolete.

Fields with identical names

 Example 2

> You want to loop over the records in the ZMEMBER02 database table and append each of them to the ITAB01 internal table. You achieve this by transferring each record from the work area of the database table into the fields with identical names for the header line of the ITAB01 internal table. Each time the header line of the internal table has been filled, you append these records to the table body of the internal table.

The internal table must contain fields with the identical name as the database table. Since the attributes must also be identical, reference is made to the fields of the database table using the TYPE addition:

```
DATA: BEGIN OF itab01 OCCURS 0,
        zzcoursetitle TYPE zmember02-zzcoursetitle,
        mfee TYPE zmember02-mfee,
      END OF itab01.
```

This internal table only has two fields that have the identical name and structure as the corresponding fields in the database table.

Also in this example, the `SELECT` loop places one record at a time in the table work area of the database table, but the processing then proceeds differently than the one used in Example 1:

```
* Read dbtab into itab01 via header line
SELECT * FROM zmember02 INTO wa_zmember02.
  MOVE-CORRESPONDING wa_zmember02 TO itab01.
    APPEND itab01.
ENDSELECT.
```

The system uses the `MOVE-CORRESPONDING` statement to find the fields with the identical name in the header line of the internal table and copies the relevant field values to that location. If the system finds two fields with the identical name (as in the example), then two field contents are transferred. For example, if there were 20 fields, then 20 field contents would be transferred. If database fields do not have counterparts with identical names in the header line of the internal table, the system does not transfer any field contents.

MOVE-CORRESPONDING

You should be careful when working with this statement because it does involve some risks. If the fields have the identical name but not the identical type, problems may occur because the system only checks for fields with the same name, not for fields with the same type, and tries, if necessary, to perform an automatic type conversion. This could result in character strings being truncated or the decimal separator being changed, for example.

Automatic type conversion

Again, it will depend on the planned further processing as to whether the automatic type conversion returns useful or harmful results. In any case, you're on safe ground if the fields of the internal table have the identical names as the relevant fields of the database table and their definitions refer to the attributes of the database fields.

The `MOVE-CORRESPONDING` statement is followed by the contents of the fields with the identical names in the header line of the internal table. The following statement appends the content of the header line to the table body as a new line:

```
  APPEND itab01.
```

Example 3

In terms of filling the internal table, you no longer want the records of the ZMEMBER02 database table to be placed line by line into the work area of the database table, then into the header line, and from there into the body of the internal table. Instead, you want to transfer all records of the database table into the internal table as a data block. The processing will no longer take place in a loop. Consequently, you avoid working with the work area of the database table and the header line of the internal table.

Unlike the two previous examples, the records are now transferred from the database table directly into the body of the internal table block by block as a closed data block. To make this easier to understand, we will first provide you with some notes about defining the internal table, which you should do like this:

```
DATA BEGIN OF itab02 OCCURS 0.
       INCLUDE STRUCTURE itab01.
       DATA min_persons TYPE i.
DATA END OF itab02.
```

INCLUDE
STRUCTURE

You should first note that this example is not about defining a chain statement. Although the structure for defining the ITAB02 internal table is the same, there are two statements in the structure. The first statement contains the existing line type of the ITAB01 internal table:

```
INCLUDE STRUCTURE itab01.
```

In the ITAB01 sample table, a line has two fields; so from now on, a line from ITAB02 will also have two fields. They have the same name and structure as the fields in ITAB01. You can use this statement to include every existing structure.

You can, of course, also include structures from the ABAP Dictionary. The following statement, for example, would include the structure of the ZMEMBER02 database table in a line of the ITAB02 internal table:

```
INCLUDE STRUCTURE zmember02.
```

This approach means that several structures could also be included in a single internal table by several consecutive INCLUDE statements. The combination with additional fields is also an option. In the example, the

MIN_PERSONS field is also defined in the line as type i and determines the minimum number of members of a course. A line from the ITAB02 internal table therefore consists of three fields.

In this example, the ITAB02 internal table is filled without a loop through a block-by-block transfer (that is, not line for line, one record at a time, but from the body of the database table into the body of the internal table). This block-by-block type of transfer is also called an *array fetch*. Note that the SELECT statement for this syntax is not a loop:

Array fetch

```
SELECT * FROM zmember02
  INTO CORRESPONDING FIELDS OF TABLE itab02.
```

The ITAB02 internal table has a field for the minimum number of members, which is not contained in the database table. This field is not filled in the lines of the internal table using the SELECT statement and remains empty; this also applies to all other similar fields. If required, they would have to be filled in a separate processing block for the internal table.

This form of SELECT statement provides the fastest option to fill an internal table. The table work area of the database table and the work area of the internal table are avoided. If you don't want to transfer all fields of a line from the database table, simply specify a list of the fields to be transferred in place of the asterisk in the SELECT statement. For example, if you only want to transfer the contents of the MNUMBER, MNAME, and MDOB fields into the ITAB05 internal table, the statement would read like this:

```
SELECT mnumber mname mdob FROM zmember02
  INTO CORRESPONDING FIELDS OF TABLE itab05.
```

The fields with the identical names must, of course, also exist in the ITAB05 internal table.

Processing an Internal Table Line by Line

Let's first process an internal table with a work area.

Processing an Internal Table with a Work Area

Like database tables, you can also process all lines consecutively, or individual lines specifically, for internal tables using a loop. However, to do this here, you must use different statements for database tables and internal tables.

LOOP ... ENDLOOP

To process all records of an internal table in a loop, you use the LOOP and ENDLOOP statements. These are structure statements similar to the structure of SELECT and ENDSELECT. The LOOP statement opens the structure and the ENDLOOP statement closes it again. In between are the statements that indicate how a line is to be processed.

The LOOP loop places the lines in the work area record by record. Since you can freely select the work area, you must specify in the LOOP statement the work area in which you want the line to be placed. If you have provided the WA_ITAB01 work area for the ITAB01 internal table, the LOOP statement is:

```
LOOP AT itab01 INTO wa_itab01.
```

 LOOP AT with References and Field Symbols

In addition to using work areas, there are two other methods for the line-by-line access to an internal table. If you use the LOOP statement with the ASSIGNING addition, then a field symbol is always assigned to another table line in each loop run.

If you use the LOOP statement with the REFERENCE INTO addition, a reference variable is always filled with a reference to another table line in each loop run. However, these advanced methods are only mentioned for the sake of completeness.

The WA_ITAB01 work area is now filled with a line of table ITAB01 in each loop run. If you want to output the fields of the WA_ITAB01 work area onto a list, write this:

```
WRITE: / wa_itab01-zzcoursetitle, wa_itab01-mfee.
```

In reality, it is usually more time-consuming to process a line. But in all cases, you must close the processing loop using the ENDLOOP statement.

To change existing entries in an internal table, use the MODIFY state-   MODIFY
ment. If the MODIFY statement is inside a LOOP loop, the current line
of the internal table is updated, indicating the relevant work area. In
this case, the content of the work area, in turn, must first be updated
inside a LOOP loop using a statement:

```
wa_itab03-fee = 567.
```

After all fields of the work area have received the updated content,
the body line of the internal table is updated using the FROM addition,
taking the relevant work area into account:

```
MODIFY itab03 FROM wa_itab03.
```

 MODIFY

> The MODIFY statement only changes the content of an existing line of the
> internal table; it doesn't create a new line here. If the MODIFY command
> is in a LOOP loop, the current line is always changed. However, the key for
> tables with a unique key must not be changed in this case. If the MODIFY
> statement is outside a LOOP loop, the line to be changed must be speci-
> fied using the index.

When you insert new lines, you must first set up the new line in the   INSERT
corresponding work area. The work area in the following example is
WA_ITAB01:

```
wa_itab01-zzcoursetitle = 'LINUX-BASICS'.
wa_itab01-mfee = '456.78'.
```

You then transfer the content of the work area into the table body of
the ITAB01 internal table. The index for the correct line is contained in
the LINES_ITAB01 field. You also determined it already:

```
INSERT wa_itab01 INTO itab01 INDEX lines_itab01.
```

As soon as you have identified the correct line of the internal table   READ
using the index, you can access the index of the line using the INDEX
addition and place the line into the work area provided, for example,
WA_ITAB03 using the INTO addition:

```
READ TABLE itab03 INDEX 3 INTO wa_itab03.
```

Index

> You can specify the index absolutely. In practice, a field name with the relevant content will appear instead of the number 3 in this example. Access via the index is the fastest access type for index tables.
>
> However, if you cannot determine the index, you can also use key fields to access data. In the case of sorted tables, you were already able to specify the key for the definition. Accordingly, you would use this key for the READ statement.

WITH KEY In our example, we are working with standard tables that always have a non-unique key. So you must consider which key fields you can use to identify a line of the internal table as uniquely as possible. Since lines may appear multiple times in standard tables, this is particularly important. The READ statement takes the first suitable record, without questioning whether there may still be other matching lines in the internal table, and places it into the corresponding work area, like this:

```
READ TABLE itab02 INTO wa_itab02
  WITH KEY zzcoursetitle = 'SAP06'.
```

Here, the INTO addition transfers the first suitable line from the body lines of the ITAB02 internal table into the WA_ITAB02 work area, for which the ZZCOURSETITLE field has the content "SAP06". However, the table could contain several lines with this field content; the READ statement no longer checks this possibility.

DELETE When you delete a body line, you can also identify the relevant line using the index or the content of the work area. If you search for the body line using the work area, you must fill the work area accordingly before the DELETE statement. Like the READ statement, the DELETE statement only searches from the beginning of the table to the first suitable record in the body lines and deletes only this record. The DELETE statement also has the problem of identically named body lines that appear multiple times, albeit in a different sense.

ADJACENT DUPLICATES One option to delete redundant lines would be to first sort the internal table accordingly, and then use the DELETE statement and ADJACENT DUPLICATES addition to delete the redundant lines except for one line. However, we won't discuss this option any further here.

If you have already filled the WA_ITAB02 work area adequately, specify the ITAB02 internal table using the TABLE addition, and the relevant work area using the FROM addition, like this:

```
DELETE TABLE itab02 FROM wa_itab02.
```

Processing an Internal Table with a Header Line

In this section, we want to highlight in particular the differences that arise with internal tables when you work with a header line rather than a work area. The same applies to the descriptions of internal tables with header lines: This method is obsolete and prohibited in the ABAP Objects environment. Nevertheless, you'll often come across it in real life, so knowledge about it is indispensible.

The reason for the prohibition of internal tables with header lines in ABAP Objects is the same as the reason for the prohibition of the TA-BLES statement: Two different data objects (header line and table body) are addressed with the same name. This and other implicit behaviors of the ABAP system in combination with tables with header lines are confusing for developers and no longer correspond to the modern programming conventions. Today, a more explicit programming style is preferred—one in which you can actually find the task the system is supposed to carry out in the source code.

The main difference in the processing by line is that the lines of the internal table must always and only be read and written using a corresponding header line. This applies to single access and loops.

In the case of an internal table with a header line, the records are transferred line by line from the table body into the header line and processed there according to the statements:

```
LOOP AT itab01.
*   Process workarea line with array fetch
ENDLOOP.
```

The statement block may only consist of a simple list output:

```
WRITE: / itab01-course_title, itab01-fee,
         itab01-max_persons.
```

After the last record has been placed in the work area and processed, the LOOP...ENDLOOP structure is closed and the next statement is executed in the source code. The table body of the internal table remains unchanged in this example.

The statement block can contain any number of ABAP statements. However, these statements only relate to the work area (in this case, the header line of the internal table but not the lines in the table body). If you want to output the field for the minimum number of members with a value in the list, for example, this value can be determined in the loop:

```
LOOP AT itab02.
  itab02-min_persons = 2.
  WRITE: / itab02-zzcoursetitle, itab02-mfee,
          itab02-min_persons.
ENDLOOP.
```

The value assignment for a processing stage in this example is rather symbolic. However, it is used to illustrate that, for the further processing of data, the field in the work area is filled with a value, but the field in the table body is not.

If you want to copy the value determined in the header line into a corresponding line and a corresponding table field, proceed as described in the following sample code. Here, the price for a particular course is changed in the header line of the internal table and written into the corresponding body line of the internal table. We have already described how the MODIFY statement works inside and outside LOOP loops. Again, note the "correct" uppercase and lowercase spelling in the literal of the condition; only one set of results meets the condition and the price is changed:

```
LOOP AT itab03.
  IF itab03-course_title = SAP05'.
    itab03-fee = 567.
  ENDIF.
  WRITE: / itab03-course_title, itab03-fee,
          itab03-max_persons.
  MODIFY itab03.
ENDLOOP.
```

For Index Tables and Tables with a Header Line Only

This form of MODIFY statement in the example is only allowed for index tables and tables with a header line. If the MODIFY statement is in a LOOP loop and no other additions are specified, the MODIFY command automatically affects the current record in the header line and the corresponding body line. Otherwise, the table index of the body line to be changed would have to be specified using the INDEX addition.

For certain processing steps, you need information about the internal table. You can use the DESCRIBE statement to query the number of table body lines, the reserved memory space, and the table type (standard, sorted, or hashed). The number of table body lines is probably the most important piece of information to know. You can determine this using the LINES addition. For example, if you want to know how many body lines are contained in the ITAB01 table, you write:

DESCRIBE TABLE

```
DESCRIBE TABLE itab01 LINES lines_itab01.
```

The statement returns an integer value for the number of lines found and places it into the LINES_ITAB01 field in this example.

You could use the number of body lines determined if you want to insert a new line into an internal index table using the INSERT statement.

INSERT

```
INSERT itab01 INDEX lines_itab01.
```

Unlike the APPEND statement, which only appends lines to the end of the table body, you can insert lines anywhere in the body using the INSERT statement. The new line is always inserted before the item that you specify using the INDEX addition. For example, if you specify INDEX 5, the new line will be inserted before the old line 5. In the example, the number of body lines is contained in the LINES_ITAB01 variables. The new line would be inserted before the last line. If the content of LINES_ITAB01 has been increased by 1, the new line is appended to the table body. In this special case, the effect of the statement is similar to the APPEND statement.

Lines can appear multiple times in standard tables. However, if you have a sorted table, you must ensure that the sorting is still error-free after the INSERT statement, because the system would otherwise generate a runtime error. If you defined the table using a unique key, the system would react in the same way.

READ   Of course, not only can you read and process the lines of internal tables in a loop, but you can also use the READ statement to specifically read individual records from the table body. If you're working with a header line, the record is placed in the header line; if you're working with a work area, you must specify this explicitly.

When working with this statement and its records, in particular, you must always consider which internal table type you want to process with which key. In accordance with the design of the internal table, the READ statement with its records looks different.

INDEX   If ITAB03 is a standard table with a non-unique standard key and header line, for example, and you want to place the third body line of this internal table into the header line for further processing, the statement is:

```
READ TABLE itab03 INDEX 3.
```

 Paying Attention to the Type and Key

As mentioned, you often don't know the correct index, just the content of particular fields. The only option available to you in this situation is to run a search using a key. If the internal table has the same structure as the database table, you can perhaps use the key fields of the database table to help you. It is important that you pay attention to the type and key of the internal table.

If you're dealing with a standard table with a non-unique standard key and header line, remember that several identical lines are allowed for this type of table. The key of the database table doesn't necessarily have to be unique for this internal table; rather, the situation will depend on which processing steps were already performed with the internal table.

If you simply assume that the key fields of the database table can be regarded as keys for the internal table, that the internal table is sorted in ascending order, and that there are no redundant lines, then you can also find the required record in the internal table using the READ statement and place it in the header line for processing. The internal table in this case is searched sequentially as of line 1, until the "correct" record is found.

The index is the fastest type of access to use for reading data in an internal table, but it is not ideal. The problem is usually finding the correct line number or index. Compared to index access, for example, access using a hash algorithm involves approximately 3 times the effort, and access using a key means that up to 14 times the effort is required.

In the following sample code, the ITAB04 internal table has the same structure as the ZMEMBER02 database table; the remaining requirements are also fulfilled. Therefore, you can search sequentially in the internal table, using the key fields of the CLIENT and MNUMBER database table:

WITH KEY

```
READ TABLE itab04 WITH KEY
  client = sy-mandt

  mnumber = 5.
```

You can also use the shown syntax of the READ statement for sorted tables and hashed tables. If the specified fields map the key completely, then a binary search is run for sorted tables, whereas, for hashed tables, a search is run using the hash algorithm. If you use fields other than the key fields, sorted tables and hashed tables are also searched sequentially.

 It All Depends on the Developer

You could also use other fields for the search, but the problem here is uniqueness. When you run the sequential search using the READ statement, the system regards the first relevant record it finds as a hit and places the record in the header line, thereby ending the sequential search. Whether the record found is also the "correct" one is your problem, not the system's problem.

You use the DELETE statement to delete an individual line or a group of lines from the internal table. Again, the table index is the quickest way to delete specific lines. Like the READ statement, this addition is not possible for hashed tables; it can only be used with standard tables and sorted tables (that is, with index tables). The same problem of identifying the correct index also applies here.

DELETE

In the following example, the ITAB01 internal table is a standard table again with a header line. You delete the body line with the index 4 (the fourth body line) using the following statement:

```
DELETE itab01 INDEX 4.
```

No effects
Deleting a line in the table body has no effect whatsoever on the header line or work area of the table, whose content remains unchanged. If the line to be deleted must be logged for documentation purposes, you need to place this line into the work area of the internal table and process it accordingly before you delete it.

We also recommend the syntax of the DELETE statement if you want the statement to delete the current record from the table body in a LOOP loop. The index is then determined using the SY-TABIX system field; the statement for the ITAB01 internal table is this:

```
DELETE itab01 INDEX sy-tabix.
```

The DELETE statement should not be used inside or outside LOOP loops without the INDEX addition. Outside LOOP loops, it generates a runtime error—a short dump. Inside LOOP loops, the INDEX addition should be specified with regard to future releases whenever possible.

WHERE
Unfortunately, sometimes you won't initially know the index of the line that is to be deleted. If you have a unique key, you can use it to find and delete the correct record. If you have a non-unique key, you have to formulate a logical condition that will restrict the number of hits you get as much as possible. After the WHERE addition, you specify a logical expression that contains these conditions for identifying the records to be deleted. The more generally you formulate the condition, the greater the number of hits.

For example, if you want to delete all lines from ITAB02 for which the content "SAP03" is contained in the ZZCOURSETITLE field, you write:

```
DELETE itab02 WHERE zzcoursetitle = 'SAP03'.
```

Not Only Can You Delete a Record, But ...

Note that not only can you use this statement to delete a record, but you can also use it to delete all lines of the internal table to which this condition applies. All table entries of the internal table, both for a standard table and a hashed table, are checked for this condition. The processing for sorted tables can, in some circumstances, be optimized internally in such a way that only the "correct" lines are actually processed.

You use the SORT statement to sort internal tables. This statement basically sorts the internal table in ascending order. Without other additions, the sorting is performed based on the defined table key. Except for the name of the internal table, do not specify any other additions for sorted tables and hashed tables.   **SORT**

If you use standard tables, the system requires statements for the sorting criteria. You must first specify the fields based on the order you want them to be sorted. You do this by using the BY addition.   **BY**

In the following example, we assume that the ITAB04 internal table contains the data of the ZMEMBER02 database table. The key in the database table consists of the CLIENT and MNUMBER fields. The data records are also contained in the internal table in ascending order according to this key. The following statement now re-sorts the internal table in such a way that the lines are sorted according to the content of the COURSE_TITLE field:

```
SORT itab04 BY zzcoursetitle.
```

The sequence in this case is sorted on a binary basis for fields of the c type, not according to the language-specific sorting criteria. Depending on the operating system of the application server, uppercase letters might be output before lowercase letters.

The language-specific sorting for all fields of the field list applies with this syntax. If the language-specific sorting only applies for certain fields, you would have to write the AS TEXT addition after each relevant field.

➕ AS TEXT

If you want the sorting to be performed according to language-specific criteria, we recommend that you use the AS TEXT addition directly after the name of the internal table:

```
SORT itab04 AS TEXT BY zzcoursetitle.
```

As the sorting criterion, you can specify several field names as a field list, up to 250 fields. For example, if you want to sort the ITAB04 internal table according to the course title and name of member, you enter the course title as the first sorting criterion. The sorting is performed according to the name of the member; the same goes for the same course title.

```
SORT itab04 AS TEXT BY zzcoursetitle mname.
```

DESCENDING

As mentioned, without other additions, the internal table is sorted in ascending order. If you require a sorting sequence in descending order (for instance, for ranking lists), the DESCENDING addition must follow immediately after the name of the internal table:

```
SORT itab04 DESCENDING AS TEXT BY zzcoursetitle mname.
```

Deleting the Contents of Internal Tables

Meaningless results

Depending on the business task and program flow control, another small problem can occur (in particular, if the filling and processing of an internal table is included in a loop): The content of the work area and table body is retained in the program until it is overwritten. However, this would result in meaningless results for certain processes. If you need to start the new processing step with an empty internal table, you must delete or initialize the work areas and table body. Several options and statements can help you do this; here, the difference between internal tables with a header line and internal tables without a header line is critical.

Deleting Work Areas and Internal Tables with a Work Area

CLEAR

You use the CLEAR statement to delete internal tables with a work area. For example, this statement deletes the body lines:

```
CLEAR itab01.
```

The CLEAR statement deletes the table body completely. All old lines no longer exist. The work area for this table must be initialized separately using this statement:

```
CLEAR wa_itab01.
```

The REFRESH statement has the same effect in the ABAP Objects environment and is thus obsolete. The work area of the internal table also remains unaffected by the REFRESH statement and must be initialized using a separate CLEAR command. The lines of the ITAB01 internal table and its WA_ITAB01 work area are deleted or initialized using two statements:

REFRESH

```
CLEAR itab01.
CLEAR wa_itab01.
```

You can also combine these statements in a chain statement:

```
CLEAR: itab01, wa_itab01.
```

As an alternative to the CLEAR statement, you can use the FREE statement:

FREE

```
FREE itab01.
```

While the initial memory requirement remains reserved with CLEAR, FREE releases the entire memory space used by the table for other requirements. Although the internal table can be accessed again at any time, the system must then reserve the memory area again, which could affect performance. Of course, the work area of the table is not affected by the FREE statement.

Deleting an Internal Table with a Header Line

If you have an internal table with a header line, for example, the ITAB01 table, you can use this statement to initialize the header line of the internal table:

CLEAR

```
CLEAR itab02.
```

The old field contents are deleted and the fields are set to their initial value. However, the entries in the table body remain unaffected by this statement.

If you want to use not only the CLEAR statement to release the header line, but also the body lines of the internal table from the old contents, you must use two square brackets after the name:

```
CLEAR itab02[].
```

 Deleting Body Lines

Note that the body lines are not initialized with this statement—they are deleted.

REFRESH The REFRESH statement works the same way for both internal table types and deletes the body lines of the table. If you want to delete the body lines of the ITAB02 internal table, for example, write this:

```
REFRESH itab02.
```

If you want to initialize both the header line and the table body, you need two statements, like these:

```
CLEAR itab02.
REFRESH itab02.
```

FREE Also for tables with header line, not only is the table body deleted, but the reserved memory area is released for other requirements with the following statement:

```
FREE itab03.
```

Like the CLEAR and REFRESH statements, the FREE statement also works the same for both internal table types. It deletes the lines of the table body, releases the reserved memory space, and leaves the content of the header line unaffected. You also need the CLEAR statement to initialize the work area.

The FREE statement doesn't affect the header line of the internal table. As an alternative for CLEAR and REFRESH, you could write this:

```
CLEAR itab03.
FREE itab03.
```

Sample Code for ITAB with Work Area

Listing 12.1 illustrates how to access internal tables with work areas.

```
1   *&---------------------------------------------*
2   *& Report   Z_MEMBERLIST12_WORK_AREA            *
3   *&                                              *
4   *&---------------------------------------------*
5   *&                                              *
6   *&                                              *
7   *&---------------------------------------------*
8
9   REPORT   Z_MEMBERLIST12_WORK_AREA.
10
11  * Define work area
12  DATA wa_zmember02 TYPE zmember02.
13
14  * Define fields
15  DATA: lines_itab01 TYPE i.   "Amount of lines in itab01
16
17  * Define data types for itab lines
18  TYPES: BEGIN OF line01_type,
19         zzcoursetitle TYPE zmember02-zzcoursetitle,
20         mfee TYPE zmember02-mfee,
21         END OF line01_type.
22
23  TYPES BEGIN OF line02_type.
24       INCLUDE TYPE line01_type.
25       TYPES min_persons TYPE i.
26  TYPES END OF line02_type.
27
28  TYPES: BEGIN OF line03_type,
29         course_title TYPE zmember02-zzcoursetitle,
30         fee TYPE zmember02-mfee,
31         max_persons TYPE i,
32         END OF line03_type.
33
34  TYPES line04_type TYPE zmember02.
35
36  * Define data types for itabs
37  TYPES itab01_type TYPE STANDARD TABLE OF line01_type.
38  TYPES itab02_type TYPE STANDARD TABLE OF line02_type.
39  TYPES itab03_type TYPE STANDARD TABLE OF line03_type.
40  TYPES itab04_type TYPE STANDARD TABLE OF line04_type.
```

```
41
42  * Define itab without header line
43  DATA itab01 TYPE itab01_type.
44  DATA itab02 TYPE itab02_type.
45  DATA itab03 TYPE itab03_type.
46  DATA itab04 TYPE itab04_type.
47
48  * Define work areas for itabs
49  DATA wa_itab01 TYPE line01_type.
50  DATA wa_itab02 TYPE line02_type.
51  DATA wa_itab03 TYPE line03_type.
52  DATA wa_itab04 TYPE line04_type.
53
54  * Define selection screen
55
56  *initialization.
57
58  *at selection screen.
59
60  *---------------------------------------------*
61  START-OF-SELECTION.
62
63  * Read dbtab into itab01 via work area
64  SELECT * FROM zmember02 INTO wa_zmember02.
65    MOVE-CORRESPONDING wa_zmember02 TO wa_itab02.
66    APPEND wa_itab01 TO itab01.
67  ENDSELECT.
68
69  * Read dbtab and fill itab02 with array fetch
70  SELECT * FROM zmember02
71    INTO CORRESPONDING FIELDS OF TABLE itab02.
72
73  * Read dbtab and move field values into itab03
         via work area
74  wa_itab03-max_persons = 10.
75  SELECT * FROM zmember02 INTO wa_zmember02.
76    wa_itab03-course_title = wa_zmember02-zzcoursetitle.
77    wa_itab03-fee = wa_zmember02-mfee.
78    APPEND  wa_itab03 TO itab03 .
79  ENDSELECT.
80
81  * Read dbtab and fill itab04 with array fetch
82  SELECT * FROM zmember02
83    INTO CORRESPONDING FIELDS OF TABLE itab04.
```

```
84
85
86   *-----------------------------------------------*
87   END-OF-SELECTION.
88
89   * Read and display amount of lines in itab01
90   DESCRIBE TABLE itab01 LINES lines_itab01.
91   SKIP.
92   WRITE: / 'Amount of lines in itab01:', lines_itab01.
93
94   * Clear work area, create new values,
        and insert in itab01
95   CLEAR wa_itab01.
96   lines_itab01 = lines_itab01 + 1.
97   wa_itab01-zzcoursetitle = 'LINUX-BASIC'.
98   wa_itab01-mfee = '456.78'.
99   INSERT wa_itab01 INTO itab01 INDEX lines_itab01.
100
101  * List. lines of itab01
102  SKIP.
103  WRITE: / 'sy-tabix, itab01-zzcoursetitle, itab01-mfee'.
104  LOOP AT itab01 INTO wa_itab01.
105    WRITE: / sy-tabix, wa_itab01-zzcoursetitle,
                  wa_itab01-mfee.
106  ENDLOOP.
107
108  * Process itab02 and list lines
109  SKIP
110  WRITE: / 'itab02-zzcoursetitle, itab02-mfee,
               itab02-min_persons'.
111  LOOP AT itab02 INTO wa_itab02
        WHERE zzcoursetitle = 'SAP05' .
112    wa_itab02-min_persons = 2.
113    WRITE: / wa_itab02-zzcoursetitle, wa_itab02-mfee,
114              wa_itab02-min_persons.
115  ENDLOOP.
116
117  * Process itab03 and modify lines
118  SKIP.
119  WRITE: / 'itab03-course_title, itab03-fee,
               itab03-max_persons'.
120  LOOP AT itab03 INTO wa_itab03.
121    IF wa_itab03-course_title = 'BASIC'.
122    wa_itab03-fee = 567.
```

```
123    MODIFY itab03 FROM wa_itab03.
124 ENDIF.
125 WRITE: / wa_itab03-course_title, wa_itab03-fee.
126          wa_itab03-max_persons.
127 ENDLOOP.
128
129 * List. a line of itab03 using line index
130 READ TABLE itab03 INDEX 3 INTO wa_itab03.
131 SKIP.
132 WRITE: / 'read itab03', sy-tabix NO-GAP, '.line:',
133          wa_itab03-course_title, wa_itab03-fee,
134          wa_itab03-max_persons.
135
136 * List. a line of itab04 using key
137 READ TABLE itab04 INTO wa_itab04
138      WITH KEY client = sy-mandt mnumber = 5.
139 SKIP.
140 WRITE: / 'read line of itab04',
141          wa_itab04-client, wa_itab04-mnumber,
142          wa_itab04-mname, wa_itab04-mdob,
143          wa_itab04-mgender.
144
145 * Read, delete and log a line of itab01 using index,
146 READ TABLE itab01 INTO wa_itab01 INDEX 3.
147 DELETE itab01 INDEX 3.
148 SKIP.
149 WRITE: / 'Line deleted in itab01',
              sy-tabix NO-GAP, '.line:',
150          wa_itab01-zzcoursetitle, wa_itab01-mfee.
151
152 * Read, delete and log a line of itab02 using key
153 READ TABLE itab02 INTO wa_itab02
154      WITH KEY zzcoursetitle = 'SAP06'.
155 DELETE TABLE itab02 FROM wa_itab02.
156 SKIP.
157 WRITE: / 'Line deleted in itab02',
              sy-tabix NO-GAP, '.line:',
158          wa_itab02-zzcoursetitle.
159
160 * Effect of clear, refresh and free statement for
161 *          internal tables without header line
162 BREAK-POINT.
163 CLEAR wa_itab01. "initalize wa
164 CLEAR itab01.    "delete all body lines
```

```
165
166  CLEAR wa_itab02. "initialize wa
167  REFRESH itab02.  "delete all body lines
168
169  CLEAR wa_itab03. "initalize wa
170  FREE itab03.     "delete all body lines
                       and release memory space
171  SKIP.
```

Listing 12.1   Listing 1.1: Report Z_MEMBERLIST12_WORK_AREA

Notes on the Source Code

Line 12

The work area for the database table is explicitly defined. The line type is already defined in the ABAP Dictionary. Like every other data object, the WA_ZMEMBER02 data object is defined using the DATA statement. You can choose to name a work area as you wish, but it is a common practice to begin the name with WA_ for readability reasons.

*Beginning work areas with WA_*

Lines 18 to 21

The line type that is later used for the work area and internal table is defined. We recommend inserting a note on the intended purpose into the name of the type (in this case, on type 01). In reality, you would select components of mnemonic names, such as "Invoice item line," for example. The line type here consists of two fields.

Mnemonic names

Lines 23 to 34

Three more line types are defined. To make this easier to understand, different definition examples were selected:

> The structure of the LINE01_TYPE line type and an additional type were integrated into the first line type. For all intents and purposes, the line type contains three fields. It is a flat structure.

> The second line type only contains elementary types, and can therefore be written as a chain statement.

> The structure of the database table for the third line type is integrated as a type.

Lines 37 to 40
The data types for the internal tables are defined.

Lines 43 to 46
The data objects (that is, the internal tables themselves) are defined.

Lines 49 to 52
The intended work area (that is, the data object) is defined for the internal tables.

Lines 64 to 67
The internal table is filled. The table is read and filled through two work areas in a loop, and a line of the database table is first placed into the work area of the database table. The identically named fields of the work area are then filled for the internal table. Finally, content of the second work area is appended to the body of the internal table as a new line.

Lines 70 to 71
In this example, the identically named columns of the internal table are filled in blocks. A work area is not required.

Lines 95 to 99
The content is initialized before the work area is filled to avoid transferring the remainder of the previous content by mistake. The work area is then rebuilt and its content inserted into the table body. The content is inserted before the index that is specified as a value in the LINES_ITAB01 field. If the value is 1 greater than the number of table lines, then the INSERT statement, by definition, works like the APPEND statement in this special case and appends the new line to the table body.

Lines 104 to 106
All lines of the internal table are transferred line by line in a loop into the work area. When the line is being further processed, a field must be accessed by its work area name instead of its table name.

Lines 113 to 117

The internal table is processed line by line in a loop. Each line that meets the condition is placed in the work area and further processed from there.

Lines 120 to 127

In this example, a work area field is changed, and the changed line is saved in the original line. The body line of the table is consequently updated.

Line 155

This statement only deletes one individual line in the table body. The content of the work area should therefore identify *only* the correct line. If the table body contains several lines with this content, only the first matching line is deleted. The search begins with line 1. You can also delete several lines using a single DELETE statement. In this case, however, you would need the WHERE addition and a logical expression to identify the group of lines.

Line 163

The work area is initialized.

Line 164

The CLEAR statement works differently for tables without a header line than it does for tables with a header line. In the example, this is a table without a header line. Here, all body lines of the internal table are deleted using the CLEAR statement.

Line 167

For tables without a header line, the REFRESH statement works identically to the CLEAR statement in line 164.

Tracing the Output of the Source Code in the ABAP Debugger

The best way you can trace the internal processes in the system is by using the ABAP Debugger. The stop sign indicates the set breakpoint, while the yellow arrow shows at which statement the ABAP Debugger is currently located and which one it will execute next. You execute this statement by executing the STEP INTO button, or F5. As shown in Figure 12.1, you can follow in the loop how the work area of the database table is refilled in each loop pass. You can display the current content of the table by pressing the STEP INTO (F5) button in the table mode of the ABAP Debugger. It allows you to monitor in detail how the statements of the program change the content of the table.

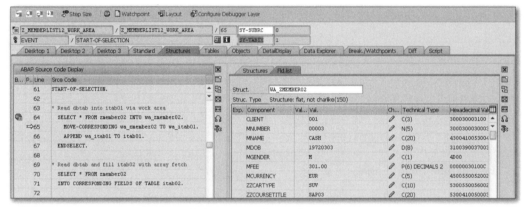

Figure 12.1 Filled Work Area for Database Table ZMEMBER02

You can also check the content of the work area for the internal table. To do this, enter the name of the work area into the input field and press the Enter key (see Figure 12.2).

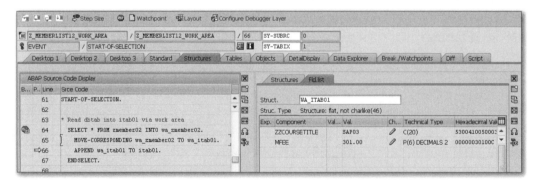

Figure 12.2 Filled Work Area for Internal Table ITAB01

When you look at the internal table, you can see how a line is appended to the table body with each APPEND statement. In Figure 12.3, you can see that the system is still located before the APPEND statement. This is clear from the yellow line before the command. After you click STEP INTO, you see that the table body has received an additional line.

Pay attention to the yellow arrow

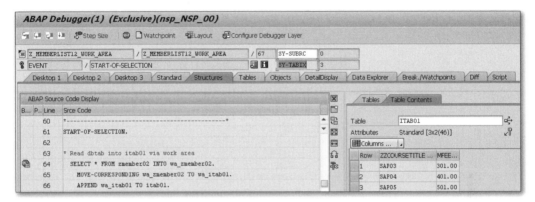

Figure 12.3 Filling an Internal Table from the Work Area

Figure 12.4 only displays the table body because the ITAB01 table doesn't have a header line. If it had a header line, the ABAP Debugger would indicate this with a hat (see Figure 12.6). The next CLEAR command will delete all body lines of the internal table. As you can see below, the effect for a table with header line would be different.

Missing hat

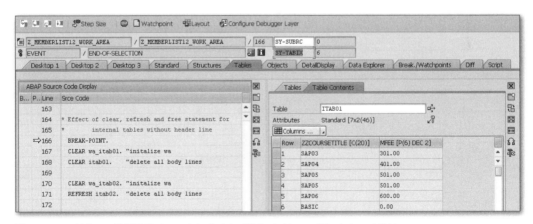

Figure 12.4 Using a CLEAR Statement to Delete All Body Lines of the Internal Table Without a Header Line

Figure 12.5 finally shows the empty internal table after all body lines have been deleted.

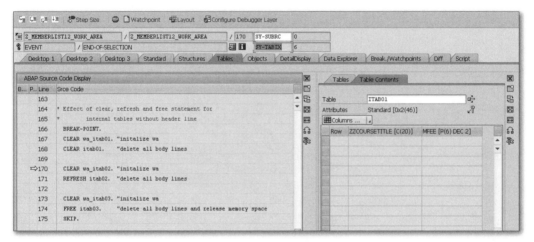

Figure 12.5 Empty Internal Tables without Body Lines

Sample Code for ITAB with Header Line

Listing 12.2 shows how to declare and access internal tables that have a header line.

```
 1  *&---------------------------------------------*
 2  *& Report   Z_MEMBERLIST12_HEADER_LINE        *
 3  *&                                             *
 4  *&---------------------------------------------*
 5  *&                                             *
 6  *&                                             *
 7  *&---------------------------------------------*
 8
 9  REPORT  z_memberlist12_header_line.
10
11  * Define table work area
12  DATA wa_zmember02 TYPE zmember02.
13
14  * Define fields
15  DATA: lines_itab01 TYPE i.
16
17  * Define internal tables with header line
18  DATA: BEGIN OF itab01 OCCURS 0,
```

```
19            zzcoursetitle TYPE zmember02-zzcoursetitle,
20          mfee TYPE zmember02-mfee,
21        END OF itab01.
22
23 DATA BEGIN OF itab02 OCCURS 0.
24          INCLUDE STRUCTURE itab01.
25          DATA min_persons TYPE i.
26 DATA END OF itab02.
27
28 DATA: BEGIN OF itab03 OCCURS 0,
29        course_title TYPE zmember02-zzcoursetitle,
30          fee TYPE zmember02-mfee,
31          max_persons TYPE i VALUE 10,
32        END OF itab03.
33
34 DATA BEGIN OF itab04 OCCURS 0.
35      INCLUDE STRUCTURE zmember02.
36 DATA END OF itab04.
37
38 * Define work areas
39
40 * Define selection screen
41
42 *initialization.
43
44 *at selection-screen.
45
46 *----------------------------------------------*
47 START-OF-SELECTION.
48 * Read dbtab into itab01 via header line
49   SELECT * FROM zmember02 INTO wa_zmember02.
50     MOVE-CORRESPONDING wa_zmember02 TO itab01.
51     APPEND itab01.
52   ENDSELECT.
53
54 * Read dbtab and fill itab02 with array fetch
55   SELECT * FROM zmember02
56            INTO CORRESPONDING FIELDS OF TABLE itab02.
57
58 * Read dbtab and move field values into itab03
     via header line
59   SELECT * FROM zmember02 INTO wa_zmember02.
60     itab03-course_title = wa_zmember02-zzcoursetitle.
61     itab03-fee = wa_zmember02-mfee.
```

```
62      APPEND itab03.
63    ENDSELECT.
64
65  * Read dbtab and fill itab04 with array fetch
66    SELECT * FROM zmember02.
67    INTO CORRESPONDING FIELDS OF TABLE itab04.
68
69  *-------------------------------------------------*
70  END-OF-SELECTION.
71  * Read and display amount of lines in itab01
72    DESCRIBE TABLE itab01 LINES lines_itab01.
73    SKIP.
74    WRITE: / 'Amount of lines in itab01:', lines_itab01.
75
76  * Clear header line, create new values and insert in
      itab01.
77    CLEAR itab01.
78    itab01-zzcoursetitle = 'LINUX-BASICS'.
79    itab01-mfee = '456.78'.
80    lines_itab01 = lines_itab01 + 1.
81    INSERT itab01 INDEX lines_itab01.
82
83  * list lines of itab01
84    SKIP.
85    WRITE: / 'itab01 sy-tabix,
                itab01-zzcoursetitle, itab01-mfee'.
86    LOOP AT itab01.
87      WRITE: / sy-tabix, itab01-zzcoursetitle,
                  itab01-mfee.
88    ENDLOOP.
89
90  * process itab02 and list lines
91    SKIP.
92    WRITE: / 'itab02-course_title, itab02-mfee,
                itab02-min_persons'.
93    LOOP AT itab02 WHERE zzcoursetitle = 'SAP05'.
94      itab02-min_persons = 2.
95      WRITE: / itab02-zzcoursetitle, itab02-mfee,
                  itab02-min_persons.
96    ENDLOOP.
97
98  * proces itab03 and modify lines of itab03
99    SKIP.
100   WRITE: / 'itab03-course_title, itab03-fee,
```

```
                     itab03-max_persons'.
101   LOOP AT itab03.
102     IF itab03-course_title = 'SAP05'.
103       itab03-fee = 567.
104       MODIFY itab03.
105     ENDIF.
106     WRITE: / itab03-course_title, itab03-fee,
                   itab03-max_persons.
107   ENDLOOP.
108
109 * List. a line of itab03 using line index
110   READ TABLE itab03 INDEX 3.
111   SKIP.
112 *  write: / 'read itab03 line', sy-tabix,
113   WRITE: / 'read line of itab03',
                 sy-tabix NO-GAP, '. line:',
114              itab03-course_title, itab03-fee,
                 itab03-max_persons.
115
116 * List. a line of itab04 using key
117   READ TABLE itab04 WITH KEY
      client = sy-mandt  mnumber = 5.
118   SKIP.
119   WRITE: / 'read line of itab04',
120              itab04-client, ib04-mnumber, itab04-mname,
121              itab04-mdob, itab04-mgender.
122
123 * Read, delete and log a line of itab01 using index
124   READ TABLE itab01 INDEX 3.
125   DELETE itab01 INDEX 3.
126   SKIP.
127   WRITE: / 'Line deleted in itab01:',
                 sy-tabix NO-GAP, '.line,',
128              itab01-zzcoursetitle, itab01-mfee.
129
130 * Read, delete and log a line of itab02 using key
131   READ TABLE itab02 WITH KEY zzcoursetitle = 'SAP03'.
132   DELETE itab02 WHERE zzcoursetitle = 'sap03'.
133   DELETE itab02 WHERE zzcoursetitle = 'SAP03'.
134   SKIP.
135   WRITE: / 'Line deleted in itab02',
                 sy-tabix NO-GAP, ' .line:',
136              itab02-zzcoursetitle.
137
```

```
138  * Sort itab
139    SORT itab04 BY zzcoursetitle.
140    SKIP.
141    WRITE: /  'itab04 sorted binary by zzcoursetitle'.
142    LOOP AT itab04.
143      WRITE: /  itab04-zzcoursetitle,
                    itab04-mfee, itab04-mnumber,
144                 itab04-mname.
145    ENDLOOP.
146
147    SORT itab04 AS TEXT BY zzcoursetitle.
148    SKIP.
149    WRITE: /  'itab04 sorted as text by zzcoursetitle'.
150    LOOP AT itab04.
151      WRITE: /  itab04-zzcoursetitle, itab04-mfee,
152                 itab04-mnumber, itab04-mname.
153    ENDLOOP.
154
155    SORT itab04 AS TEXT BY zzcoursetitle mname.
156    SKIP.
157    WRITE: /'itab04 sorted as text
                 by zzcoursetitle and mname'.
158    LOOP AT itab04.
159      WRITE: /  itab04-zzcoursetitle, itab04-mfee,
160                 itab04-mnumber, itab04-mname.
161    ENDLOOP.
162
163    SORT itab04 DESCENDING AS TEXT BY zzcoursetitle mname.
164    SKIP.
165    WRITE: /'itab04 sorted descending as text by
                 zzcoursetitle and mname'.
166    LOOP AT itab01.
167      WRITE: /  itab04-zzcoursetitle, itab04-mfee,
168                 itab04-mnumber, itab04-mname.
169    ENDLOOP.
170
171    BREAK-POINT.
172  * Effect of clear, refresh and free statement for
173  *        internal tables with header line
174    CLEAR itab01.    "initialize header line
175    CLEAR itab01[].  "delete  all body lines
176
177    CLEAR itab02.    "initialize header line
178    REFRESH itab02.  "delete  all body lines
```

```
179
180    CLEAR itab03.       "initialize header line
181    FREE itab03.        "delete  all body lines and release
                           memory space
182    SKIP.
```

Listing 12.2   Report Z_MEMBERLIST12_HEADER_LINE

Notes on the Source Code

Lines 17 to 21
The ITAB01 internal standard table is defined and the system determines the initial memory space requirements. The internal table has two fields that refer to the ABAP Dictionary for their definitions.

Lines 23 to 26
The ITAB02 internal table is defined. It must contain the structure of the lines from ITAB01 and an additional field (that is, a line therefore has three fields in total).

Lines 34 to 36
The structure of the database table is implemented into the ITAB04 table. Therefore, a line of the internal table has the same structure as a line of the database table.

Lines 49 to 52
The database table is read record by record into its work area. Fields with identical names are transferred from there into the header line of the internal table. After the fields are transferred, the content of the header line is appended to the table body as a new line. The content of the header line is retained and overwritten (in this case, by a new line from the database table). The last content of the header line is no longer overwritten.

Lines 55 to 56
An array fetch transfers the content of the database table in blocks into the identically named fields of the internal table. Only fields with

identical names are filled. The work area of the database table and the header line of the internal table are not required.

Line 72
The number of body lines of the internal table is determined and placed in a variable for further processing.

Line 77
The header line of the internal table is initialized. This is always useful if you want to ensure that none of the older contents of the header line remain because, in certain circumstances, they would make the new line that is about to be set up unusable.

Lines 78 to 81
The new body line is set up in the header line. The item before which the new line is to be inserted is determined. The content of the header line is then written as a new line into the determined area in the table area.

Lines 86 to 88
In a loop, each record of the internal table is transferred consecutively into the header line so that they can be further processed from there. The statement block for the processing is symbolized by a list output.

Line 93
The loop must only transfer the lines of the internal table that meet a certain condition into the header line. Only the transferred records can be further processed from the header line.

Lines 101 to 105
The loop places all body lines into the header line record by record. Processing takes place there. If a certain condition is met for the current record, the content of the header line is changed. The content of the changed header line is transferred into the current body line. All other body lines, for which the condition is not fulfilled, are not modified.

Line 110
The third body line is transferred into the header line.

Line 117
A line is read from the internal table. The key in this case is to reduce the risk to such an extent that the correct record is read. The developer chooses the key fields for standard tables, and must select the fields and contents in such an astute way that the description leads the system to finding the "correct" record.

 Imagining a Key as a WHERE Condition

It might help to think of the key as a WHERE condition instead of thinking of it in the context of database tables (though there is no READ statement with a WHERE condition in ABAP).

Line 125
The third body line of the internal table is deleted.

Line 133
All body lines to which this condition applies are deleted.

Line 139
The internal table is sorted in ascending order in binary format according to the content of the ZZCOURSETITLE field.

Line 147
The internal table is sorted in ascending order in lexical format according to the content of the ZZCOURSETITLE field, based on country-specific settings.

Line 155
The internal table is sorted according to first the ZZCOURSETITLE and then the MNAME fields. That is, the ZZCOURSETITLE field is the first sorting criterion. The sorting for the same field content of ZZCOURSETITLE is performed as the second sorting criterion in accordance with the content of the MNAME name.

Line 163

The sequence is sorted in descending order so that the lexically highest value appears in the first line of the internal table.

Line 174

The header line of the internal table is initialized. In other words, each field receives its type-specific initial value. Even if the fields in the DATA statement were predefined with a value using VALUE, for example, the field doesn't receive the default value. Instead, it receives its type-specific initial value. This would be a blank space (" ") for c type fields, for example.

Line 175

All body lines of the internal table are deleted. Note the difference between deleting and initializing here.

Line 178

The statement works the same as the CLEAR statement in line 175.

Line 181

The body lines are also deleted using this statement. The initial memory space is also released for the internal table. If you want to fill the internal table again, the FREE statement is less suitable (less efficient) than the REFRESH statement.

Tracing the Output of the Source Code in the ABAP Debugger

With or without a hat
In the table mode of the ABAP Debugger, you can specifically trace, step by step, how a line is transferred from the database table into the header line of the internal table and then into the table body. As previously mentioned, the presence of a header line of the internal table is indicated with a hat icon (see Figure 12.6). If the hat icon is missing, as in Figure 12.4, the table must be an internal table without a header line.

Stop sign and yellow arrow
Again, you use the ABAP Debugger to monitor the program flow. The ABAP Debugger that appears before the internal table is filled block by

block and is identified by the yellow arrow in front of the statement
(see Figure 12.7).

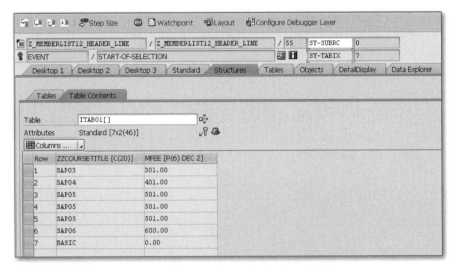

Figure 12.6 Reading Data Record by Record into the Database Table

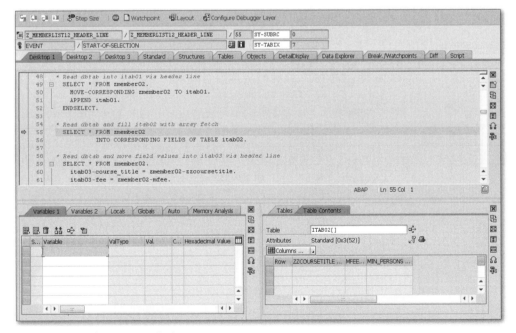

Figure 12.7 Reading Data in Blocks

433

All lines of the database table were transferred into the body lines of the table using a single command. The header line is still initial (see Figure 12.8).

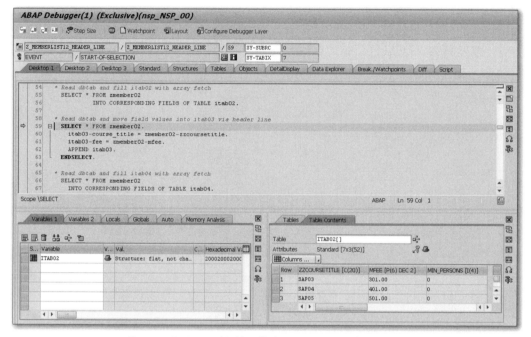

Figure 12.8 Internal Table Filled Using Array Fetch

The READ statement was used to identify a unique line and transfer it into the header line (see Figure 12.9).

The literal of the condition 'sap03' also contains lowercase letters. In the example, the content of the literal cannot be found in the internal table because the ZZCOURSETITLE field only contains uppercase letters. And so the statement in this example doesn't delete any body lines (see Figure 12.10).

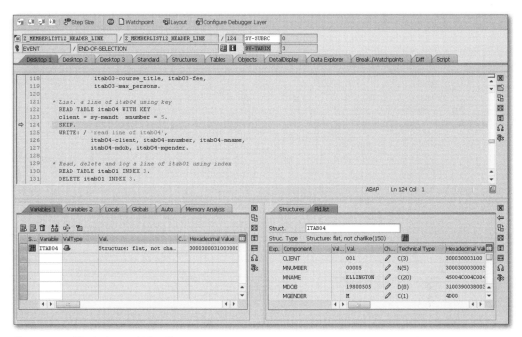

Figure 12.9 Single Access Using Key

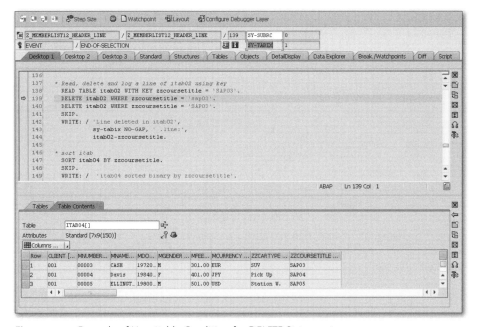

Figure 12.10 Example of Unsuitable Condition for DELETE Statement

Since the DELETE statement could not delete any lines, it issues return code 4 and places it in the SY-SUBRC field (see Figure 12.11).

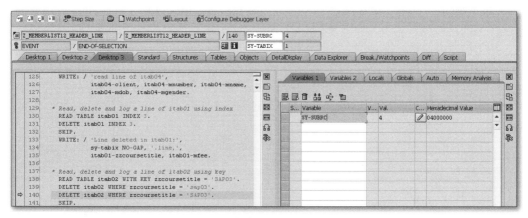

Figure 12.11   Return Code for DELETE Statement

After the SORT statement, the internal table is available, sorted in ascending order in binary format according to the code table in question (see Figure 12.12).

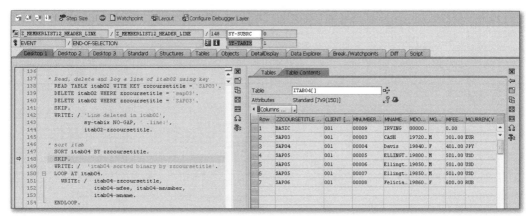

Figure 12.12   Sorted Standard Table

Capturing Errors

If you want this error to be caught, the content of SY-SUBRC must be queried immediately after the DELETE statement with an IF or CASE structure, and a corresponding statement block must follow.

As shown in Figure 12.13, the header line was already initialized with the first CLEAR statement. You can clearly see the difference in the initial value for ZZCOURSETITLE and MFEE. The first is a type c field, the second a type p field. The second CLEAR statement is next in order to delete the table body.

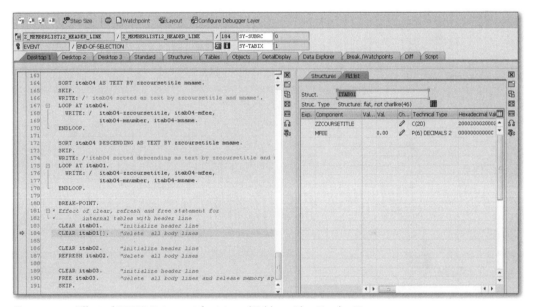

Figure 12.13 Effect of CLEAR Statement for Internal Tables with a Header Line

The last statement executed, CLEAR itab01[], deleted all body lines (see Figure 12.14). Neither the line number, the index, nor the initial value was retained.

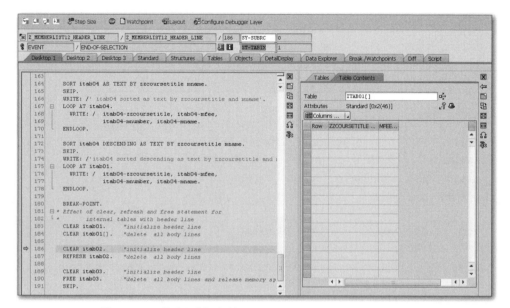

Figure 12.14 Deleted Body Lines

13

Modularizing Programs

Clearly delineated packages with limited tasks are the ideal of the modular principle. When you split complicated solutions into small, encapsulated components, you'll appreciate the high level of transparency and changeability of the components. In ABAP, this is called *modularization*, and in this chapter, you'll learn the important techniques that support it.

First, a small but not unimportant comment: you structure each solution in your head, not in the source code. The source code only maps the solution, whether or not it is well structured. The tools of a development environment are no substitute for a good solution concept. A bad solution remains a bad solution even if it uses the most refined modularization techniques and runs even faster on a supercomputer.

Garbage in, garbage out

 First Design, Then Program

> So, starting from the very first line of your source code, you should design and structure your program, perform the required research, and check the draft of the solutions. Then—and only then—should you start writing source code in the ABAP Editor.

Overview

SAP provides a variety of technologies for modularization. The use of global and local ABAP classes enables you to deploy modern modularization and encapsulation technologies, create reusable units, and apply clear structure in your programs.

Function groups are similar reusable units. They don't provide all of the advantages of global classes, but are widespread because they are easy to create and use.

By their very nature, the processing blocks of every ABAP report give the program a modular structure. The runtime environment independently calls processing blocks (events like START-OF-SELECTION or dialog modules like a selection screen).

ABAP source code also allows you to use additional modularization techniques. For ABAP novices, two techniques are especially useful:

> **Modularization of source code**
> The modularization of source code into different and separately maintainable source texts can improve the manageability of large programs and facilitate simultaneous processing by several developers. The modules contain ABAP source code that is integrated in program generation as if it were in the main program.
>
> This modularization technique is used by function groups, for example. The function group (the subroutine) includes numerous include programs, which contain the actual function modules, subroutines, and global data definitions.

> **Procedures**
> Procedures are units that can be called and have interfaces for the data transfer to the calling program. They can also contain their own local data declarations. For getting started with ABAP, the following procedures are important:

> – **Methods**
>   Methods are procedures within global or local classes. They primarily help with internal modularization tasks in programs, such as ensuring that a specific process block is executed in a loop. To keep the loop manageable and to isolate the required local

variables from the global variables of their class, the processing block is placed in its own subroutine. You can define the visibility for methods. This way you determine whether the methods can be used only within the respective class or also by other calling programs.

– **Subroutines**
The function that methods fulfill for classes corresponds to the function that subroutines fulfill for programs. They are procedures that can be called explicitly but, in comparison to methods, have some weaknesses: The interface definition is not very exact, and you cannot specify their visibility. Consequently, subroutines can only be called within the corresponding main program to provide functions for other programs.

– **Function modules**
Unlike program-specific subroutines, function modules are used for general tasks that repeat frequently. For example, imagine that the print output of various programs should always create a PDF file rather than an SAP list. To build this conversion into various programs as easily as possible, you would use a central function module that performs this task. The function module must simply be called in the program and the data interface must be populated with data. The function module takes care of the rest (the actual conversion).

The standard delivery of SAP software includes many function modules that can be used in customer-specific programs as needed. SAP also provides a special tool to manage function modules (see "Function Modules").

 Not for Reuse

Although you may be tempted, do not use source code modularization with include programs to create reusable source text units. If an include program is used in multiple subroutines, the maintainability of both the include program and the main program decreases. It becomes very difficult to make changes to the include program without damaging the main program. If you want to program a function that can be reused, you should use global classes instead.

Historically Grown

Historically speaking, function modules and function groups are the predecessors of ABAP classes. They play a similar role but don't have the object orientation attributes. Whether you find function modules or classes in your working environment will depend on how old the respective SAP application is and whether it has been modernized in the last few years. More recent applications are composed almost exclusively of classes; function modules are used in specifically justified exceptions only. In older applications that have not been updated lately, it's the other way around.

The following section examines modularization techniques in more detail.

Source Code Modules

Listing 12.1, for report Z_MEMBERLIST12_WORK_AREA, with about 170 lines of code, can hardly be called manageable or well organized (see Listing 13.2, later in the chapter). How would this kind of "spaghetti programming" look after 2,000 lines?

Include principle

To give the report a better structure and organization, copy it to report Z_MEMBERLIST13. For the definition part, create an include report (Z_MEMBERLIST_DEFINITIONS) in the copied program. This include report contains all the data definitions. The following statement links the contents of report Z_MEMBERLIST_DEFINITIONS to your report, Z_MEMBERLIST13, so that a single runtime object exists after generation:

```
INCLUDE z_memberlist_definitions.
```

You should always select a name for the include that enables you to easily identify the respective assignment to the main program. (Remember that you can theoretically also use an include in several main programs; however, this is rather disadvantageous for reasons already mentioned.)

The effect of the statement is identical to having copied the source code of the include program instead of the INCLUDE statement into the main program.

Special Rule

Note this special rule for the INCLUDE statement: The entire INCLUDE statement must be written to one line, and this line cannot contain any other statements.

When it is finished, the definition part of the main program should consist only of comment lines and INCLUDE statements, as follows:

Only comment lines

```
* Definitions
INCLUDE z_memberlist_definitions.
```

You have two options to create the include report. First, you can create the report with the ABAP Workbench and the initial screen of the ABAP Editor, just as you have created new reports so far. The only difference is that you must use the program attributes to ensure that you create an include report, not an executable program (see "ABAP Editor Overview" in Chapter 3).

The second option is to work directly from the ABAP Editor of report Z_MEMBERLIST13 and use forward navigation to reach the editor of the include report. Double-click on the name of the include report to start forward navigation. The object does not yet exist, and the system asks if it should be created. Of course, you answer the question with YES. In this example, you then create the object as a local object. In the real world, you can, of course, either use an existing request number or create a new transport request. After you click on the name of the report, the ABAP Editor reopens immediately, but you are in a new report and can now edit the include report (see Figure 13.1).

Creating an include report

You will probably notice that the source code doesn't include a REPORT statement. This is because you aren't working with an executable report. But if you follow GoTo • ATTRIBUTES to change to the program attributes of the report, you will also see that the system has created a program of the INCLUDE PROGRAM type (see Figure 13.2). You would have had to specify this type yourself if you'd created the include report directly with the ABAP Workbench.

In the include program, you now write all the required definitions, which used to take up almost an entire page in report Z_MEMBERLIST12

443

_WORK_AREA (lines 12-52). After you have written all the required statements in the include report or have copied them, check and activate the report so that you can actually use it. Use the BACK button to return to your main program.

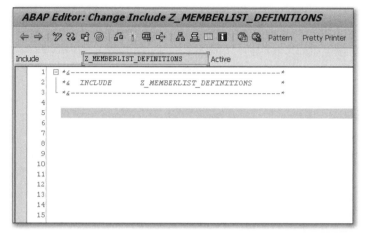

Figure 13.1   Editing the Include Report

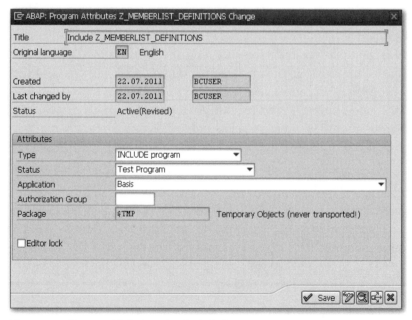

Figure 13.2   Program Attributes of an Include Report

Nesting Possible

Include reports can be nested, so one include program can call another include program. Any number of INCLUDE statements can appear in such a report. For this example, you theoretically could have created a specific INCLUDE for every internal table. Just make sure that the INCLUDE statement is located at the logically correct place in the source code.

You can find (deterrent) examples of standard SAP programs in which the first two program levels consist only of INCLUDE statements and familiar statements like DATA appear only in the third level or later. For clarity and maintainability reasons, you should avoid nesting includes and only use them for modularization at the highest program level.

The include report is included in the syntax check for the main program, just as if the lines of source code were in the main program.

Procedures

Unlike source code modules, procedures have interfaces for transferring data between the calling program and the procedure. As noted, procedures can also have their own data definitions that are known only with the procedure.

Subroutines

Subroutines primarily help with program-internal modularization of tasks. For example, you could call a limited task from various places in the main program, or you could bundle related tasks in a single subroutine. Report Z_MEMBERLIST12_WORK_AREA (see Listing 13.2, later in the chapter) has only one level that includes definitions, events, and statements for flow control in the program and for processing.

Modularizing tasks

If you want to call subroutine ITAB01_FILL, use this statement:

PERFORM

```
PERFORM itab01_fill.
```

Only Controlling Components on the First Level

For better manageability, the uppermost program level should contain only controlling components and no processing components. Populating an internal table involves processing. According to this principle, that's why the START-OF-SELECTION event contains only four statements: four subprogram calls. The processing should then occur in the subprogram. If processing consists of several steps, each individual processing step should be located in its own subprogram. In the real world, the depth of processes depends on the complexity and scope of the tasks.

The easiest way to create a subroutine is to use forward navigation. Double-click on the name of the subroutine; answer YES when the system asks if you want to create the object, and it will provide you with several options.

 Main Program

In the current example, you should create the subroutines in the main program (see Figure 13.3), because the task of populating an internal table with content does not belong to the definitions, and you don't want to have to create a new include program for this example. In practice, subroutines are frequently moved into specific include programs for the same reasons that apply to definitions and selection screens. As noted, an include program doesn't contain a data interface and works just like copying source code to the calling location.

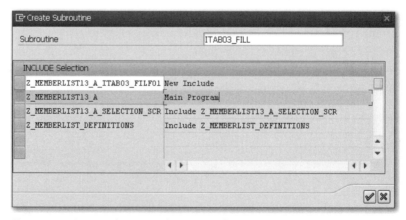

Figure 13.3 Creating the New Subroutine in the Main Program

To create the subroutine in your Z_MEMBERLIST13 program, check the corresponding line header and click CONTINUE.

At the end of your main program, the system inserts comment lines and two statements: FORM and ENDFORM (see Figure 13.4).

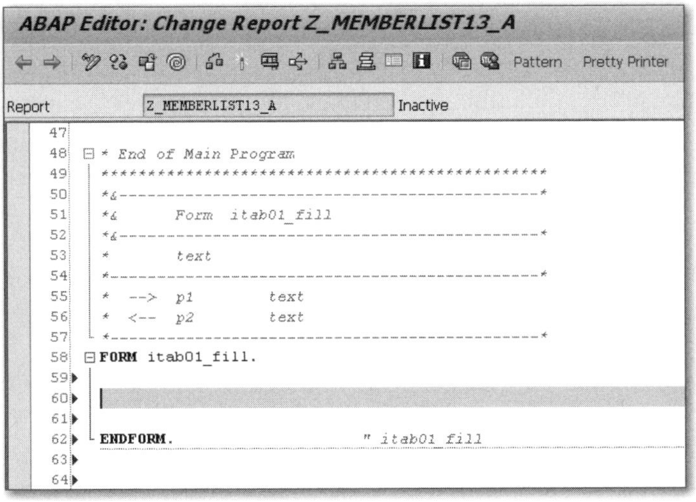

FORM ...
ENDFORM

ABAP Editor: Change Report Z_MEMBERLIST13_A

Report   Z_MEMBERLIST13_A   Inactive

```
47
48  ⊟ * End of Main Program
49    ************************************************
50    *&----------------------------------------------*
51    *&        Form   itab01_fill
52    *&----------------------------------------------*
53    *         text
54    *-----------------------------------------------*
55    *    -->  p1         text
56    *    <--  p2         text
57    *-----------------------------------------------*
58  ⊟ FORM itab01_fill.
59 ▶
60 ▶ |
61 ▶
62 ▶ ⌐ ENDFORM.                    " itab01_fill
63 ▶
64 ▶
```

Figure 13.4 Structure of a Subroutine

The FORM statement defines the beginning of the subroutine, and the ENDFORM statement defines its end. The PERFORM statement branches from the calling program to the FORM statement of the corresponding subroutine. After processing the ENDFORM statement, the system continues with processing in the calling structure, after the PERFORM statement. The ABAP statements to be executed in this subroutine are located between FORM and ENDFORM.

In our example, those are the statements to populate internal table ITAB01. After you insert the statements, return to the calling location with the BACK button.

Global and Local Variables

So far, you have worked exclusively with *global variables*, which means that all the variables have the same name and contents in the subroutine that they do in the main program. Global variables are therefore

In the main program

447

defined in the main program. As you can trace later with the ABAP Debugger, global variables are known in all the deeper calling structures and levels of this program.

At the level only

The opposite is true of *local variables*, which are known only at the level at which they were defined (in this case, in the subroutine). They are not known at higher or lower levels. On one hand, local variables are used because fields are often needed in only specific modules, and the fragmentation of all required variables into several areas reduces complexity. On the other hand, such fields let you decouple a module from the calling module, making them universally usable as modules, which is a major advantage.

The distribution and assignment of global and local variables means that you can call such modules from any location. The global names are assigned to the local names over the data interfaces, and the content is transferred. So the names in the calling structures can be completely different. The distribution into global and local variables lets you more easily test procedures individually and change them separately: You can change both the controlling level of the main program and the processing level of individual procedures without affecting the other level.

You have two options for the definition of local variables: *explicit* and *implicit*.

Defining local variables explicitly

With explicit definition, you write one or more DATA statements in the FORM procedure and they define the required fields. You work similarly with data types and other data objects. As noted, the data objects and their contents within this FORM routine remain isolated. Further processing must begin from here:

```
FORM itab03_fill .
  DATA lok_tmax TYPE i VALUE 10.
* Statement block
ENDFORM.
```

The LOK_TMAX variable is defined locally in this code sample. If the variable is modified and its contents are to be output to a list, the statement block of the subroutine must contain the corresponding WRITE statement.

You define local variables implicitly when you use the data interface. When you call the subroutine, the PERFORM statement and the USING addition indicate a list of fields and tables as operands.

Unlike with methods and function modules, a special feature of subroutines is that the parameters are position operands, so the sequence of fields is important:

```
* Call the subroutine
PERFORM itab04_list USING par04     lines_itab04.
* Definition of the subroutine
FORM itab04_list USING loc_par04 loc_lin_count.
* Statement block
   ...
   CHECK loc_par04 IS NOT INITIAL.
   ...
ENDFORM.
```

Both the PERFORM and the FORM statements must contain an identical number of fields in terms of the field list, but the names can be completely different. The first field in the list of the FORM statement is defined in the subroutine, just as the first field is in the list of the PERFORM statement. The second field and all additional fields are defined according to their assignments. The LOC_LIN_COUNT field of the subroutine is therefore defined just as the LINES_ITAB04 field. You can think of the effects here much like you would the TYPE addition of the DATA statement.

At the PERFORM statement, the PAR04 and LINES_ITAB04 are defined and known to the system. Calling the subroutine copies the field contents from the fields of the list to the corresponding fields of the subroutine.

As you can see in the example of a CHECK statement (see Figure 13.5), the fields in the subroutine are addressed with their local names. If the contents of the local variables change in the subroutine, the content of the higher-level (global) variables also changes automatically.

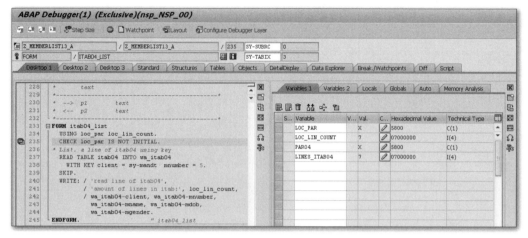

Figure 13.5   Global and Local Fields in the Subroutine

After passing through the ENDFORM statement, the local variable and its content are no longer known to the system. That's not a bad approach, because the PARO4 and LINES_ITAB04 variables contain the field contents, as you can see in Figure 13.6.

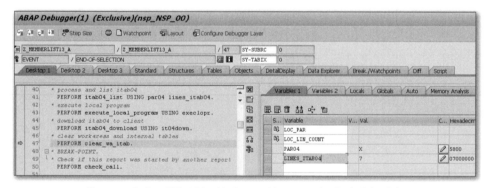

Figure 13.6   Local Variables No Longer Known at the End of the Subroutine

Transferring Internal Tables

Sequence of the
assignment

You can also transfer internal tables to a subroutine. The PERFORM statement requires the USING addition. If the table that is supposed to be transferred has a header line, then be careful: If you do something wrong, you only transfer the header line and not the table body. This is explained further in the following section.

The example defines internal table ITAB02 without a header line. If you want to process it in the encapsulated subroutine, use the following statement:

```
PERFORM itab_fill USING itab02.
```

The FORM statement must have a similar structure:

```
FORM itab_fill USING itab_universal TYPE table.
```

 Note the Header Line

If internal table ITAB02 was defined with a header line, then the PERFORM statement would make only the header line available to the subroutine. But if the example is supposed to also make the rest of the table available to the subroutine, you must work with square brackets (just like you would do with a CLEAR statement). The PERFORM statement would then look like this:

```
PERFORM itab_fill USING itab02[].
```

Figure 13.7 is missing the hat (Chapter 12 has more details about the hat icon), which means that internal table ITAB02 was defined without a header line and is still empty.

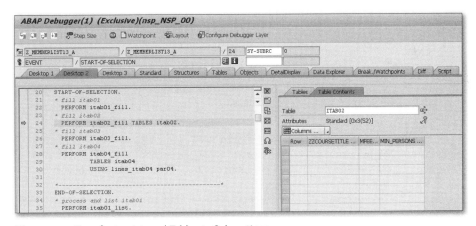

Figure 13.7 Transferring Internal Tables to Subroutines

Although the corresponding local internal table (see Figure 13.8) is defined with a header line, only the body lines are transferred to the subroutine with the USING addition and returned to the calling program with the ENDFORM statement.

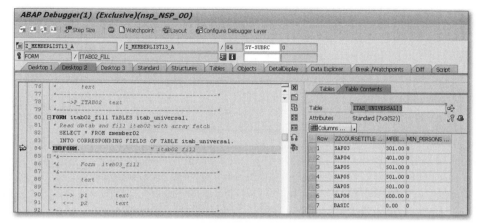

Figure 13.8 Local Internal Table

The internal tables and their fields are addressed exclusively by their local names in the subroutine. The WRITE statement must look like this:

```
WRITE: / itab_universal-zzcoursetitle.
```

And not like this:

```
WRITE: / itab04-zzcoursetitle.
```

Internal Tables in the Subroutine

You might stumble upon another issue: The processing of internal tables with header lines follows different rules and uses different mechanisms than the processing of internal tables without header lines. Even some commands, like CLEAR, work differently (see Chapter 12). If your main program uses tables with header lines (against the modern convention), you may have to think a little differently in the subroutine—another reason for avoiding header lines.

External Subroutines

Apart from letting you use your own subroutines, ABAP also allows you to call the subroutines of other reports and to call other reports in their entirety as "subprograms."

You can go to the calling program and remain there, or return to your report after executing the program you have called. You can also start the called program with a selection screen or bypass the selection screen. If you bypass the selection screen, we recommend that you transfer the settings or start the report with a variant.

After processing an external subroutine, the system returns to your report and continues processing after the point at which the subroutine was called. This works exactly like an internal subroutine. You need the name of the subroutine, the name of the report, and information on the data interface. Of course, you should be very familiar with the functions and workings of the external program.

Calling an external subroutine

For example, if you want to call external subroutine ITAB04_LIST from report Z_MEMBERLIST13_A from your report (Z_MEMBERLIST13_B), you must check the parameter list of the called subroutine. Doing so could look like this:

```
FORM itab04_list USING loc_par04 loc_lin_count.
```

If it contains two position operands, as is the case here, you must know what the operands do to design their parameter list accordingly when you call it.

The PERFORM statement requires the IN PROGRAM addition. The statement in your report could then look like this:

IN PROGRAM

```
* Modern notation
  PERFORM itab04_list IN PROGRAM z_memberlist13_a
          USING nvml lines_itab04.
```

External Reports

If you want your program to call an external executable report, first decide whether you want your report to continue working after the call, or whether you want it to end with the call of the external report. You should also determine whether you want to execute the called report with a selection screen, or whether it should run in the background.

The selection screen offers more options for dialog but slows down the flow. If you don't use the selection screen of the called report, you should still consider the required selections. Here you can start the

SUBMIT

report with a variant or transfer the values for the selection screen from within your program. To start an external report, always use the SUBMIT statement; only the additions differ.

The following sections explain the various options and offer some examples.

Terminating the call of an external report

 Example 1

You want to end your report with the call of an external report. The external report should appear with its selection screen, Z_MEMBERLIST13_A.

VIA SELECTION-SCREEN

The solution involves the VIA SELECTION-SCREEN addition:

```
SUBMIT z_memberlist13_a VIA SELECTION-SCREEN.
```

You first see the selection screen of your own report. As soon as the SUBMIT command is executed in your source code, your reports ends and you see the selection screen of the called report. The following statements in your report are not executed. You then continue to work in the called report.

Controlling the section screen of the follow-up report

 Example 2

As you probably noted in Example 1, intermediate results or content that has been calculated is accessible up to the SUBMIT statement, but not after it. In other words, you must have processed these results up to that point; otherwise, they are lost.

You might also want to use the selection screen of the follow-up report for population or control.

WITH

To solve the problem, you once again use the SUBMIT command, but this time with the WITH addition for each parameter or section table of the follow-up report that should be transferred.

For example, if you want to call report Z_MEMBERLIST13_A, you must check whether its selection screen is set up, verify the technical names of the corresponding selection parameters, and confirm which values you want to transfer.

In the following sample code, you transfer values for two parameters of the follow-up selection screen. Their technical names in the follow-up report are PAR02 and PAR03. Both parameters involve checkboxes that should be checked. As described in Chapter 11; the checkboxes are one-character fields that contain either a space or an X. Therefore, you transfer the literal 'X' for each parameter. To check the results, display the selection screen. The SUBMIT statement then looks like this:

```
SUBMIT z_memberlist13_a
  WITH par02 = 'X'
  WITH par03 = 'X'
  VIA SELECTION-SCREEN.
```

 Example 3

Assuming that the subject-matter flow of Example 2 is correct, you would slow down the selection screen of the follow-up report only during work. You want to avoid this problem.

Calling the report without selection screen

You can avoid the selection screen of the follow-up report with the SUBMIT statement by omitting the VIA SELECTION-SCREEN addition. When executing your report, you won't even notice that another report has taken on the work and produced the results.

If you want to transfer only the PAR02 parameter and that the report should run in the background, write this:

```
SUBMIT z_memberlist13_a
  WITH par02 = 'X'.
```

 Example 4

The first three examples in this chapter apply if you want to end your report and have another report continue the work. But now you want to call the external report like a subprogram so that your own report continues to work after the external report.

Own report continues to work

You can use the SUBMIT statement to meet your requirements with the AND RETURN addition. The following example calls external report

AND RETURN

Z_MEMBERLIST13_A. When the report has ended, the system returns to the original report and continues processing with the next statement after the SUBMIT command:

```
SUBMIT z_memberlist13_a VIA SELECTION-SCREEN
       AND RETURN.
```

However, the data consistency of both reports will become difficult over time. Report A doesn't know anything about the data and field contents of report B (and vice versa) because each report runs independently of the other by design.

Searching for and finding meaningful data

To solve this minor problem, use working memory areas that can be accessed by several programs. Your only concern is that the correct report populates the correct area at the correct time so that the report finds meaningful data when it requires it. "Memory Areas for Data Transfer" covers this common problem.

Function Modules

Don't reinvent the wheel

Like subroutines, *function modules* are procedures that differ significantly in how they are maintained and used. Function modules are used for limited subtasks that are repeatedly needed at various places throughout the entire SAP system. For example, this section covers the download of an internal table to a local file, which is a task that might be performed daily in every department and area of a company. If you don't want to reinvent the wheel, you need to be able to access a reusable component. You will come to appreciate the advantages of function modules.

A variety of ready-to-use function modules are delivered as standard with the SAP software. You can also create your own customer-specific function modules.

Function Builder

Function library

Function modules are managed in a dedicated function library and with a dedicated tool, the *Function Builder*. You use this tool to develop, manage, and test function modules. Function modules that belong to a specific work area are combined in function groups, which the Function Builder will also help you create and manage.

To get started with ABAP, you only need to know these things: how to use the tool to search for function modules in the library, how to understand the documentation and interfaces of function modules, and how to test and link function modules in your ABAP program. You can access the Function Builder via SAP MENU • TOOLS • ABAP WORKBENCH • DEVELOPMENT • FUNCTION BUILDER or with Transaction SE37.

In the initial screen of the Function Builder, first follow menu path UTILITIES • FIND to call the Repository Info System (see Figure 13.9) to search for function modules. You can use this info system across all SAP objects to search for other objects. It's already integrated here automatically.

Searching for function modules

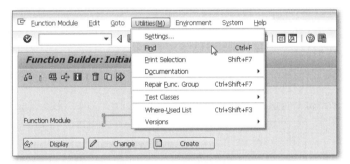

Figure 13.9 Searching for Function Modules in the Function Builder

 No Labor of Sisyphus

We recommend that you think about what exactly you are looking for in a function module before you start searching for it. Given the large number of function modules—the standard delivery contains several hundred thousand—the search might seem like a labor of Sisyphus. Tips from experienced developers about naming components and other search criteria can be very helpful here.

Function Modules for Starting a Program

As an initial exercise, you search for a function module that starts a local program on the presentation server. Because executable programs are called .exe files (from "execute"), it's clear that one of these words could be part of the name of the function module that we're searching for. It's best to search generically by specifying wildcards such as "*". As shown in Figure 13.10, enter "*EXECUTE*" in the FUNCTION MODULE field as the search argument and click EXECUTE ($\boxed{\text{F8}}$).

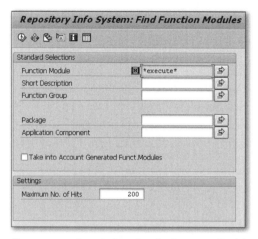

Figure 13.10   Generic Searches for Function Modules

In the real world, of course, no one starts a program so blindly. The vast majority of developers repeatedly work with specific modules and applications and therefore know the common packages, function groups, and so on. But that level of work is too demanding for just getting started with ABAP.

Generic search   If the generic search argument is too general, you will see a very comprehensive list that has as many as 300 possible hits. To shorten the process, use "*WS_EXEC*" as the next search argument and you'll get a much more manageable list of possible hits (see Figure 13.11).

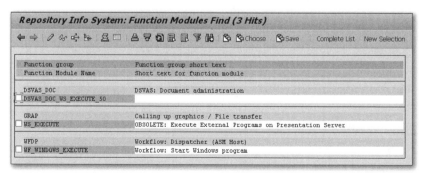

Figure 13.11   Hit List When Searching for *WS_EXEC*

Note that you should not use function modules with a short description that begins with "obsolete." You can look at the remaining modules for your information and select the one that best meets your requirements. For this example, select function module DSVAS_DOC_WS _EXECUTE_50 and use the Show button to return to the Function Builder (see Figure 13.12).

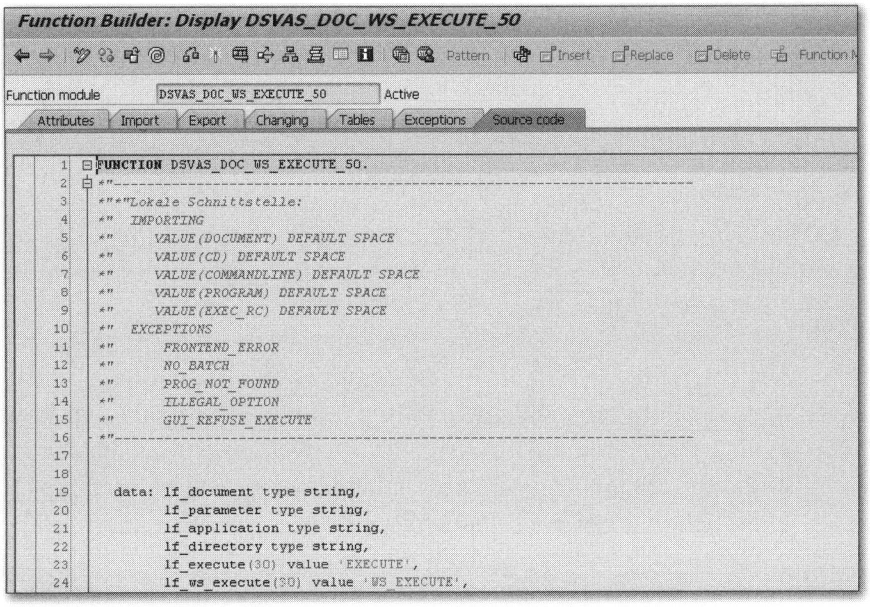

Figure 13.12　Source Code of the Function Module in the Function Builder

Various tabs are displayed. If you want to use the function module without any changes and strictly for information purposes, the Source code tab will suffice. The other tabs, however, are more important.

Source code

The Attributes tab (see Figure 13.13) displays the general properties or attributes of the module. In this example, the Processing Type is a normal function module, which can be used just like a subroutine. It's not designed to be called from outside its own SAP system, and it's not designed as a special update function module that performs posting activities in the database in a particular type of program task. You can change this setting for function modules that you yourself have created.

Attributes

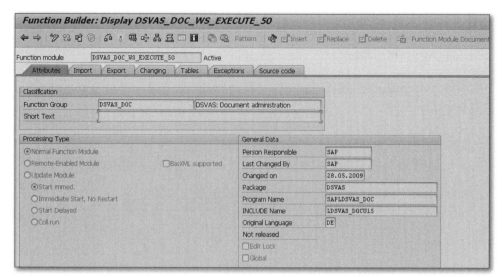

Figure 13.13 Attributes of the Function Module

Import The IMPORT tab (see Figure 13.14) describes the data interface on the input side of the module (that is, the information that the function module needs from your ABAP source code). You can see the names of the corresponding parameters in the function module, their types, and whether they have been populated with suggested values.

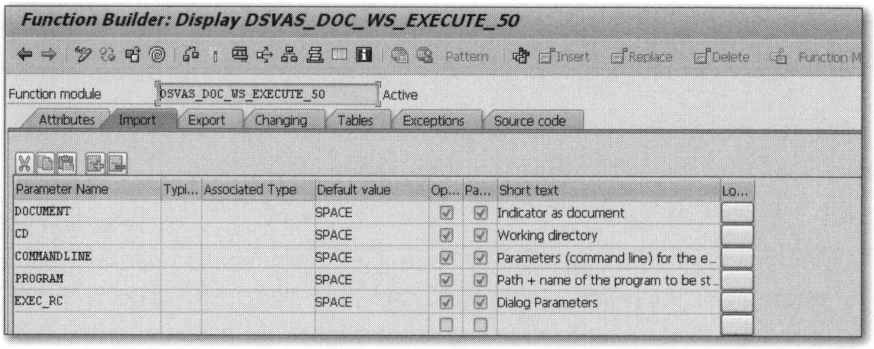

Figure 13.14 Import Parameters of the Function Module

The OPTIONAL and PASS VALUE columns are also important. If the parameter is checked in the OPTIONAL column, you don't have to specify the parameter when calling the function module. If the parameter is not declared as optional in this column (as is the case in this example), you must assign a value to the parameter when calling the function module.

The PASS VALUE option controls whether the calling program passes the parameter *by value* or *by reference*:

> Passing data by value means that, when being called, the function module has a copy of the transferred parameter value from the calling program. The function module can use this copy in any way and change it without affecting the calling program.

> Passing data by reference means that the function module is granted access to the actual data object of the calling program. So the data doesn't need to be copied (which the system only does for optimization reasons if and when the transferred parameter is changed). Within the called function module, reference parameters are protected against overwriting in order to avoid unpleasant side effects.

The EXPORT tab (see Figure 13.15) displays the parameters that the function module makes available to the calling ABAP report. If the tab is blank, the function module doesn't provide any values to the calling ABAP report.

Export

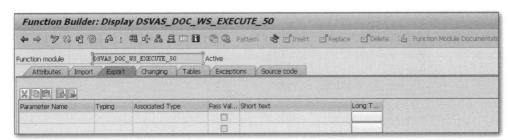

Figure 13.15 Export Parameters of the Function Module

The CHANGING tab (see Figure 13.16) contains parameters that serve as import and export parameters between the calling ABAP report and the function module. When the function module is called, the calling program transfers the value to the function module. The values might be changed during execution of the function module. At the end of

Changing

the function module, the values are transferred back to the calling program. A blank tab indicates that no data interfaces exist for these kinds of parameters.

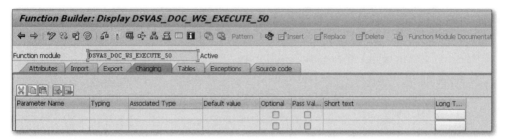

Figure 13.16 Changing Parameters of the Function Module

Tables   The TABLES tab (see Figure 13.17) displays the internal tables that the function module uses as import and export parameters. Once again, for the usability of the function module, it's important whether the assignment of an internal table is declared as mandatory or optional: If a tables parameter is marked as mandatory, it must be assigned a value by the caller. Otherwise, the function module can be called without providing a value for this parameter.

If the tab is left blank, as is the case here, the function module doesn't have any tables parameters.

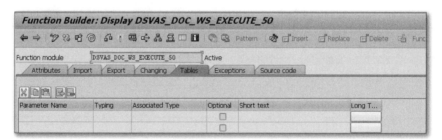

Figure 13.17 Transfer of Internal Tables in the Function Module

Exceptions   The entries in the EXCEPTIONS (see Figure 13.18) tab map the errors defined for the function module. You can see which errors are supported. The calling program queries and analyzes the expected errors with the SY-SUBRC return code. In this example, the tab is blank, which means that the ABAP program does not support error handling.

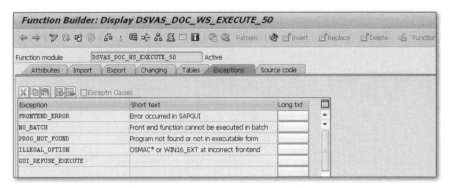

Figure 13.18 Parameters for Exceptions in the Function Module

> ### ▶ Elegant Function Module
>
> The interface of this function module is appropriate for getting started in ABAP. It is not complicated, has no internal tables, and has only a few parameters, and doesn't do error handling. Of course, not all function module interfaces have such an elegant construction, as you'll discover in later examples.

Assuming that this function module can handle the task at hand, you should test it in the next step just to ensure that it actually works as you expect it to. Click the TEST/EXECUTE button (F8) (see Figure 13.19) to reach the test environment of the Function Builder (see Figure 13.20).

Testing function modules

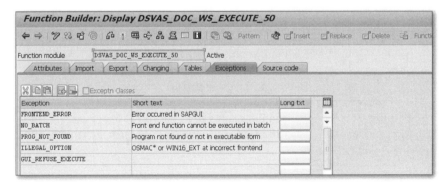

Figure 13.19 Calling the Test Environment of the Function Builder

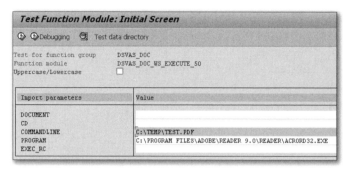

Figure 13.20 Testing Import Parameters

Testing is easy with only three parameters. For the PROGRAM parameter, you enter the path to a local program; for the COMMANDLINE parameter, you enter the path to the file to be opened. The OUT_FILE parameter stays empty because it is unnecessary. It is only required if the local program outputs to a file.

Sample call

This example starts *Acrobat Reader* to open the *TEST.PDF* file. Start the test with the EXECUTE button. After the system prompts you to confirm that you intentionally left the OUT_FILE parameter empty, Acrobat Reader starts and displays the desired file. The functionality is the same for all local programs, but it's important that the directories are present and the program and file names are correct. You can also use network drives and network paths (assuming, of course, that you have the required read and write authorizations).

 Path Name May Be Enough

> When you do a little more testing with the function module, you'll find that it's enough to enter the path name to the *C:\TEMP\TEST.PDF* file for the PROGRAM parameter. The other parameters can remain empty. But that works only when the local operating system (the registry in Windows) links the suffix of the file name to the corresponding program. The operating system then knows that it should always open a PDF file with Acrobat Reader.

Calling the function module

If testing convinces you that the function module is appropriate for your needs, you can include it in your ABAP source code. It's best to let the system support you here. Place the cursor at the place in the source code where you want to call the function module and click PATTERN (⌜Ctrl⌝ + ⌜F6⌝) (see Figure 13.21).

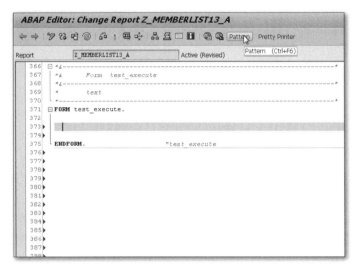

Figure 13.21 Inserting a Pattern in ABAP Source Code

In the INSERT STATEMENT screen, check CALL FUNCTION and enter the name of the function module that you wish to insert. In this case, this is tested function module DSVAS_DOC_WS_EXECUTE_50 (see Figure 13.22). Then click CONTINUE.

Pattern

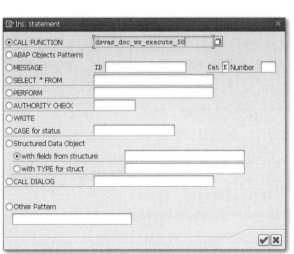

Figure 13.22 Inserting Function Modules with Patterns

The system enters the complete call of the function modules in the ABAP source code, including all parameters, tables, and exceptions. Optional entries are given asterisks and become comments.

```
CALL FUNCTION 'DSVAS_DOC_WS_EXECUTE_50'
  EXPORTING
    commandline
    program
        . . .

    .
```

CALL FUNCTION

As you can see, a function module is called with the CALL FUNCTION statement and its name. The name is output as a literal, and the characters in the literal must be given in uppercase. You can use a variable instead of the literal.

Position of the period

The CALL FUNCTION statement can be quite comprehensive. Numerous parameters, tables, and exceptions can make the command fill an entire screen, but the statement always ends with a period. That might sound quite trivial here, but it can also be a stumbling block because the system inserts a period at the end of every line, and it's easy to miss it. If that annoys you, you must position the period accordingly.

▶ **Import-Export and Export-Import**

Another seemingly insignificant note is that perspective matters. In this context, your point of view can be critical. For example, what constitutes an import for a function module is an export for our ABAP program. That's why the import parameters of the function modules are next to the export parameters in the ABAP source code. And the opposite also holds true: The export parameters of a function module are located next to the import parameters of your ABAP source code. You'll see that more clearly in other examples.

Mandatory parameters must contain a value assignment. In the example, assign the path name of the file to be opened to the COMMAND-LINE parameter as a literal. Enter the path name for the program to be started into the PROGRAM parameter as a literal:

```
CALL FUNCTION 'DSVAS_DOC_WS_EXECUTE_50'
  EXPORTING
    commandline = 'C:\TEMP\TEST.PDF'
    program     = 'C:\Programs\Adobe\Reader 8.0\
                   Reader\AcroRd32.exe'
  .
```

Of course, you can enter any type of file (a text document, for example) on your presentation server instead of a PDF file. The notation in the example requires only that the link between the file suffix and the application program be correct. If you want, try other combinations and experiment with your local programs and files.

Function Module for Downloading an Internal Table

To shorten the initially cumbersome selection procedure for this example, let's assume that you have decided on function module DSVAS_DOC_WS_DOWNLOAD_50. In terms of its parameters, this function module is somewhat more complex. In the IMPORT tab, you can see one mandatory and several optional parameters (see Figure 13.23). You can view information on individual parameters with the corresponding button in LONG TEXT. Click the FUNCTION MODULE DOCUMENTATION button for a description of the function modules and examples of calls.

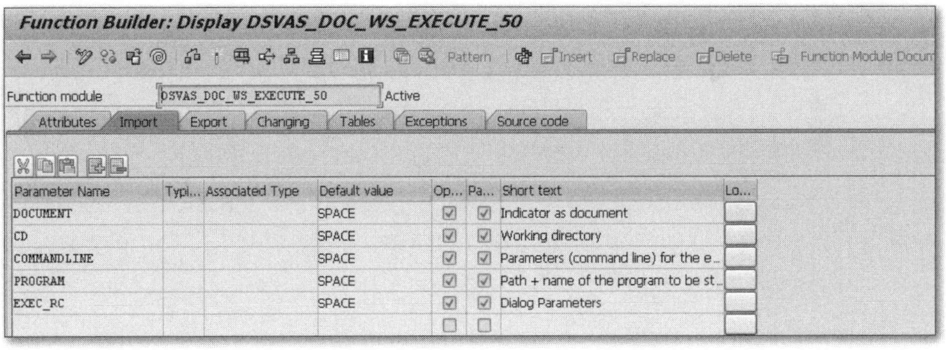

Shortcut

Function Builder: Display DSVAS_DOC_WS_EXECUTE_50

Parameter Name	Typi...	Associated Type	Default value	Op...	Pa...	Short text	Lo...
DOCUMENT			SPACE	☑	☑	Indicator as document	
CD			SPACE	☑	☑	Working directory	
COMMANDLINE			SPACE	☑	☑	Parameters (command line) for the e...	
PROGRAM			SPACE	☑	☑	Path + name of the program to be st...	
EXEC_RC			SPACE	☑	☑	Dialog Parameters	
				☐	☐		

Figure 13.23 Function Module: Import Parameters

For example, if you want more information on the APPEND parameter, click DISPLAY in the LONG TEXT column. The long text displays the possible values and effects of the parameter (see Figure 13.24). Proceed similarly with the parameters, tables, and exceptions on the other tabs.

Documentation of the function module

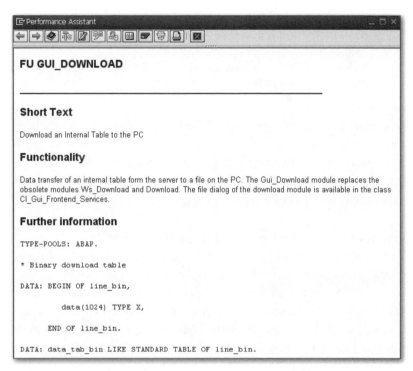

Figure 13.24 Long Text on the APPEND Import Parameter of the GUI_DOWNLOAD Function Module

Pattern function

Check which function module is best suited to your requirements. As you can see in the GUI_DOWNLOAD and DSVAS_DOC_WS_DOWNLOAD_50 examples, there are significant differences regarding quantity and quality of the documentation transferred.

Insertion of the call of the function module in the ABAP source code is easiest with the PATTERN function. The inserted call would appear as shown in Listing 13.1.

```
      CALL FUNCTION 'DSVAS_DOC_WS_DOWNLOAD_50'
        EXPORTING
*       BIN_FILESIZE                 = ' '
          filename                   = ' '
          filetype                   = ' '
          mode                       = ' '
*     IMPORTING
*       FILELENGTH                   =
```

```
    TABLES
        data_tab                    =
    EXCEPTIONS
        file_open_error             = 1
        file_write_error            = 2
        invalid_filesize            = 3
        invalid_type                = 4
        no_batch                    = 5
        unknown_error               = 6
        invalid_table_width         = 7
        gui_refuse_filetransfer     = 8
        customer_error              = 9
        no_authority                = 10
        OTHERS                      = 11
IF sy-subrc <> 0.
* MESSAGE ID SY-MSGID TYPE SY-MSGTY NUMBER SY-MSGNO
* WITH SY-MSGV1 SY-MSGV2 SY-MSGV3 SY-MSGV4.
   WRITE: / 'Download itab04 to local file failed,',
           'sy-subrc =', sy-subrc.
ENDIF.
```

Listing 13.1 DSVAS_DOC_WS_DOWNLOAD_50 Function Module

You can see that the call is somewhat more complex. The optional parameters are given asterisks to make them comments, but the mandatory parameters are not. If you want to use the optional parameters, you must remove the asterisks and supply the parameters with values (see Listing 13.2).

Supplying values

```
   CALL FUNCTION 'DSVAS_DOC_WS_DOWNLOAD_50'
      EXPORTING
*     BIN_FILESIZE                = ' '
        filename                    = locfile
        filetype                    = 'DAT'
        mode                        = ' '
*  IMPORTING
*     FILELENGTH                  =
      TABLES
        data_tab                    = itab04
      EXCEPTIONS
        file_open_error             = 1
        file_write_error            = 2
        invalid_filesize            = 3
        invalid_type                = 4
```

469

```
        no_batch                        = 5
        unknown_error                   = 6
        invalid_table_width             = 7
        gui_refuse_filetransfer         = 8
        customer_error                  = 9
        no_authority                    = 10
        OTHERS                          = 11
IF sy-subrc <> 0.
* MESSAGE ID SY-MSGID TYPE SY-MSGTY NUMBER SY-MSGNO
* WITH SY-MSGV1 SY-MSGV2 SY-MSGV3 SY-MSGV4.
  WRITE: / 'Download itab04 to local file failed,',
           'sy-subrc =', sy-subrc.
ENDIF.
```

Listing 13.2 DSVAS_DOC_WS_DOWNLOAD_50 Function Module Populated with Transfer Values

In the example, enter a variable that contains the name for the name of the local file at the export parameter. The data type is DAT for spreadsheet programs. If the file already exists, it should be overwritten, and the columns separated by a tab. For the table parameters, use internal table ITAB04 once again.

 Exception Handling

Exception handing is interesting. This function module has eleven different error exits and one general error exit. It delivers suggested values for the error exits (for example, the value 1 if problems occur when writing the file to the presentation server, which might happen if another program currently has the file open).

You can change the suggested values as needed. In all cases, they are entered as a return code in SY-SUBRC. You query the content of SY-SUBRC directly after the CALL FUNCTION statement and then evaluate it. That's why the IF structure for error handling is inserted along with the pattern—you can design error handling as you wish. If necessary, you can use a CASE structure instead of the IF structure.

ABAP Classes

ABAP has been object-oriented since the introduction of ABAP Objects. In addition to *procedural constructs*, you can use *object-oriented constructs* (classes) for modularization.

Object orientation

Classes and Function Groups

Actually, classes are similar to function groups in many ways:

Similarity between classes and function groups

> A function group is a main program with global variables that are not deleted when one of their function modules has been processed. Function groups have an internal state that does not expire until the calling program has been fully processed. Similarly, classes have class attributes (variables) and, consequently, an internal state as well.

> The function modules of a function group correspond to the methods of a class. Just as logically and functionally related function modules are bundled in a function group, the methods of a class belong together and operate together in an internal state.

However, there are also differences between classes and function groups:

> Classes do not only have one state; you can generate any number of independent copies of them, which are called *object instances*, *objects*, or *instances*. Each object can be addressed separately and has (and only views) its own state. Imagine having a class called "Employees." Your program can generate as many objects of this class as there are employees. Each object of the Employees class has its own values for the following variables (called *attributes* for classes): name, date of birth, career level, salary, and department. The methods of the Employees class describe the operations that you can carry out for an employee: edit, pay, determine remaining leave, and so on.

Object instances

> You can define the *visibility* for each part of a class (that is, all attributes and methods). This enables you to control whether a method can be called outside the class (PUBLIC), or whether it is only available within the class (PRIVATE and PROTECTED), for example. By

Visibility

hiding all internal methods whose call from the outside wouldn't make sense, you make it considerably easier for other programmers to use your newly manageable class interface.

Scope > All methods have a *scope*. They are either *instance methods* or *class methods* (also known as *static methods*). Instance methods are always called with reference to a single object instance. This means that you can only call an instance method when you have access to an object instance of the class. This kind of method (for example, "determine remaining leave") would be useful in the Employees class example with reference to a single employee. Class methods or static methods are not called with reference to a single object instance, so they don't require an existing instance. Class methods often have a cross-application character and can refer to all object instances (for example, starting the payroll run, outputting a list of all employees), or they can be used to generate, delete, or merge object instances. The same applies to the attributes that are defined for a class: They are either class attributes (and thus generally valid) or instance attributes, which can have a different value for each object instance.

 More Information on Object Orientation

Describing object-oriented programming in detail goes beyond the scope of this book. If you haven't already become an expert in object-oriented programming due to your experiences in another programming language, you should read *Object-Oriented Programming with ABAP Objects* (SAP PRESS, 2009).

Global and Local Classes

Cross-system or program-internal visibility

Global and local classes have a similar relationship as function modules and subroutines: Like function modules, global classes are available across the system and can be called in any program. Local classes are defined within a program and are only available there.

It makes sense to use a local class if the tasks that it performs are very specific to the surrounding program and if it won't be used by other programs for other purposes. Such special classes, which carry out local auxiliary work, are also called *helper classes*.

If you want the functions of your class to be available to other programs, you should create it as a global class.

Class Builder

You create and manage global classes in the Class Builder. You can access the Class Builder via SAP Menu • Tools • ABAP Workbench • Development • Class Builder or with Transaction SE24.

To search for classes, carry out the same steps you performed in the Function Builder. To view a class, for example, enter the name of the CL_GUI_FRONTEND_SERVICES class (see Figure 13.25), or search for the class via the info system. Then, click Display to take a closer look at the class.

Searching for classes

Figure 13.25   Initial Screen of the Class Builder

The most important tab lists the methods of the ABAP class. Every method is a procedure that can be called, but not every method is available. You can only call methods with the PUBLIC visibility outside of the class.

Methods

This tab also indicates which methods are static methods and which are instance methods (see Figure 13.26); the former can be called across the system, and the latter can only be called with reference to an object instance.

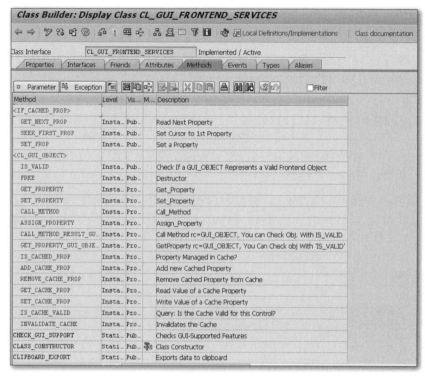

Figure 13.26   Methods of a Class

 Adapting the Presentation

You can adapt the screen to fit your needs using the UTILITIES • SETTINGS menu path. For example, for classes that you only want to use but not edit, it makes sense to hide all private components and only display the methods and attributes that are visible to the outside (see Figure 13.27).

Parameters   Let's now take a closer look at a certain method. Scroll down the list of the methods until you reach the EXECUTE method. The method is static—so it doesn't require an object instance—and public (that is, it can be called outside of the class). Select the method by clicking on it once, and click on PARAMETER. Like in the Function Builder, the system now displays an overview of the parameters of this method (see Figure 13.28).

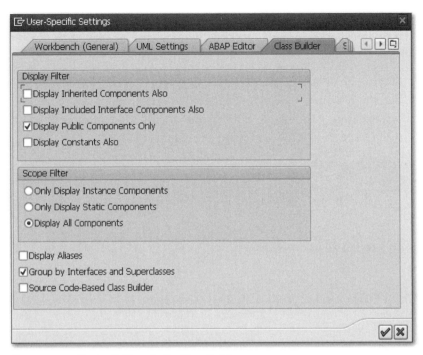

Figure 13.27 Display Settings in the Class Builder

Class Builder: Display Class CL_GUI_FRONTEND_SERVICES

← → | 🈁 🈂 🈳 ◎ | 🔄 ┊ 🖳 🈶 | 🔃 🈵 □ 🈚 🈸 | 🈷 🖺 Local Definitions/Implementations | Class documentation

| Class Interface | CL_GUI_FRONTEND_SERVICES | Implemented / Active |

Properties | Interfaces | Friends | Attributes | Methods | Events | Types | Aliases

| Method parameters | EXECUTE | ▲ ▼ |

← Methods | ⚡ Exceptions | 🖹 | 🖺 | 🖥🖥 | ✂️🗐🗏

Parameter	Type	P...	O...	Typing ...	Associated Type	Default value	Description
DOCUMENT	Importi..	☑	☑	Type	STRING		Path+Name to Document
APPLICATION	Importi..	☑	☑	Type	STRING		Path and Name of Application
PARAMETER	Importi..	☑	☑	Type	STRING		Parameter for Application
DEFAULT_DIRECTORY	Importi..	☑	☑	Type	STRING		Default Directory
MAXIMIZED	Importi..	☑	☑	Type	STRING		Show Window Maximized
MINIMIZED	Importi..	☑	☑	Type	STRING		Show Window Minimized
SYNCHRONOUS	Importi..	☑	☑	Type	STRING		When 'X': Runs the Application..
OPERATION	Importi..	☑	☑	Type	STRING	'OPEN'	Reserved: Verb für ShellExecute
		☐	☐	Type			

Figure 13.28 Method Parameters

The EXECUTE method enables you to execute a program on the presentation server or call a document. To test the method, select CLASS • TEST in

Testing the method execution

the menu. Accept the default values for the replacement of the generic parameter types without checking them by clicking on NEXT.

The system displays a view of all available components of the class. Because no object instance exists, the system only displays static attributes and methods; because you view the class from the outside, the system merely shows the public components. Click on the EXECUTE icon next to the EXECUTE method (see Figure 13.29).

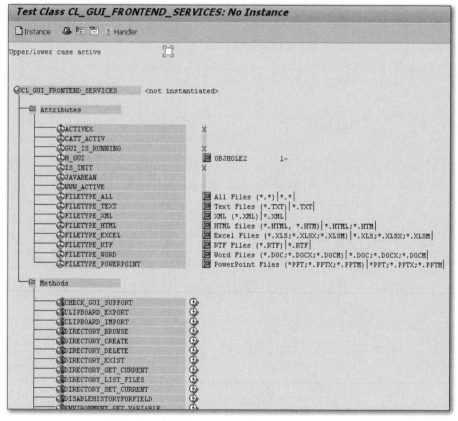

Figure 13.29 Testing the CL_GUI_FRONTEND_SERVICES Class

Entering test values

Now enter the values from the previous example (in which you opened a PDF document in Acrobat Reader), and click on EXECUTE (see Figure 13.30).

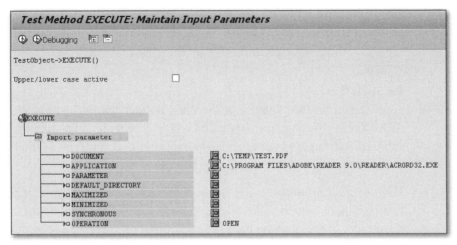

Figure 13.30 Transferring Parameters for Testing Purposes

If the call has been successful, you can now take the next step and embed it in an ABAP program.

In the ABAP Editor, call the PATTERN function, select the ABAP OBJECTS PATTERN radio button in the next dialog box (see Figure 13.22), and click CONTINUE. In the OO STATEMENT PATTERN dialog screen, enter the name of the class and method that you want to call, and click OK.

Using patterns

As it did for the pattern for the function module, the system now generates the code for calling the method; again, optional information is given an asterisk and becomes comments.

```
CALL METHOD cl_gui_frontend_services=>execute
    EXPORTING
        document              =
        application           =
        ...
    .
```

In contrast to the previously used function module, the method expects that you fill either the document parameter or the application parameter but not both of them. Enter the path to the document here:

```
CALL METHOD cl_gui_frontend_services=>execute
    EXPORTING
        document                    = 'C:\TEMP\TEST.PDF'.
```

The call is now complete. In addition to the function modules of the SAP standard, you can also use the corresponding global classes (although you are currently only able to call static methods).

Local Classes

Local classes
Local classes are not defined in the Class Builder but exclusively via ABAP keywords. They are developed within a program and—like the subroutines, data types, and global variants defined in this program—are only available within that program.

The surrounding program can be an ABAP report, a function group, or a class pool (which is the main program of a global class). So local classes are, in a way, appendages of other programs. As helper classes, they usually carry out minor, routine tasks for this program.

Common usage
Programmers who prefer object-oriented programming to mere procedural programming (which can be often found in the ABAP world) like to use local classes to encapsulate as much of the functionality of an ABAP report as possible into classeses. Due to the use of object-oriented concepts, such as access control, they can create a more transparent program structure and improve the maintainability of the program.

Definition and implementation are simply embedded into the program code. Here, the definition should be embedded at the beginning of a program (near the type definitions) and the implementation should be embedded at the end (near the subroutines):

```
CLASS lcl_my_local_class DEFINITION.
  PUBLIC SECTION.
    CLASS-METHODS main.
ENDCLASS.
CLASS lcl_my_local_class IMPLEMENTATION.
  METHOD main.
    WRITE: / 'Hello World!'.
  ENDMETHOD.
ENDCLASS.
```

You can now access the functions of the class in the main part of the program, for example, during START-OF-SELECTION:

```
START-OF-SELECTION.
  CALL METHOD lcl_my_local_class=>main( ).
```

Although this topic is very interesting, further details about the use of object orientation in real life exceed the scope of this book. If you have already gained experience with object-oriented programming in other object-oriented programming languages, then hopefully this example taught you some special features in ABAP. For more information, refer to the SAP PRESS book recommended earlier in this section.

Memory Areas for Data Transfer

To solve the problem of data transfer between various reports, you can use files, database tables, and working memory areas.

For getting started in ABAP, we'll look at data transfer with the help of working memory areas. We will use working memory areas that can be accessed by several programs. You must ensure that only the correct report uses the correct area at the right time so that it finds the significant data that it needs. The working memory areas are called *global SAP memory*, *local SAP memory*, *ABAP memory*, and *shared memory*.

Memory areas

Global SAP Memory

The content of global SAP memory is available to users between the time they log on and the time they log off. Field contents can be written to and read from this area. The content is uniquely identified by a parameter ID of up to 20 characters. These parameters are also often used to populate the selection screens of programs with suggested values.

During logon

You use the SET PARAMETER ID statement to write to global SAP memory and the GET PARAMETER ID statement to read from SAP memory.

For example, if you want to write the contents of the PROGNAME field to the Z_TEST parameter ID, the statement looks like this:

SET PARAMETER ID

```
SET PARAMETER ID 'Z_TEST' FIELD progname.
```

If you want to read the contents of the Z_TEST parameter from SAP memory into the PROGNAME variable of the program, write:

GET PARAMETER ID

```
GET PARAMETER ID 'Z_TEST' FIELD progname.
```

With the SET PARAMETER and GET PARAMETER statements, you can use only an existing parameter ID, but you can create these parameter IDs easily with the ABAP Editor and forward navigation, or with the ABAP Workbench.

Local SAP Memory

During a transaction

Local SAP memory is available only during the length of a transaction. If you call additional reports from the report with the SUBMIT statement, the reports you call can access local SAP memory. The SET PARAMETER ID and GET PARAMETER ID statements write to both memory areas. Local SAP memory guarantees only that the parameter IDs that apply to it remain unchanged during the runtime of a transaction, whereas the contents of the global SAP memory can change during this time based on events in another transaction.

ABAP Memory

Shortest lifespan

ABAP memory has the shortest lifespan of the three memory areas. The content stored there remains available only as long as an external session with its internal sessions remains active. If a user closes a session, the contents of this memory are deleted. This area is typically used to transfer data to a called program.

You write data to ABAP memory with the EXPORT TO MEMORY ID statement. You read data from ABAP memory into your ABAP program with the IMPORT FROM MEMORY ID statement.

EXPORT TO MEMORY

You use the EXPORT statement to write objects like fields, work areas, and internal tables to ABAP memory. The objects are entered as field lists. There is also a variant of this statement without the specification of the memory ID (which can have up to 60 digits); in this variant, the same memory area is always used for write or read processes. The memory ID is the cluster name.

The objects are stored in ABAP memory as clusters (series of binary characters), so it's very important that the structure of the objects agrees during writing and reading. During reading with the IMPORT statement, the structure is filled incrementally.

Responsibility for Assignment

No automatic check occurs to determine whether the structure agrees during writing and reading. As the developer, you are responsible for the correct assignment. With internal tables, only the body lines of the table are written to ABAP memory as a cluster, even when the table is defined with a header line.

For example, if you want to write internal table ITAB04 to ABAP memory as a cluster, you can enter the cluster name as a literal or a variable. In the following example, the cluster name contains the variable PROGNAME, so the EXPORT statement looks like this:

```
EXPORT itab04 TO MEMORY ID progname.
```

This example exports only one internal table. If it exported several tables or a combination of fields, work areas, and tables, then all exports would be in the specified cluster as binary figures. Within the 32-character limit for names, ABAP memory can contain any number of clusters, and all are available to all of the programs in the call chain.

For example, if you want the called program to reimport internal table ITAB04 from the cluster in ABAP memory that contains the variable PROGNAME and to put it in internal table ITAB05, you would use this statement:

IMPORT FROM MEMORY

```
IMPORT itab04 TO itab05 FROM MEMORY ID progname.
```

You now know how to transfer large and complex data structures to programs in the call chain.

Shared Objects

If you know how to use advanced object-oriented programming in ABAP—that is, if you can generate and manage object instances appropriately—then shared objects provide an additional technology for accessing shared memory. These technologies are only described briefly here. The objective of the following section is to give you a first insight into these and provide another reason for becoming acquainted with ABAP Objects.

Shared objects are object instances of ABAP classes that do not exist in the memory of their internal session (as other objects do) but are managed in the shared memory of the ABAP application server—in the same memory area in which the ABAP memory is located. To be able to distinguish between the different users (multiple SAP applications, for instance) of the shared memory, the stored content is structured with *areas*, which you can create and manage in Transaction SHMA.

To store objects in the shared memory and read them from there, some requirements must be met: First, the used classes must have the *shared memory-enabled* property in the Class Builder. Second, the used area must exist in Transaction SHMA. Third, you have to create a special class (the area root class) and assign it to the area in Transaction SHMA. This class is used as the access class for the data that is stored in the shared memory. This means that you should select attributes and methods that enable you to directly or indirectly access all of the data and objects that you want to manage in the shared memory.

When these requirements are met, you can access the shared memory with only a few lines of code, and can benefit from the advantages of object-oriented programming.

Sample Code for Modularization

```
1   *&---------------------------------------------*
2   *& Report   Z_MEMBERLIST13_A                   *
3   *&                                             *
4   *&---------------------------------------------*
5   *&                      .                      *
6   *&                                             *
7   *&---------------------------------------------*
8
9   REPORT   z_memberlist13_a.
10
11  * Definitions
12  INCLUDE z_memberlist_definitions.
13  INCLUDE z_memberlist13_a_selection_scr.
14
15  *initialization.
16
```

```
17  *at selection-screen.
18
19  *-----------------------------------------------*
20  START-OF-SELECTION.
21  * fill itab01
22    PERFORM itab01_fill.
23  * fill itab02
24    PERFORM itab02_fill USING itab02.
25  * fill itab03
26    PERFORM itab03_fill.
27  * fill itab04
28    PERFORM itab04_fill USING itab04
29      lines_itab04 par04.
30
31  *-----------------------------------------------*
32  END-OF-SELECTION.
33  * process and list itab01
34    PERFORM itab01_list.
35  * process and list itab02
36    PERFORM itab02_list.
37  * process and list itab03
38    PERFORM itab03_list.
39  * process and list itab04
40    PERFORM itab04_list USING par04 lines_itab04.
41  * call a program on presentation server
42    PERFORM execute_loc_prog USING execlopr.
43  * Download itab04 to presentation server
44    PERFORM itab04_download USING it04down.
45  * clear workareas and internal tables
46    PERFORM clear_wa_itab.
45  * Check if this report was started by another report
46    PERFORM check_call.
47
48  * End of Main Program
49  *************************************************
50  *&----------------------------------------------*
51  *&      Form  itab01_fill
52  *&----------------------------------------------*
53  *       text
54  *-----------------------------------------------*
55  *  --> p1        text
56  *  <-- p2        text
57  *-----------------------------------------------*
58  FORM itab01_fill .
```

```
59   * Read dbtab into itab01 via work area
60     SELECT * FROM zmember02 INTO wa_zmember02.
61       MOVE-CORRESPONDING wa_zmember02 TO wa_itab01.
62       APPEND wa_itab01 TO itab01.
63     ENDSELECT.
64   ENDFORM.                       " itab01_fill
65   *&---------------------------------------------*
66   *&      Form  itab02_fill
67   *&---------------------------------------------*
68   *       text
69   *---------------------------------------------*
70   *  -->P_ITAB02  text
71   *---------------------------------------------*
72    FORM itab_fill USING itab_universal TYPE table.
73   * Read dbtab and fill itab02 with array fetch
74     SELECT * FROM zmember02
75       INTO CORRESPONDING FIELDS OF TABLE itab_universal.
76   ENDFORM.                       " itab02_fill
77   *&---------------------------------------------*
78   *&      Form  itab03_fill
79   *&---------------------------------------------*
80   *       text
81   *---------------------------------------------*
82   *  --> p1         text
83   *  <-- p2         text
84   *---------------------------------------------*
85   FORM itab03_fill .
86     DATA loc_max_persons TYPE i VALUE 10.
87     CHECK par03 IS NOT INITIAL.
88   * Read dbtab and move field values
       into itab03 via work area
89     wa_itab03-max_persons = loc_max_persons.
90     SELECT * FROM zmember02 INTO wa_zmember02.
91       wa_itab03-course_title =
         wa_zmember02-zzcoursetitle.
92       wa_itab03-fee = wa_zmember02-mfee.
93       APPEND  wa_itab03 TO itab03 .
94     ENDSELECT.
95     PERFORM test.
96   ENDFORM.                       " itab03_fill
97   *&---------------------------------------------*
98   *&      Form  itab04_fill
99   *&---------------------------------------------*
100  *       text
```

```
101  *-------------------------------------------------*
102  *  -->  p1        text
103  *  <--  p2        text
104  *-------------------------------------------------*
103   FORM itab04_fill USING lok_itab TYPE table
104                               lin_count
105                               loc_pararameter.
106    CHECK loc_parameter IS NOT INITIAL.
107  * Read dbtab and fill itab04 with array fetch
108    SELECT * FROM zmember02
109      INTO CORRESPONDING FIELDS OF TABLE itab.
110    DESCRIBE TABLE itab LINES loc_lin_count.
111  ENDFORM.                      " itab04_fill
112  *&------------------------------------------------*
113  *&      Form   test
114  *&------------------------------------------------*
115  *        text
116  *-------------------------------------------------*
117  *  -->  p1        text
118  *  <--  p2        text
119  *-------------------------------------------------*
120  FORM test .
121  * Break-point.
122  * global field glob_max_persons exists in form
123  * local  field loc_max_persons  exists not
124  ENDFORM.                       " test
125  *&------------------------------------------------*
126  *&      Form   itab01_list
127  *&------------------------------------------------*
128  *        text
129  *-------------------------------------------------*
130  *  -->  p1        text
131  *  <--  p2        text
132  *-------------------------------------------------*
133  FORM itab01_list .
134    CHECK par01 IS NOT INITIAL.
135  * Read and display amount of lines in itab01
136    DESCRIBE TABLE itab01 LINES lines_itab01.
137    SKIP.
138    WRITE: / 'Amount of lines in itab01:', lines_itab01.
139  * Clear work area, create new values
         and insert in itab01
140    CLEAR wa_itab01.
141    lines_itab01 = lines_itab01 + 1.
```

```
142    wa_itab01-zzcoursetitle = 'LINUX-BASIC'.
143    wa_itab01-mfee = '456.78'.
144    INSERT wa_itab01 INTO itab01 INDEX lines_itab01.
145  * List. lines of itab01
146    SKIP.
147    WRITE: / 'sy-tabix, itab01-zzcoursetitle,
                  itab01-mfee'.
148    LOOP AT itab01 INTO wa_itab01.
149      WRITE: / sy-tabix,
                    wa_itab01-zzcoursetitle, wa_itab01-mfee.
150    ENDLOOP.
151  * Read, delete and log a line of itab01 using index
152    READ TABLE itab01 INTO wa_itab01 INDEX 3.
153    DELETE itab01 INDEX 3.
154    SKIP.
155    WRITE: / 'Line deleted in itab01', sy-tabix NO-GAP,
                  '.line:',
156              wa_itab01-zzcoursetitle, wa_itab01-mfee.
157  ENDFORM.                       " itab01_list
158  *&---------------------------------------------*
159  *&      Form   itab02_list
160  *&---------------------------------------------*
161  *        text
162  *----------------------------------------------*
163  *  -->  p1         text
164  *  <--  p2         text
165  *----------------------------------------------*
166  FORM itab02_list .
167    CHECK par02 IS NOT INITIAL.
168  * Process itab02 and list lines
169    SKIP.
170    WRITE: / 'itab02-zzcoursetitle, itab02-mfee,
                  itab02-min_persons'.
171    LOOP AT itab02 INTO wa_itab02 WHERE
       zzcoursetitle = 'SAP05' .
172      wa_itab02-min_persons = 2.
173      WRITE: / wa_itab02-zzcoursetitle, wa_itab02-mfee,
174                wa_itab02-min_persons.
175    ENDLOOP.
176  * Read, delete and log a line of itab02 using key
177    READ TABLE itab02 INTO wa_itab02
178        WITH KEY zzcoursetitle = 'SAP06'.
179    DELETE TABLE itab02 FROM wa_itab02.
180    SKIP.
```

```
181    WRITE: / 'Line deleted in itab02',
                  sy-tabix NO-GAP, '.line:',
182              wa_itab02-zzcoursetitle.
183  ENDFORM.                    " itab02_list
184  *&---------------------------------------------*
185  *&       Form  itab03_list
186  *&---------------------------------------------*
187  *        text
188  *---------------------------------------------*
189  *  --> p1         text
190  *  <-- p2         text
191  *---------------------------------------------*
192  FORM itab03_list .
193    CHECK par03 IS NOT INITIAL.
194  * Process itab03 and modify lines
195    SKIP.
196    WRITE: / 'itab03-course_title, itab03-fee,
                  itab03-max_persons'.
197    LOOP AT itab03 INTO wa_itab03.
198      IF wa_itab03-course_title = 'BASIC'.
199        wa_itab03-fee = 567.
200        MODIFY itab03 FROM wa_itab03.
201      ENDIF.
202      WRITE: / wa_itab03-course_title, wa_itab03-fee,
                  wa_itab03-max_persons.
204    ENDLOOP.
205  * List. a line of itab03 using line index
206    READ TABLE itab03 INDEX 3 INTO wa_itab03.
207    SKIP.
208    WRITE: / 'read itab03', sy-tabix NO-GAP, '.line:',
209              wa_itab03-course_title, wa_itab03-fee,
210              wa_itab03-max_persons.
211  ENDFORM.                      " itab03_list
212  *&---------------------------------------------*
213  *&       Form  itab04_list
214  *&---------------------------------------------*
215  *        text
216  *---------------------------------------------*
217  *  --> p1         text
218  *  <-- p2         text
219  *---------------------------------------------*
220  FORM itab04_list
221    USING loc_par loc_lin_count.
222    CHECK loc_par IS NOT INITIAL.
```

```
223  * List. a line of itab04 using key
224    READ TABLE itab04 INTO wa_itab04
225      WITH KEY client = sy-mandt  mnumber = 5.
226    IF sy-subrc = 0.
227      SKIP.
228      WRITE: / 'read line of itab04',
229              / 'amount of lines in itab:', loc_lin_count,
230              / wa_itab04-client, wa_itab04-mnumber,
231                wa_itab04-mname, wa_itab04-dob,
232                wa_itab04-mgender.
233    ENDIF.
234  ENDFORM.                    " itab04_list
235  *&---------------------------------------------------*
236  *&      Form  clear_wa_itab
237  *&---------------------------------------------------*
238  *       text
239  *----------------------------------------------------*
240  *  -->  p1         text
241  *  <--  p2         text
242  *----------------------------------------------------*
243  FORM clear_wa_itab .
244  * Effect of clear, refresh and free statement for
245  * internal tables without header line
246  *  BREAK-POINT.
247    CLEAR wa_itab01.    " initalize wa
248    CLEAR itab01.       " delete all body lines
249
250    CLEAR wa_itab02.    " initalize wa
251    REFRESH itab02.     " delete all body lines
252
253    CLEAR wa_itab03.    " initalize wa
254    FREE itab03.        " delete all body lines and
                             release memory space
255  SKIP.
256  ENDFORM.                    " check_call
257  *&---------------------------------------------------*
258  *&      Form  check_call
259  *&---------------------------------------------------*
260  *       text
261  *----------------------------------------------------*
262  *  -->  p1         text
263  *  <--  p2         text
264  *----------------------------------------------------*
265  FORM check_call .
```

```
266    GET PARAMETER ID 'Z_TEST' FIELD progname.
267    IF progname IS NOT INITIAL.
268      repname = 'Z_MEMBERLIST13_A'.
269      SKIP.
270      WRITE: / 'Report', repname,
                   'was called by:', progname.
271       IMPORT itab04 TO itab05 FROM MEMORY ID progname.
272      SKIP.
273      LOOP AT itab05 INTO wa_itab05.
274        WRITE: / 'itab05-mname:', wa_itab05-mname.
275      ENDLOOP.
276      progname = space.
277      SET PARAMETER ID 'Z_TEST' FIELD progname.
278    ENDIF.
279  ENDFORM.                      " clear_wa_itab
280  *&---------------------------------------------------------*
281  *&      Form   execute_loc_prog
282  *&---------------------------------------------------------*
283  *       text
284  *---------------------------------------------------------*
285  *  -->  p1        text
286  *  <--  p2        text
287  *---------------------------------------------------------*
288   FORM execute_loc_prog USING par_sel.
289     CHECK NOT par_sel IS INITIAL.
290     CALL FUNCTION 'DSVAS_DOC_WS_EXECUTE_50'
291       EXPORTING
292  *    DOCUMENT                 = ' '
293  *    CD                       = ' '
294         commandline              = 'C:\TEMP\TEST.PDF'
295         program                  = 'C:\Programs\Adobe\
                           Reader 8.0\Reader\AcroRd32.exe'
296  *    EXEC_RC                  = ' '
297  * EXCEPTIONS
298  *    FRONTEND_ERROR           = 1
299  *    NO_BATCH                 = 2
300  *    PROG_NOT_FOUND           = 3
301  *    ILLEGAL_OPTION           = 4
302  *    GUI_REFUSE_EXECUTE       = 5
303  *    OTHERS                   = 6
304              .
305     IF sy-subrc <> 0.
306  * MESSAGE ID SY-MSGID TYPE SY-MSGTY NUMBER SY-MSGNO
307  *         WITH SY-MSGV1 SY-MSGV2 SY-MSGV3 SY-MSGV4.
```

```
308     ENDIF.
309   ENDFORM.                      " execute_loc_prog
310   *&---------------------------------------------------------*
311   *&      Form   itab04_download
312   *&---------------------------------------------------------*
313   *        text
314   *---------------------------------------------------------*
315   *  -->  p1         text
316   *  <--  p2         text
317   *---------------------------------------------------------*
318   FORM itab04_download USING par_sel.
319     CHECK NOT par_sel IS INITIAL.
320     CALL FUNCTION 'DSVAS_DOC_WS_DOWNLOAD_50'
321       EXPORTING
322   *    BIN_FILESIZE                 = ' '
323         filename                     = locfile
324         filetype                     = 'DAT'
325         mode                         = ' '
326   * IMPORTING
327   *    FILELENGTH                   =
328       TABLES
329         data_tab                        = itab04
330       EXCEPTIONS
331         file_open_error              = 1
332         file_write_error             = 2
333         invalid_filesize             = 3
334         invalid_type                 = 4
335         no_batch                     = 5
336         unknown_error                = 6
337         invalid_table_width          = 7
338         gui_refuse_filetransfer      = 8
339         customer_error               = 9
340         no_authority                 = 10
341         OTHERS                       = 11
342               .
343     IF sy-subrc <> 0.
344   * MESSAGE ID SY-MSGID TYPE SY-MSGTY NUMBER SY-MSGNO
345   *          WITH SY-MSGV1 SY-MSGV2 SY-MSGV3 SY-MSGV4.
346       WRITE: / 'Download itab04 to local file
                    failed, sy-subrc =', sy-subrc.
347     ENDIF.
348   ENDFORM.                      " itab04_download
```

Listing 13.3 Report Z_MEMBERLIST13_A

```
1   *&----------------------------------------------*
2   *&  INCLUDE       ZMEMBERLIST13_A_SELECTION_SCR*
3   *&----------------------------------------------*
4   * Block on selection screen with frame and frame title
5   SELECTION-SCREEN BEGIN OF BLOCK member
6     WITH FRAME TITLE text-001.
7   PARAMETERS: par01 AS CHECKBOX,
8               par02 AS CHECKBOX,
9               par03 AS CHECKBOX,
10              par04 AS CHECKBOX.
11              execlopr as checkbox,
12              it04down as checkbox,
13              locfile TYPE c length 20
                      default 'C:\TEMP\TEST.XLS'.
14  SELECTION-SCREEN END OF BLOCK member.
```

Listing 13.4 Include Report ZMEMBERLIST13_A_SELECTION_SCR

```
1   *&------------------------------------------------*
2   *&  INCLUDE       Z_MEMBER_DEFINITIONS    *
3   *&------------------------------------------------*
4
5   * Define table work area
6    DATA wa_zmember02 TYPE zmember02.
7
8   * Define fields
9    DATA: glob_tmax TYPE i VALUE 12,
10         local_file TYPE string,
11         nvml TYPE c LENGTH 1, fill "itab04
                              and process in
                              Z_MEMBERLIST13_A
12         progname TYPE c LENGTH 25,
13         repname LIKE progname,
14         lines_itab01 TYPE i,
15         lin_count_itab04 TYPE c LENGTH 1.
16
17  * Define data types for itab lines
18   TYPES: BEGIN OF line01_type,
19         zzcoursetitle TYPE zmember02-zzcoursetitle,
20         mfee TYPE zmember02-mfee,
21         END OF line01_type.
22
23   TYPES BEGIN OF line02_type.
24   INCLUDE TYPE line01_type.
25   TYPES min_persons TYPE i.
```

```
26    TYPES    END OF line02_type.
27
28    TYPES: BEGIN OF line03_type,
29           course_title TYPE zmember02-zzcoursetitle,
30           fee TYPE zmember02-mfee,
31           max_persons TYPE i,
32           END OF line03_type.
33
34    TYPES line04_type TYPE zmember02.
35
36  * Define data types for itabs
37    TYPES itab01_type TYPE STANDARD TABLE OF line01_type.
38    TYPES itab02_type TYPE STANDARD TABLE OF line02_type.
39    TYPES itab03_type TYPE STANDARD TABLE OF line03_type.
40    TYPES itab04_type TYPE STANDARD TABLE OF line04_type.
41
42  * Define itab without header line
43    DATA itab01 TYPE itab01_type.
44    DATA itab02 TYPE itab02_type.
45    DATA itab03 TYPE itab03_type.
46    DATA itab04 TYPE itab04_type.
47    DATA itab05 TYPE itab04_type.
48
49  * Define work areas for itabs
50    DATA wa_itab01 TYPE line01_type.
51    DATA wa_itab02 TYPE line02_type.
52    DATA wa_itab03 TYPE line03_type.
53    DATA wa_itab04 TYPE line04_type.
54    DATA wa_itab05 TYPE line04_type.
```

Listing 13.5   Include Program Z_MEMBERLIST_DEFINITIONS

Notes on the Source Code

Different program organization

The program in Listing 13.3 doesn't solve any new business problem. It offers almost the same functionality as the report in Chapter 12, Internal Tables (see Listing 13.2). What's different is its organization. While working with report Z_MEMBERLIST12_WORK_AREA was somewhat unstructured and unmanageable, report Z_MEMBERLIST13_A focuses on the structure and legibility for the sake of comparison. Among other things, this is achieved by using the include reports shown in Listing 13.4 and Listing 13.5.

Line 12

All definitions of data types and data objects were stored in a dedicated include report. The following report, Z_MEMBERLIST13_B (see " Sample Code for Calling an Export"), accesses these definitions. The include report could serve as a central definition object for several reports or for a group of tasks.

Line 13

The definitions for the selection screen were also placed in an include report for the sake of manageability.

Lines 20 to 30

No more processing commands are found beneath the START-OF-SE-LECTION event. There you find only controlling statements and calls of subroutines in the example. This approach gives the event a clear structure and makes it much more manageable.

A clear structure ensures better manageability

Lines 33 to 46

Only calls of subroutines are located beneath the END-OF-SELECTION event for the same reasons. This approach also applies to all other events.

Line 48

The main program contains only 48 lines. The events stand out; the functionality is encapsulated. If the program is changed or has to be modified, it's easy to find the appropriate location with forward navigation from the related subroutine.

Lines 58 to 64

The subroutine works with global variables that were defined in the include program (line 12) and that are known at all levels of the report.

Lines 72 to 76

The subroutine works with a local table name that is known only within the subroutine. The FORM statement defines the local name. The name in the calling structure must be delivered with the PERFORM statement;

the structure (e.g., the table fields and type) used in this subroutine str inherited from the definition of the table that is actually passed to the subroutine in the PERFORM statement. The encapsulation means that the subroutine can populate any internal table with the values of database table ZMEMBER02, as long as the internal table shares all or some of its field names with the database table. As such, it can be used globally.

Lines 85 to 96

A local variable is defined and processed in the subroutine. An additional subroutine is called to make the report more understandable. As you can see in the ABAP Debugger, only the global variables are known there.

Lines 105 to 113

A table and several variables are transferred to the subroutine. Because position operands are being transferred, the PERFORM and FORM statements must have identical structures.

Lines 265 to 280

This subroutine checks to see if another report calls the report. It reads the parameter ID from SAP memory. The calling report already populated SAP memory. If the subroutine finds a value that is anything other than a blank, this means that the report was called by an external report. In this case, it populates and processes an internal table from ABAP memory. The calling report must have already stored the body of the internal table in ABAP memory. Next, the parameter ID is initialized and rewritten to SAP memory. Otherwise, it would be impossible to tell during runs of the program whether it was started directly (the parameter ID is blank) or called by a different program (the parameter ID is not blank).

Lines 288 to 309

This subroutine calls Acrobat Reader on the local computer—that is, on the presentation server—and indicates which file Acrobat Reader is supposed to open. For both specifications, you have to define the name of the path. Regarding the issue of case sensitivity in literals, please consider the requirements of your personal computer's operating system. Some operating systems differentiate between uppercase and lowercase letters and some don't. Also, please check the actual file system path in which your Adobe Acrobat installation resides. It may vary from the one assumed in this example.

Lines 318 to 348

This section saves the content of the internal table, itab04, on the local computer by downloading it and storing it as a file. The name of the target file needs to be specified as a path name. The easiest way of doing this is to use a selection screen. Depending on the further use of the file, you can choose between various formats. Because this file is supposed to be further processed with Excel, 'DAT' was selected as the file type. This is a format that most personal computer spreadsheet programs can process.

Program Output

Another way of thinking about modularization also applies to the redesigned selection screen (see Figure 13.31). Only selected subtasks should be processed in the program. You use checkboxes to enable multiple selection.

Multiple selection possible

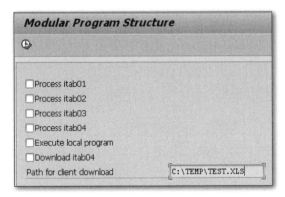

Figure 13.31 Z_MEMBERLIST13_A Selection Screen

Sample Code for Calling an External Report

```
 1  *&---------------------------------------------*
 2  *& Report   Z_MEMBERLIST13_B                  *
 3  *&                                            *
 4  *&---------------------------------------------*
 5  *&                                            *
 6  *&                                            *
 7  *&---------------------------------------------*
 8
 9  REPORT   z_memberlist13_b.
10
11  * Definitions
12  INCLUDE z_memberlist_definitions.       "DATA, TYPES ...
13  INCLUDE z_memberlist13_b_selection_scr.
     "Selection screen statements
14
15  *initialization.
16
17  *at selection-screen.
18
19  *---------------------------------------------*
20  START-OF-SELECTION.
21  * start report no return, different kinds
22     PERFORM start_no_return.
23  * start report and return
24     PERFORM start_and_return.
25  *---------------------------------------------*
26  END-OF-SELECTION.
27     SKIP.
28     WRITE: / 'Report z_memberlist13_b finished'.
29  * End of Main Program
30  **********************************************
31  *&---------------------------------------------*
32  *&      Form   start_no_return
33  *&---------------------------------------------*
34  *       text
35  *---------------------------------------------*
36  *  -->  p1        text
37  *  <--  p2        text
38  *---------------------------------------------*
39  FORM start_no_return .
40     IF rsow IS NOT INITIAL.
```

```
41  * Start report via empty selection screen, no return
42      SUBMIT z_memberlist13_a VIA SELECTION-SCREEN.
43    ENDIF.
44    IF rsowas IS NOT INITIAL.
45  * Using parameters for default values
      in selection screen
46      SUBMIT z_memberlist13_a
47        WITH par02 = 'X'
48        WITH par03 = 'X'
49        VIA SELECTION-SCREEN.
50    ENDIF.
51    IF rsowih IS NOT INITIAL.
52  * Using parameters for default values but
      without selection screen
53      SUBMIT z_memberlist13_a WITH par02 = 'X'.
54    ENDIF.
55  ENDFORM.                       " start_no_return
56  *&---------------------------------------------*
57  *&      Form   start_and_return
58  *&---------------------------------------------*
59  *       text
60  *----------------------------------------------*
61  *  -->  p1        text
62  *  <--  p2        text
63  *----------------------------------------------*
64  FORM start_and_return .
65    CHECK rsmw IS NOT INITIAL.
66    GET PARAMETER ID 'RID' FIELD progname.
67    SET PARAMETER ID 'Z_TEST' FIELD progname.
68    nvml = 'X'.
69    PERFORM itab04_fill IN PROGRAM
                              z_memberlist13_a
70              USING itab04
71                    lines_itab04
                      nvml.
72    READ TABLE itab04 INTO wa_itab04 WITH KEY
                                    client = sy-mandt
                                    mnumber = 3.
76    IF sy-subrc = 0.
77      WRITE: / Output from program Z_MEMBERLIST13_B',
78             / Member number', wa_itab04-mnumber,
                                  '=', wa_itab04-mname .
79    ENDIF.
```

```
80    EXPORT itab04 TO MEMORY ID progname.
81    SUBMIT z_memberlist13_a AND RETURN.
82  ENDFORM.                       " start_and_return
```

Listing 13.6   Z_MEMBERLIST13_B Report

```
 1  *&--------------------------------------------*
 2  *&  INCLUDE       Z_MEMBERLIST_DEFINITIONS    *
 3  *&--------------------------------------------*
 4
 5  * Define work area
 6   DATA wa_zmember02 TYPE zmember02.
 7
 8  * Define fields
 9   DATA: glob_tmax TYPE i VALUE 12,
10         local_file TYPE string,
11         nvml TYPE c LENGTH 1, "fill itab04
                                  and process in
                                  Z_MEMBERLIST13_A
12         progname TYPE c LENGTH 25,
13         repname LIKE progname,
14         lines_itab01 TYPE i,
15         lin_count_itab04.
16
17  * Define data types for itab lines
18   TYPES: BEGIN OF line01_type,
19          zzcoursetitle TYPE zmember02-zzcoursetitle,
20          mfee TYPE zmember02-mfee,
21          END OF line01_type.
22
23   TYPES BEGIN OF line02_type.
24   INCLUDE TYPE line01_type.
25   TYPES min_persons TYPE i.
26   TYPES   END OF line02_type.
27
28   TYPES: BEGIN OF line03_type,
29          course_title TYPE zmember02-zzcoursetitle,
30          fee TYPE zmember02-mfee,
31          max_persons TYPE i,
32          END OF line03_type.
33
34   TYPES line04_type TYPE zmember02.
35
```

```
36    * Define data types for itabs
37    TYPES itab01_type TYPE STANDARD TABLE OF line01_type.
38    TYPES itab02_type TYPE STANDARD TABLE OF line02_type.
39    TYPES itab03_type TYPE STANDARD TABLE OF line03_type.
40    TYPES itab04_type TYPE STANDARD TABLE OF line04_type.
41
42    * Define itab without header line
43    DATA itab01 TYPE itab01_type.
44    DATA itab02 TYPE itab02_type.
45    DATA itab03 TYPE itab03_type.
46    DATA itab04 TYPE itab04_type.
47    DATA itab05 TYPE itab04_type.
48
49    * Define work areas for itabs
50    DATA wa_itab01 TYPE line01_type.
51    DATA wa_itab02 TYPE line02_type.
52    DATA wa_itab03 TYPE line03_type.
53    DATA wa_itab04 TYPE line04_type.
54    DATA wa_itab05 TYPE line04_type.
```

Listing 13.7 Include Program Z_MEMBERLIST_DEFINITIONS

```
1    *&---------------------------------------------------*
2    *&  Include              ZMEMBERLIST13_B_SELECTION_SCR
3    *&---------------------------------------------------*
4    SELECTION-SCREEN BEGIN OF BLOCK v13b
                      WITH FRAME TITLE text-001.
5    PARAMETERS: rsmw AS CHECKBOX,   " Start report and
                                       return
6             rsow AS CHECKBOX,      " Start report no
          return, via empty sel.screen
7             rsowas AS CHECKBOX,   " Start report no
          return, via presel. sel.screen
8             rsowih AS CHECKBOX.   " Start report no
          return, via black sel.screen
9    SELECTION-SCREEN END OF BLOCK v13b.
```

Listing 13.8 Include Program Z_MEMBERLIST13_B_SELECTION_SCR

Notes on the Source Code

Report Z_MEMBERLIST13_B (see Listing 13.6) calls external reports **External calls** by subroutines in external reports and by function modules. It also transfers data between reports in various memory areas. Analogous to the example from Listing 13.3, this report also contains an include report for selection parameters (see Listing 13.7) and an include report for definitions (see Listing 13.8).

 Business Tasks Take Second Place

Because the focus of this report is on the call and flow logic and on data transfer, business tasks take second place.

Lines 11 to 36

The data definition accesses the common include report. The definitions for the selection screen are located in a dedicated include report. Only calls of individual subtasks are located beneath the events. The events and the levels of the report should have as clear a structure as possible.

Lines 46 to 63

Integrated components

External report Z_MEMBERLIST13_A is called as an integrated component. Report Z_MEMBERLIST13_B ends with the call of this report. In other words, report A is the alternative end of report B. The system won't jump back to report B after the end of report A.

The selection screen of report B determines how to jump back to report A. The sample source code has three options:

> Report A is called with its selection screen. The user must complete the selection screen and start the report with the EXECUTE button. Two selection screens appear, one after the other: report B and then report A.

> Report A is called with its selection screen, but the selection parameters for report A are transferred. The selection screen of report A contains suggested values. The user can check the suggestions and change them as desired. Then the user then starts report A with the EXECUTE button.

> Report A receives the transferred selection parameters without a display of selection screen of the report. The user then completes only the selection screen of report B. Report A runs invisibly in the background.

Note that none of the three cases returns to report B after the end of report A.

Lines 72 to 82

First, the parameter ID that contains the program name of report B is read from SAP memory. The program name is then written to parameter ID Z_TEST. After using an external subroutine to populate the internal table, the body lines of the internal table are written to the cluster that contains the PROGNAME field in ABAP memory. Report A is then called so that it branches back to report B after the end of the report. Processing resumes with the statement right after the SUBMIT statement.

The called report (A) checks the content of the Z_TEST parameter ID. If it contains a program name, report A is called by another program. In this case, the cluster is read from ABAP memory and placed in an internal table. Then the internal table is processed and the parameter ID is initialized. Report A can use the content of the parameter ID to determine whether it was called by a user or by an external report.

Report A reacts based on the type of call. If it was called by an external report, the report generates a specific list. The BACK button takes the user to the list output of report B and then to its selection screen. In this case, the selection screen of report A is not redisplayed.

If a user starts report A, the report also generates a list. But in this case, the BACK button takes you to the selection screen of report A, where you can either restart report A or end it.

Program Output

The selection screen of this report (see Figure 13.32) doesn't focus on data selection, but on flow control. Think of this report as the root of

Root of a tree structure

a tree structure. Additional processing steps are triggered. They are controlled and executed by the calling components, procedures, and reports. You can use this kind of root to build a central control component for reports with related subjects.

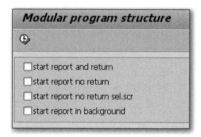

Figure 13.32   Z_MEMBERLIST13_B Selection Screen

14

Advanced Topics

The Chinese proverb "May you live in interesting times" is a two-edged sword: Interesting times are not necessarily good times, and so the wish is traditionally intended as more of a curse than a blessing. Thankfully, we as ABAP developers can find it much easier to enjoy the interesting times we live in, because they are good times indeed.

Although this is a book for beginners, we want to take a look at some advanced topics you'll encounter in your (hopefully) long and illustrious career as an ABAP developer. This chapter aims to address several topics that have a broader perspective and to give you a taste of some interesting tools and technologies that you'll probably come across in real life. We briefly describe these advanced topics and, when possible, recommend additional literature for further reference.

Interesting Times for the ABAP Programming Language

In the last decade, the ABAP programming language has changed considerably. What was once a purely procedural programming language based on the COBOL host language—which today is rather outdated—

ABAP over time

has become a modern, object-oriented language that has incorporated numerous ideas, concepts, and language constructs from other modern programming languages (for example, from Java). A new generation of programmers is putting its mark on the ABAP world and introducing elements from various modern programming languages.

Modern programming language

Some years ago, the typical ABAP developer was either a former CO-BOL programmer or an expert in the business domain but without broad background knowledge of software development; today, developers from various modern programming languages and environments contribute their knowledge to the ABAP community.

Hybrid of procedural and object-oriented programming

Despite the change inherent in becoming an object-oriented language, ABAP has not forgotten its origin: For compatibility reasons, language constructs from "ancient" days have been supported for years, whether the person responsible for the development of the language likes it or not. The result is a hybrid language in which you can address any problem using either the procedural way or the object-oriented way; in fact, the solution is often a combination of both ways. (This may also be a necessity as you find that the ABAP system doesn't always support the object-oriented way of programming, and certain subtasks can only be solved with classic, procedural ABAP.)

If you're particularly interested in the new, modern options of the ABAP language and the SAP NetWeaver Application Server, we recommend that you read *Next Generation ABAP Development* (SAP PRESS, 2nd edition, 2011).

Programming Using Frameworks

Frameworks are everywhere

A frequent phenomenon in object-oriented programming has also become part of the ABAP world: *Frameworks* support developers in carrying out recurring tasks. To avoid solving the same problem again and again in similar ways, you can use libraries that solve the actual problem with a general, reusable method.

You then only have to program the special feature of the current problem, which could not be considered in the general library.

So how can you ensure that your problem-specific, non-reusable code and the generic code of the framework interact smoothly? Popular frameworks are very powerful and accordingly comprehensive. They consist of many individual components that are integrated like puzzle pieces and have to be called at the right place and time, respectively. Due to the generic programming of frameworks, their internal structure is often complicated and hard to understand. So shifting the responsibility for the correct call of all components of a complex framework to the user (that is, to the programmer who uses it) isn't very helpful, because the framework is supposed to make his work easier and not more complicated.

Instead, the typical solution is that the framework itself controls the overall process. Once called, the framework assumes control and calls all necessary components for a smooth process. This also includes the problem-specific (that is, non-generic) components that you have programmed and which run smoothly in the overall framework process; they need to be called by the framework at the right time. Two prerequisites have to be met in this context:

> The component that is supposed to be called (for example, an ABAP class) must be known to the framework. In the ABAP environment, this is usually done by entering the class name into a Customizing table. At runtime, the framework uses this table to determine the ABAP classes that need to be called to call them at the appropriate time. Alternatively, you can call a specific method of the framework and transfer the name of the ABAP class or the corresponding object instance during this process. This way you, the application developer, have registered your code successfully and enabled the framework to call it when required.

> The application code that is called by the framework must meet the framework's interface requirements. When the framework calls the user code, it expects that certain parameters, which are necessary for the communication with the application code, are available. The framework usually ensures this by pretending that the application code exists in an ABAP class that implements a specific class interface defined by the framework; this way, the methods and parameters defined in this class interface are available.

Interaction between framework code and application code

Frameworks control the overall process

Software Built with Timber Frame Construction

Imagine framework programming as the construction of a timber house or modern wooden-frame house. First, you create the frame that supports the entire construction, provides stability, and defines the internal and external shape of the building. Then you fill the spaces in the frame. The structure of the frame is critical: You cannot build a load-bearing wall with only insulation because you need a frame that provides structure.

This analogy also applies to the quality and stability requirements for development. You can repair rotten fillings in a timbered construction, but unsound buttresses can't support a house. So framework development in particular requires a stable and persistent frame that provides as much flexibility as possible and leaves room for maneuvering.

Inversion of control or Hollywood principle

The method of letting the framework deal with the flow control and, in particular, call the problem-specific application code is called *inversion of control*. Sometimes, it is also facetiously referred to as the Hollywood principle: "Don't call us—we'll call you."

Example of an Archiving Solution

Why archiving?

As an example, let's take a look at an archiving solution. Archiving is necessary because, in many tables of an application system, the data cannot be stored forever. If the content of a table becomes too comprehensive over the course of time, write and read accesses become increasingly slower and the system's operability will be jeopardized. In addition, a large volume of old, unnecessary data can be problematic for users if, for example, they can't find relevant data that needs to be processed in the selection dialogs, because they're bogged down by old, already processed data. On one hand, you want to remove this fallow data so that it doesn't decelerate or impede running processes. On the other hand, you don't want to simply delete it for a variety of reasons. You may need it in the future in order to check an individual case, or because you are governed by legal retention periods that prohibit the deletion of data.

Basic principles of archiving solutions

With data archiving, data that you no longer require is collected, exported, and stored on an external storage medium outside the SAP system. This way, the data in the SAP system can be safely deleted.

However, the "deleted data" can't be completely deleted, per se; the SAP system will retain information that enables the user to find relevant, archived data records according to specific search criteria and retrieve them from the archive. For this purpose, you have to create an *archive index* in the SAP system. This index refers to the exact position of the data records in the archive, and additionally contains a small selection of data fields from the records—just enough to determine whether the data records in the archive are still relevant and to make sure that they don't vanish into obscurity altogether.

Archive index for finding data

If you now analyze the concrete task for several tables that are supposed to be archived, you will notice that there are more similarities than differences between the various application scenarios. A general solution makes sense here:

> The basic process (identifying data that is supposed to be archived, collecting the data, storing the data in the archive, generating an archive index, and deleting the data) is always the same.

> The search process in the archive (searching for archived data according to a selection of data fields, exporting found data records from the archive, and displaying the data in a display interface) is also always the same.

The following attributes vary in the various archiving scenarios and need to be implemented individually:

> The technical logic that is used to identify the data records that are no longer required and need to be archived is different for each customer and scenario.

> The tables that are supposed to be archived and their structures tend to vary.

> The fields of the archive index that are required to find archived data records are also always different between records.

> The dialog interface for displaying a data record that is stored in the archive varies for the different tables.

Draft of a Possible Archiving Solution

The following sections describe a possible solution for the archiving problem, which illustrates how you can use frameworks to solve recurring problems—either by developing a framework yourself or by using a framework that has been developed by others.

Differentiating between general aspects and problem-specific aspects

> The reusable solution for the archiving problem consists of a framework that solves the general, application case-independent aspects. At certain critical points in time, it calls the specialized application code for which no general solution can be created. One example is a special method for selecting the data records that need to be archived; another is a special dialog for displaying a data record from the archive.

Framework controls the process

> The framework itself controls the overall process, as described above, and calls the application-specific code at the appropriate time.

> You enter the names of the application-specific ABAP classes in a Customizing table (for example, the ABAP classes that are responsible for the data selection).

The long-awaited call from Hollywood

> These application-specific ABAP classes have to implement specific class interfaces provided by the framework so that their interface corresponds to the expectations of the framework at runtime. In a manner of speaking, they have to ensure that they speak the same language when Hollywood finally calls.

Important Frameworks in the SAP Standard

How do you recognize a good and experienced ABAP programmer? This question can result in many interesting discussions. One of the essential characteristics is probably a working knowledge of the frameworks that can be used in the ABAP server.

The frameworks that are introduced in the following sections are mainly interesting for you as the user, because you might use them in a project soon. In addition, there's another advantage of dealing with these frameworks: You can think of them as a pool of ideas, and you might solve a totally different but structurally related problem in a similar way in future.

Web Dynpro ABAP

Web Dynpro ABAP is one of the most important innovations of the last ten years in the SAP world. It is a user interface technology and a tool for creating SAP application user dialogs. Chapter 11 introduced the creation of selection screens and briefly described the closely related screen programming technology. But the classic user interface technology no longer covers the entire range of requirements that a modern application has to meet. Consequently, it is increasingly replaced by the more modern Web Dynpro ABAP technology. As an ABAP programming freshman, you should therefore also learn how to program Web Dynpro-based applications as soon as you are familiar with the basics.

Successor of classic screens

The "web" in the name already implies that applications programmed using Web Dynpro do not require specific client software on the user side, but can run in a regular web browser. This is a considerable advantage if you want to provide applications for users who work in the SAP system only occasionally, and you don't want to install hundreds of megabytes of software on users' personal computers just so they can submit occasional leave requests or settle travel expenses.

No client installation required

However, Web Dynpro not only scores high points because it is browser-enabled, but also because it is suited for cross-system applications:

Suited for cross-system applications

> First, it can be smoothly integrated with SAP NetWeaver Portal and SAP NetWeaver Business Client and enables the data exchange with other portal applications, even when they are located in a different SAP system.
> Second, Web Dynpro ABAP has a counterpart on the Java side: Web Dynpro Java. You can create applications whose dialogs are located partly in the ABAP system and partly in the Java system and that still provide a uniform look-and-feel and continuous user navigation.

> Third, SAP NetWeaver Business Process Management (SAP NetWeaver BPM), a Java-based workflow environment for cross-system applications, can also integrate Web Dynpro ABAP. This facilitates the use of your application in cross-system and cross-department scenarios and thus increases its value. Eventually, the more often a software is used to support a process, the more valuable it is.

➕ Model View Controller

Web Dynpro is based on the Model View Controller (MVC) principle. This popular architecture pattern for application distinguishes between model (technical data model as maintained in the application), view (user interface, display), and controller (flow control) so that you can program these three parts separately.

> For example, the model of your application would contain the most important data structures and functions for loading, storing, and validating.

> A view A of your application would exclusively contain the layout and code that is required to display specific data of the model and allow for certain input.

> A different view, B, could contain another dialog screen.

> It is important to note that neither view A nor view B know anything about the sequence of input process in its entirety—in which at first view A is called and then, after data has been entered successfully, view B is called.

> The controller is responsible for these controlling aspects—displaying view A first, calling the check function of the model afterwards, and then displaying view B.

This architecture might seem confusing at first glance because you first must learn how to assign the tasks that belong to the model, the view, and the controller. However, soon you'll be used to it and be able to make these assignments easily. Then the advantages of this popular architecture pattern will be obvious: Due to the delegation of duties, model, view, and controller have an internal structure that is less complex. Furthermore, the approach unlocks reuse potentials. Oftentimes, it is possible to reuse the same model in several different contexts where the view and controller have to be implemented anew, but the model can remain unchanged.

If you develop your ABAP applications with Web Dynpro ABAP, a world of potential users and integrations with other applications opens up. The applications can even run outside your system and be based on different technologies. Nevertheless, Web Dynpro ABAP is adapted to the typical SAP design and uses classic screen interfaces. Of course, all that glitters is not gold, and Web Dynpro still leaves something to be desired. For example, the highly standardized and business-like appearance of Web Dynpro applications doesn't suit everyone's tastes, and the performance of browser-based applications can rarely reach that of applications with a heavier client footprint in the form of a native client software installed on the user's desktop computer. But in most companies that use SAP, Web Dynpro ABAP plays an important role and will continue to become more important.

When talking about Web Dynpro ABAP, we must mention Floorplan Manager (FPM), an additional framework that helps you create standards-compliant Web Dynpro dialogs. The FPM framework supports you in creating the different charts whose combination constitute the overall dialog. It is the frame that combines everything to form a functioning solution at runtime—just as if it had been programmed by the SAP system directly.

You can find more information on Web Dynpro programming for beginners in *Getting Started with Web Dynpro ABAP* (SAP PRESS, 2010).

Web Services

Web services allow communication between applications beyond system boundaries. A web service enables an application on one system to call a function of an application on another system. For these *remote calls,* there have always been various technologies and communication protocols. For this purpose, many platforms provide proprietary protocols, which are optimized for the corresponding platform—for example, SAP systems prefer to communicate through the SAP-proprietary Remote Function Call (RFC), and SAP also offers libraries for

Communication beyond system boundaries

non-SAP systems so that these systems can communicate with SAP systems through RFC.

Restrictions of proprietary approaches

Ultimately, however, these proprietary approaches lead to a lot of problems if each system needs to speak the languages of all other systems in a heterogeneous system landscape with multiple different platforms. If a function moves from one system to another (that is, if it is implemented on a different platform), all users of the function must change to a new communication protocol. This is as if not only the telephone number of a contact person changes, but this contact partner suddenly only speaks a language from another planet. This hurdle can impose considerable restrictions on software architecture.

Web services as the lingua franca

So web services were developed as the solution to these problems. Web services provide a standard (strictly speaking, a bundle of standards) that tries to create a *lingua franca* — that is, a language that can be spoken and understood by every IT system. This approach allows Oracle systems to communicate with ABAP systems as easily as with Microsoft servers or Java Enterprise servers. The user of a function that is provided as a web service doesn't notice and doesn't have to consider on which platform that service runs. The platform could change at any time without the user having to care about it. If the service moves to another platform, only the address and nothing else might change from the user's perspective. So the telephone number of a contact person changes, but their language does not. Good things happen when software architecture has more room to maneuver.

How does the web service manage to be universally available and used on virtually all software platforms that both provide and use services? The answer lies in the selection of the tools and standards used:

Web services are a standard that is based on common standards

> Web services are usually based on the exchange of data via Hypertext Transfer Protocol (HTTP). HTTP is the communication protocol of the World Wide Web and is understood by every web browser and web server.

> The data that is transferred during this process — service description, call, and response — are coded in XML format, which is also part of the basic set of IT systems today.

Abstraction of Platform and Backend

When you find a solution to a problem that reduces a certain aspect of the problem enough to be ignored, this is called abstraction. For example, database accesses in ABAP are implemented via OpenSQL, the database-independent SQL variant that is integrated with ABAP and always stays the same, regardless of the database system on which the SAP server runs. In this context, OpenSQL *abstracts* from the database system—that is, you no longer have to know which database system is used.

Web services are used to abstract from two other aspects:

> First, you use them to abstract from the platform, so that the developer of a program calling a web service doesn't have to know on which type of server platform the service runs, in which programming language it is implemented, and so on.

> Second, you can use them to abstract from the backend. The backend is the server that provides the used service. An abstraction from the backend is successful if the calling program of a service no longer needs to know on which server and under which address the service is exactly provided. This way, the service can move anytime without the users noticing.

Web services allow for this kind of backend abstraction in one of two ways. The first is by requesting the call address from a directory server at runtime. The second is by sending the call to a system that acts as a central hub and forwards all calls to the corresponding backends. Oftentimes the system that serves as a hub can translate service calls between different structures and key directories. You can change the interface of a called service without having to move all users to the new interface structure at the same time; instead, you implement a translation step for service calls in the central hub.

The directory server for web services is called the Universal Description Discovery and Integration (UDDI) server; the hub is called an Enterprise Service Bus. In the SAP environment, the SAP NetWeaver Process Integration (SAP NetWeaver PI) solution provides this function.

> The data types within the exchanged XML documents are described using XML schema, a commonly used standard that can be found almost anywhere XML is used.

The newly defined web services standards and specifications are based on these widespread standards and were (or are) easier to implement for platform providers than standards that reinvent the wheel (for example, for communication, data format, and interface description).

For more information on this topic, refer to Developing Enterprise Services for SAP (SAP PRESS, 2009) for a comprehensive and detailed overview of the creation and use of web services — including the special, SAP-specific "web service dialect," *Enterprise Services*.

Frameworks for Enhancements

Usually, individual software doesn't have to be adapted to the customer-specific needs retroactively, since it is often already tailored to the customer's requirements. But most SAP applications are standard, out-of-the-box software that is developed and provided for all customers.

Tailored and customized application systems

Just like when you have to shorten ready-made pants or the sleeves of a new jacket so that your new clothes fit you properly, SAP applications must be adapted to each customer's specific requirements before they can be used. Over time, various tools and technologies have been developed in the SAP environment that can be used to implement such adaptations.

Customizing

Control tables for customer-specific settings

The most commonly used technology is *Customizing*, in which the adaptation is implemented by creating customer-specific table entries. These table entries can be customer-specific key directories and master data (such as company codes, cost centers, subsidiaries, and regions) but can also include control entries that define how the system is supposed to behave in certain situations. For example, you can use a table entry to determine whether an electronic vendor invoice that the system identified as incorrect is supposed to be automatically returned via an error message or submitted to a human agent for further checks and processing.

Modification

Overwriting standard code

Not every adaptation can be implemented via table entries. If program code needs to be adapted, you can use *modification*: You simply change the source code of the SAP standard application. This is the adaptation method with the most inherent disadvantages because the standard SAP code can be changed and provided again by SAP at any time. In this event, what would happen to your code modification? It would either be overwritten, or you would need to merge it; this last option would involve a great deal of effort because you'd have to merge the changes made by SAP with your own. SAP upgrades are nearly impossible due to the involved merging effort when customers make complicated or numerous modifications to their SAP systems. These customers use outdated SAP releases and wind up paying SAP huge amounts of money to maintain these releases long after they're no longer supported.

Business Add-Ins

When adapting SAP systems to customer requirements through programming, you can save some effort by using *business add-ins* (BAdIs), which replace the formerly used user exits or customer exits. BAdIs are specific extension points provided by SAP that enable you to insert program logic at a certain place in the processing logic to manipulate the flow (though to a limited extent). The SAP standard can provide a BAdI, for example, that lets you influence the result of an input verification using particular customer-specific checks, or lets you overwrite calculation results after the processing of a calculation function if the standard technology for calculations doesn't fit your needs. Compared with modifications, the major advantage here is that SAP guarantees release stability for BAdIs; it promises that once a BAdI is implemented, it will also work in future SAP releases. What's more, your BAdI implementations won't be overwritten by SAP deliveries in the future.

Release stability owing to predefined extension points

Switch and Enhancement Framework

The most modern tool for the adaptation of the SAP system is the Switch and Enhancement Framework. Actually, it is an entire toolbox whose components can also be used separately: the Switch Framework, the Enhancement Framework, and the elements of the Enhancement Framework (BAdIs, for instance) without the framework.

Comprehensive package of extension technologies

The purpose of this framework is to create a variety of enhancement options. Imagine software manufacturer A developing an application. Developer B supplements this software by developing and delivering extensions for it. The Switch and Enhancement Framework ensures that the extensions provided by developer B supplement manufacturer A's code either by being inserted at certain places during execution, or by superimposing the code so that developer B's code is executed instead manufacturer A's code.

These extensions can be implemented at places predefined by the manufacturer of the enhanced software A, or embedded at will at (nearly) any place. In the first case, manufacturer A can establish long-term interface stability and guarantee the smooth operation of the predefined extension point in follow-up releases. In the second case (in which the extension is not inserted at a predefined point but instead embedded at will), you can hardly achieve 100% release stability. Although the extension cannot be overwritten by new releases of the extended code of manufacturer A like a modification, you have to check and, as necessary, adapt the extension with each new release like a modification.

The Switch and Enhancement Framework enables you to make this kind of extension switchable—that is, deliver them with a switch so that system administrators activate or deactivate the extensions. This enables customers to execute only the original code of manufacturer A or use it together with developer B's extensions. This part, which deals with switchability, is assumed by the Switch Framework.

 Different Scenarios

You might have realized that "manufacturer A" in the above scenario is SAP implementing basic functions, and "developer B" is the customer extending the SAP code. However, other scenarios are also possible:

> Different departments of software manufacturer SAP can play the roles of A and B, which means that SAP provides enhancements for its own products. These SAP-specific enhancements are delivered in enhancement packages (EHPs), which contain numerous functions, some of which can be activated at extra charge.

> Third parties can enhance the SAP code with their own functions and, consequently, integrate their products with the SAP standard, without actually changing any part of the SAP standard. Instead, the original SAP code and the third party enhancement are blended together by the Enhancement Framework at runtime.

> A customer extends the code of a third party.

For more information on this topic, refer to *Implementing SAP Enhancement Packages* (SAP PRESS, 2010).

Discover!

The mentioned technologies and frameworks are only a small selection of the numerous challenging and interesting topics you can discover as your ABAP development skills advance. It can be taken for granted that new topics will have emerged between the time that this book was written and the moment that you first hold it in your hands: The innovation speed of the ABAP platform is very high, and interested ABAP experts are permanently provided with new tools that support them in successfully managing daily challenges to development.

Continuous development of the ABAP platform

In fact, today's innovation speed is so high that it is vital for every developer to expand his knowledge—continuous development is in demand!

In this context, we want to share some tips on how to stay up to date and informed of the current developments in the ABAP and SAP worlds:

Tips for SAP knowledge workers

> Use SAP Community Network (SCN). You can find the most comprehensive portal for SAP experts at *http://scn.sap.com/*. More than one million users visit this portal each month, and many of these users provide useful tips in the forums and blogs, contributing their ideas in interesting discussions. This platform is also used to announce and discuss new technologies and tools and provide step-by-step instructions for beginners.

Using SAP Community Network

> To get as much experience in real life as possible, try new things! A lot of businesses have sandbox systems of the various SAP system types in which you can delete data without any problem and gain experience with the current innovations and applications. In addition, ABAP trial systems are delivered with the SAP books or made available in SCN. We recommend that you download offers that let you install SAP system for learning purposes. Finally, there are also trial systems (for example, to test SAP's software-as-a-service offers) that don't require installation at all.

Using test systems

Establishing contact
with interested
SAP experts

> Maintain a network of dedicated SAP experts who willingly share their knowledge and with whom you can discuss interesting and complex issues. Social media provide good contact points; with Twitter and Facebook, you can easily get in touch with the corresponding SAP community and get to know the whizzes personally. Events (such as *SAP Inside Tracks*, which is voluntarily organized by highly committed members) and large meetings (such as *SAP TechEd* and *SAPPHIRE NOW*) are ideal for establishing and maintaining a network of contacts.

Marketing
techniques
and skills

> Do you want to prove your newly learned techniques in real-life projects? Some developers moan that their projects don't require new technologies. One of the reasons is that the new technologies are not known to their businesses' decision makers, or management doesn't know that it already has employees who are familiar with the new technologies.

Contact the decision makers in your business who are responsible for or can influence the use of recent technologies. These decision makers can be end customers, project leads, product managers, or sales employees who often don't have the chance to keep themselves up to date about technological developments. They'll probably be thankful when you indicate new opportunities for programming better IT solutions for end users. Don't forget to market your skills and commend yourself for interesting tasks.

Index

Work process, 29, 247
WRITE, 83, 88, 89, 119
WRITE UNDER, 120

X

X buffer, 81

Y

Y buffer, 81

Z

Z buffer, 81
ZIP code, 108

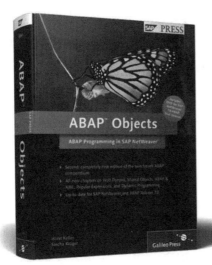

Second, completely new edition of the benchmark ABAP compendium

All-new chapters on Web Dynpro, Shared Objects, ABAP & XML, Regular Expressions, Dynamic Programming, and more!

Up-to-date for SAP NetWeaver 2004s (ABAP release 7.0)

Horst Keller, Sascha Krüger

ABAP Objects

ABAP Programming in SAP NetWeaver

This completely new third edition of our best-selling ABAP book provides detailed coverage of ABAP programming with SAP NetWeaver. This outstanding compendium treats all concepts of modern ABAP up to release 7.0. New topics include ABAP and Unicode, Shared Objects, exception handling, Web Dynpro for ABAP, Object Services, and of course ABAP and XML. Bonus: All readers will receive the SAP NetWeaver 2004s ABAP Trial Version ("Mini-SAP") on DVD.

1059 pp., 2. edition 2007, with DVD 5, 79,95 Euro / US$ 79.95
ISBN 978-1-59229-079-6

>> www.sap-press.com

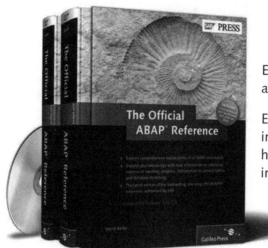

Explore comprehensive explanations of all ABAP statements

Expand your knowledge with new information on extended expression handling, pragmas, introduction to internal tables, and database streaming

Horst Keller

The Official ABAP Reference

This book is your official reference for all ABAP statements. Sorted by topic, it provides an explanation of the function, the syntax listing in pseudo code, a description, notes on special usage, and an example for each statement. In addition, every chapter includes an introduction that recapitulates the essential concepts for that topic, such as character string processing, dynpro development, and more. This new edition is updated for release 7.0, but also covers the new functions of releases 7.02 and 7.2.

1677 pp., 3. edition 2011, with DVD 5, 149,95 Euro / US$ 149.95
ISBN 978-1-59229-376-6

>> **www.sap-press.com**